Multi and Management

Activities

Susan E. L. Lake
Former Technology Education Specialist
Lubbock-Cooper ISD
Lubbock, Texas

Karen Bean
Information Management Instructor
Blinn College
Brenham, Texas
Former Teacher
Killeen Independent School District
Killeen, Texas

THOMSON

SOUTH-WESTERN

Australia · Canada · Mexico · Singapore · Spain · United Kingdom · United States

Multimedia and Image Management Activities
Susan Lake and Karen Bean

Vice President/Executive Publisher:
Dave Shaut

Team Leader:
Karen Schmohe

Acquisitions Editor:
Jane Congdon

Project Manager/Consulting Editor:
A. W. Kingston

Executive Marketing Manager:
Carol Volz

Marketing Manager:
Mike Cloran

Production Editor:
Todd McCoy

Production Manager:
Patricia Matthews Boies

Manufacturing Coordinator:
Charlene Taylor

Compositor:
Lachina Publishing Services

Printer:
Quebecor World
Dubuque, Iowa

Design Project Manager:
Stacy Shirley

Cover Designer:
Robb & Associates

Contents

UNIT 2 PROFESSIONAL VISUAL COMMUNICATIONS SKILLS   86

UNIT 3 PRINT PUBLISHING 144

UNIT 4 PRESENTATION STRATEGIES 244

UNIT 5 WEB PUBLISHING SYSTEMS 353

UNIT 6 ORAL AND OTHER PROFESSIONAL COMMUNICATION SKILLS 431

Preface

USING THIS BOOK WITH MACINTOSH COMPUTERS

Most of the applications discussed within this book are available for both the Windows and Macintosh operating systems, and the activities described can be worked easily on either system. However, the following applications are not available to Macintosh users.

Unit 1	Part 1	Jasc Paint Shop Pro
Unit 2	Part 5	Microsoft MapPoint
Unit 3	Part 1	Microsoft Publisher
Unit 4	Part 1	Microsoft Sound Recorder
	Part 4	Jasc Animation Shop
Unit 6	Part 1	Dragon NaturallySpeaking
	Part 4	MGI Cinematic

At different points within the activity instructions, there are references to Windows keyboard shortcuts. These can be converted to Macintosh keyboard shortcuts by using the following substitutions.

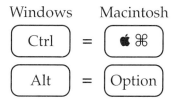

Apple provides the additional label of "Alt" on the Option key on their current keyboards to aid in adapting cross-platform instructions like these.

Image Management Procedures

Image management begins with basic software skills and knowledge in understanding what tools and software to use for a desired result, just as a doctor knows what prescription you need for your symptom. Your goal is to become familiar enough with image management software that you will be able to write a "prescription."

We don't anticipate that you will become experts in these tools, but merely familiar. Basic skills are offered in the unit, but our desire is for you to unleash your creativity and explore what may be beyond basic skills.

In this unit, you will experience tutorials in the image management software that is widely considered the business standard. Both Jasc Paint Shop Pro and Adobe Photoshop each have their own advantages. Both of them are able to produce professional and yet "cool-looking" images. With the help of a scanner, a digital camera, and your own creative ability, you will be able to produce images that will be used on Web pages, in desktop publishing documents, and in PowerPoint presentations. You will also have an opportunity to experience vector software, such as Adobe Illustrator or Macromedia FreeHand. Producing crisp, sharp images for logos and other business solutions has never been more challenging. Take the challenge! You will be amazed at what you can accomplish—and the best part is that you can have fun being productive!

Part 1

Jasc Paint Shop Pro

Jasc Paint Shop Pro
Publisher: Jasc Software, Inc.
Paint Shop Pro is image management software that began as shareware and has quickly become a leader in the market. The relative quality for the low price of the software has made it a popular choice in some schools.

ACTIVITY 1 • BASIC IMAGE EDITING

In this activity, you will become familiar with:

- Opening an Image
- Using the Selection Tool
- Cutting and Pasting an Image
- Viewing an Image
- Resizing an Image

Opening an Image

1. Open *Capital.jpg* from your CD.

Using the Selection Tool

1. Click on the Selection Tool.
2. Select the image with the Selection Tool to view only the dome and the floors under the dome in the new image. The person should not be in the image. Different shapes are available with the Selection Tool. For this activity, use the Rectangle. When you click on a tool, the Tool Options Palette is often a floating menu on your screen. If it is not visible, go to the menu bar and choose View > Toolbars, then click in the box to turn on the Tool Options Palette.

Selection Tool

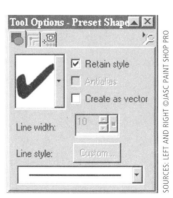

SOURCES: LEFT AND RIGHT ©JASC PAINT SHOP PRO

Tool Options

Cutting and Pasting an Image

1. After selecting the area, go to the menu bar and choose Edit > Cut. Then go to the menu bar and choose Edit > Paste > As New Image. Save as *CutCapital.jpg*. When you save an image as a JPG or GIF, most of the time you will get a warning message about the limitations of the color or merging it into one layer. Click Yes to accept this change.

Viewing an Image

1. Open *Flowers.gif* from your CD.
2. Before you save an image, it is a good idea to view it in Normal Viewing to check that it is the size you need. Go to the menu bar and choose View > Normal Viewing. If it is dimmed, then you are in Normal Viewing.

Resizing an Image

1. To resize an image, go to the menu bar and choose Image > Resize. Adjust the percentage to increase or decrease the image.
2. Decrease the size of the image to 50% of its original size.
3. Save as *ResizedFlowers.gif*.

CutCapital.jpg

ACTIVITY 1 • MINI-PROJECT

Create an Image for a Poem

1. Go to http://www.inform.umd.edu. Search for Emily Dickinson. Several links are available to many of her poems.
2. Choose a poem to illustrate with an image.
3. Type the poem in a word processing document.
4. Create your image using a digital or scanned photograph, clip art from the Internet, or another source available to you.
5. From your original image, create four slightly different images using the Selection Tool and the various shapes from the Selection Tool.
6. Resize some of the images for variety.
7. Insert all five of your images into the second page of the word processing document. Label each with a description of what was done to the image. Illustrate the poem on the first page of your document with the best image.
8. Save the images as *01Poem.jpg*, *02Poem.jpg*, *03Poem.jpg*, *04Poem.jpg*, and *05Poem.jpg*.
9. Save the word processing document as *IllustratedPoem.doc*.
10. The following criteria should be met:
    - ☐ Original image appropriate to the topic of the poem.
    - ☐ Each of the four revised images are different and creative.
    - ☐ At least two images resized.
    - ☐ Poem typed accurately in the word processing document.
    - ☐ Poem placed on the word processing document so that it presents an attractive appearance.
    - ☐ Each image labeled with attention to detail on how the image was created.
    - ☐ Chosen image for illustration is appropriate.

ACTIVITY 2 • CREATING IMAGES

In this activity, you will become familiar with:

■ Defaults in Creating an Image
■ Preset Shapes Tool
■ Strokes and Fill
  ○ Solid
  ○ Gradient
  ○ Pattern
  ○ Null
■ Patterns and Textures

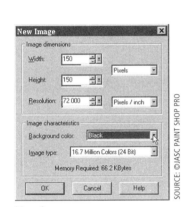

New Image

Shapes Tool

Defaults in Creating an Image

1. Create a new image of 150 × 150 pixels, using the defaults for resolution, background, and image type. (Unless otherwise instructed, all files should be created using pixels.)
2. The default is a transparent background. Note that you may change Background colors.

Preset Shapes Tool

1. Click on the Preset Shapes Tool on the Tool Palette docked on the left side. If the Tool Palette is not visible, go to the menu bar and choose View > Toolbars, then click in the box to turn on the Tool Palette.
2. Locate Check 4 in the Tool Options—Preset Shapes dialog box. The Tool Options will not be set to Preset Shapes if that tool is not selected.
3. Create an image with Check 4 and Retain style checked. Create the same image with Check 4 and Retain style unchecked. Be sure Line style is solid. Notice that when Retain style is unchecked, the shape takes on the attributes of the fill color.
4. Compare and contrast the two images.

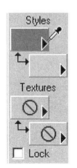

Shapes Example

Stroke and Fill

5. Save as *Check4.gif*. Insert into a word processing document and explain the differences.
6. Save the word processing document as *Check4Comparison.doc*.
7. Practice creating at least three other images using different shapes. Put an image with Retain style checked next to an image with Retain style unchecked.
8. Save as *01Shape.gif*, *02Shape.gif*, and *03Shape.gif*.

Stroke and Fill

The Stroke and Fill may be adjusted using the right arrow on the corresponding color box. The choices are Solid, Gradient, Pattern, and Null. In the following exercises, you should adjust the stroke to use each type.

Style Choices

Solid

1. Create a new 150 × 150 pixel image with a black background.
2. Click on the Preset Shapes Tool and locate the Triangle. Change the Line width to 15. Note in the figure to the right that Retain style is not checked.
3. Change the Foreground Solid Color to blue and the Background Solid Color to white. In the Styles area, click on the arrow on the Stroke color box and select Solid. Draw the Triangle on the black background. (See figure labeled Solid.gif)
4. If the Triangle does not take up most of your image space, use your selecting, cutting, and pasting skills to create a smaller image before saving.
5. Save as **Solid.gif**.

Gradient

1. Create a new 150 × 150 pixel image with a black background.
2. Click on the Preset Shapes Tool and locate the Triangle. Change the Line width to 15. (See "Solid," step 3.)
3. Click on the arrow on the Stroke color box and select Gradient. Leave the Foreground Solid Color at blue and the Background Solid Color at white.
4. Draw the Triangle on the black background.
5. If the Triangle does not take up most of your image space, use your selecting, cutting, and pasting skills to create a smaller image before saving.
6. Save as **Gradient.gif**.

Pattern

1. Create a new 150 × 150 pixel image with a black background.
2. Click on the Preset Shapes Tool and locate the Triangle. Change the Line width to 15.
3. Click on the arrow on the Stroke color box and select Pattern. Leave the Background Solid Color at white.
4. Click on the Foreground Pattern color box to open the Pattern dialog box. Select the Yarn pattern.
5. Draw the Triangle on the black background.
6. If the Triangle does not take up most of your image space, use your selecting, cutting, and pasting skills to create a smaller image before saving.
7. Save as **Pattern.gif**.

Null

1. Create a new 150 × 150 pixel image with a black background.
2. Click on the Preset Shapes Tool and locate the Triangle. Change the Line width to 15.
3. Click on the arrow on the Stroke color box and select Null. Leave the Background Solid Color at white.
4. Draw the Triangle on the black background.
5. If the Triangle does not take up most of your image space, use your selecting, cutting, and pasting skills to create a smaller image before saving.
6. Save as **Null.gif**.
7. Experiment with the four types of Stroke styles. Now leave the Stroke on Solid and change the Fill colors.
8. Save as **01Fill.gif**, **02Fill.gif**, **03Fill.gif**, and **04Fill.gif**.

Patterns and Textures

1. Create a new 300 × 300 pixel image. Select a background color of your choice.
2. Use the Preset Shapes Tool to draw shapes using different Stroke and Fill Textures.

SOURCE: ©JASC PAINT SHOP PRO

Triangle Options

Solid.gif

Gradient.gif

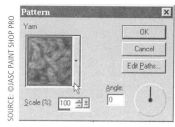

SOURCE: ©JASC PAINT SHOP PRO

Pattern Dialog

Pattern.gif

Null.gif

3. Click on the Stroke Texture arrow key to change Null to Texture as shown below. Choose a Texture.

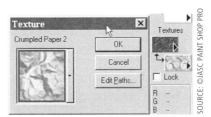

Texture

4. Click on the Fill Texture arrow key to change Null to Texture. Choose a Texture.
5. Repeat this process to create three different designs using Stroke, Texture, and/or Fill Texture.
6. Save as *01Texture.gif*, *02Texture.gif*, and *03Texture.gif*.
7. Using the Preset Shapes, Styles, and Fill, create a personal logo using your initials. Be sure you have used the following elements:
   - Minimum of three different shapes
   - Minimum of one with Retain style
   - Minimum of two different Textures and/or Fill
8. Save as *MyLogo.gif*.
9. Insert the image into a word processing document and explain the process you used to create your image and why you chose the textures or shapes you chose.
10. Save the document as *LogoExplanation.doc*.

MyLogo.gif

ACTIVITY 2 • MINI-PROJECT

Create an Image from Words

1. Given the following words, create an image that illustrates all of them.
   - Star
   - Country
   - Flag
   - Patriotism
   - War

Each word must have an element in the image, any size, that illustrates the word. The element could be a color to create an image of that word.

2. Save as *WordIllustration.jpg*.
3. In a word processing document, insert the image you created. List each of the five words with an explanation as to what element in the image illustrates the word.
4. Save the document as *WordExplanation.doc*.
5. The following criteria should be met:
   - ☐ Background changed from the default.
   - ☐ Preset Shapes Tool used effectively.
   - ☐ Strokes and Fill used effectively.
   - ☐ Color variations such as Gradient, Solid, or Patterns and Textures are used as needed.
   - ☐ All five words are illustrated appropriately.
   - ☐ Explanation in word processing document is organized.
   - ☐ Explanation in word processing document has a logical illustration of the word.

ACTIVITY 3 • SELECTING IMAGES

In this activity, you will become familiar with:

■ Selection Tool
■ Freehand Tool
■ Wand Tool
■ Mover Tool

Selection Tool

1. Open *WhiteCat.jpg* from your CD.
2. Click on the Selection Tool. If the Tool Options Palette is not visible, go to the menu bar and choose View > Toolbars, then click in the box to turn on the Tool Options Palette.
3. You may choose to select the image in a specific shape. Settings may be adjusted for Feather, Antialias, and Sample Merged. Note that Antialias and Feather should be set before making a selection. Find the Circle in the shapes list in the Tool Options—Selection dialog box. Using the Circle, select the White Cat image.
4. Click on Feather and adjust the feathering to 6 in the Tool Options—Selection dialog box. Go to the menu bar and choose Edit > Cut. Then go to the menu bar and choose Edit > Paste > As New Image. You may close the image you cut from without saving it.
5. Save the new image as *Circle.jpg*.
6. Open *WhiteCat.jpg* from your CD.
7. Using the Selection Tool, cut and paste a Pentagon-shaped cat into a new image. There should not be any feathering. Save as *Pentagon.jpg*.

Freehand Tool

The Freehand Tool creates irregular shapes. You can select using one of three methods: Freehand, Smart Edge, or Point to Point.

1. Open *Swans.jpg* from your CD.
2. Click on the Freehand Tool.
3. Select the swans using the Freehand Tool. When you have selected everything for the new image, double-click to end the selection. Cut and paste to a new image.
4. Save the new image as *Freehand.jpg*.
5. Click on the title bar of the original *Swans.jpg*. Click Undo until the image is back to its original state. The Undo button is located under the menu bar. It looks like a left curved arrow and is the fifth icon over.
6. Select the swans using the Point to Point Selection type. Double-click to end the selection. Cut and paste to a new image. Save the new image as *PointtoPoint.jpg*.
7. Click on the title bar of the original *Swans.jpg*. Click Undo until the image is back to its original state.
8. Select the swans using the Smart Edge Selection type. Double-click to end the selection. Cut and paste to a new image.
9. Save the new image as *SmartEdge.jpg*.
10. Insert all three images into a word processing document. Evaluate which Selection type worked best on this image and explain your reasoning. Save as *SelectionTypes.doc*.

Selection Tool

Circle.jpg

Pentagon.jpg

Freehand Tool

Freehand Options

Magic Wand Tool

Wand Tool

The Wand Tool selects based on Color, Hue, or Brightness. The Control Palette for the Wand has Match Mode, Tolerance, and Feather Options.

1. Open **Clouds.jpg** from your CD.
2. Click on the Magic Wand Tool. Set the Tolerance to 20.
3. Click on one of the sets of clouds. Make sure the tolerance setting picked up most of the cloud.
4. Go to the menu bar and choose Edit > Cut.
5. Go to the menu bar and choose Edit > Paste > As New Image.
6. Save the new image as **MagicClouds.jpg**.

Mover Tool

Mover Tool

The Mover Tool enables you to move the marquee. To do this, hold down the left mouse button inside the marquee and drag the marquee where you want it. Release the mouse button. By holding down the Shift key, you may add a new selection to an existing one. By holding down the Ctrl key, you may remove a selection from an existing one.

1. Open **Clouds.jpg** from your CD.
2. Use the Magic Wand Tool to select the top cloud on the left side. Set the Tolerance to 20.
3. With the Magic Wand tool still selected, click on the cloud, hold down the left mouse button and drag the cloud over to the right side of the image. Notice that when you hold down the left mouse button on the selected cloud, the pointer becomes a Mover Tool icon.
4. Save as **MovedCloud.jpg**.

ACTIVITY 3 • MINI-PROJECT

Create a Story with Words and Pictures

1. Create five pictures of similar items (such as five different cats or five different flowers). You may use a digital camera, scanned pictures, or clip art from the Internet.
2. Crop and resize the pictures as needed.
3. Save as **01Pic.jpg**, **02Pic.jpg**, **03Pic.jpg**, **04Pic.jpg**, and **05Pic.jpg**.
4. Write a short story to describe the pictures with words. Insert the pictures into the word processing document with the story to illustrate.
5. Save as **WordStory.doc**.
6. The following criteria should be met:
   - ☐ Pictures are good quality.
   - ☐ Pictures are cropped and resized appropriately for a word processing document.
   - ☐ Five pictures of a similar topic.
   - ☐ Story is well-written and demonstrates some creativity.
   - ☐ Story is error-free.
   - ☐ Files saved as instructed with no errors in file names.
   - ☐ Selection Tool used with different shapes.
   - ☐ Minimum of one use of the Freehand Tool with either Freehand, Smart Edge or Point to Point.
   - ☐ Minimum of one use of Wand Tool.
   - ☐ Minimum of one use of Mover Tool.

ACTIVITY 4 • USING DRAWING TOOLS

In this activity, you will become familiar with:

- Lines
  - ○ Single Line
  - ○ Multisegmented Line
- Bezier Curve
  - ○ Curve
  - ○ S Shapes
- Freehand Line
- Point to Point Line

Lines

Single Line

The Drawing Tool may be used to draw lines as Raster objects or layers and Vector objects or layers. You may use the tool in Vector Mode to move, deform, and edit the objects without affecting the rest of the image.

1. Create a new 400 × 400 pixel image with a transparent background.
2. Click on the Draw Tool.
3. To draw a line, first decide on type, width, line style, and color. To make these choices, use the Tool Options—Draw dialog box and the Foreground Color palette. You can customize these lines to give a greater variety of lines.

Draw Tool

SOURCE: ©JASC PAINT SHOP PRO

Draw Options

Line Options

SOURCES: LEFT AND RIGHT ©JASC PAINT SHOP PRO

4. Practice drawing a box of straight lines. Click the left mouse button and drag to begin the line draw. To end the line, release the mouse button. The line will then be created. Be creative using different types, widths, line styles, and colors.
5. Save as *StraightLines.gif*.

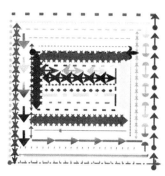

StraightLines.gif

Multisegmented Line

1. To draw a Multisegmented Line, hold down the Alt key to connect your line segments. Click the mouse at the corner, hold down the mouse button, and continue to draw the next side. Do not release the Alt key as you form the angles and draw.
2. Create a new 500 × 500 pixel image with a blue background.
3. Click on the Draw tool.
4. Choose Single Line for Type, 15 for Width, and Opposing Arrowheads Equal for Style.
5. Choose a color that is at the darker end of the scale.
6. Draw a square. Within that square, change the Width to 10 and choose a color that is the same color except lighter.
7. Draw another square within that first square.
8. Change the Width to 5, choose an even lighter color, and draw another square within the other color.

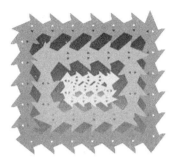

MultiBox.gif

Bezier Example

S-Shape.gif

9. Choose a lighter color and draw a straight line in the middle.
10. Select as close around the image as possible and cut and copy to a new image.
11. Save as **MultiBox.gif**.

Bezier Curve

Curve

1. Create a new 400 × 400 pixel image with a transparent background.
2. Choose a Foreground/Stroke Style and Texture. If you have no Foreground/Stroke Style selected from the Color palette before you draw, the curve is filled with the Background/Fill choices but no line is visible.
3. Click on the Draw Tool.
4. In the Tool Options—Draw dialog box, choose Bezier Curve in the Type drop-down list.
5. Draw a line about two inches long.
6. Click the mouse button where you want to position the top of the curve and then click again to bring the curve from the endpoint up to it.
7. The example to the left shows two curves on top of each other. You can adjust so there is no gap between them and stretch the image to fit the other one if needed. To create the upside-down curve, draw another two-inch line, click below the line where you want to position the bottom of the curve, and click again.
8. Save as **Curves.gif**.

S Shapes

1. To create an S shape, draw a vertical bezier line.
2. Click the mouse button and drag once on one side of the line and once on the other, dragging different directions. The sample is a Solid Style with no Fill and no Textures and a Customized Arrowhead Ball Line.
3. Save as **S-Shape.gif**.
4. Create a new 1000 × 1000 pixel image with your choice of background color.
5. Practice using the Draw Tool to create the letters of the alphabet. Determine the best type of line to use for each letter of the alphabet. Draw as many letters as space allows.
6. Save as **Alphabet.gif**.

Freehand Line

1. Create a new 500 × 500 pixel image with a transparent background.
2. Click on the Draw Tool.
3. In the Tool Options—Draw dialog box, choose Freehand Line from the Type drop-down list.
4. Draw the shape of any type of hat without releasing the mouse button. Note the dotted line. The dots will connect once the mouse button is released.
5. Once you have released the mouse button, the hat or drawn image will have a box around it. You can hover the pointer over the edge of the box to resize or rotate the image.
6. Practice drawing several different hats. Save one of the images as **Hat.gif**.

Point to Point Line

1. Create a new 500 × 500 pixel image with your choice of background color.
2. Click on the Draw Tool.
3. In the Tool Options—Draw dialog box, choose Point to Point Line from the Type drop-down list. Change the Width to 5 and choose a Line style of Solid. Use colors of your choice.
4. Click on the new image file somewhere near the top left. Click again directly across from it in the far right corner. Click about a quarter inch underneath

where you clicked on the left the first time. Then go to the right side and click about a quarter inch underneath where you clicked on the right the first time. Continue until there are at least six white squares on the left and six white squares on the right.

5. Hover the pointer over the last place you clicked until the pointer has the word "END" on it. Click and drag the square further out. This allows you to increase or decrease the length of the last line you drew. Do this before you click off the image.

6. After clicking off the image, hover the pointer over one of the points. When the pointer turns into a sheet of paper, drag the line down. This stretches out the space between the lines.

7. Hover the pointer over the last point. When the pointer changes to a wavy line, click and drag to move the image around on your background. Experiment to find any other changes you can make to the image by hovering the pointer over the points.

8. Using the Point to Point drawing method, create a maze on a new 500 × 500 pixel image.

9. Continue to use the Point to Point drawing method to draw your way out of the maze. Use different colors for the maze and for getting out of the maze.

ACTIVITY 4 • MINI-PROJECT

Create a Table of Geometric Shapes

1. Using a geometry book or Internet research, find ten different angles or shapes. If you are not currently taking geometry, here is a sample Web site: http://www.stetson.edu/~efriedma/packing.html. If that one is no longer available, use a search engine to search for "geometric shapes."

2. Seven of the shapes must have a source. You may come up with three of the shapes on your own if you choose. Once you have chosen ten different shapes, use your drawing tools to replicate those shapes.

3. Create a folder titled **Geometric Shapes**. Save the shapes in the folder as **01Geo.gif, 02Geo.gif, 03Geo.gif, 04Geo.gif, 05Geo.gif, 06Geo.gif, 07Geo.gif, 08Geo.gif, 09Geo.gif,** and **10Geo.gif**.

4. The following criteria should be met:
   - ☐ Ten appropriate shapes used.
   - ☐ Shapes saved as instructed with no errors in folder name or file name.
   - ☐ Line and multisegmented line used with creativity in color, type, and line style.
   - ☐ Bezier curves used with creativity in using Foreground/Stroke Style and Texture.
   - ☐ Images cropped and resized as needed.
   - ☐ Other tools from previous activities used appropriately.

ACTIVITY 5 • WORKING WITH TEXT

In this activity, you will become familiar with:

■ Adding Text
■ Bending Text

Adding Text

1. Open **Squirrel.jpg** from your CD.
2. Click on the Text Tool.

Text Tool

SOURCE: ©JASC PAINT SHOP PRO

3. Click on the point on the image where you want to place the text to open the Text Entry dialog box. Make font style, size, and color changes in the Text Entry dialog box.

Text Entry

4. Create two different text entries as shown in the figure to the left. If you place text on the image and do not like it, you can press the Delete key to remove it. You can also use the Mover Tool to place it appropriately after the text is created. Be sure when you edit text that your text is selected. If it is not selected, you can hover the pointer over the text until the pointer becomes an icon of text with brackets around it, then click.
5. Save as *AustinSquirrel.jpg*.

AustinSquirrel.gif

Bending Text

1. Create a new 900 × 150 pixel image with a transparent background.
2. Click the Draw Tool, choose a Bezier Curve with a Width of 6 and a Line style of your choice, and draw two curved lines. (See below.)

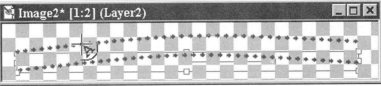

Text Bend

SOURCE: ©JASC PAINT SHOP PRO

3. Click on the Text Tool.
4. Hover the pointer over the left end of the bezier curve until the pointer turns into a rocking A. (See above.)
5. In the Text Entry dialog box, type "Roller Coasters, Etc." Change the color to red for Fill and blue for Stroke. Change the font size to 48.
6. Click in the middle of the text and move it so it is centered over the line.
7. Save as *RollerCoastersEtc.gif*.

RollerCoastersEtc.gif

8. Use the Text Tool, Shape Tool, and Draw Tool to create logos for the following companies. Use at least two colors in each logo and one shape, one line, and one text entry. Change the text font size, color, and type.
   - ShareWare House, Inc., Save as **ShareWare.gif**.
   - Paint By Us, Inc., Save as **PaintByUs.gif**.
   - ABC Day Care, Save as **ABC.gif**.
   - Circle Y Drive-In, Save as **CircleY.gif**.

ACTIVITY 5 • MINI-PROJECT

Create a Nameplate for a Company

1. Call the chamber of commerce in your community or visit their Web site to find out the names of the top five employers in your area. Research each of these companies to find the colors used in their logos. For each company, create a nameplate in their colors.
2. As a part of this activity, you may also want to take a field trip to the chamber of commerce or invite one of its members to speak to the class on the top five employers in the community and their businesses. The more you know about a company, the easier it is to create an image for it—even an image as simple as a nameplate in which font and color choices are the most important.
3. Save the logos as **01Nameplate.gif**, **02Nameplate.gif**, **03Nameplate.gif**, **04Nameplate.gif**, and **05Nameplate.gif**.
4. The following criteria should be met:
   - ☐ Research on each company accurate and thorough.
   - ☐ Nameplates saved as instructed without errors in the file names.
   - ☐ Creativity demonstrated in adding and bending text.
   - ☐ No errors on the nameplate.
   - ☐ Nameplate colors used in a way that complements the text.
   - ☐ Nameplate is an appropriate size.

ACTIVITY 6 • USING OTHER TOOLS

In this activity, you will become familiar with:

- ■ Airbrush Tool
- ■ Fill Tool
- ■ Picture Tubes
- ■ Dropper Tool
- ■ Clone Brush

Airbrush Tool

SOURCE: ©JASC PAINT SHOP PRO

Airbrush Tool

1. The Airbrush Tool can be used to create backgrounds and other fill-in effects. Create a new 400 × 400 pixel image with a transparent or white background.
2. Click on the Airbrush Tool.
3. Create two textured backgrounds. Experiment with Styles and Textures with both Stroke and Fill. You can also use Solid, Gradient, and Pattern choices. Use the options available in the Tool Options—Airbrush dialog box.
4. Save as **01Background.gif** and **02Background.gif**.
5. Create a new 460 × 60 pixel image. This size image is most commonly used to create banners for Web pages or newsletters.

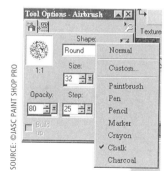

SOURCE: ©JASC PAINT SHOP PRO

Airbrush Options

6. Create a company name to use on the banner. Use the Airbrush Tool to create a textured background and use other tools for the business name and logo. Some tools you may want to consider are the Preset Shapes Tool and the Draw Tool.

7. A banner should convey a positive image of the business and a message about the product of the business. For instance, a banner for Star Clothing would produce an image that the business carries trendy, casual clothing.

Star Clothing Example

8. Save as *MyImage.gif*.
9. Insert the image into a word processing document and include an explanation of the type of business image you are attempting to produce.
10. Save the word processing document as *BusinessImage.doc*.

Fill Tool

To use the Fill Tool, the image should have a transparent background and should not be created as Vector.

1. Create a new 400 × 400 pixel image with a transparent background.
2. Use the Draw Tool to create an image similar to the figure to the left.
3. Click on the Fill Tool. Use various colors in the color palette to fill in the shapes and color the image.
4. Use the Rectangle Selection Tool to cut as close around the image as possible and save as *FillImage.gif*.

Picture Tubes

Picture Tubes can be used to add to an image or to create an image by themselves. More tubes can be found on the Internet, or you can create your own tubes.

1. Create a new 400 × 400 pixel image with a transparent background.
2. Use the Fill Tool to create a solid background for your image.
3. Click on the Picture Tube Tool. In the Tool Options—Picture Tube dialog box, choose a Picture Tube that represents your favorite holiday. Experiment with changing the scale.
4. Click on the second tab in the Tool Options—Picture Tube dialog box. Experiment with changing Placement mode and Selection mode.
5. Use a Picture Tube to add a border around your image.

Fill Example

Fill Tool

SOURCE: ©JASC PAINT SHOP PRO

Picture Tubes Tool

SOURCE: ©JASC PAINT SHOP PRO

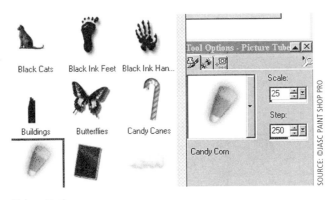

Tubes Options

6. Use the Text Tool to add a holiday message to your image.
7. Save as *Holiday.gif*.

Dropper Tool

The Dropper Tool can pick up the color in an image to match another color. This is useful to correct blemishes on old photographs or to get the red out of eyes in a photograph.

1. Open *Texas.jpg* from your CD.
2. Click on the Dropper Tool. You can Zoom 5:1 by going to the menu bar and choosing Views > Zoom In By 5.
3. Click on a red in the image. Choose one that seems to be the predominant color. Note that doing so made your choice the foreground color.
4. Click the toggle arrow between the Background Solid Color and Foreground Solid Color boxes to change it to the background color, then click on a blue in the image.
5. Hover the pointer over the color and write down the RGB number.

Holiday.gif

Dropper Tool

Color Options

6. Create a banner-size image with a white background.
7. Type "Business Image and" on the first line. Use the red you created with the Dropper Tool.
8. Type "Multimedia Management" on the second line. Use the blue you created with the Dropper Tool.
9. Drag the text image you created and the logo image you opened so that they are side by side to compare the matched colors.
10. Save as *MatchedColors.gif*.

Clone Brush

The Clone Brush is used to copy part of an image to another location. The image must be grayscale or 24-bit in order to use this tool. You are working with two image areas: the target and the source.

1. Open *RedBarn.jpg* from your CD to use as the source of the clone.
2. Open *SculptedDog.jpg* from your CD to use as the target of the clone.
3. Click on the Clone Brush.
4. In the Tool Options—Clone Brush dialog box, you can set the brush tip shape and other options. Use the default settings for now.
5. On the second tab of the Tool Options—Clone Brush dialog box, set the Clone mode to Aligned.
6. Shift-click on the dog, then paint it in an appropriate spot on the Red Barn image.
7. Use previously learned skills to get rid of the white around the dog.
8. Save as *ClonedDog.jpg*.

Clone Brush Tool

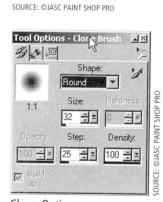

Clone Options

ACTIVITY 6 • MINI-PROJECT

Create an Image for a CD Cover

1. You have been invited to enter a contest to create a CD cover for your favorite singer's latest album.
2. Decide on the singer and choose at least one song to market on the CD.
3. Create three CD covers (front only) to submit for the contest. Save as **01CD.jpg**, **02CD.jpg**, and **03CD.jpg**.
4. Each image must be 4.75 × 4.75 inches.
5. Use only tools practiced up to this point.
6. Create a word processing document with an enumerated explanation of the tools used on each CD cover. Before the enumerated list, include an explanation of the elements in the CD cover that describe the song being marketed. Save as **Documentation.doc**.
7. The following criteria must be met:
   - ☐ No ready-made images used.
   - ☐ Airbrush Tool, Fill Tool, Picture Tubes, Dropper Tool, Magic Wand Tool, and Clone Brush each used at least once on one of the three images. They may be used more than once.
   - ☐ Text used at least once on all three CD covers.
   - ☐ Effective use of tools.
   - ☐ Explanation of tools used and the elements describing the song being marketed clear and organized.
   - ☐ No errors in the word processing document.

ACTIVITY 7 • CREATING SPECIAL EFFECTS

In this activity, you will become familiar with:

- ■ Layers
  - ○ Background with Text
  - ○ Opening a Paint Shop Pro Layered Image
  - ○ Creating a Layered Image
  - ○ Using an Image in Layers
- ■ Filters and Effects
  - ○ Reflection Effects
  - ○ Geometric and 3-D Effects
  - ○ Textures
  - ○ Artistic Effects on Images
- ■ Channels
- ■ Masks

Layers

Background with Text

1. Open **Rain.jpg** from your CD. Turn on the Layer Palette by typing "l." (You can also use the Caps Lock key to toggle all floating menus off your screen.) Note that this image becomes your Background layer on your Layer Palette.
2. Change your foreground and background colors to a blue and a green that match the colors in your background image. You may want to use the Dropper Tool to get exact matches. Change Style and Textures to None and Fill to Gradient.
3. Click on the Text Tool to add a text layer to this image.

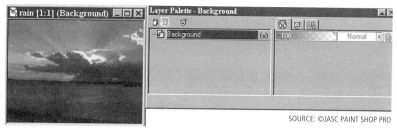

Basic Layers Options

4. Click on the image at the point where you want the image centered both vertically and horizontally. You can adjust this later if needed. It will automatically add text as a vector layer.
5. Change the font to Impact and the font size to 24. Type "Partly Cloudy" for the text, then click OK.
6. Click on the text and drag it around so it is centered at the bottom of the lake area.

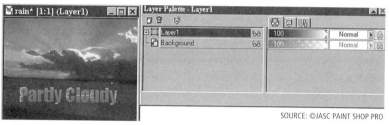

Palette Text Layer

7. On the Layer Palette, right-click on the words Layer 1 and Rename the layer as "Text."
8. Save as *Weather.jpg*. A message will appear that the layered image needs to be merged. Click Yes to merge the image. Some programs call this Flatten.

Opening a Paint Shop Pro Layered Image

1. Open *JazzMan.psp*, which came with your Paint Shop Pro program.
2. It has three layers with several objects on each layer.
3. In the Layer Palette, click the plus sign next to each layer to open the layer and name all objects.
4. Click on the Layer Visibility Toggle (looks like a pair of glasses) for each object one at a time and note what disappears from the image. Continue doing this with each layer.
5. Click on the toggle for the layer rather than the toggle for each object to make the entire layer invisible. Note that when an object or layer is invisible, its Layer Visibility Toggle is marked with a red X.
6. Turn off all layers except the Background. Add text to the Background in appropriate colors. Type "The Jazz Store."
7. Save the new image as *JazzStore.psp*.

Creating a Layered Image

1. Create a new 400 × 400 pixel image.
2. Layer 1 is a brown color. Use the Fill Tool to create this layer.
3. Create Layer 2 by clicking on the Create layer icon on the floating Layer Palette. Name the layer "Shapes." Layer 2 has three different shapes on it. One shape is the sun. Make it an appropriate color. The second shape is the Triangle for tents. The third shape is Dodecagon for the text.

New Layers

4. Layer 3 is the text. Each line of text is a different object. Rename the layer as "Text."
5. Save as *PeacefulSunrise.gif*.
6. Note the symbols in front of each of the layers. The text is automatically created as a Vector layer. The symbol is different for Vector and Raster layers.
7. Create your own layered image with at least three layers similar to the practice image. Decide what you are advertising and use shapes and a background to bring your theme to life.
8. Save as *Advertising.gif*.
9. Insert *Advertising.gif* into a word processing document and explain the steps used in creating the image. Save as *AdSteps.doc*.

Peaceful Sunrise Palette

Peaceful Sunrise Layers

Using an Image in Layers

1. Open *Lake.jpg* from your CD. This image will be the Background layer.
2. Open *Museum.psd* from your CD. Copy and paste it as a new layer to the *Lake.jpg* Background.
3. Use the Mover Tool to place it in an appropriate place. Repeat this process for *TrainDepot.psd*.
4. Add a shape to the image with text, as shown in the figure to the left, below.

LakeLang.jpg

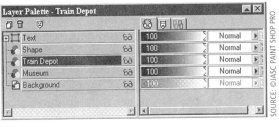

Lake Lang Layers

5. Save as *LakeLang.jpg*.
6. Create a layered image of your own. Use an image of your school, a building in your school, or a sign as the background image. Add two other images of activities within the school or other images within the building. You may add text and other shapes. Save as *HighSchool.jpg*.

Filters and Effects

Reflection Effects

1. Open *BirthdayPaper.jpg* from your CD.
2. Go to the menu bar and choose Effects > Reflection Effects > Kaleidoscope. Try the other Reflection Effects. Save one that you think looks best. Save as *BestReflection.jpg*.
3. Take at least four digital pictures of wrapping paper or scan the wrapping paper. Create your own backgrounds using some of the Reflection Effects. Save as *01Back.jpg*, *02Back.jpg*, *03Back.jpg*, and *04Back.jpg*.

BirthdayPaper.jpg

Geometric and 3-D Effects

1. Open **Placemat.jpg** from your CD.
2. Apply the Circle Geometric Effect.
3. Use the Selection Tool to select as closely around it as you can. Cut and paste into a new image.
4. Save as **Circle.jpg**.
5. Create a new 200 × 200 pixel image.
6. Turn on the Layer Palette.
7. Use the Dropper Tool to choose a color from the placemat image for the background. Fill the new image with the chosen background color.
8. Copy the new placemat image and paste it as a layer on the newly created background image. Go to the menu bar and choose Layers > Merge > Merge All (Flatten) the layers.
9. Use the Selection Tool to select as closely around the now-flattened image as possible. Cut and paste it as a new image.
10. Using 3-D Effects, Buttonize the image. Resize the image to 50%.
11. Save as **PlacematButton.jpg**.

Textures

1. Open **GreenWallpaper.jpg** from your CD. Apply the Texture Effect of Blinds. Save as **Blinds.jpg**.
2. Open **ButterflyWallpaper.jpg** from your CD. Apply the Texture Effect of Weave. Save as **Weave.jpg**.
3. Use scanned or digital pictures of cloth, wallpaper, wrapping paper, or other materials to experiment with the Texture effects. Save at least two other textures. Save as **01Texture.jpg** and **02Texture.jpg**.

Artistic Effects on Images

1. Open **Sunset.jpg** from your CD. Apply different Artistic Effects to the image.
2. Save at least two Artistic Effects that worked effectively. Save as **01Artistic.jpg** and **02Artistic.jpg**.
3. Insert the saved images into a word processing document. Write an explanation as to which Artistic Effects were tried and could not be used. Save as **ArtisticEffects.doc**.
4. Open **PurpleFlower.jpg** from your CD.
5. Add the Circle effect and save as **Circle.jpg**.
6. Add the Erode effect and save as **Erode.jpg**.
7. Add the Meridian effect and save as **Meridian.jpg**.

Channels

Colors can be split using the following options:
- RGB
- HSL
- CMYK (print)

1. Open *RedLeaf.jpg* from your CD.
2. Go to the menu bar and choose Colors > Split Channel > Split to RGB. The original image will still be on the screen as well as three grayscale images.

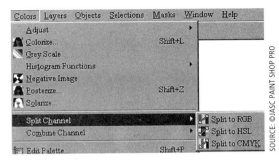

Split Channel

Combined RGB

RGB Splitting

3. Use the Paintbrush Tool to make a few changes to the Red grayscale image. You may use the Fill Tool or Airbrush Tool as well.
4. Go to the menu bar and choose Colors > Combine Channel > Combine from RGB.
5. Save the combined image as *RGBSplit.jpg*.
6. Repeat this process to split for HSL, then combine the split. Save as *HSLSplit.jpg*.
7. Repeat this process to split for CMYK, then combine the split. Save as *CMYKSplit.jpg*.
8. Insert the images into a word processing document and write a summary of what happens in channel splitting.
9. Save as *ChannelSplitting.doc*.

Masks

Masking is like a paint that you can brush on or off. It comes in three different colors:
- Black for transparent.
- Gray for partly transparent.
- White for fully opaque.

Any of the Paint Shop Pro tools can be used on the mask.

1. Open *MallEntrance.jpg* from your CD. Open *MallFountain.jpg* from your CD.

Mask Applied

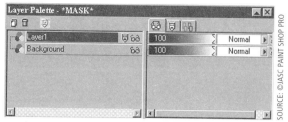

Mask Edit

2. Copy and paste Mall Fountain to Mall Entrance as a new layer. To do this, click on Mall Fountain. In the Layer Palette, drag the word Background on the palette and drop it into the open image of *MallEntrance.jpg*. You can now close Mall Fountain.

3. Make the layer transparent by clicking on the layer name in the Layer Palette.

4. Go to the menu bar and choose Masks > New > From Image. Choose This Window from the Source window drop-down list.

5. Leave the default at Source luminance to make the mask from the varying brightness of the image. Click OK.

6. Notice that a tiny mask appears next to the Layer Visibility Toggle on the Layer Palette. In order to use the mask, the layer must be in Edit mode.

7. Go to the menu bar and choose Masks > Edit. Note the word MASK in the title bar. Clicking on another layer will automatically take you out of Edit mode.

8. Use black paint and the Paintbrush Tool to make the people in the image transparent.

9. To import the mask's transparency to the layer's image, go to the menu bar and choose Mask > Delete.

10. Paint Shop Pro will ask, "Would you like this mask merged into the current layer?" If you click Yes, the mask's transparency becomes a part of the image. Choose Yes.

11. Save as *Mall.jpg*.

Add Mask

ACTIVITY 7 • MINI-PROJECT

Create an Image for a Magazine Cover

1. Choose your favorite actor and actress.
2. Research sites about each of them on the Internet. In a word processing document, write a list of traits and accomplishments about each of them. Save as *Traits.doc*.
3. Create two different images for a magazine cover.
4. The images must be at least 600 × 600 pixels and cannot exceed 1000 × 1000 pixels. Save as *Actor.jpg* and *Actress.jpg*.
5. The following criteria must be met:

☐ A variety of tools used to create the image effectively.
☐ Filters and effects used at least once on both images.
☐ Image has at least two layers.
☐ Appropriate size used for the images.
☐ Images saved as instructed without errors in file names.
☐ Image adequately describes the traits and accomplishments listed in the word processing document.
☐ Word processing document is error-free.

Using Paint Shop Pro to Restore Photographs

1. You have decided to use your image management skills to open a business that restores photos. The first thing you need to do is create some images to place in a portfolio for marketing purposes. You will also create some images to use as advertising. After much thought, you decide to name the business Restore-It, Inc.

2. Collect at least five photos in need of some repair. They may have creases in them, red eyes, discoloration, and so on.

3. Scan each of the photos. Save all images for this project in a folder titled *Restore*. Save as *01or.jpg, 02or.jpg, 03or.jpg, 04or.jpg*, and *05or.jpg*.

4. Repair as much as possible on each of the photographs. Crop and resize as needed. Save as *1re.jpg, 2re.jpg, 3re.jpg, 4re.jpg*, and *5re.jpg*.

5. Create a table in a word processing document with two columns. In the top cell on the left, insert the original photograph. In the next cell, insert the restored photograph. To merge the two columns in the second row, select the row then go to the menu bar and choose Table > Merge Cells. Write an explanation of what tools were used in the restoration process. Remember that this may be used on a poster for advertising purposes or in the shop window. The font needs to be fairly large in a color that matches the photograph. Save the documents as *01ph, 02ph, 03ph, 04ph*, and *05ph*.

6. Your other task is to create some images with the company name in it that can be used for advertising. Some of the images may be used on T-shirts, mugs, coasters, or keychains. Others may be used for the newspaper. Using as many tools as you can that you learned in Paint Shop Pro, create five images with the company name in it. Save as *01im.jpg, 02im.jpg, 03im.jpg, 04im.jpg*, and *05im.jpg*.

7. The following criteria should be met:
   - [ ] Images collected appropriate for the project.
   - [ ] Images scanned and saved as instructed with no errors in file names.
   - [ ] Effective restoration made on the images. Obvious use and knowledge of the proper tools for the task.
   - [ ] Word processing documents prepared as requested with no errors. Formatting of the document effective for promotional use.
   - [ ] Five images created using effectively most of the tools learned in Paint Shop Pro.
   - [ ] Creativity evident in the five images created for marketing use.

Adobe Photoshop

> **Adobe Photoshop**
> **Publisher: Adobe Systems Incorporated**
> Adobe Photoshop has been a software leader in creating professional images for many years. It continues to be in the forefront by staying ahead of the latest technology and allowing greater creative flexibility.

ACTIVITY 1 • BASIC IMAGE EDITING

In this activity, you will become familiar with:

- Opening and Cropping an Image
- Resizing an Image
- History Tab
- Viewing an Image
- Showing Rulers and Guides

Cropping Tool
SOURCE: ©ADOBE PHOTOSHOP

Opening and Cropping an Image

1. Open *Capital.jpg* from your CD.
2. Click on the Crop Tool. The capital image needs to be cropped so that only the dome and the floors under the dome are in the new image. The person should not be in the image.
3. Click and drag to select the area you want in the picture. The marquee surrounds the area you have selected.
4. Right-click on the cropped area and choose Crop.
5. Save the new image as *CutCapital.jpg*.

Capital.jpg

CutCapital.jpg

Daisies.gif

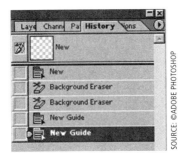

History Tab

View

Resizing an Image

1. Open *Daisies.gif* from your CD.
2. Go to the menu bar and choose Image > Image Size.
3. Change the size of the flowers to 100 pixels wide. The height will be automatically calculated to keep it in proportion.
4. Save the new file as *ResizedDaisies.gif*.

History Tab

The History tab is used much like Undo and Redo in other programs. In the example, the current image has been edited five times. You can click on any of these to redo them or click on them again to undo them.

Viewing an Image

You can easily change the view to magnify it by going to the Navigator tab in one of the floating palettes. To open this palette, go to the menu bar and choose Window > Open Navigator. In the bottom left figure, the view is at 100%. Slide the triangle to the right to increase the view size.

Showing Rulers and Guides

Rulers and Guides can also be viewed on an image to help balance the image.
To view Rulers, go to the menu bar and choose View > Show Rulers. This is a toggle.
New Guides can be added by choosing View > New Guide and typing in the placement in inches for where you want the guide. (Note: You can also specify guide placement using points, picas, or pixels.)

ACTIVITY 1 • MINI-PROJECT

Create People Pictures

1. In business one of the things that creates interest is images of people. Sometimes these are the most difficult pictures to take or images to create.
2. In a team of three or four students, take two pictures of each student. You may want to take one as a full-length shot by turning the camera. In a team of three, each student would then have six pictures to crop and resize. Create a folder titled *Crop and Resize*. Save the pictures in the folder as *01Original.psd*, *02Original.psd*, *03Original.psd*, *04Original.psd*, *05Original.psd*, and *06Original.psd*. Remember that it is best to save your original in the native format. Once you have saved it as a JPG and it is compressed, the image may lose quality each time you make changes.
3. Take the first picture and crop it two times and resize it two times. You will have four images when you are finished. Be sure to crop so that the picture is usable. Pay attention to details of items you want to crop out. Take them out of the picture altogether. Center on your focus object. Resize the picture at 75% and then at 50%. Save as *01Crop.jpg*, *02Crop.jpg*, *01Resize.jpg*, and *02Resize.jpg*.
4. Continue cropping and resizing the other pictures. When you have finished, you will have the following file names in your folder: *03Crop.jpg*, *04Crop.jpg*, *05Crop.jpg*, *06Crop.jpg*, *07Crop.jpg*, *08Crop.jpg*, *09Crop.jpg*, *10Crop.jpg*, *11Crop.jpg*, and *12Crop.jpg*, (Continue this pattern of numbering if you have more team members.) *03Resize.jpg*, *04Resize.jpg*, *05Resize.jpg*, *06Resize.jpg*,

07Resize.jpg, 08Resize.jpg, 09Resize.jpg, 10Resize.jpg, 11Resize.jpg, and *12Resize.jpg*. (Continue this pattern of numbering if you have more team members.)

5. Meet as a team for team members to assess your work. Make any corrections that are suggested and save again.

6. Create a table in a word processing document. The table should have three columns: the first column for the original image, the second column for the cropped image, and the third column for the second cropped image. On the next row of the table, the left cell will be empty, the middle cell will have the first resized image, and the right cell will have the second resized image. Save as *CropandResize.doc*.

7. The following criteria should be met:

☐ Correct number of images and saved as instructed with no errors in file names.

☐ Proper amount was cropped out of picture.

☐ Picture was centered after cropping was completed.

☐ Proper resizing was completed for each image as instructed.

☐ Team members gave a good assessment of the cropping and resizing.

☐ Table was completed properly as instructed with sizing adjusted as needed.

ACTIVITY 2 • CREATING IMAGES

In this activity, you will become familiar with:

New Dialog Box

■ Using Defaults When Creating an Image
■ Custom Shape Tools
■ Stroke a Selection
■ Gradient Application

Using Defaults When Creating an Image

1. Create a new 150 × 150 pixel image using the defaults for resolution, background, and image type. The default is a transparent background. Note that you can change background colors. At this time, the image can be named or you can wait until later.

2. Set the foreground color to one of your favorite colors.

Foreground Color

Custom Shape Tools

1. Hold down the left mouse button on the Rectangle Tool located in the toolbox docked on the left side of your screen. Choose Custom Shape Tool. If the toolbox is not visible, go to the menu bar and choose Window > Show Tools. In the example, the choice is the filled star.

Shapes Choices

2. Draw a filled star to fit the background you chose. There are many available shapes from which to choose. Use Unconstrained mode which means that the star's size and placement will be determined by clicking and dragging the mouse. Save the image as *Filled Star.gif*.

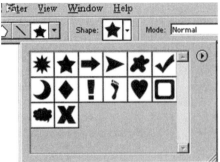
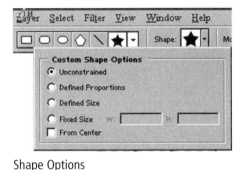

Shapes Available

Shape Options

3. Create a new 300 × 300 pixel image. Choose a custom shape from the Tool Options bar. Select a style to fill the image. Load other styles by clicking on the right arrow to access the menu.

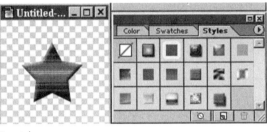
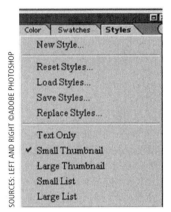

Swatches

Style Options

4. Use several different custom shapes. Click and drag to draw shapes, but note the other options when you press Ctrl, Alt, or Shift. Save the practice image as *CustomShape.gif*.

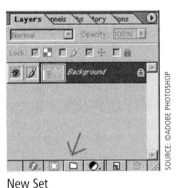

New Set

Stroke a Selection

1. Open *Parade.jpg* from your CD. Create a stroke, as shown on the following page, around the heads of three people on the float.
2. Use one of the Marquee Selection Tools to select the head of the first person. Decide whether the rectangular or the elliptical would be better for this job.

3. Go to the menu bar and choose Edit > Stroke. Create a 6 pixel stroke using the defaults. Use a blue stroke.
4. On the next stroke, change the color to red and set the location to Center. Note the difference.
5. On the final stroke, choose white for the color and set the location to Inside. Note the difference. Save the graphic as *EditedParade.jpg* and insert it into a word processing document. Explain the procedures used to create the strokes and the differences made when choosing outside, inside, or center. Save the document as *Parade.doc*.

Parade.jpg

Stroke

Gradient Application

1. Create a new 460 × 60 pixel image. Apply a gradient fill to this image.
2. Click on the Gradient Tool. A tool option bar will appear under the menu, as shown below.
3. Linear is the default. This can be changed by clicking on one of the other icons on the Tool Options bar. Choose a gradient. Drag the mouse pointer across the blank image. Release the mouse button to fill the area with the gradient.

Gradient Tool

SOURCE: ©ADOBE PHOTOSHOP

Gradient Options

SOURCE: ©ADOBE PHOTOSHOP

4. Experiment with the options available on the Tool Options bar for creating gradients. Create three different images. Save the files as *01Gradient.gif*, *02Gradient.gif*, and *03Gradient.gif*. Insert the three images into a word processing document. Explain what you did to create each gradient. Save the document as *Gradient.doc*.
5. Open *ForSale.jpg* from your CD. Select part of the sky over to the right of the image. Apply a gradient that looks good with the colors of the entire image. Save as *Edited Sky.jpg*.

For Sale Example

ACTIVITY 2 • MINI-PROJECT

Create a Business Identity with Color, Shapes, and Background

1. Use the skills you learned in the Custom Shape Tools and Gradient Application activities to create business identities for the following business names:
    GE Alloy, Inc.
    Saunas Galore
    Sandy Hills Apartments
    Sew Fine Fabrics, Inc.
    Lake Louey Resorts
2. For each business name, think of some words that immediately come to mind when you look at it. Include in these words some colors that come to mind. If you get a visual image when you look at the business name, try to associate a word or phrase with that image.
3. Look at the list of words and determine a background color or gradient that might give someone a visual image of the word. You can be creative in your backgrounds and scan foil, wrapping paper, cloth, and so on. Use at least two gradients as backgrounds.
4. Use the Custom Shapes Tool to continue to add to the business identity. There will be no text on this image. The image you create should be fairly simple, but should have a minimum of two elements that describes the business name.
5. Crop and resize each image as appropriate.
6. Save as *Alloy.gif*, *Saunas.gif*, *Sandy.gif*, *Sew.gif*, and *Lake.gif*.
7. Insert each image into a word processing document. Explain the background used, colors used, and shape used for that particular image. Save as *ExAlloy.doc*, *ExSaunas.doc*, *ExSandy.doc*, *ExSew.doc*, and *ExLake.doc*.
8. The following criteria should be met:
    - ☐ Minimum of two gradients used as backgrounds.
    - ☐ Creativity used on backgrounds.
    - ☐ Colors associated with businesses were appropriate.
    - ☐ Shapes associated with businesses were appropriate.
    - ☐ Explanation of business identity was clear and well-written with no errors.
    - ☐ Crop and resize used appropriately.
    - ☐ Files saved as instructed with no errors in the file names.

ACTIVITY 3 • WORKING WITH TYPE

In this activity, you will become familiar with:

- ■ Adding Type
- ■ Putting Type in a Bounding Box
- ■ Warping Type

Adding Type

1. Open *ForSale.jpg* from your CD.
2. Click on the Type Tool.
3. Click on the image where you want the text to appear then type "For Sale."
4. Change the font size, type, color, and other attributes using the Tool options bar. You can also use the floating Character palette. If the character window is not

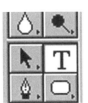

Type Tool
SOURCE: ©ADOBE PHOTOSHOP

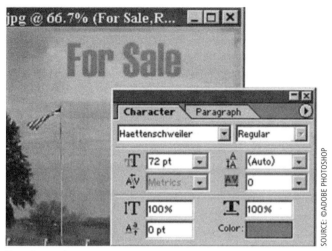

Text Example

showing, go to the menu bar and choose Window > Show Character. Select
"For Sale." Change the text to Verdana, Bold, 48 pt.

5. Move the pointer away from the text until the pointer changes into a right arrow
   with a plus sign. At this point you can click and drag the text to change the
   placement. Press the Enter key on the numeric keypad or select any other tool
   to accept the changes you made to the text.
6. Save as *LandForSale.jpg*.

Putting Type in a Bounding Box

1. Putting type in a bounding box allows you more control over the placement and
   how the text wraps. Create a new 300 × 300 pixel image. On the image use the
   background color. Be sure to change the background color of your image to
   your school colors.
2. In the box, type: "your school name" (Enter) "your city, state, and zip code"
   (Enter) and "your school phone number." Change the font to your other school
   color for this information. Change the font, size, type, and other text attributes
   as needed.
3. Experiment with changing the size of the bounding box. Hover the pointer over
   one of the squares on the edges of the images. When the pointer turns into a
   horizontal arrow, click and drag to resize the box.
4. Create an announcement for an FBLA (Future Business Leaders of America)
   meeting. Begin with a new 300 × 300 pixel image.
5. Make the background a blue metal gradient.
6. Add a bounding text box for the FBLA headline. Use a font that will attract
   attention but is readable. Change the font to bold, change the font color to white,
   and use a large font size to fit across most of the space.
7. Add a second bounding text box with the information for the meeting. Use a
   plain font such as Arial and a smaller size so the lines fit. Change the font to a
   dark blue color.
8. Hover the pointer around the second bounding text box until the pointer
   becomes a curved arrow. This enables you to place the text at an angle. Angle
   the text to create interest in your image.
9. Save as *FBLA.jpg*.

FBLA.jpg

Warp Tool

SOURCE: ©ADOBE PHOTOSHOP

Warping Type

1. Click on the Create warped text icon on the Tool Options bar (far right). If the Tool Options bar is not visible, be sure you have clicked on the Type Tool first. If it is still not visible, go to the menu bar and choose Window > Show Options.
2. The Warp Text dialog box will open. Choose a Style from the drop-down list. Note that the default is None.

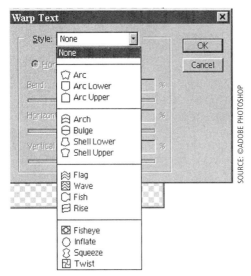

SOURCE: ©ADOBE PHOTOSHOP

Warp Styles

Marketing Seminar

Saturday
February 12, 2xxx
Call 245-555-0110

Warp Example

3. Create the box shown to the left. It does not need to be exactly like the example. Experiment with the different styles, bending, and horizontal and vertical distortion.
4. Save the image as *Marketing Seminar.gif*.

ACTIVITY 3 • MINI-PROJECT

Create School Banners with Text, Color, and Backgrounds

1. Your school is hosting the University Interscholastic League (UIL) Academic District Meet within the next two weeks. You have been assigned the task of designing a banner for each high school to place in the auditorium for the opening ceremony.
2. Design a banner for each high school in your district. Use their school colors and high school name. Be sure to create one for your own school.
3. Use the skills you learned in the Adding Type, Putting Type in a Bounding Box, and Warping Type activities.
4. Save each image as the school name initials. For instance, one of the schools may be Bellville High School. Then the file name would be *bhs.gif*. You will have a file for each school in your district.
5. The following criteria should be met:
   - ☐ Correct colors used for each school.
   - ☐ School names spelled correctly, including capitalization.
   - ☐ Warped text used effectively on at least two images.
   - ☐ A bounding box used on at least two images.
   - ☐ Backgrounds are creative and appropriate to the school.

ACTIVITY 4 • USING SELECTION TOOLS

In this activity you will become familiar with:

- Marquee Selection Tools
- Lasso Tool
- Magnetic Lasso Tool
- Magic Wand

Marquee Selection Tools

1. Open *Clouds.jpg* from your CD.
2. Click the Rectangular Marquee Tool. Drag the mouse pointer diagonally across the image to select part of the clouds to use as a layer. Hold down the Shift key while you click and drag to create a square selection; hold down the Alt key to create a selection from the center out. Practice each of these selections.
3. Cut the part of the image you selected. Create a new image and paste the cut part of the image to the new image. Save as *LayeredClouds.jpg*.
4. Open *Azaleas.jpg* from your CD. Choose the Rectangular Marquee Tool, but hold down your mouse button on it. The drop-down menu shown below appears. Choose the Elliptical Marquee Tool.

Marquee Selection

SOURCE: ©ADOBE PHOTOSHOP

Selections

SOURCE: ©ADOBE PHOTOSHOP

5. Using the Elliptical Marquee Tool, select a part of the azaleas in the middle. Go to the menu bar and choose Filter > Stylize > Emboss. This is just one example of what you can do once you have selected part of an image. You will learn more about filters later.
6. Use the Elliptical Marquee Tool again. This time select the embossed part of the flowers and an edge of flowers around the embossed part. Cut the selection and paste to a new image. Save as *Elliptical.jpg*.

Elliptical.jpg

Lasso Tool
SOURCE: ©ADOBE PHOTOSHOP

Magnetic Lasso
SOURCE: ©ADOBE PHOTOSHOP

Magic Wand
SOURCE: ©ADOBE PHOTOSHOP

Lasso Tool

1. Open *LassoExample.jpg* from your CD. Using the Lasso Tool, select the head of the cat. Be sure to end the lasso at the same place you began.
2. Cut the selection and paste it to a new image. Save as *EditedCat.jpg*.

Magnetic Lasso Tool

1. Open *Poodle.jpg* from your CD.
2. Use the Magnetic Lasso Tool to trace around the image. If needed, increase the view size so that you can accurately trace around the image. End the tracing at the same point the tracing started. When using this tool, be sure you have a high contrast in the image.
3. Cut the selected image. Create a new image and paste the cut image onto the new image. Save as *EditedPoodle.jpg*.

Magic Wand

1. Open *Clouds.jpg* from your CD.
2. The Magic Wand Tool selects areas of pixels that are similar in color. It works best on areas of solid color. Click the Magic Wand Tool.
3. Type a number from 1 to 255 in the Tolerance field on the Tool Options bar. If you want a small area of color, type a small number. If you want a large area of color, type a large number. The default is a low number (32). If you choose 255, the Magic Wand Tool will probably select the entire image.

Tolerance Field

SOURCE: ©ADOBE PHOTOSHOP

4. Experiment with the tolerance numbers and selecting areas of the blue sky. If you want to add to your selection, hold down the Shift key while selecting other areas.
5. Change the background color to black so that you can easily see what happens when you replace or delete the color. Press the Delete key and note what happens to the sky. Continue to remove other similar blue areas of the sky using the Magic Wand Tool if desired.
6. Save as *BlueSky.jpg*.

ACTIVITY 4 • MINI-PROJECT

Create a Collection of Pictures

1. Review the uses for the Marquee Selection Tool, Lasso Tool, Magnetic Lasso Tool, and Magic Wand.
2. Use various resources to find or create images that are appropriate for using these tools. Your resources could be creating an image with a digital camera, scanning an image, or using clip art or other ready-made images. You could also use previously learned tools and create your own image. Vary the type of images used.
3. Create two images using each tool. Decide whether to save the image as a GIF or a JPG.
4. Save in a folder titled *Collection* as *01Marquee*, *02Marquee*, *01Lasso*, *02Lasso*, *01Magnetic*, *02Magnetic*, *01Magic*, and *02Magic*.

5. The following criteria should be met:
   - ☐ Appropriate use of images used for each tool.
   - ☐ Variety of resources used.
   - ☐ Images saved as an appropriate type.
   - ☐ Images saved with correct file name and no errors.
   - ☐ Tool used properly to create a usable image.

ACTIVITY 5 • USING OTHER TOOLS

In this activity you will become familiar with:

- Airbrush Tool
- Rubber Stamp Tool
- Eraser Tool and Eyedropper Tool
- Blur and Sharpen Tools
- Dodge Tool

Airbrush Tool

1. The Airbrush Tool can be used to create backgrounds and other fill-in effects. Create a new 400 × 400 pixel image with a transparent or white background. Click the Airbrush Tool. Choose a foreground color.
2. Click the brush on the Tool Options bar and choose a brush size and type. If the Tool Options bar is not visible, go to the menu bar and choose Window > Show Options.

Airbrush Tool
SOURCE: ©ADOBE PHOTOSHOP

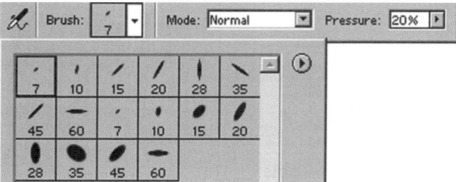

Brush Options

SOURCE: ©ADOBE PHOTOSHOP

3. Experiment with varying the brush type and size, the Mode, and the Pressure for your new image. Change the foreground color as well for variety. Save as *Background.bmp*.
4. Open *AirbrushExample.jpg*. from your CD. Use the Airbrush Tool to add some color to this image. Save as *EditedAirbrush.jpg*.

Rubber Stamp Tool

1. Open *RubberStampExample.jpg* from your CD.
2. Click on the Rubber Stamp Tool, holding the left mouse button down. Slide the mouse over to the Clone Stamp Tool to select it.
3. Choose a brush size and type using the Tool Options bar.
4. Holding the Alt key down, click on a leaf. Using the Clone Rubber Stamp Tool, paint leaves on the faucet to hide it. Save as *HiddenFaucet.jpg*. Leave this file open for the next step.

Rubber Stamp Tool
SOURCE: ©ADOBE PHOTOSHOP

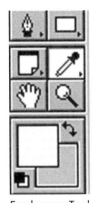

Eyedropper Tool

SOURCE: ©ADOBE PHOTOSHOP

5. Hold down the left mouse button on the Rubber Stamp Tool and choose Pattern Stamp Tool. Paint at least four of the bricks different patterns. Note that on the Tool Options bar for Patterns, if you click the right arrow at the top right, a menu unfolds that enables you to choose more sets of patterns.

6. Save as *PaintedBricks.jpg*.

Eraser Tool and Eyedropper Tool

1. The Eraser Tool allows you to remove part of an image, although you can not change the background layer with the eraser. Open *EraserExample.jpg* from your CD.

2. In this example, a customer is making a decision on refinishing the dresser. This customer wants to see what the dresser would look like without the mirror. Click on the Eyedropper Tool and click on the color around the mirror to pick up the color.

3. Click the blue area of the image. Be sure this color is your background color.

4. Click the Eraser Tool. Experiment with some of the options: Brush, Mode, Opacity, and Wet Edges. (If the Tool Options bar is not open, go to the menu bar and choose Window > Show Options.) Erase the top part of the dresser. It may be beneficial to use the Eyedropper Tool to pick up a different color blue pixel every so often. Also, you may want to change to a smaller brush as you get closer to where the mirror and the bottom part of the dresser meet so you can erase finer lines.

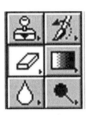

Eraser Tool

SOURCE: ©ADOBE PHOTOSHOP

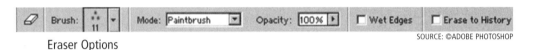

Eraser Options

SOURCE: ©ADOBE PHOTOSHOP

5. Save the image as *Dresser.jpg*.

6. Open *EraserExample.jpg* again. This time hold down your mouse button on the Eraser Tool and choose the Magic Eraser Tool.

7. Make the wall, the floor, and the piece of furniture that you can partly see all transparent. The Magic Eraser Tool makes transparent all the pixels that are near the color you click on. Change the tolerance, if needed. It is best to use a low tolerance and click several times to get the desired effect.

Blur and Sharpen Tools

1. Click the Blur Tool. On the Tool Options bar, select a brush size. You can also change the pressure of the tool. Hold down the mouse button on the Blur Tool for the other choices—the Sharpen Tool and the Smudge Tool.

2. Open *Castle.jpg* from your CD. Use the Blur Tool to blur the windows of the castle. Note: If you are going to blur an entire image, there are filters that do this effectively.

3. Use the Smudge Tool on the area to the left of the castle that is not part of the main castle. Save as *BlurredCastle.jpg*.

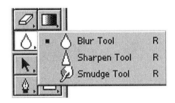

Blur Tool

SOURCE: ©ADOBE PHOTOSHOP

Dodge Tool

1. Click the Dodge Tool. This tool can be used to lighten an image.

2. Open *Sunset.jpg* from your CD. Use the Dodge Tool to lighten the background below the sunset. Experiment with different brushes, the range, and the exposure.

3. Hold down the mouse button on the Dodge Tool to access the Burn Tool. Apply a burn to the sunset on the image.

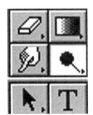

Dodge Tool

SOURCE: ©ADOBE PHOTOSHOP

4. Hold down the mouse button on the Dodge Tool to access the Sponge Tool. Apply a sponge to the car in the image.
5. Save as *DodgeSunset.jpg*.

ACTIVITY 5 • MINI-PROJECT

Create What-If Scenarios

1. In business, many times it is necessary to project what something might look like with changes. Many tools enable us to do this. Use the following tools in this activity: Airbrush Tool, Rubber Stamp Tool, Eraser Tool, Eyedropper Tool, Blur Tool, Sharpen Tool, and Dodge Tool.
2. Review the uses of each of these tools. Using a digital camera or scanner, get pictures to create "what-if" scenarios. For instance, in your classroom, there is probably a wall with a clock on it. What if the clock were gone—what would the wall look like then? You can use more than one tool on a picture, but the focus in the picture, should be on one particular tool.
3. Crop and resize as needed.
4. Save the images in a folder titled *What If* as *02Air.jpg, 02Stamp.jpg, 02Eraser.jpg, 02Eye.jpg, 02Blur.jpg,* and *02Dodge.jpg*. Include the original photos in the folder as well. Save the originals as *01Air.jpg, 01Stamp.jpg, 01Eraser.jpg, 01Eye.jpg, 01Blur.jpg,* and *01Dodge.jpg*.
5. Using word processing software, write documentation explaining each picture. Include in the documentation:
     Was the image scanned or digital?
     What tool did you use to create your "what-if" scenario? Describe exactly what you did with the tool and what you were trying to achieve.
     Did you use other tools in the newly created image? Name them and explain what you did with them.
6. The following criteria should be met:
   - [ ] Appropriate images used.
   - [ ] Tool used effectively on the image.
   - [ ] Images saved as instructed with no errors in the file names.
   - [ ] Documentation was clear and well-written with no errors.
   - [ ] Cropping and resizing used as needed.
   - [ ] Some creativity used in creating "what-if" scenarios.

ACTIVITY 6 • CREATING SPECIAL EFFECTS

In this activity, you will become familiar with:

- Layers
  - ○ Creating and Adding to Layers
  - ○ Using an Image in Layers
- Filters
  - ○ Distort
  - ○ Textures
  - ○ Using Artistic Filters on Images
  - ○ Stylize
- Channels
- Masks
  - ○ Creating a Mask
  - ○ Using Selection Tools in a Mask
  - ○ Quick Masks

Layer Tab

Layers

Creating and Adding to Layers

1. Open *Rain.jpg* from your CD. Note that this layer is the background.
2. Using the Eyedropper Tool, click somewhere in the sky until you have a color that you would like to use for text. On the Layers palette, click on the Create a new layer button at the bottom of the Layers tab. Turn the visibility off for the background layer by clicking on the eye icon.

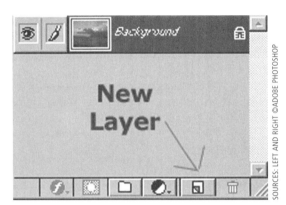

New Layer

Layer Visibility

3. Create a text bounding box on the new layer. Type "Partly Cloudy" in the bounding box with an appropriate font size. Resize the text bounding box as appropriate and place it by using the Move Tool if necessary. If you accidentally add a layer you did not intend, right-click on the layer name to delete it.
4. Save the image as *RainLayer.psd*. When you save it as a .psd file, the image is still in layers. Saving it in another format will flatten the layers.

Partly Cloudy

Lake Lang

Using an Image in Layers

1. Create the image shown using the following images. Open *Lake.jpg* from your CD and use it for the background image. Open *Museum.psd* from your CD and copy and paste it as a new layer to the lake image. Use the Move Tool to place it in an appropriate place. Repeat this process for *TrainDepot.psd*. Add a shape and text to finish the image as shown.
2. Save as *LakeLang.psd*.
3. Create a layered image of your own. Use an image of your school, a building in your school, or a sign as the background image. Add two other images of activi-

ties within the school or other images within the building. Add text and other shapes if you desire. Be creative! Save as your school name.

Filters

Distort

1. Open *BirthdayWrappingPaper.jpg* from your CD. Go to the menu bar and choose Filter > Distort. Experiment with each of the Distort filters. Save those that have made a real change and give interesting effects.
2. Add text on each image explaining which filter was used. Save as *Distort1.jpg*, *Distort2.jpg*, and *Distort3.jpg*.
3. Insert the images into a word processing document. Save the word processing document as *Distort.doc*.

Distort Glass

Textures

1. Open *GreenWallpaper.jpg* from your CD. Go to the menu bar and choose Filter > Texture > Stained Glass. Save as *StainedGlass.jpg*.
2. Open *ButterflyWallpaper.jpg* from your CD. Go to the menu bar and choose Filter > Texture > Craquelure. Save as *Craquelure.jpg*.
3. Using scanned or digital pictures of cloth, wallpaper, wrapping paper, or other materials, experiment with the texture effects. Save as *01Texture.jpg* and *02Texture.jpg*.

Using Artistic Filters on Images

1. Open *Sunset.jpg* from your CD. Apply different artistic filters to the image. Save at least two of those that worked effectively and could be used.
2. Insert the saved images into a word processing document. Write an explanation as to which artistic effects were tried and could not be used.

Stylize

1. Create a minimum of five pictures with a digital camera, a video camera, or a scanner.
2. Experiment with the stylize filters on these pictures. Save each picture as a JPG.
3. Insert the images into a word processing document. Explain whether the picture was digital or scanned and where the picture was taken.

Channels

Colors can be split between either RGB colors or CMYK (print) colors.

1. Open *RedLeaf.jpg* from your CD. Go to the menu bar and choose Image > Mode > RGB color if you are not already viewing the image in RGB mode.

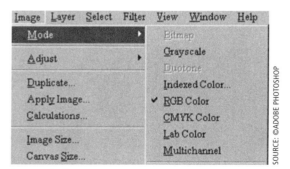

Image Mode

2. Be sure that the Channels tab is visible. Click the Indicates channel visibility button (the eye icon) to turn off visibility on all the images except red. This button is a toggle and is located to the left of the thumbnail of each image on the Channels tab.

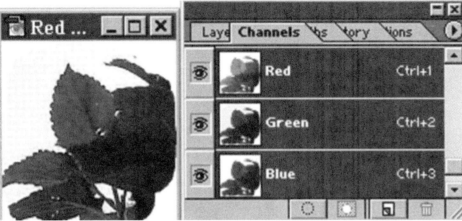

RGB Channels

SOURCE: ©ADOBE PHOTOSHOP

3. Experiment with adjusting the colors on the red image, using the Paint Bucket Tool, Paintbrush Tool, or Airbrush Tool. Make a few minor changes to the red picture first, then combine the channels to write observations about the changes. Save the image and insert it into a word processing document and explain what you have done to the image and what difference it made.
4. Continue experimenting with making changes to each of the grayscales and combining the channels for RGB. Save at least four of the images, insert them into a word processing document, and record your observations of channel splitting. Save the word processing document as *RGBChannels.doc*.
5. Repeat this process using CMYK mode.

Masks

Masking is like a paint that you can brush on or off. It comes in three different colors:
1. Black for transparent
2. Gray for partly transparent
3. White for fully opaque
Any of the Adobe Photoshop tools can be used on a mask.

Creating a Mask

1. Open *MallEntrance.jpg* and *MallFountain.jpg* from your CD. Click on the Layers pallette thumbnail of the Mall Fountain image and drag it into the Mall Entrance image. If you hold down the Shift key while doing so, the image will drop onto the other image centered. You can also use the Move Tool to slide it around until it is centered. Close the Mall Fountain image.
2. Click on the Paintbrush Tool. Type "d." This will give you the default colors in your palette. Note that the background color is now black and the foreground color is now white. Remember that black makes something transparent in a mask so that the background image will show through. Set the Paintbrush Tool to a large size.
3. Go to the menu bar and choose Layer > Add Layer Mask > Reveal All. You are now ready to start painting. The people need to be painted out of the image. You can paint out as much as you desire, but leave the mall fountain in the image with the greenery around it.
4. Save as *MallMask.jpg*.

Mask Image

Using Selection Tools in a Mask

1. Open *Flowers.psd* from your CD. This will be the background on this image. Open *Windmill.jpg* from your CD. Drag and drop the thumbnail of Windmill onto the background. Close *Windmill.jpg*.

2. Using the Rectangular Marquee Tool, select a similar area on the right side of the windmill as shown in the example. It does not have to be exactly the same.

Marquee Selection

3. Go to the menu bar and choose Layer > Add a Mask Layer > Reveal All. Use the Paintbrush Tool to paint over the selected area. By creating a selection, you don't have to worry about painting too much. The Paintbrush Tool will paint only the selected area.

4. Select another area on the right side of the windmill and paint over that selection.

Second Selection

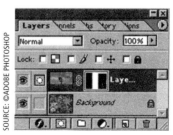

Link

5. On the Layers tab, click on the Link icon between the thumbnails of the layer and the mask. This breaks the link. Use the Move Tool to move the mask around on the background where you would like it placed. Experiment with moving with the link on and with it off.

6. Go to the menu bar and choose Layer > Flatten Image. Save the image as *Flattened.psd*.

Selection Mask

Quick Masks

1. Open *Squirrel.jpg* from your CD. Double-click on the Magic Wand Tool. Adjust the Tolerance if needed and choose one of the more common colors in the squirrel. You can adjust the Tolerance again if necessary to attempt to get an outline of the squirrel. It does not have to be perfect as you can make changes in the next step.
2. Click on the Quick Mask Mode toggle. To select a brush, click on the Paintbrush tool, then go to the Tool Options and choose a brush size and type. Use the brush to touch up to add or take away from the squirrel. Remember that if you accidentally uncover something with black you didn't intend to, you can change the foreground to white to remove it again. Practice adding to and taking away from the mask.
3. Toggle back to standard mode so you are no longer in Quick Mask Mode. Click on the Layers tab if it is not already visible. Double-click on the name of the layer, which is probably Background. Give it a name. This is promoting it from a background to a layer.
4. Go to the menu bar and choose Layer > Reveal Selection. Save the Quick Mask as *Squirrel.psd*.

Quickmask Icon

SOURCE: ©ADOBE PHOTOSHOP

ACTIVITY 6 • MINI-PROJECT

Create an Image for a College

1. Consider three colleges or universities that you may want to attend. Research those schools on the Internet, collecting some images from their Web sites. Save the images in a folder titled *Colleges*. Try to incorporate in the image what the college is known for.
2. Create an image of each school by using the collected images. Use layers, filters, and masks to create an eye-catching design. Save the images as *01College.jpg*, *02College.jpg*, and *03College.jpg*.
3. Share your images with a partner. Exchange feedback on your first impressions when looking at each others images. What kind of feeling does it leave you

with? Is it a positive or negative feeling? Are you interested in learning more about the college or not? Decide if changes need to be made from each other's reactions. Save again if changes are made.

4. The following criteria should be met:

    - ☐ Collection of images was appropriate and demonstrated evidence of research on the college.
    - ☐ Appropriate and effective use of layering.
    - ☐ Appropriate and effective use of filters with a variety of filters attempted.
    - ☐ Appropriate and effective use of masks.
    - ☐ Images saved as instructed with no errors in file names.
    - ☐ Partnership effort was productive in creating a positive image of the colleges.

PART 2 • SIMULATION

Using Adobe Photoshop to Create Images for a Folder Cover

1. Have you ever noticed the variety of folders you can purchase for your classes? Someone has to design these covers. Many have several different designs on the front and back of your favorite cartoon characters, favorite foods, favorite drinks such as Coke, and so on.

2. Choose an item that is your favorite that you would like to see on a folder cover. If you need to, visit a store that sells this item to get some ideas of what is on the market. Create four images using as many tools as possible that you learned in Adobe Photoshop. Collect pictures of the item, either scanned, digital, from the Internet, or from a clip art package. Use the tools to draw your own shapes. Be creative. Save the images in a folder titled *Folder Cover*.

3. In a word processing document, keep an accurate list of each tool you use and how you created each layer. Save the document as *Documentation.doc*.

4. Begin with creating a background that uses something unusual. If necessary, go to the Internet and research tutorials to give you some ideas. There are many tutorials at http://www.adobe.com; you can also search for "tutorials using Adobe Photoshop."

5. Save as *01Favorite.jpg*, *02Favorite.jpg*, *03Favorite.jpg*, and *04Favorite.jpg*.

6. Insert the four images in a word processing document where you would like to see them on a folder cover. Save as *FolderCover.doc*.

7. The following criteria should be met:

    - ☐ Four different images created, centering the idea on one product.
    - ☐ Images used a variety of tools.
    - ☐ Images demonstrated creativity.
    - ☐ Documentation of how the image was created was clear and well-written with no errors.
    - ☐ Images saved in the correct folder with no errors in file name.
    - ☐ Images inserted into a word processing document in an effective manner.

Part 3

Adobe Illustrator

Adobe Illustrator
Publisher: Adobe Systems Incorporated
Adobe Illustrator is the industry standard in vector graphics programs. Illustrator makes it easy to produce high-quality graphics with minimal time and effort. Logo creation is one of its specialties, although the program can integrate with many other programs as well as produce Web pages.

ACTIVITY 1 • SETTING UP THE WORK AREA

In this activity, you will become familiar with:

- File Creation
- View Options
- Status Bar
- Screen Modes
- Opening and Placing Files
  - ○ Importing a Bitmap Image
  - ○ Opening an Adobe Photoshop file
  - ○ Placing an Adobe Photoshop file

File Creation

1. Go to the menu bar and choose File > New. Name the file *Practice.ai*.

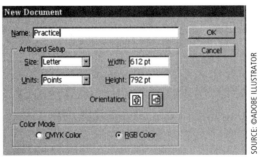

New Document

2. In this dialog box you can change the default document size from Letter to a number of other choices. You can also create a custom document size. The orientation can be changed from portrait to landscape. You can also work in RGB color or CMYK color. The default color option is RGB color. Do not change any of the defaults. Click OK to accept the defaults and move to the work area. You

can change the size of the paper after you have already started the new document by going to the menu bar and choosing File > Print Setup and selecting a page type in the Print Setup dialog box.

3. You can change the color of the page. This will not change the print color, but the color you view.
   a. Choose File > Document Setup.
   b. Select Transparency from the drop-down list.
   c. Select the Simulate Paper check box. Click the top color box and select a new color in the Color dialog box. Click OK to accept the color.
   d. Click OK to close the Document Setup dialog box.

View Options

1. The document opened to 60% size for viewing. This can be changed in a number of different ways. It tells you what view size you are in, along with the name of the file in the title bar. You can also see this at the bottom left corner, as shown in the top, right figure. The view size can go as high as 6400%. To change the size, click the arrow next to the 60% and choose a size.

2. The Navigator tab can be used to change the size of viewing. Use the slide to change the view size or click on the triangles to change the view size. The triangle on the left is for zooming out and the triangle on the right is for zooming in. The Navigator shows a thumbnail of the current document.

3. The Zoom Tool changes view size. Click on the tool, then click on your document. This allows you to zoom out each time you click to the next view size. If you right-click, you can change to zoom in. The two most commonly used views are Fit in Window and 100%. If you double-click the Zoom Tool, the view will change to 100%. If you double-click the Hand Tool to the left of the Zoom Tool, the view will change to Fits in Window. Practice using the Zoom Tool.

Status Bar

1. The status bar is located at the bottom left of the screen between the view window and the scroll bar.

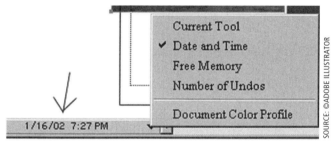

Status Bar

2. There are five options. Try each of them and determine which one would be most helpful to you. You may change your mind later or at different times when you need different information available quickly.

Screen Modes

1. The Screen Mode is located on the last row of your toolbar. There are three choices.

2. The leftmost choice is Standard Screen Mode, which is the default. The middle choice is Full Screen Mode with Menu Bar, which takes away some of your menus and toolbars and gives you more work space. The rightmost choice is

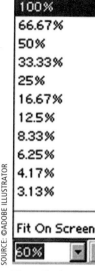

View Choices

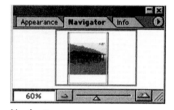

Navigator
SOURCE: ©ADOBE ILLUSTRATOR

Zoom Tool
SOURCE: ©ADOBE ILLUSTRATOR

Screen Mode
SOURCE: ©ADOBE ILLUSTRATOR

Linked Image

SOURCE: ©ADOBE ILLUSTRATOR

Links Palette

SOURCE: ©ADOBE ILLUSTRATOR

Full Screen Mode, which takes away all menus. You can quickly toggle between Screen Modes by typing "f."

Opening and Placing Files

Importing a Bitmap Image

1. Go to the menu bar and choose File > New. Create a new 300 × 300 pixel document.
2. Go to File > Place. Browse to the CD and click on *Cactus.bmp*. On the Place dialog box, choose Link. Note in the figure to the left that a linked image has a blue X across it. The X can be removed by clicking on the image. If the file is embedded then it is included in the Illustrator file, which makes the file much larger. If it is linked to the Illustrator file then the file will be much smaller.
3. You can now make changes to the image using transformation tools and image filters. Experiment using a few transformation tools and image tools on the imported cactus image. Do not save.
4. The Links palette allows you to identify, select, monitor, and update objects in Illustrator that are linked to external files. To turn the Links palette on, go to the menu bar and choose Window > Links.

Opening an Adobe Photoshop File

1. Go to the menu bar and choose File > Open. Open *Apple.pdf* from your CD.
2. Save as *Apple.eps*.

Placing an Adobe Photoshop File

1. Go to the menu bar and choose File > New. Create a 300 × 300 pixel document.
2. Go to the menu bar and choose File > Place. Select the file you want to place and choose Place. Open *Apple.pdf*.
   a. Placing EPS or PDF files with the Link check box selected will not allow you to modify the linked object.
   b. With the Link check box not selected, the file is embedded and you can edit each part as an object.

ACTIVITY 1 • MINI-PROJECT

Create Images from BMP or EPS Formats

1. Go to http://www.google.com or your favorite search engine and search for BMP and EPS files. Locate three of each file type or convert them to the specified type. The images should be business-related. Save in a folder titled *Placing Images* as *01.bmp*, *02.bmp*, *03.bmp*, *01.eps*, *02.eps*, and *03.eps*.
2. Place each image in a 200 × 200 pixel Illustrator document. Experiment with filters on each image until you have a usable image. Save only two of the filtered images for each image. Save in the *Placing Images* folder as *01BMP.ai*, *02BMP.ai*, *03BMP.ai*, *04BMP.ai*, *05BMP.ai*, *06BMP.ai*, *01EPS.ai*, *02EPS.ai*, *03EPS.ai*, *04EPS.ai*, *05EPS.ai*, and *06EPS.ai*.
3. The following criteria should be met:
   ☐ Appropriate file types found as requested.
   ☐ Document size as instructed.
   ☐ Creativity used in experimenting with filters.
   ☐ Filters saved were appropriate for use in business.
   ☐ Files saved as instructed with no errors in file names.

ACTIVITY 2 • USING THE DRAWING TOOLS

In this activity, you will become familiar with:

- Selection Tools
- Pencil Tool
  - ○ Freeform Path
  - ○ Closed Path
- Smooth Tool
- Erase Tool
- Pen Tool
  - ○ Straight Line
  - ○ Closed Path
  - ○ Curved Segments
  - ○ Adding and Deleting Endpoints
  - ○ Converting Anchor Points
  - ○ Resizing
  - ○ Splitting Paths
- Drawing Shapes
- Drawing Symbols
  - ○ Creating a Symbol
  - ○ Symbol Sprayer Tool
- Using Brushes
  - ○ Selecting Brushes
  - ○ Creating a Closed Brush
  - ○ Creating a Custom Brush
- Auto Trace Tool

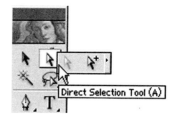

Selection Tools

SOURCE: ©ADOBE ILLUSTRATOR

Selection Tools

There are three selection tools in Illustrator.
1. The Selection Tool is used to select entire objects.
2. The Direct Selection Tool is used to select portions or segments of objects.
3. The Group Selection Tool is used to select portions or sections of objects that you have defined as a group.

Pencil Tool

Freeform Path

1. Click the Pencil Tool. At any time, if you need the Pencil Tool to change to a crosshair for more precise drawing, press the Caps Lock key. Try that now.
2. Place the pointer where you want to begin the path. Drag to draw.
    a. The Pencil Tool will show a small × to show that you are drawing a freeform path.
    b. A dotted line appears as you drag.
    c. Anchor points are on either end of the line.
    d. The path takes on the current paint color.
    e. The path remains selected until you begin another freeform path.
3. Place your pointer at the end of the anchor point and begin dragging again. This will add to the freeform path. The path must be selected first.
4. Go to the menu bar and choose File > New. Create a 300 × 300 pixel document. Draw several freeform paths, experimenting with adding to paths and beginning new paths.
5. Add some open arcs or curves, similar to the top left figure on the following page, in your practice. To change color on an arc or curve, use the Selection Tool. To change color on more than one at a time, click on the first freeform

Pencil Tool

SOURCE: ©ADOBE ILLUSTRATOR

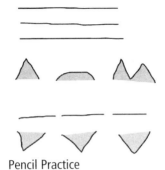

Pencil Practice

Fill Color

path, then hold down the Shift key and click on others. Click the color you want them to be in the color palette.

Closed Path

1. Go to the menu bar and choose File > New. Create a 300 × 300 pixel document.
2. Select the Pencil Tool.
3. Place the pointer where you want to begin and start dragging. At some point while dragging, hold down the Alt key. Do not hold down the Alt key before beginning the path. The pointer will have stripes, indicating that you are drawing a closed path. Do not release the Alt key until the path has been closed.
4. Draw the bottom part of an ice cream cone. It will look like a triangle. Double-click the fill color to access the Color Picker. Choose a brown color for the bottom of the ice cream cone by clicking on a brown in the Color Picker then clicking OK.

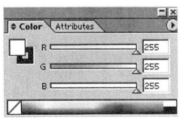

Color Palette

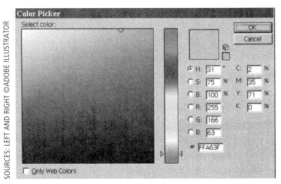

Color Picker

5. Using the Pencil Tool, draw an open path for the ice cream on top of the cone. Choose a color of ice cream you would like. Drag the ice cream and set it on top of your cone by clicking on the Selection Tool then holding the left mouse button down and dragging the shape to the bottom of the ice cream cone. If the ice cream does not fit the cone, use the pencil to shave off some of the ice cream on the side. Practice using the Pencil Tool to add to or take away from the shape drawn.
6. Pick up a black color for your Pencil Tool and add some lines on the cone to make it look more real. Save as *IceCream.ai*.
7. Using your own creativity, draw another object that includes drawing a freeform path, drawing a closed path, reshaping the closed path with the pencil, changing colors, and moving drawn objects. Save as *Object.ai*.

Smooth Tool

1. Draw a tulip similar to the one shown to the far left. Use the drawing skills you learned in the previous exercise.
2. Using the Selection Tool, select the bloom on the tulip.
3. Click and drag on the Pencil Tool to select the Smooth Tool. You can also hold down the Alt key while selecting the Pencil Tool to change it to the Smooth Tool. Note that you can also tear off these tool choices so they are a floating toolbar.
4. Trace the tulip bloom and compare the differences to your original drawing.
5. Continue using the Selection Tool to select each leaf and smooth the leaves as needed.
6. Save as *Tulip.ai*.

Ice Cream.ai

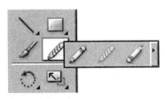

Tulip.ai

Smooth Tool

Note: Setting Preferences on the Pencil and Smooth Tools
1.   Double-click the Pencil or Smooth Tool to open the Preferences dialog box.

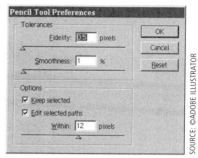

Pencil Preferences

2.   You can use the sliders or enter values for Fidelity and Smoothness.
a.   For a more angular curve, the Fidelity value should be low. The higher the value, the smoother the curve.
b.   For a coarser path, the Smoothness value should be lower. The higher the value, the more smooth the path.

Erase Tool

1.   Go to the menu bar and choose File > New. Create a 300 × 300 pixel document.
2.   Draw several closed and open paths.
3.   Select one of the paths. Click on the Pencil Tool then drag across to select the Erase Tool. Drag along the path until you have chosen the amount you want to erase.
4.   Continue experimenting with this tool on other paths you have drawn.

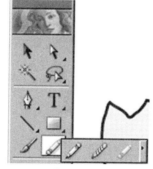

Erase Tool
SOURCE: ©ADOBE ILLUSTRATOR

Pen Tool

Straight Line

1.   The Pen Tool enables you to create straight lines and smooth curves with exactness.
2.   Go to the menu bar and choose File > New. Create a 300 × 300 pixel document.
3.   Click on the Pen Tool.
4.   Click with the Pen Tool to create a beginning anchor point. Click a little away from it to create another anchor point. You do not need to drag to create the straight line. Do not save your work.
5.   Note: A quick method of undoing a pen draw is to hold down the Ctrl key while typing "z."

Pen Tool
SOURCE: ©ADOBE ILLUSTRATOR

Closed Path

1.   If at any time some of your paths try to connect to one another, click and then click again to begin a new line that is separate from the other. Note that you can click to create multiples of 45-degree angles.
2.   Create straight lines to form a box. When you get ready to close the box with the fourth line, the Pen Tool cursor shows a hollow circle. This means you have it positioned correctly to close the shape.
3.   Create a square, a rectangle, a triangle, a diamond, an octagon, and a pentagon. Save as *Shapes.ai*.

Pen's Hollow Circle
SOURCE: ©ADOBE ILLUSTRATOR

Curved Segments

1. Go to the menu bar and choose File > New. Create a 250 × 250 pixel document.
2. Click on the Pen Tool.
3. Place the pen tip where the curve should begin. Hold down the left mouse button. The first anchor point is placed, and the pen tip changes to an arrowhead.
4. Drag to extend the direction line.
   a. The angle determines the slope of the curve.
   b. The length determines the height of the curve.
5. Practice the following:
   a. Place the pen tip and drag to create a horizontal direction line about one inch long. Release the mouse button. Click about one inch below the anchor point. Repeat, except this time click above the horizontal line to create a curve.
   b. Place the pen tip and drag to create a vertical direction line about one inch long. Release the mouse button. Click about one inch to the right of the anchor point. Repeat, except this time click to the left of the anchor point on the vertical line to create a curve.
   c. Practice drawing S shapes and birds flying in the air. Save as *CurvedSegments.ai*. You can use the Reshape Tool to help with creating S shapes and birds by selecting the object with the Selection Tool, then choosing the Reshape Tool and clicking on an anchor point and dragging the shape.

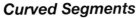

S Curves
SOURCE: ©ADOBE ILLUSTRATOR

Reshape Tool
SOURCE: ©ADOBE ILLUSTRATOR

Adding and Deleting Endpoints

1. Open *CurvedSegments.ai*. This is the file that you created in the last activity.
2. Using the Selection Tool, select the paths where you want to add or delete anchor points.
3. Select the Pen Tool that is appropriate for what you want to do (add or delete). You can also select the proper tool by hovering the pointer over the anchor point that you want to add or delete.

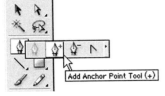

Add or Delete Anchor Point Tools
SOURCE: ©ADOBE ILLUSTRATOR

Converting Anchor Points

1. Create a new 150 × 150 pixel document.
2. With the Pen Tool, draw a straight line in the shape of a V.
3. Using the Direct Selection Tool, select the path you want to modify if it is not already selected.
4. With the Convert Anchor Point Tool selected (see bottom, left figure), click at the base of the V and drag a horizontal direction line. Notice the shape changing. Release the mouse button and you now have converted the V to a smooth point.

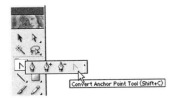

Convert Anchor Point Tool
SOURCE: ©ADOBE ILLUSTRATOR

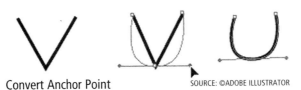

Convert Anchor Point   SOURCE: ©ADOBE ILLUSTRATOR

5. With the Convert Anchor Point Tool still selected, click at the anchor point and watch it convert back to a corner point.
6. Draw three straight and three rounded shapes and practice using this tool. Save as *Convert.ai*.

Resizing

1. For a straight segment, use the Direct Selection Tool and drag the anchor point on either end. For rectangles, you can select the shape with the Selection Tool then resize using one of the handles on the sides of the bounding box.

2. For curved segments, use the Direct Selection Tool and select an anchor point on either end. Drag the anchor point or drag a direction point. You can change directions by using the Convert Anchor Point Tool.

> Note: For more choices on making changes to pen-drawn paths, go to the menu bar and choose Object > Path.

Splitting Paths

1. Create a new 250 × 250 pixel document.
2. Click on the Scissors Tool. Click on the path where you would like to split it.
3. Using the Direct Selection Tool, drag the blue square that indicates the split to the shape you would like.
4. Create several other closed and straight line segments to practice splitting. Save as *SplittingPractice.ai*.
5. Using what you have learned with the Pen Tool, draw three cattle brands. You can research cattle brands on the Internet or, if available, use the following site: http://www.viptx.net/victoria/history/brands.

Scissors Tool

SOURCE: ©ADOBE ILLUSTRATOR

Drawing Shapes

1. Create a new 300 × 300 pixel document.
2. Click on the Rectangle Tool.
3. Position the pointer where you want to begin and drag diagonally to create a rectangle. Hold down the Shift key while dragging to create a square. Drag to the desired shape or, when you are finished, double-click on the rectangle and type in the values you desire for the height and length.
4. A shape can also be created by dragging from the center by holding down the Alt key while creating the shape.
5. Repeat steps 2 through 4, using the Rounded Rectangle and Ellipse Tools to draw them. Access the Ellipse Tool by clicking on the Rectangle Tool and dragging the mouse over to the Ellipse Tool icon. Do not save your work.
6. Click on the Polygon Tool.
7. Drag to create a polygon.
   a. Rotate the polygon by dragging in an arc.
   b. Press the up arrow or down arrow key to increase or decrease the number of sides. You can also double-click the shape to change the number of sides by typing in the value.
8. Draw shapes of varying numbers of sizes for practice.
9. Click on the Star Tool. Draw several stars using some of the shortcuts you learned in creating other shapes.
10. Click on the Flare Tool.
11. Note that the Flare Tool has two handles—a center handle and an end handle. Practice adjusting each by clicking on the Direct Selection Tool then dragging the center or end handle.
12. Double-click on the Flare Tool or the flare image to access the Flare Tool Options dialog box.

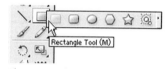

Shapes Tools

SOURCE: ©ADOBE ILLUSTRATOR

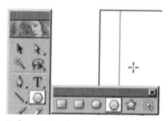

Polygon Tool

SOURCE: ©ADOBE ILLUSTRATOR

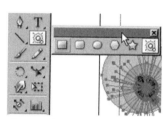

Flare Tool

SOURCE: ©ADOBE ILLUSTRATOR

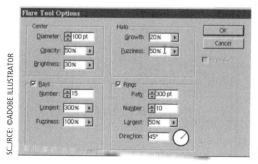

Flare Tool Options

13. Create a new 500 × 500 pixel document. Using at least three different shapes, draw a floor plan of your classroom. Save as *FloorPlan.ai*.

Drawing Symbols

Creating a Symbol

1. Open *Tulip.ai*. This is the file you created and saved when learning the Smooth Tool. Select the artwork.
2. Drag the artwork to the Symbols palette. If the Symbols palette is not visible, go to the menu bar and choose Window > Symbols.
3. You can duplicate a symbol by choosing Duplicate Symbol on the Symbols palette menu. This menu can be accessed by clicking the right triangle on the Symbols palette.
4. Open *IceCream.ai*. This is the file you created and saved when learning the Color Picker. Add this symbol to the palette by dragging it to New Symbol. Duplicate the symbol in the document.

Symbols Palette

Symbol Sprayer

Symbol Sprayer Tool

1. The Symbol Sprayer Tool creates multiple image sets on your document.
2. Create a new 500 × 500 pixel document. Click on the Symbol Sprayer Tool.
3. Double-click on the Symbol Sprayer Tool to access more options.
4. Practice using the sprayer on several different symbols.
5. Practice using the other symbols you found when you double-clicked to the Symbol Sprayer Tool. Note that each time you click with the sprayer, the image gets larger. Make a list of any other tricks you learn while practicing. Try using the Ctrl and Alt keys while using the sprayer. Type your list of tips in a word processing document. Save as *SymbolTips.doc*.
6. Save this document as *SymbolPractice.ai*.

Using Brushes

Selecting Brushes

1. Create a new 500 × 500 pixel document. Double-click on the Paintbrush Tool to open the Paintbrush Tool Preferences dialog box. These preferences were introduced in a previous activity. For this exercise, accept the default preferences by clicking OK.
2. On the Brushes palette, click on New Brush. If the Brushes palette is not visible, go to the menu bar and choose Window > Brushes. You will note that there are four different types of brushes: Calligraphic Brush, Scatter Brush, Art Brush, and Pattern Brush. For this activity, leave it on Calligraphic Brush.

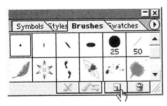

New Paintbrush

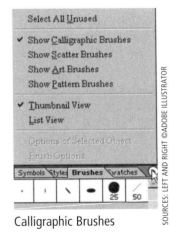

Calligraphic Brushes

Creating a Closed Brush

1. To create a closed brush, begin dragging the paintbrush, hold down the Alt key, and do not release the Alt key until you have the desired size. Experiment with this by drawing numbers from 0 through 9 on your new document. For the numbers 6, 8, 9, and 0, use the closed brush. (You can create them without the closed brush, but for the benefit of this activity use the closed brush.) Save this document as *NumberPractice.ai*.

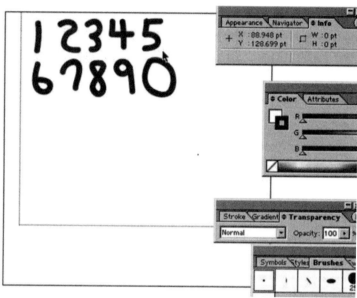

Number Practice

SOURCE: ©ADOBE ILLUSTRATOR

2. Create a new 500 × 500 pixel document. You can use any drawing tool in Illustrator to draw a path, and then add a brush to it. Use the Pencil Tool to draw an open path. On the Brush palette, choose the 12 pt Oval. The closed path drawn with the pencil should now appear to have been drawn with a brush, as illustrated to the right. An open path does not connect in all places. At least one end is not connected to anything. A closed path is connected.

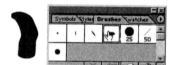

Applying Brushes

SOURCE: ©ADOBE ILLUSTRATOR

3. Use the Pen Tool and add different brushes to open and closed drawings. Save your practice as *ApplyingBrushes.ai*.

4. Brushes can also be removed from a path. Create a brushed path in the shape of an L. Use a pencil, then apply a brush to it. Now remove the brush by choosing Remove Brush Stroke on the Brushes palette menu.

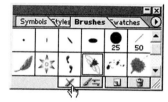

Remove Brush

SOURCE: ©ADOBE ILLUSTRATOR

Creating a Custom Brush

1. You can create any of the four types of brushes. For this activity, we will create a Scatter Brush.

2. Using the Pencil Tool, draw an eye. Put some color into it.

3. Select the entire eye. You can do this easily by pressing Ctrl and typing "a."

4. Click on the New Brush button on the Brushes palette menu. Choose New Scatter Brush in the New Brush dialog box.

5. Name the New Scatter Brush "Eye." You should now see the brush among the thumbnails.

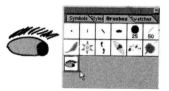

Eye Brush

SOURCE: ©ADOBE ILLUSTRATOR

6. Create a new 500 × 500 pixel document. Experiment with the new Scatter Brush. Save as *EyeBrush.ai*.

7. Using your own idea, create an object to add to the Brushes palette as a Scatter Brush, following the same steps 1 through 6. Save as *MyScatterBrush.ai*.

Auto Trace Tool

SOURCE: ©ADOBE ILLUSTRATOR

Auto Trace Tool

1. You can bring an image into Illustrator and trace over it so that you can use the image or part of it in another piece of artwork.
2. Open *Clarinet.jpg* from your CD. Click on the Auto Trace Tool. Click anywhere on the outside edge of the clarinet. Copy and paste the clarinet into the same document several times. Save as *AutoTrace.jpg*.

ACTIVITY 2 • MINI-PROJECT

Create Logos for Businesses Using Drawing Tools

1. In a team of four, create a business plan for each of three businesses. The business plan should include business name, purpose of the business, location of the business (city, state), targeted market (what type of people will shop at the business or frequent the business as a consumer or client), and a simple mission statement of no more than fifteen words.
2. Break into partners within your team. Partners will work together to create a logo for each of the businesses. Save as *01Logo.ai*, *02Logo.ai*, and *03Logo.ai*.
3. Create a word processing document with a table. The table should have four columns. Create a list of the following drawing tools in the first column: Selection Tool, Direct Selection Tool, Group Selection Tool, Pencil Tool, Smooth Tool, Erase Tool, Pen Tool, Rectangle Tool, Polygon Tool, Flare Tool, Symbols palette, Symbol Sprayer Tool, Brushes, and Auto Trace Tool. In the second, third, and fourth column headings, type the name of the files in step 2. Use this table to keep a record of which tools you use in each of the files. Save as *LogoRecord*.
4. Compare logos within your team. In a word processing document, summarize differences in the logos and logo records. In your summary, include which partnership used more tools, ideas you might have obtained from the other partnership, and what you might have done differently after comparing. Save as *PartnershipComparison.doc*.
5. The following criteria should be met:
   - ☐ Team created a business plan for each business with all required elements.
   - ☐ Partners created three logos using a preponderance of the tools listed.
   - ☐ Table of tools used was created as instructed and accurate as far as tools used for each logo.
   - ☐ Creativity used in creating logos.
   - ☐ Comparison summary was detailed and well-written, and contained no errors.

ACTIVITY 3 • TRANSFORMING OBJECTS

In this activity, you will become familiar with:

- ■ Rotating
- ■ Scaling
- ■ Reflecting
- ■ Shearing
- ■ Transform Palette
- ■ Warp Effects

Rotating

1. Create a new 250 × 250 pixel document. Add a star shape to the document. Copy and paste another star shape. Click on the Hand Tool and slide the star shape directly on top of the first star.

2. Click on the star that is on top so that it is chosen. Click on the Rotation Tool.
3. Rotate the star so that the image now looks like a 10-sided star. Save as *10-sidedStar.ai*.

Scaling

1. Open *10-sidedStar.ai*. This is the file you created and saved when learning the Rotation Tool. Select one of the stars. Click on the Shift key and select the other star so that both stars are selected. Click on the Scale Tool.
2. Hover the pointer over one of the points, then drag to increase the size of the star so that it is almost the size of the Artboard. Hold down the Shift key while dragging to keep the star in proportion. Repeat for the other star. Save as *10-sidedStar.ai*, replacing the other file.

Reflecting

1. Open *Face.jpg* from your CD.
2. Click the face with the Selection Tool.
3. Select the Reflect Tool.
4. Click above the face to set the point of origin. It does not necessarily have to be the same amount of space as the example.

Step 1 Reflect
SOURCE: ©ADOBE ILLUSTRATOR

5. Imagine a line from the point of origin that you just created at an angle downward between the original and the reflection. Click at the end of the imaginary line. See Step 2, below. You can also hold down the Alt key while clicking and make a copy, rather than move the reflection.
6. Save as *ReflectionExample.ai*. It should look similar to the Reflection Copy below.

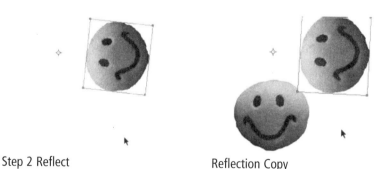

Step 2 Reflect   Reflection Copy
SOURCES: LEFT AND RIGHT ©ADOBE ILLUSTRATOR

Shearing

1. To *shear* means to slant or skew an object. Create a new 400 × 400 pixel document.
2. Using the pencil, draw a leaf. Look at the symbol leaf for an example if necessary.
3. Make sure the leaf is selected.

Rotation Tool
SOURCE: ©ADOBE ILLUSTRATOR

Scale Tool
SOURCE: ©ADOBE ILLUSTRATOR

Reflect Tool
SOURCE: ©ADOBE ILLUSTRATOR

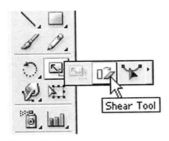

Shear Tool

SOURCE: ©ADOBE ILLUSTRATOR

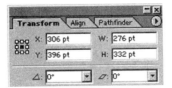

Transform Palette

SOURCE: ©ADOBE ILLUSTRATOR

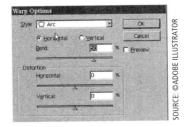

Warp Options

SOURCE: ©ADOBE ILLUSTRATOR

Removing Warps

SOURCE: ©ADOBE ILLUSTRATOR

4. Select the Shear Tool. The leaf will have a point of origin set. Click outside the leaf and drag to skew the leaf. Practice this several times until you have your desired result.
5. Repeat this process with your leaf. This time, hold down the Alt key while skewing the leaf. By doing this you create a copy of the leaf with the original still intact.

Transform Palette

1. You can make some of the changes that you have just learned about by using the Transform palette. If the Transform palette is not visible, go to the menu bar and choose Window > Transform.
2. Open *Building.jpg* from your CD. Using the Selection Tool, select the building.
3. Make the following changes:
   a. For a new horizontal orientation, enter a value in the X text box on the Transform palette. No changes are necessary in this activity. You can try it, but choose Undo when you are finished.
   b. For a new vertical orientation, enter a value in the Y text box.
   c. For width change, enter a value in the W text box. Change this to 300.
   d. For height change, enter a value in the H text box. Change this to 200.
   e. For rotation changes, enter a value between 0 and 360 in the Rotate text box. Change this to −30.
   f. For shearing, enter a value in the Shear text box. Experiment with a few different numbers, then decide on one.
4. To reset the bounding box, Choose Object > Transform > Reset Bounding Box.
5. Save as *TransformExample.ai*.

Warp Effects

1. Open *Flower.jpg* from your CD.
2. Go to the menu bar and choose Effect > Warp > Arc to open the Warp Options dialog box.
3. Leave the warp options at the default settings for now. You will have a chance to experiment with them in the next activity. Be sure to select the Preview check box.
4. Undo the preset warp effect arc and try several others. When you have found one you like, save the document as *WarpedFlowers.ai*.
5. Open *Roses.jpg* from your CD.
6. Click on the image *Roses.jpg* then go to the menu bar and choose Effect > Warp > then choose a warp effect.
7. In the Warp Options dialog box, set the Horizontal and Vertical Distortion by typing in values to determine the amount of horizontal and vertical distortion you want. Click OK.
8. Click on the Appearance palette. Click on the warp you would like to remove. Click and drag it to the trash can in the lower right corner of the Appearance palette.

ACTIVITY 3 • MINI-PROJECT

Create a Transformed State Seal

1. Go to http://www.google.com and search for the state seals for Texas, Florida, Oklahoma, Washington, and Maine. State seals are similar to logos in a business, except they are governed by law to authenticate official documents of the state.

2. Save the images in a folder titled *State Seals*. Save as *Texas*, *Florida*, *Oklahoma*, *Washington*, and *Maine*. Each image should have been saved on the Internet as a GIF or JPG. Do not change this file format. Save it as the same file format as it was on the Internet.

3. On each of the state seals, use the Rotate, Scale, Reflect (create a reflection copy), and Shear effects and one Warp effect. Save the transformed images as *TransTexas*, *TransFlorida*, *TransOklahoma*, *TransWashington*, and *TransMaine*.

4. The following criteria should be met:

   ☐ Images saved as instructed with no errors in file names.
   ☐ Required tools used effectively for the Texas seal.
   ☐ Required tools used effectively for the Florida seal.
   ☐ Required tools used effectively for the Oklahoma seal.
   ☐ Required tools used effectively for the Washington seal.
   ☐ Required tools used effectively for the Maine seal.

ACTIVITY 4 • USING THE LIQUEFY TOOLS

In this activity, you will become familiar with:

- Warp Tool
- Twirl Tool
- Pucker Tool
- Other Liquefy Tools
- Blends

Warp Tool

1. You cannot use any liquefy tools on objects that contain text, graphs, or shapes. Keep this in mind as you learn the tools.
2. Open *WaterLily.jpg* from your CD.
3. Use the Selection Tool and select the object.
4. Click on the Warp Tool.
5. Drag the area around the water lilies to distort them.
6. Save as *DistortedLilies.ai*.

Twirl Tool

1. Create a new 400 × 400 pixel document.
2. Using what you learned with the Paintbrush Tool, create an object. It does not have to be exactly like the example.
3. Click on the Twirl Tool.
4. Apply the Twirl Tool to the artwork you created. Save as *TwirlExample.ai*.
5. Think of a type of object that would make an impact if the Twirl Tool were used on it. Search the Internet for a free image of that type and apply the Twirl Tool to it. Save as *Twirl.ai*.

Pucker Tool

1. Access the Pucker Tool by clicking on the Warp Tool then dragging across to the Pucker Tool icon. Take a digital picture or scan a picture of an object.
2. Open the object that you have chosen to use.
3. Select the object with the selection tools.
4. Apply the pucker effect using the Pucker Tool.
5. Save as *Pucker.ai*.

Warp Tool

SOURCE: ©ADOBE ILLUSTRATOR

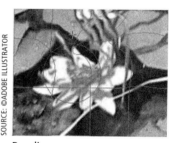

SOURCE: ©ADOBE ILLUSTRATOR

Bending

Twirl Example

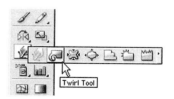

Twirl Tool

SOURCE: ©ADOBE ILLUSTRATOR

Other Liquefy Tools

1. Continue using your own digital images, scanned images, or images from the Internet. Create two examples of each of the liquefy tools.
2. Insert these examples into a word processing document with an explanation of how they would be used in business.
3. After creating each example in Illustrator, open the example in Adobe Photoshop or Jasc Paint Shop Pro and save it as a JPG before inserting it into the word processing document. Save the word processing document as *LiquefyTools.doc*.

Blends

1. Create a new 400 × 400 pixel document.
2. Click on the Polygon Tool.
3. Draw a small polygon and then a much larger polygon far to the right of it.
4. Select each of the shapes you drew with the Selection Tool, then click on the Blend Tool.
5. Drag from the large shape to the small shape. Notice that the program fills in the missing sizes for you.

Blends Tool

SOURCE: ©ADOBE ILLUSTRATOR

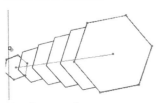

Blends Example

SOURCE: ©ADOBE ILLUSTRATOR

ACTIVITY 4 • MINI-PROJECT

Create Special Effects with State Flowers

1. Search on the Internet for the following state flowers: New York, Georgia, Michigan, Ohio, Tennessee. Save in their original file type from the Internet in a folder titled *State Flowers*. Save as *NewYork*, *Georgia*, *Michigan*, *Ohio*, and *Tennessee*.
2. Use a different tool on each image from the following list: Warp Tool, Twirl Tool, Pucker Tool, and two liquefy tools.
3. Save in the *State Flower* folder as *Warp*, *Twirl*, *Pucker*, *01Liquefy*, and *02 Liquefy*.
4. The following criteria should be met:
   - ☐ Correct state flower located for each state requested.
   - ☐ Warp image demonstrates an effective use of the Warp Tool.
   - ☐ Twirl image demonstrates an effective use of the Twirl Tool.
   - ☐ Pucker image demonstrates an effective use of the Pucker Tool.
   - ☐ Liquefy images demonstrates an effective use of the liquefy tools.
   - ☐ Images saved as instructed with no errors in the file names.

ACTIVITY 5 • LEARNING MORE ABOUT APPLYING COLOR

In this activity, you will become familiar with:

- Color Palette
- Stroke Palette
- Swatches Palette
- Color Picker
- Gradients
- Meshes

Color Palette

1. Create a new 500 × 500 pixel document. Using the shape tools, draw six shapes.

2. If the Color palette is not visible, go to the menu bar and choose Windows > Color to open it.
3. Select the Fill box.
4. Position the pointer over the color bar and when the pointer turns into an eyedropper, click. If the color you have chosen is *out of gamut*, then you will see an exclamation point in a yellow triangle. Out of gamut means that the color cannot be printed using CMYK colors. If the color you have chosen is not Web-safe, you will see a cube. Click the cube so that it will find the closest match that is Web-safe. Do the same for CMYK colors.
5. Click on the Fill box and drag the color to one of the shapes. There are other ways to color a shape, but this is the quickest. For instance, if you have the shape selected and click on a color, the shape will automatically change to that color.
6. Color the rest of your shapes. Color at least two of them using Web-safe colors and two using CMYK (print) colors. Save as *Fill.ai*. Leave the document on your screen for the next activity.

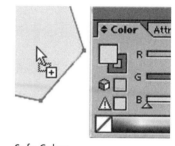

Safe Colors

SOURCE: ©ADOBE ILLUSTRATOR

Stroke Palette

1. The *Fill.ai* document should be on your screen. If not, open it.
2. Click on the Stroke box on the tool bar. The Stroke box is found in the lower right corner of the Toolbar. It is at an angle to the Fill box.
3. Select one of the objects.
4. Go to the menu bar and choose Windows > Stroke.
5. Change the stroke Weight to 10 and then drag the Stroke to one of the filled shapes. Continue to do this until all have been outlined. Experiment with the weights of the strokes. Do not worry about the Web-safe or CMYK colors this time.
6. Save as *FillandStroke.ai*.

Stroke

SOURCE: ©ADOBE ILLUSTRATOR

Swatches Palette

1. Open *FillandStroke.ai*. This is the file you created in the last activity. Use this document to practice using swatches.
2. Go to the menu bar and choose Windows > Swatches.
3. Click a swatch in the Swatches palette.
4. Click on the Fill box to apply this fill to any selected object.

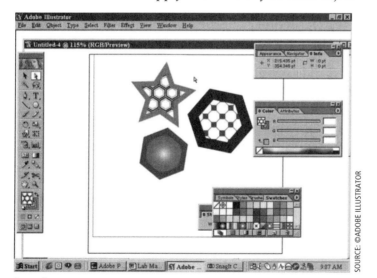

SOURCE: ©ADOBE ILLUSTRATOR

Swatches

5. Draw a picture using the Pencil Tool. Draw a sun, a person, flowers, a tree, and a house. Using fill, strokes, and swatches, color your picture. Save as *Picture.ai*.

Color Picker

1. Create a new 400 × 400 pixel document.
2. Using the Pencil Tool, draw a bouquet of five balloons.
3. To access the Color Picker, double-click on the Fill box.

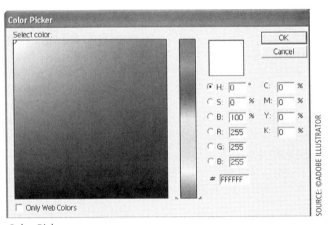

Color Picker

4. These balloons are going to be placed on a Web site to advertise for a business that plans parties. Be sure that the colors are Web-safe.
5. After choosing a color in the Color Picker, click OK.
6. Drag the color to the balloon. Continue until all balloons are filled with color.
7. Save as *Balloons.ai*.

Gradients

1. Create a new 400 × 400 pixel document.
2. Draw a shape, then fill it with color.
3. Using the Gradient palette, set the gradient the way you would like it. If the Gradient palette is not visible, go to the menu bar and choose Window > Gradient. Choose between the two types of gradients. Linear blends one color into another from one side to the other. Radial blends one color into another from the center out. You can use the sliders on the Gradient palette to make changes in the overall appearance of the gradient. Click the gradient box to apply the gradient to your shape on the Artboard.
4. To apply color to the gradient, choose a color on the slider from the Color palette. Drag the color down to the slider on the Gradient palette. You can adjust the color of the gradient by sliding it to the left or right once you have it on the slider.
5. You can also add more than one color by dragging multiple colors from the color slider to the gradient slider. Experiment with this.
6. Create at least five different shapes with five different gradients. Some gradients should be radial and some linear. Some should be one color and some should be more than one color. Save as *Gradients.ai*.

Meshes

1. Create a new 400 × 400 pixel document.
2. Draw a rectangle and fill it with color.

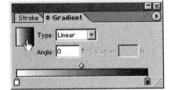

Gradient Palette

SOURCE: ©ADOBE ILLUSTRATOR

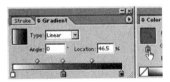

Applying Color

SOURCE: ©ADOBE ILLUSTRATOR

3. Click on the Mesh Tool.
4. Click on the object with the Mesh Tool. An explanation of the lines follows:
    a. Mesh lines crisscross the object and allow you to manage color across the lines.
    b. A mesh point is the intersection of two mesh lines.
    c. Anchor points can be placed on any mesh line and then moved around to modify it.
    d. A mesh patch is the area between any four mesh points.
5. Click several times on the mesh object to add more points. You can also drag the lines around and bend them. Experiment with making these changes.
6. Click on a different color on the Color palette.
7. Click in a different place on the mesh object.
8. Click on a different color again. Continue practicing this with several drawn shapes. Save the practice as *MeshPractice.ai*.

Mesh Tool
SOURCE: ©ADOBE ILLUSTRATOR

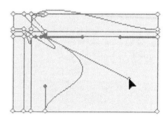

Mesh Example
SOURCE: ©ADOBE ILLUSTRATOR

ACTIVITY 5 • MINI-PROJECT

Create a Stained-Glass Effect

1. Create a new 250 × 250 pixel document.
2. Using the Polygon Tool, draw a polygon shape on the document. Copy the shape eight times for a total of nine polygons that are the same size.
3. Fit the polygons together much as you would a puzzle.
4. Fill each polygon with color. Make sure that you do not repeat a color and that the colors are Web-safe. Use stroking on the outer edge of each polygon that is a different color than the fill color.
5. Group all nine polygons by clicking on the first polygon then holding the Shift key down while selecting each of the other polygons. Go to the menu bar and choose Object > Group.
6. Draw a rectangle around the entire group of polygons.
7. Fill the rectangle with color and arrange the rectangle so that it is behind the polygons.
8. Save as *StainedGlass.ai*.
9. The following criteria should be met:
    ☐ Correct document size.
    ☐ Nine polygons all same size.
    ☐ Polygons fit together appropriately.
    ☐ Colors in the polygons all different, with Web-safe colors.
    ☐ Polygons grouped.
    ☐ Rectangle drawn around all polygons and filled with a color.
    ☐ Rectangle arranged so that it is behind the polygons.
    ☐ Image saved as instructed with no errors in file name.

ACTIVITY 6 • USING TYPE

In this activity, you will become familiar with:

■ Entering Type
■ Type in a Box
■ Type on a Path

Entering Type

1. Open *Park.jpg* from your CD.

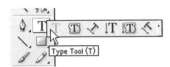

Type Tool

SOURCE: ©ADOBE ILLUSTRATOR

Park Example

Type Alignment

SOURCE: ©ADOBE ILLUSTRATOR

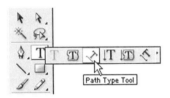

Path Type Tool

SOURCE: ©ADOBE ILLUSTRATOR

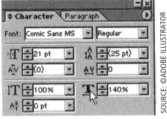

Character Palette

SOURCE: ©ADOBE ILLUSTRATOR

2. Click on the Type Tool.
3. Click somewhere in the bottom right quadrant of the image. Type "Come join us at the park!"
4. Click and drag to select all of the type. Right-click and change the font to Impact (or another font if that one is not available). Also change the size of the font to 21. Change the color of the font to white.
5. Save as *Park.ai*.

Type in a Box

1. Open *Daffodils.jpg* from your CD.
2. Click on the Type Tool. Drag a box over the middle of the vase. Right-click to change the size of the type and the format. Experiment to get the right effect. Choose a color for the type. Type "Wedding Rehearsal" (Enter) "Friday 6 p.m." (Enter) "San Miguel Steak House." One advantage of putting type in a box is that it will wrap if you are typing a paragraph.
3. If the Paragraph palette is not visible, go to the menu bar and choose Window > Type > Paragraph and Alignment. Change the alignment, for this purpose, to centered.

Type on a Path

1. Create a new 300 × 300 pixel document.
2. Using the Ellipse Tool, draw a circle. The circle should be about three inches in circumference.
3. Click on the Path Type Tool.
4. Click on the outside of the circle, along the line and type "Texas Computer Education Association." Use the spacebar to space so that the type moves around the way you would like it to point.
5. Using the Character palette, adjust the horizontal spacing so the words fit perfectly around the circle. You may also need to adjust the size of the font.
6. Save as *TCEA.ai*.

ACTIVITY 6 • MINI-PROJECT

Create an Annotation of Art

1. Search the Internet for art museums. Find at least five pieces of interesting art. Save each piece of art in a folder titled *Art*. Save the files as *01Art*, *02Art*, *03Art*, *04Art*, and *05Art*.
2. Scale the art if needed. Using the Type Tool, add notes on the art about the artist and where the art may be found. You must at least have the artist's name added with the Type Tool. Type directly on the art, in a box, and in a path for variety. Change font, size, and color to work with the piece of art.
3. Save as *06Art.ai*, *07Art.ai*, *08Art.ai*, *09Art.ai*, and *10Art.ai*.
4. The following criteria should be met:
   - ☐ Five pieces of art saved and in the correct folder.
   - ☐ Art scaled appropriately to use for annotating the piece of art.
   - ☐ Notes on the art thorough and accurate.
   - ☐ At least one piece of art uses typing directly on the art.
   - ☐ At least one piece of art uses typing in a box.
   - ☐ At least one piece of art uses typing on a path.
   - ☐ Annotated art saved as instructed with no errors in file names.

Using Adobe Illustrator to Create an Image for a Program Cover

1. Your principal has asked you to create a program cover for graduation. He wants you to submit at least three possibilities for him to choose from. His last statement to you was, "I want it to be something that gives a positive image of our school, with as many elements of our school depicted in the image as possible."

2. If there is a theme to this year's graduation, use it in your program cover. Include the date, time, and location.

3. Create a new document. The Artboard Setup should be Custom Size, Units in Inches, Width 5.5, and Height 8.5. Choose CMYK Color Mode.

4. Create your program covers, using as many tools as possible. Be creative.

5. Save as *01GradProgram.ai*, *02GradProgram.ai*, and *03GradProgram.ai*.

6. The following criteria should be met:
   - ☐ Document setup correct.
   - ☐ When and where information for graduation is accurate.
   - ☐ School name and colors displayed somewhere on the program cover.
   - ☐ Image paints a positive image of the school and the variety of activities within the school.
   - ☐ Colors used are all CMYK print-ready.
   - ☐ Program cover contains no errors.
   - ☐ Creativity demonstrated throughout the program cover, with original ideas and evidence of effort.

Part 4

Macromedia FreeHand

> **Macromedia FreeHand**
> **Publisher: Macromedia, Inc.**
> FreeHand is an image management program that enables you to create extraordinary illustrations. It hosts a multiple page workspace and even enables you to create Macromedia Flash movies and test them in the software. Drawing freeform paths has never been easier than in this program.

ACTIVITY 1 • THE WORK AREA

In this activity, you will become familiar with:

- File Creation
- View Options
- Moving the Document
- Opening and Importing Files
  - Opening a File
  - Importing a File
  - Importing Clip Art
- Grids, Gridlines, and Rulers
- Master Pages

File Creation

1. When you open FreeHand, the Wizard enables you to create a new document, open a document, go to a previous document, use a template, or get help. The Wizard can be turned off if you do not find it useful. For now, turn the Wizard off by clearing the "Show this screen when starting FreeHand" check box.
2. To create a new document, go to the menu bar and choose File > New or click on the New icon. You can also press Ctrl and type "n."
3. Document options are available using the Document inspector. If the Document inspector is not on your screen, go to the menu bar and choose Window > Inspectors > Document.
4. Change the size of the document to Custom. Set x to 400 and y to 500 pixels.
5. On the Document inspector, click on the Landscape icon next to the custom drop-down box to select Landscape orientation
6. On the bottom right corner of the Document inspector, there are three choices for thumbnail view. Leave the setting at the default middle view.
7. To add pages, click the right arrow in the upper right corner of the panel to display the shortcut menu, and choose Add pages.
8. On the Add Pages dialog box, click OK. See the Add Pages figure on the following page.

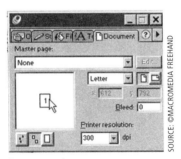

Opening Wizard

SOURCE: ©MACROMEDIA FREEHAND

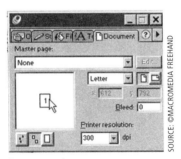

Document Inspector

SOURCE: ©MACROMEDIA FREEHAND

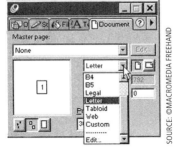

Page Size

SOURCE: ©MACROMEDIA FREEHAND

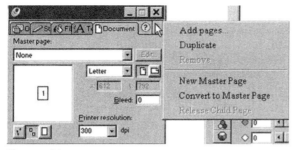

Shortcut Menu

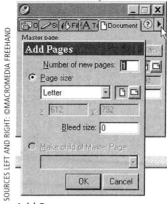

Add Pages

View Options

1. Click on the Zoom tool.
2. Using the Zoom tool, enlarge the document by clicking on it.
3. To reduce the page, hold down the Alt key and click on the document with the Zoom tool.
4. To enlarge or reduce an area, drag the selection.
5. You can also change the zoom in the lower left corner by clicking on the arrow and choosing a percentage.

Moving the Document

Use the Hand tool to move the document around on the work area.

Opening and Importing Files

Opening a File

1. Go to the menu bar and choose File > Open and double-click on *Cactus.bmp*.
2. Close the file by going to the menu bar and choosing File > Close.

Importing a File

1. Go to the menu bar and choose File > New.
2. Go to the menu bar and choose File > Import.

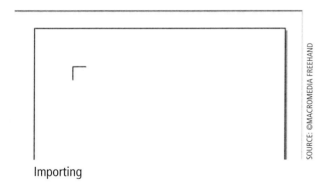

Importing

3. Place the pointer over the place marker, as shown above, and click to place the image.
4. Using the corner handles, stretch the image to fit the full page.
5. Save as *Apple.fh10*.

Zoom Tool

SOURCE: ©MACROMEDIA FREEHAND

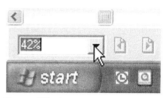

Zoom Window

SOURCE: ©MACROMEDIA FREEHAND

Hand Tool

SOURCE: ©MACROMEDIA FREEHAND

Clipart Viewer

Viewer Screen

Importing Clip Art

1. FreeHand comes with a clip art folder that contains many graphics. These images can be resized, rotated, recolored, and manipulated in many ways. You can open the Clipart Viewer from a shortcut on the desktop if available or by choosing Start > Programs > Macromedia FreeHand 10 > Freehand 10 Clipart Viewer.

2. The clip art folder does not copy to the hard drive when FreeHand is installed. You will need to add the clip art folder to the hard drive, or pull clip art from the CD that comes with the program.

3. Minimize the FreeHand program so that you can see both the FreeHand Clipart Viewer and the FreeHand program. Find the clip art you want to use and drag it to the FreeHand document window. The figure below shows the Clipart Viewer with the FreeHand program behind it. One of the graduation images is being moved to the FreeHand document window by clicking and dragging.

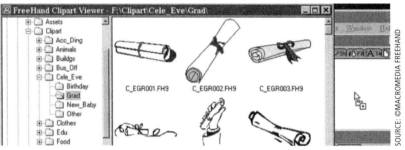

Moving Clipart

4. Choose a piece of clip art to move to the document window. Save as *ClipartViewer.fh10*.

5. The clip art can also be opened as a file from the FreeHand program. If you open it as a file, you can not place more than one piece of clip art on the page unless you do so by copying and pasting other clip art or using the Clipart Viewer for the other clip art. You also will need to ungroup to do some manipulation of the image.

Grids, Gridlines, and Rulers

1. To turn grids on, go to the menu bar and choose View > Grid > Show.

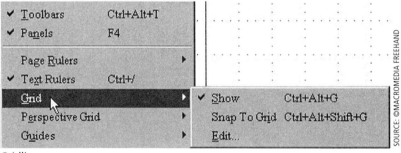

Gridlines

2. The color of the grids or gridlines can be changed by going to the menu bar and choosing Edit > Preferences > Colors. Click on the Guide color or Grid color box and select a new color. Click OK.

3. Grid options can be set by going to the menu bar and choosing View > Grid > Edit. Choose the way you want yours to snap. If you want it to snap to relative position, then select the Relative grid check box. If you want to force snapping to precise grid intersections, then clear the Relative Grid check box.

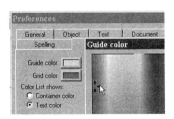

Grid Color

4. To add guides, be sure that rulers are turned on first. To turn rulers on, go to the menu bar and choose View > Page Rulers. Set the rulers to 0 by grabbing the crosshairs at the top left corner where they intersect and dragging them to the upper left and top corner of the document. To set a vertical guide, click anywhere on the left vertical ruler and drag the guide to 64 on the horizontal ruler. To set a horizontal guide, click anywhere on the horizontal ruler and drag the guide down to 64.

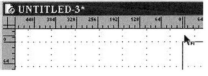

Zero Setting

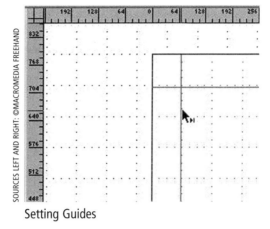

Setting Guides

Master Pages

1. Go to the menu bar and choose Window > Inspectors > Document. Click on the right arrow in the upper right corner of the Document inspector and choose New Master Page.

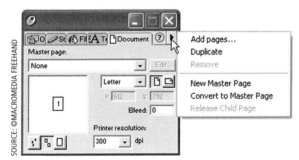

Master Pages

Library

2. Go to the menu bar and choose Window > Library. Click on the right arrow in the upper right corner of the window and choose New Master Page.
3. Be sure that the guides, grids, and rulers are on. Using the crosshairs, set the left and top margin to 0. Turn on snap to grid. Go to the menu bar and choose View > Grid > Snap to Grid. Import *Dog.jpg* from the CD and place the image at the top left corner inside the guides. Set a Bleed of 10 in the Document inspector.
4. Close the Master Document window.
5. In the Library window, drag or double-click the Master Document you just created to your current document. Save as *DogMaster.fh10*. The bottom right figure shows the icon that is a FreeHand document.
6. Using an image you have created, scanned, or taken with a digital camera, create another Master Document. Place the image anywhere on the page. Save as *MyImage.fh10*.

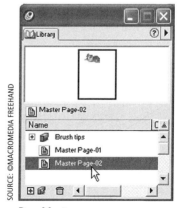

Dog Master

ACTIVITY 1 • MINI-PROJECT

Create a Collage of Images

1. You are an assistant to the marketing specialist and have been given the task of locating some images that can be used for a flyer. The flyer is for one of your clients who is going to host a barbecue at the country club for potential buyers of their product. You decide the product.
2. Create three custom 400 × 500 pixel FreeHand documents with at least five possible images for use on the flyer. Use a variety of sources, including the Clipart Viewer that comes with FreeHand, the Internet, and digital or scanned images.
3. Resize the images as needed so that five images fit on each document.
4. Save the documents as *01Potentials.fh10*, *02Potentials.fh10*, and *03Potentials.fh10*.
5. No labeling is necessary on the document, although you should be prepared to justify your choices of images.
6. The following criteria should be met:
   - ☐ Thought was evident in choosing the product to be marketed.
   - ☐ Documents set up as instructed.
   - ☐ Variety of sources used for the images.
   - ☐ Images resized and placed in an organized manner in the document.
   - ☐ Images appropriate for the type of business, activity, and product.
   - ☐ Documents saved as instructed with no errors in file names.

ACTIVITY 2 • USING THE DRAWING TOOLS

In this activity, you will become familiar with:

- Shapes
  - ○ Rectangle Tool
  - ○ Line Draw
  - ○ Polygon or Star Tool
  - ○ Spirals
  - ○ Arcs
- Freeform Paths
- Pen Tool
  - ○ Pen Tool Smart Cursors
  - ○ Closed Paths
- Bezigon Tool
  - ○ Drawing with the Bezigon Tool
  - ○ Grouping a Path
  - ○ Freeform Tool
- Charts and Pictographs
  - ○ Creating a Chart
  - ○ Importing a Chart and Setting a Chart Type
  - ○ Creating a Pictograph
- Graphic Hose Tool

Shapes

Rectangle Tool
1. Go to the menu bar and choose File > New.
2. Change the document settings to Custom, 800 × 800 pixels.

3. Double-click the Rectangle tool. This allows you to create curved corners on your drawing. Change the Corner radius to 50.
4. Draw a rectangle on your document by clicking and dragging. Double-click on the Rectangle tool again. Change the corner radius to 100, which is the maximum curve, and draw two more rectangles.
5. Choose the first rectangle by using the Selection tool. Click on the Stroke tab in the Inspectors panel. If the Stroke tab is not visible, go to the menu bar and choose Window > Inspectors > Stroke to turn it on. Choose a color by double-clicking on the color box for stroke.

Rectangle Tool

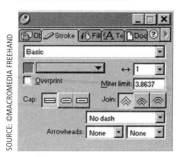

Stroke

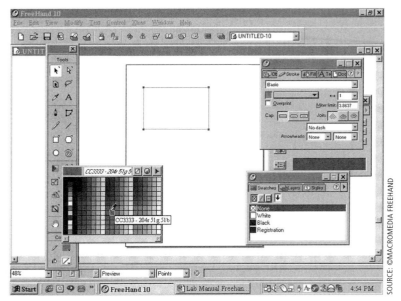

Color Box

6. On the Inspectors palette, click on the Fill tab. Double-click the color box to select a color. You can also drag the color and drop it into the rectangle to fill it with color. Do not use the same color twice on any rectangle for the stroke or the fill.
7. Repeat this procedure for the other two rectangles. Change the stroke to 6 pt for rectangle 2. You can do this on the Stroke inspector. The stroke weight is the box with the double arrow to the left of it. Change the stroke to 12 pt on rectangle 3.
8. Save as *Rectangles.fh10*.
9. Draw ellipses by repeating steps 1 through 8, using the Ellipse tool. Save as *Ellipses.fh10*.

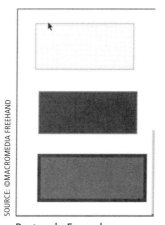

Rectangle Examples

Line Draw

1. Lines are drawn much the same way as rectangles and ellipses. In this activity, you will practice a couple of basic techniques that can be used in drawing any shape. Create a new document using the default document settings.
2. Click on the Line tool. To keep a line constrained so that it is straight, hold down the Shift key while drawing the line. Draw a line using the Shift key so that it is straight. You can also set the constrain angle by using the menu. Go to the menu bar and choose Modify > Constrain and enter a value in the Angle text box or use the wheel.
3. Draw a second line. This time hold down the Alt key while drawing the line to draw from the center out.
4. While the second line is selected, add a stroke color to it. Go to the Stroke inspector and change the stroke to 4 pt.
5. Select the first line with the Pointer tool and add a stroke color to it and a weight of 12 pt. The Pointer tool is located in your Tools panel. It is the top left tool. You can double-click the tool to open the dialog box with the tool name.

Line Draw

6. Draw at least five other lines of varying stroke weights and colors.
7. Save as *Lines.fh10*.

Polygon or Star Tool

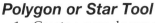

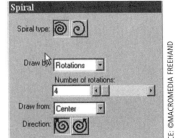

Polygon Tool

1. Create a new document using the default document settings.
2. Double-click the Polygon tool.
3. You can choose Polygon or Star for Shape in the dialog box shown at left. You can also set the Number of Sides, how many sides for the star or polygon, and change the Star Points settings for the star.
4. Use the same techniques for constraining as you learned in the previous activity and the Polygon Tool dialog box to draw at least three polygons and three stars. None of the stars or polygons should look the same.
5. Use the stroke and fill to add color to each of them.
6. Save as *PolygonsandStars.fh10*.

Spirals

1. Create a new document using the default document settings.
2. Go to the menu bar and choose Window > Toolbars > Xtra Tools.

Xtra Tools

SOURCE: ©MACROMEDIA FREEHAND

3. Double-click on the Spiral tool.
4. In the dialog box shown at left, you can change the Spiral type, Number of rotations, Draw from settings (center, edge, or corner), and Direction.
5. Draw at least six different spirals, experimenting with changing types, rotations, and direction. No two spirals should look the same.
6. Add color to the spirals.
7. Save as *Spirals.fh10*.

Spiral Tool

Arcs

1. Create a new document using the default document settings.
2. Double-click on the Arc tool on the Xtra Tools toolbar.
3. In the Arc dialog box, choose the following setting combinations and draw an arc on your document using each combination. If necessary, use a second document.
   a. open arc
   b. flipped arc
   c. concave arc
   d. open, flipped arc
   e. open, concave arc
   f. flipped, concave arc
   g. open, flipped, concave arc
4. Save as *Arcs.fh10*.

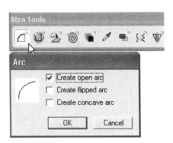

Arc Tool

SOURCE: ©MACROMEDIA FREEHAND

Freeform Paths

1. Create a new document. Change the document settings to Custom, 500 × 500, Landscape.
2. Double-click on the Pencil tool. There are three types of Tool Operations: Freehand, Variable stroke, and Calligraphic pen. Click on each one and notice the changes in the Pencil Tool dialog box. Select Freehand.

3. With Freehand you have two choices to make. For Precision, a high number follows minor variations as you draw, and a low value smooths minor variations as you draw. The other choice is Draw dotted line. The dotted line enables you to draw faster, but the final result is still a solid line. Experiment with this tool, changing the precision and drawing using a solid line and a dotted line.
4. Select Variable stroke and draw numbers from 0 to 9. Select the Auto remove overlap (slow) check box and change the Width to Min 12 and Max 24. To make Auto remove overlap work, the number must be written in one movement without lifting the pencil. Add a fill color to each of the numbers. Save as *Numbers.fh10*.
5. Select Calligraphic Pen and set Width and Angle options. Write as many letters of the alphabet on one page as you can. Save as *Alphabet.fh10*.

Pencil Tool

Freehand

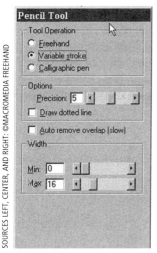

Variable Stroke

Calligraphic Pen

Pen Tool

Pen Tool Smart Cursors

1. Create a new document using the default document settings.
2. Click on the Pen tool. As you move the Pen tool, the pointer changes to show you what action you can expect with the next click.
3. Click somewhere near the middle of the document. Notice that when you click on the document, new menu options appear in the Object inspector. The panel should look similar to the one in the Pen Options figure. If the Object inspector is not on your screen, go to the menu bar and choose Window > Inspectors > Object.
4. Click away from the anchor point that you set when you clicked on the document. You can hold down the Shift key while clicking on the ending point to draw a straight line. If you want to start a separate line from the first one, hold down the Ctrl key and click anywhere on the document. Practice drawing straight lines and some that are not straight.
5. Hold down the Alt key and right-click to place a connector point. Dragging as you place a connector point will extend the point's handle.
6. Hold down the Ctrl key as you drag to move the curve point to a new location.
7. Double-click on the last point or press Tab to create an open path, or click on the first point to create a closed path.

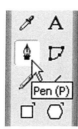

Pen Tool

Pen Options

Closed Paths

1. Create a new document using the default document settings.
2. Click on the Pen tool.
3. Click three places on the screen as if you are drawing a triangle, except do not draw the closing line.
4. Select the Closed check box in the Object inspector.
5. Practice drawing other shapes and using the Object inspector to close them.
6. With a partner, draw a tic-tac-toe board and then play the game, filling in the squares with "O" and "X" using the Pen tool. Save as *TicTacToe.fh10*.

Bezigon Tool

Drawing with the Bezigon Tool

1. Create a new document using the default document settings.
2. Click on the Bezigon tool.
3. Place corner points by clicking on the document.
4. Hold down the Alt key as you click to place a curve point.
5. You can move the point and point handles by holding down the Ctrl key and dragging the point to a new location.
6. To connect a straight path with a curved path, hold down the Ctrl key and drag the point to a new location.

Grouping a Path

1. Create a new document using the default document settings.
2. Click on the Pen tool.
3. Press the Shift key and click on the document to create the starting point. The Shift key causes the line to be straight.
4. Press the Shift key and click across from the starting point to create an ending point.
5. The path should still be selected, but if it is not, use the Pointer tool to select the path. You should see the selection points on the path.
6. Go to the menu bar and choose Modify > Group. The selection points cannot be seen while they are grouped.
7. The Object inspector should be visible. If it is not, go to the menu bar and choose Window > Inspectors > Object. In the Object inspector, change the line length to twice its original size by typing in the value in the "w:" (width) box. Press Enter.
8. Repeat steps 2 through 7, except place the ending point below the starting point to create a vertical line. Change the height to twice its original height.

Freeform Tool

1. Create a new document using the default document settings.
2. Using the Ellipse tool, draw a circle on your document.
3. The Freeform tool can be used to modify a path by pushing, pulling, or reshaping.
4. Double-click on the Freeform tool.
5. In the Freeform Tool dialog box, select Push/Pull. When the Freeform tool is in Pull mode, the pointer shows a small "s" beside it.
6. In the Freeform Tool dialog box, you can adjust pointer size, tool precision, and a bend option. For this exercise, leave the adjustments at the default. Pull the top of the circle down until it is the shape of a half moon. Begin pulling at the top middle of the circle.
7. Use the fill color box to add a blue color to the moon. Add a darker blue stroke to the outside of the moon.

Bezigon Tool
SOURCE: ©MACROMEDIA FREEHAND

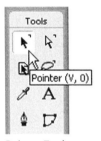

Pointer Tool
SOURCE: ©MACROMEDIA FREEHAND

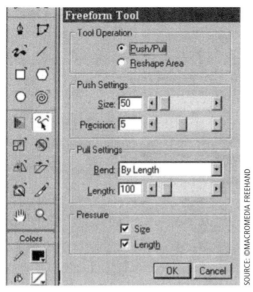

Freeform Tool

8. With the moon still selected, go to the menu bar and choose Modify > Transform > Rotate and change the Rotation angle to 55 degrees. Move the moon to the upper left corner of your document.

9. Add a few stars to the document.

10. Save as *Moon.fh10*.

11. You may want to try some more tips in using the Freeform tool.
    - While pushing or pulling, hold down the Shift key to constrain the pointer movement.
    - You can switch between the By Length and Between Points options by holding down the Alt key.
    - To increase the width of the push pointer, press the right arrow key. To decrease the width, press the left arrow key.

12. Create a new document using the default document settings.

13. Draw a circle. You will draw four circles on the document, so leave enough room for the other three. They will not all need to be the same size.

14. Double-click on the Freeform tool.

15. Select Reshape Area.

16. Place your pointer near the path and click the left mouse button. The pointer changes to the reshaping pointer. The inner circle represents the strength setting.

17. Push to reshape the top of the circle so that it looks like the top of a heart.

18. Double-click on the Freeform tool and change to Push/Pull.

19. Pull to reshape the bottom of the circle so that it looks like the bottom of a heart. Push in the sides to finish the shape of the heart. Color the heart. Repeat this for three other hearts in varying colors and sizes.

20. Save as *Heart.fh10*.

Charts and Pictographs

Creating a Chart

1. Go to the menu bar and choose Window > Toolbars > Xtra Tools.

2. Click on the Chart tool.

3. Click and drag the pointer to the size you want for your chart. This can easily be revised later. Once you stop dragging the pointer, the Chart dialog box appears.

Chart Tool

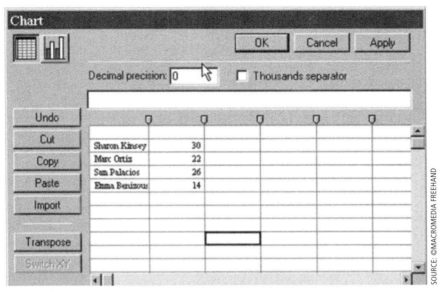

Chart Dialog Box

4. Type the following information into the Chart dialog box.

Sharon Kinsey	30
Marc Ortiz	22
Sam Palacios	26
Emma Benizous	14

5. Change the Decimal precision to 0.
6. Drag the markers to the right of each column out to resize the column.
7. Click on Apply, then OK.
8. You can make some formatting changes on the chart itself. Click on the chart. Go to the menu bar and choose Text > Size > 10. This will change the text for the X and Y axes.
9. This chart would work better if it were in landscape orientation. If the Document inspector is not visible, go to the menu bar and choose Window > Inspectors > Document. Change the orientation to landscape.
10. With the Pointer tool, click on each of the bars for the four employees. Change the color. Use red, blue, green, and yellow in that order. (Charts are created in grayscale. It is up to you to add color.)
11. Click on the Text tool.
12. Drag the pointer to draw a bounding box for the text. Type "Hours Worked" on the title line. Type "September 14–18, 2XXX" on the second line.
13. Go to the menu bar and choose Text > Align > Center.
14. Change the font color by selecting the text you typed. Double-click the color box on the bottom of the Tool panel and choose a color.
15. Resize your chart so that it uses the space on the page.
16. Save as *HoursWorked.fh10*.

Importing a Chart and Setting a Chart Type

1. Create a new document using the default document settings. Go to the menu bar and choose Window > Toolbars > Xtra Tools.
2. Click on the Chart tool.
3. Go to the Document inspector and change the orientation to landscape.
4. Drag the pointer on the screen to set the size of the chart.

Text Tool

Chart Tool

5. In the Chart dialog box, choose a Chart type of Line. Change Data markers to Diamond. Select the Gridlines check boxes for X axis and Y axis. Click Cancel when you are finished.

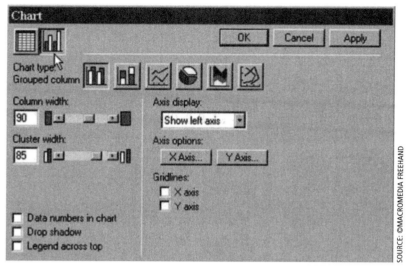

Chart Type Dialog Box

6. Double-click on the Chart tool. Click on the Import button.
7. Import the *Rain.txt* file from your CD. Click on Apply and OK.
8. Use the Hand tool if necessary to move the document around on your screen so you can see all the parts of the chart.
9. Use the Pointer tool to select the chart and reposition it on the document. The chart is selected when it has a black dot marking each corner.
10. Use the Subselect tool to select each part of the legend and delete the legend. You can use the Shift key to select and delete them all at once.
11. Add a text box with an appropriate title. Format the text for color, font type, and size.
12. Save as *Rainfall.fh10*.

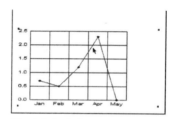

Chart Selected

SOURCE: ©MACROMEDIA FREEHAND

Creating a Pictograph

1. Create a new document using the default document settings. Add a chart to the new document by clicking on the Chart tool on the Xtra tools floating toolbar. If the Xtra tools are not visible on your screen, go to the menu bar and choose Window > Toolbars > Xtra Tools. After clicking on the Chart tool, drag the pointer on your document to set the size of the chart and open the Chart dialog box. Make the chart approximately half the size of the document. The chart should consist of four students in the room that you have interviewed. Ask them how many phone calls they make on a school evening on the average. Input this information in the chart.
2. Find the graphic you would like to use for your pictograph. You can use the Freehand Clipart Viewer or open the clip art folder from your CD. There are some telephones in the *Bus Ofc* directory under *Equip Sup*. Copy the image you want to use.
3. Use the Subselect tool to choose one of the bars to add to the pictograph.
4. Go to the menu bar and choose Xtras > Chart > Pictograph. On the Pictograph dialog box, click Paste and then OK. Repeat this procedure for each bar on the chart.
5. Save as *PhoneCalls.fh10*.

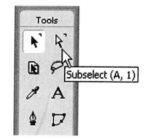

Subselect Tool

SOURCE: ©MACROMEDIA FREEHAND

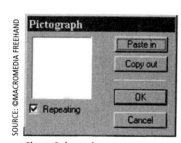

Chart Selected

Hose Tool

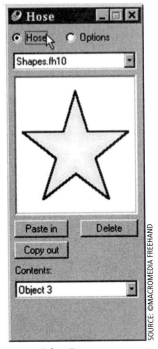

Hose Dialog Box

Hose Image

Graphic Hose Tool

1. Create a new document using the default document settings.
2. If the Xtra Tools toolbar is not visible, go to the menu bar and choose Window > Toolbars > Xtra Tools.
3. Double-click on the Graphic Hose tool to open the Hose dialog box.
4. Select Hose to display images that are available. This should be the default. You may not need to click on it.
5. Choose an image from the drop-down list.
6. Click on the document. Experiment with several other images. (Images can be imported from other sources. Find some on the Internet or create your own.)
7. To change the defaults, select Options in the Hose dialog box. You can change the Order, Spacing, Scale, and Rotate settings. Experiment with these features.

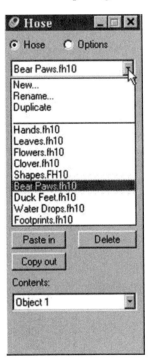

Hose Choices

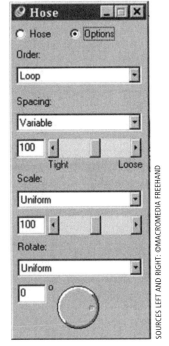

Hose Options

8. Save as *HosePractice.fh10*.
9. Create an image advertising a fund-raising product for one of the organizations in your school. Use at a minimum one graphic hose and text. You could also use shapes and other tools. Each of the hose objects can be resized and recolored by clicking on them. They act as separate objects. Experiment with this.
10. Save as *Fund-Raising.fh10*.

ACTIVITY 2 • MINI-PROJECT

Create a Sketch of Your Classroom

1. Create a new letter-sized document.
2. Draw your classroom. Include details such as trash can, clock, tables, chairs, and people.
3. Use as many of the following tools as possible: Rectangle tool, Line tool, Polygon or Star tool, Spiral tool, Arc tool, Freeform tool, Pen tool, Bezigon tool. Keep a tally of when and how you used each tool.

4. Save the image as *Classroom.fh10*.
5. Create a chart with three columns. List the preceding tools in the first column. In the second column, type an explanation of what you drew with each tool. In the third column, place a number representing how many times you used the tool. Decide whether the chart should be landscape or portrait.
6. Format the chart for no decimals. Use other formatting you have learned to add color and other additions such as titles.
7. Save the chart as *Chart.fh10*.
8. The following criteria should be met:
   ☐ Document size as requested.
   ☐ Most of the details included from the classroom.
   ☐ Tools used effectively.
   ☐ Chart included all required information and was organized.
   ☐ Formatting of chart showed creativity.
   ☐ Files saved as instructed with no errors in file names.

ACTIVITY 3 • WORKING WITH OBJECTS

In this activity, you will become familiar with:

■ Hiding and Locking Objects
■ Moving Objects
■ Copying Objects
■ Rasterizing an Object
■ Grouping Objects
■ Arranging Objects
■ Transforming Objects
   ○ Creating Composite Paths
   ○ Adjusting Transparent Sections
   ○ Using the Union Command
   ○ Using the Divide Command
■ Adding Special Effects
   ○ Drop Shadows
   ○ Embossing
   ○ 3-D Rotation
■ Distorting Objects
   ○ Creating Envelopes
   ○ Creating Patterns
■ Creating Perspectives

Hiding and Locking Objects

1. Open *HidingObjects.fh10* from your CD.
2. In some cases, you may want to hide an object so that it does not get modified. To do this, select the object you want to hide. In this case, select the duck feet.
3. Go to the menu bar and choose View > Hide Selection. This object will still print, but you cannot see it on your screen.
4. To unhide the selection, go to the menu bar and choose View > Show All.
5. To lock a selected object, go to the menu bar and choose Modify > Lock, or click on the Lock button on your main toolbar. The Lock button is now dimmed and the Unlock button is available.
6. You cannot edit a locked object. However, you can fill and stroke the objects. To unlock an object, go to the menu bar and choose Modify > Unlock, or click on the Unlock button on your main toolbar.

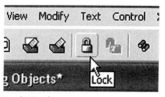

Lock Tool
SOURCE: ©MACROMEDIA FREEHAND

7. Lock the feet in the *HidingObjects.fh10* file. Attempt to resize the object. Resize the other objects on the document.
8. Save the file as *LockedObjects.fh10*.

Moving Objects

You can move selected objects by dragging, pressing an arrow key, or using the Transform panel.

1. Create a new document using the default document settings. Draw a shape on the document. Add some objects inside using the Graphics Hose.
2. Click on one of the objects to select it. If you are using another tool, you can use the Ctrl key to toggle to the Pointer tool. Then select the object.
3. Drag the selected object outside your shape.
4. You can also move by using the arrow keys. Select an object within the shape. Using the arrow keys (left, right, up, down), move the object until it is outside your drawn shape.
5. You can also move using the Transform panel. Select an object. Go to the menu bar and choose Window > Panels > Transform. Click on the first button on the left side (move distance).
6. Experiment typing a number in the Move distance: x box until you have the moved object outside the shape. Practice this with at least three of your other shapes until you have moved them outside your drawn shape.

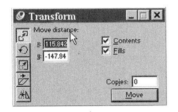

Transform Panel

Copying Objects

1. Create a new document using the default document settings.
2. . Using the Graphics Hose tool, place one of each kind of leaf on the document. If you do not have this object, open *Leaves.fh10* from your CD.
3. Using the Marquee Selection tool, select all the leaves.
4. Go to the menu bar and choose Edit > Copy.
5. Open Adobe Photoshop, Jasc Paint Shop Pro, or other image editing software.
6. Go to the menu bar and choose Edit > Paste. In Adobe Photoshop, you will need to place the image after pasting. You can do this when you close Photoshop. Save as *Leaves.jpg*.

Marquee Selection

Rasterizing an Object

1. Open *Rasterizing.fh10*.
2. Select the grouped object.
3. Go to the menu bar and choose Modify > Rasterize to open the Rasterize dialog box.
4. Change the Resolution to 300 dpi for a better bitmap image. Anti-aliasing will smooth the edges. Change it to None. It is not necessary to have smoother edges on this object. Click OK.
5. Save as *RasterImage.fh10*.

Rasterize Dialog Box

Grouping Objects

1. Create a new document using the default document settings.
2. Double-click on the Spiral tool to display the Spiral dialog box.
3. Change the spiral to how you would like it displayed. Click on OK.
4. On your document, draw two different spirals.
5. Select one of the spirals. Go to the menu bar and choose Modify > Group.
6. Select both spirals by selecting the first spiral, holding down the Shift key, and selecting the second spiral. Note the difference in a grouped and ungrouped object.

Grouped Ungrouped

Grouped Selection

7. Ungroup the object by selecting the object. Go to the menu bar and choose Modify > Ungroup.
8. Group both objects as one object by selecting both objects, then go to the menu bar and choose Modify > Group.
9. Save as *Grouping.fh10*.

Arranging Objects

Arranging objects is used only for objects within the same layer.
1. Open *StackedObjects.fh10* from your CD.
2. Click on the green triangle on top. Go to the menu bar and choose Modify > Arrange > Bring to Front.
3. Click on the red triangle to select it. Go to the menu bar and choose Modify > Arrange > Bring to Front.
4. Click on the blue triangle to select it. Go to the menu bar and choose Modify > Arrange > Send to Back. Notice that your pyramid is the exact opposite of the way it started.
5. Add fill color to all of the triangles so that they are all green.
6. Draw a brown rectangle under the bottom triangle.
7. Add a text box to the triangle and type "Arranging Objects." Change the font type, size, and color (white).
8. Save as *ArrangingObjects.fh10*.

Transforming Objects

Creating Composite Paths
1. Create a new document using the default document settings.
2. Use the Pencil tool to draw four shapes. Be sure the shapes are each closed and fill them with different colors.
3. Select two of the shapes. They do not have to be side by side or near each other on the document.
4. Go to the menu bar and choose Modify > Join. Note that the composite path now takes the fill attributes of the backmost path. A composite path is formed when two or more closed paths are joined to form one path.
5. Click on the newly formed path and drag it around the document. Notice that it does not move the other objects.
6. Select the other two objects. For less confusion, you may want to drag one near the other. Go to the menu bar and choose Modify > Join.
7. Save as *CompositePaths.fh10*.

Adjusting Transparent Sections
1. Open *Circles.fh10* from your CD.
2. Select each circle and fill it with a different color.
3. Select all three circles by using the Marquee Selection tool.
4. Go to the menu bar and choose Modify > Join.

Overlapping Subpaths

SOURCE: ©MACROMEDIA FREEHAND

5. The overlapping subpaths of the composite paths are transparent based on their path direction. To change this, go to the menu bar and choose Window > Inspectors > Object. Clear the Odd/Even Fill check box. Notice that your three circles are all filled now.
6. Save as *OverlappingSubpaths.fh10*.

Using the Union Command

1. Open *Union.fh10* from your CD.
2. Select both rectangles. Go to the menu bar and choose Modify > Combine > Union.
3. Draw two more similar rectangles. Fill them with color.
4. Group them. Compare the difference between Group and Union in overlapping paths.
5. Save as *Rectangle Union.fh10*.

Using the Divide Command

1. Open *Divide.fh10* from your CD.
2. Select both shapes. Go to the menu bar and choose Modify > Combine > Divide.
3. Pull the three new shapes apart. Notice that the overlapping shape took on the fill attributes of the topmost layer. If you want the other fill color, you would need to select that shape last.
4. Select the middle section that was the overlap.
5. Go to the menu bar and choose Modify > Transform > Rotate. Rotate the shape 15 degrees so that it is pointed up. You may need to make some adjustments in the rotation.
6. Save as *OverlappingPaths.fh10*.

Adding Special Effects

Drop Shadows

You can add one of three drop-shadow effects to an image: Hard Edge, Soft Edge, and Zoom.

1. Create a new document using the default document settings.
2. Draw three rectangles. Add a different color to each one.
3. Choose one of the rectangles.
4. If the Shadow tool is not visible, go to the menu bar and choose Window > Toolbars > Xtra Tools.
5. Double-click the Shadow tool on the Xtra Tools toolbar. Change the Offset to 15 for both x and y.
6. Experiment with the Fill settings so you can see the difference in each. Note that Color is gray, Shade is black, and tint takes on the color of the object. Leave the color as it is.
7. Paste the object to the document. Apply the Soft Edge shadow with an Offset of 15 for both x and y. Repeat these steps for a Zoom shadow.

Shadow Tool

SOURCE: ©MACROMEDIA FREEHAND

8. Observe any differences in the three types of shadows. They may be minimal differences, but they exist.
9. You should have four objects on your document.
10. Save as *ShadowArrow.fh10*.

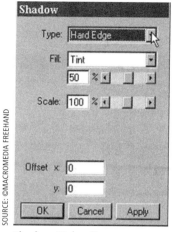

Shadow Dialog Box

Embossing

1. Create a new document using the default document settings.
2. Draw a basic rectangle filled with a color.
3. Copy the rectangle and paste it into the document so there are five rectangles. You will use a different type of embossing on each one. The choices are Emboss, Deboss, Chisel, Ridge, and Quilt.
4. Select the first rectangle.
5. To add embossing, go to the menu bar and choose Xtras > Create > Emboss. Experiment with the Contrast, Depth, Angle, and Soft Edge settings.
6. Save as *Embossing.fh10*.

3-D Rotation

1. Create a new document using the default document settings.
2. Using shapes and the Pen or Pencil tool, draw a face on the document.
3. Select all the objects in the face by pressing Ctrl and typing "a."
4. Group the face by going to the menu bar and choosing Modify > Group.
5. Select the face.
6. Double-click the 3D Rotation tool to open the 3D Rotation dialog box.
7. In the 3D Rotation dialog box you can select Easy or Expert, change where you rotate from, and change the distance of rotation. For this activity, leave it on the default settings.
8. Click in the middle of the face and drag to the left until you have a 3-D effect. Do not drag too far or the object will become distorted. If you drag too far, press the Ctrl key and type "z" to Undo.
9. Save as *Face.fh10*.
10. Use shapes and the Pen, Pencil, and Text tools to create a logo for one of your favorite places to shop. Repeat steps 1 through 9 to add a 3-D effect to your finished logo.
11. Save as *Favorite.fh10*.

3D Tool

SOURCE: ©MACROMEDIA FREEHAND

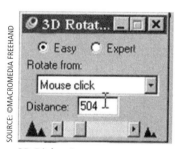

3D Dialog Box

Distorting Objects

Creating Envelopes

1. Create a new document using the default document settings.
2. Go to the menu bar and choose Window > Toolbars > Text.
3. Create a text box and type "Business Professionals of America."
4. Format the font type, size, and alignment using the Text toolbar.
5. Go to the menu bar and choose Window > Toolbars > Envelope.
6. Click on the Create button on the Envelope toolbar.

Create Envelope

7. Experiment with the different distortions. Decide on one that looks good with your text.
8. Save as *DistortingText.fh10*.

Fractalize

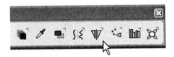

Mirror Tool

Creating Patterns

1. Create a new document using the default document settings.
2. Using the Ellipse tool, draw a circle. Leave the object selected.
3. Go to the menu bar and choose Window > Toolbars > Xtra Operations.
4. Click on the Fractalize button several times. Each application of fractalizing increases the file size. (Fractals are transformations of patterns in an object to their natural shape. A good example of this would be mountains. Fractalizing a vector object results in a jagged edge.)
5. To set the Mirror tool options, go to the menu bar and choose Window > Toolbars > Xtra Tools.
6. Double-click on the Mirror tool.

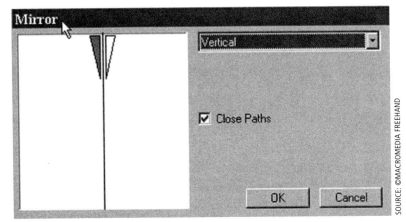

Mirror Dialog Box

7. You can make several choices in the Mirror dialog box. Horizontal reflects from top to bottom, Vertical reflects from left to right, Horizontal and Vertical reflects both ways at once and Multiple reflects around multiple axes. If you choose Multiple, there are even more options to choose from. Experiment with the options to develop a pattern.
8. Save as *Pattern.fh10*.

Creating Perspectives

Perspective Tool

1. Create a new document using the default document settings.
2. Go to the menu bar and choose View > Perspective Grid > Show.
3. Using the Polygon tool, draw four stars in varying sizes outside the document.
4. Click on the Perspective tool.
5. Using the Perspective tool, drag the stars you drew to the grid. Place them on the bottom grid. Do not release the mouse button until you have pressed the down arrow key to attach the star to the grid. You may want to zoom in so you can see the stars lying flat on the floor of the grid better. Change the zoom back to about 31%. It is easier to attach objects to the grid when you can see the entire grid at once.
6. Draw two rectangles outside the document.
7. Drag the rectangles one at a time to the vertical grid and press the left arrow key to attach them to the grid.
8. You can move the objects around by dragging. Be sure the Perspective tool is selected and not the Subselect tool or Pointer tool. The Pointer tool detaches the object from the grid.
9. Go to the menu bar and choose View > Perspective Grid > Release With Perspective.
10. Go to the menu bar and choose View > Perspective Grid > Show.
11. Save as *PerspectivesPractice.fh10*.

ACTIVITY 3 • MINI-PROJECT

Create Logos for Caps

1. Visit http://www.copycaps.com or search for other "caps" sites. Using some of the examples, create three logos for caps of your own. Use the default document settings for your design.
2. Use the skills you have learned for manipulating objects, such as moving, copying, grouping, arranging and transforming.
3. Create some special effects on caps, such as embossing and 3-D rotations.
4. Try using distortion and creating some perspectives on one of your designs.
5. Save the cap logos as *01Cap.fh10*, *02Cap.fh10*, and *03Cap.fh10*.
6. The following criteria should be met:
   - ☐ Skills used in manipulating objects used with at least one logo grouped, arranged and/or transformed.
   - ☐ Special effects used.
   - ☐ Distortion or a perspective created on at least one logo.
   - ☐ Logos saved as instructed with no errors in file names.
   - ☐ Creativity and research of cap logos evident.
   - ☐ Logos create a positive image for the business or product.

ACTIVITY 4 • MORE ABOUT COLOR

In this activity, you will become familiar with:

- Pattern Strokes and Fills
- Custom Fills
- Gradient Fills

Pattern Strokes and Fills

1. Create a new document using the default document settings.
2. Draw at least five shapes. Leave one of the shapes selected.
3. Go to the menu bar and choose Window > Inspectors > Stroke.
4. On the Stroke tab, choose Pattern from the drop-down list. You can also change the stroke width. The default is 1.

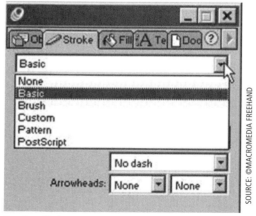

Stroke Choices

5. Scroll through the patterns to see what is available and choose one.
6. Add color from your color boxes.

7. Click on the next tab, which is the Fill tab.
8. Choose Pattern from the drop-down list.
9. Scroll through the patterns to see what is available and choose one.
10. Choose a color from the color box.
11. Repeat these steps for the other shapes you drew.
12. Save as *PatternFill.fh10*.

Custom Fills

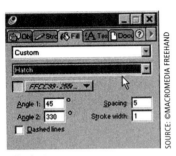

Fill Choices

1. Create a new document using the default document settings.
2. Draw some shapes.
3. Go to the menu bar and choose Window > Inspectors > Fill.
4. Choose Custom from the drop-down list on the Fill tab.
5. Scroll through the fill choices. Note that some selections cannot have color change or any other changes, whereas many have a variety of options for color, spacing, angle, width, and other attributes. Fill the shapes you drew with five different choices, experimenting with the options.
6. Save as *CustomFill.fh10*.

Gradient Fills

1. Create a new document using the default document settings.
2. Draw some shapes. Leave one of them selected.
3. Choose Gradient in the Fill inspector.
4. Choose the type of gradient you would like to use. You can choose from graduated fill, radial fill, and contour fill. On the Fill inspector, these are the three buttons below where you chose the gradient.
5. Choose a color from the color box.
6. Experiment with different types and attributes of gradients.
7. Fill all of your shapes, demonstrating use of different gradients.
8. Save as *GradientFills.fh10*.

ACTIVITY 4 • MINI-PROJECT

Create Web Image Sets

1. The Webmaster has asked you to create three sets of images to use on Web pages. Each set should include a button, a banner, and a horizontal rule.
2. Create each set in a letter-sized document.
3. Use drawing shapes to assist in creating the sets as well as pattern strokes and fills, custom fills, and gradient fills. Adjust pattern strokes for variety.
4. Do not place any text on the images.
5. Save as *01WebSet.fh10*, *02WebSet.fh10*, and *03WebSet.fh10*.
6. The following criteria should be met:
   ☐ Variety of drawing shapes used for buttons, horizontal rules, and banners.
   ☐ Variety of color fill, stroke, gradient, and custom fills used.
   ☐ No text on any image.
   ☐ Files saved as instructed with no errors in file names.
   ☐ Colors in sets complement each other.
   ☐ Buttons, horizontal rules, and banners appropriate size.
   ☐ Creativity used in shapes and colors.

ACTIVITY 5 • WORKING WITH TEXT

In this activity, you will become familiar with:

- Importing Text
- Attaching Text to a Path
- Wrapping Text

Importing Text

1. Create a new document using the default document settings.
2. FreeHand can import text in Rich Text Format (.rtf) or plain text. Go to the menu bar and choose File > Import. Import *ImportingText.rtf* from your CD.
3. Notice that the pointer has changed to a place marker. Click on the document where you would like to place the text.
4. Save as *Text.fh10*.

Attaching Text to a Path

1. Create a new document using the default document settings.
2. Draw a circle.
3. Create a text box. Type in the box "There will be a roundtable discussion about the BIMM course at the July conference."
4. Position the box at the top of the circle.
5. Select both objects by selecting the first object, then holding down the Shift key and selecting the second object.
6. Go to the menu bar and choose Text > Attach to Path.
7. Double-click on the path and select the text if necessary to change the size of the text.
8. Be sure all the text fits in the circle. Make adjustments if necessary.
9. Save as *CircleText.fh10*.
10. Create a design for the front of a t-shirt for one of your favorite businesses. Use text, shapes, and other tools learned in this tutorial. The design must have text attached to a path.
11. Save as *T-shirtDesign.fh10*.

Wrapping Text

1. Open *CircleRose.jpg* from your CD.
2. Click on the Circle Rose object and move it to the center of the document.
3. Go to the menu bar and choose File > Import.
4. Import *Roses.rtf* from your CD. The pointer will change into a place marker.
5. Place the text over the object. Drag the bottom of the text box so that the text fits over the rose.
6. Select the rose. Go to the menu bar and choose Modify > Arrange > Bring to Front.
7. With the rose still selected, go to the menu bar and choose Text > Run Around Selection to open the Run Around Selection dialog box.
8. Choose Word Wrap and a Standoff of 5 for Left, Right, Top, and Bottom. See right.
9. Zoom in on the finished story to make sure that all words are wrapped and can be read.
10. Save as *RoseStory.fh10*.
11. Create your own story of interest. Choose an object that coordinates with your story and write two paragraphs about the topic. You may need to use the Internet to look up information on the topic you choose.
12. Save as *MyStory.fh10*.

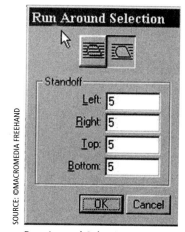

SOURCE: ©MACROMEDIA FREEHAND

Run Around Selection

ACTIVITY 5 • MINI-PROJECT

Create Interest in Student Organizations

1. Use your favorite search engine to search for "student organizations."
2. Read about and take notes on at least three student organizations at either the high school or college level that interest you. Include in your notes the Web address of each student organization. The notes should include a diagram of the emblem or logo if there is one and the mission statement for that student organization.
3. In a word processing document, save at least two of the mission statements as *01Mission.rtf* and *02Mission.rtf*.
4. Create a letter-sized document that includes a sketch of the logo of the student organization and the mission statement imported into the document. If you found no logo, sketch a simple logo using the tools you have learned in FreeHand. Save as *01StuOrg.fh10*.
5. Create a letter-sized document that includes a sketch of the logo of the student organization. Add text from the saved mission statement and wrap it around the logo. Save as *02StuOrg.fh10*.
6. Using a letter-sized document, draw a simple logo for one of the student organizations that you found. Attach text to paths in the logo. Save as *03StuOrg.fh10*.
7. Turn in your notes to your instructor.
8. The following criteria should be met:
   - ☐ Notes thorough and all requested elements included.
   - ☐ Mission statements typed in a word processing document without error and saved appropriately.
   - ☐ Mission statement imported into the document appropriately.
   - ☐ Mission statement wrapped around the logo appropriately.
   - ☐ Logo sketch demonstrates creativity and knowledge of the basic FreeHand tools.
   - ☐ Use of attaching text to paths used effectively.

PART 4 • SIMULATION

Using FreeHand Create an Illustrated History of an Olympic Event

1. Go to http://www.olympics.com or another Web site with Olympic information and statistics. Note symbols and other logos that are associated with the Olympics as you follow links. Sketch out any that you think would be fairly easy to create with the tools in Illustrator. Turn in your sketch to your instructor. You should sketch at least three to draw using FreeHand. After drawing them in FreeHand, save them in a folder titled *Olympics* as *01Olympics.fh10*, *02Olympics.fh10*, and *03Olympics.fh10*.
2. Follow the links to "All the Games Since 1896." Choose one particular event that interests you. Read the history of the event and write a summary of that history in a word processing document. Save in your *Olympics* folder as *History.rtf*. In a letter-sized document, place the official emblem of the event and wrap the history text around that image. Save in your *Olympics* folder as *HistoryEmblem.fh10*.

3. Create a chart using the top six nations who won and their number of gold, silver and bronze medals. Format the text in a table and the numbers in proper format. Include headings as needed to further explain the table. Save in your *Olympics* folder as *Winners.fh10*.

4. Using your own sketched images, the Clipart Viewer in FreeHand, and other images from the Internet, create a program cover for the Olympic event you chose. Be sure to include the place of the event and specific dates. The program cover should be in Landscape setup as a custom size of 396 × 306 pixels. Save in your *Olympics* folder as *Program.fh10*.

5. The following criteria should be met:

   ☐ Sketch turned in to instructor.
   ☐ Three logos or emblems appropriate to the Olympics; drawing tools used extensively.
   ☐ History written in own words and contains no grammatical errors.
   ☐ History saved as requested and contains no typing errors.
   ☐ History wrapped around an appropriate image.
   ☐ RTF and FreeHand history files saved as instructed without error in the file names.
   ☐ Table contains accurate information as requested.
   ☐ Table formatting demonstrates effort and creativity.
   ☐ Program cover contains accurate and thorough information, with a variety of FreeHand tools used effectively.
   ☐ Program design is eye-catching.

Unit 2

Professional Visual Communications Skills

Part 1 • HP PrecisionScan
Part 2 • ScanSoft PaperPort
Part 3 • Microsoft Excel Charts
Part 4 • MapScape.com
Part 5 • Microsoft MapPoint

Visual communication is constantly moving forward in new directions, making it even easier for us to communicate faster and more effectively. If you think for a moment, you can probably come up with many instances where you have seen the skills in this unit used in the businesses you frequent.

You will learn to use scanning software to create or reproduce images and text. Scanning allows you flexibility in manipulating images and text. This flexibility has caused us to move ahead in huge strides in the medical profession as well as other business areas. Activities using PrecisionScan by Hewlett-Packard and PaperPort by ScanSoft are included in this unit.

You will learn to create charts and graphs to visually communicate statistics, profits, and other important numbers in business. Effectively creating charts that make an impact is an important business skill today. How many of us today look at the simple pie chart on our computer to determine how much space we have left on our hard drive? It is a more efficient method than looking at the numbers. It gives us the information that we need at a glance and frees our time for acting on that information. You will use Excel to create bar, column, pie, stock, and other types of charts and graphs.

You will also learn to create and interpret maps. Mapping is useful in determining sales territories, planning a new business location, or planning a business trip. Being able to interpret a map and make good business decisions from that information is a necessity in business today. The mapping software focused on is MapScape from the Internet and MapPoint by Microsoft.

This unit will definitely give you some skills necessary to proceed into the next units. You will be able to use your scans, charts, and maps to solve business problems and create effective visuals for publications, Web pages, and presentations.

HP PrecisionScan

HP PrecisionScan
Publisher: Hewlett Packard Company
HP PrecisionScan is an optical character reader software that drives the scanner for Hewlett Packard OfficeJet and some other Hewlett Packard products. The image has to be opened in an image management software for editing.

ACTIVITY 1 • SCANNING AN IMAGE

In this activity, you will become familiar with:

- Getting Ready
- Scan To
- Preview Scan
- Save the Scan

PrecisionScan

Getting Ready

1. Bring several photographs from home to scan.
2. Get instructions from your instructor on the steps to open the scanning software on your computer. This will differ depending on whether you are on a network or stand-alone computer and also as to how the network is set up.
3. See the top right figure for the opening screen on the PrecisionScan software.

Scan To

Scan To.gif

4. Choose where the document or image will be scanned to. Your choices are Image and Text File, Image File, Mail, Microsoft Outlook, Microsoft PowerPoint, Paint, Printer, Text File, and WordPad. Choose Image File.

Preview Scan

5. Choose type of Preview Scan. In this case, leave it on "Yes, you can select entire page or parts."
6. Choose to Scan in Color. Leave it on Yes.
7. Click the Scan button. You should see the Preparing to scan box on your screen. See figure at right.
8. The image will scan to the Viewer. See figure at far right.
9. Click Accept. The Save as dialog box comes up.

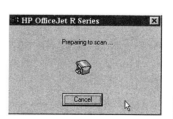

Preparing to Scan
SOURCE: ©HP PRECISIONSCAN

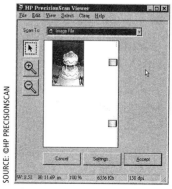

Viewer

Save the Scan

10. Click on the Save In drop-down list. If you have not already done so, you may want to create a folder to save your scanned images in. Follow instructions from your instructor as to how to organize your scanned images and documents.

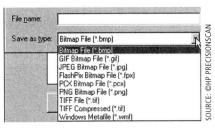

Save as type

11. Click on the File name box. Name the file *MyImage.bmp*.
12. Click on the Save as type drop-down list. Choose .bmp, which is the default. The scanned image should be saved in .bmp format first. By doing this, if you then save it as a .jpg and have to go back and make changes or use it again, it is best to open the .bmp format and make the changes to the original. Otherwise, the image may not be as clear due to being compressed several times.

ACTIVITY 1 • MINI-PROJECT

Create a Scan of Pet Images

1. Gather five photos of household pets from home or a friend.
2. Scan each photo.
3. Save in a folder titled *PetProject* as *01Pet.bmp*, *02Pet.bmp*, *03Pet.bmp*, *04Pet.bmp*, and *05Pet.bmp*.
4. Use your image management software to crop each of the photos. Remember that any part of the photo that is unnecessary will save file size if you crop it out.
5. Resize the file until it is less than 15K.
6. Save in the *PetProject* folder as 01 followed by the name of the type of pet and the .jpg extension. For example, if it is a dog, the file name would be *01Dog.jpg*. If it is a cat, the file name would be *01Cat.jpg*.
7. The following criteria should be met:
   - ☐ Five photos of household pets as instructed.
   - ☐ Scanner glass clean and image placed straight on the glass.
   - ☐ Scans saved as requested with no errors in the file names.
   - ☐ Crop performed effectively.
   - ☐ Resize performed effectively with each file less than 15K in size.
   - ☐ JPG files saved as instructed with no errors in file names.

ACTIVITY 2 • CHANGING SETTINGS

In this activity, you will become familiar with:

- ■ Resolution
- ■ Scan Speed
- ■ Page Size
- ■ Photo Quality

HP PrecisionScan

HP PrecisionScan
Publisher: Hewlett Packard Company
HP PrecisionScan is an optical character reader software that drives the scanner for Hewlett Packard OfficeJet and some other Hewlett Packard products. The image has to be opened in an image management software for editing.

ACTIVITY 1 • SCANNING AN IMAGE

In this activity, you will become familiar with:

- Getting Ready
- Scan To
- Preview Scan
- Save the Scan

SOURCE: ©HP PRECISIONSCAN

PrecisionScan

Getting Ready

1. Bring several photographs from home to scan.
2. Get instructions from your instructor on the steps to open the scanning software on your computer. This will differ depending on whether you are on a network or stand-alone computer and also as to how the network is set up.
3. See the top right figure for the opening screen on the PrecisionScan software.

Scan To

4. Choose where the document or image will be scanned to. Your choices are Image and Text File, Image File, Mail, Microsoft Outlook, Microsoft PowerPoint, Paint, Printer, Text File, and WordPad. Choose Image File.

SOURCE: ©HP PRECISIONSCAN

Scan To.gif

Preview Scan

5. Choose type of Preview Scan. In this case, leave it on "Yes, you can select entire page or parts."
6. Choose to Scan in Color. Leave it on Yes.
7. Click the Scan button. You should see the Preparing to scan box on your screen. See figure at right.
8. The image will scan to the Viewer. See figure at far right.
9. Click Accept. The Save as dialog box comes up.

Preparing to Scan
SOURCE: ©HP PRECISIONSCAN

SOURCE: ©HP PRECISIONSCAN

Viewer

Save the Scan

10. Click on the Save In drop-down list. If you have not already done so, you may want to create a folder to save your scanned images in. Follow instructions from your instructor as to how to organize your scanned images and documents.

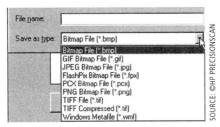

Save as type

11. Click on the File name box. Name the file *MyImage.bmp*.
12. Click on the Save as type drop-down list. Choose .bmp, which is the default. The scanned image should be saved in .bmp format first. By doing this, if you then save it as a .jpg and have to go back and make changes or use it again, it is best to open the .bmp format and make the changes to the original. Otherwise, the image may not be as clear due to being compressed several times.

ACTIVITY 1 • MINI-PROJECT

Create a Scan of Pet Images

1. Gather five photos of household pets from home or a friend.
2. Scan each photo.
3. Save in a folder titled *PetProject* as *01Pet.bmp*, *02Pet.bmp*, *03Pet.bmp*, *04Pet.bmp*, and *05Pet.bmp*.
4. Use your image management software to crop each of the photos. Remember that any part of the photo that is unnecessary will save file size if you crop it out.
5. Resize the file until it is less than 15K.
6. Save in the *PetProject* folder as 01 followed by the name of the type of pet and the .jpg extension. For example, if it is a dog, the file name would be *01Dog.jpg*. If it is a cat, the file name would be *01Cat.jpg*.
7. The following criteria should be met:
   - ☐ Five photos of household pets as instructed.
   - ☐ Scanner glass clean and image placed straight on the glass.
   - ☐ Scans saved as requested with no errors in the file names.
   - ☐ Crop performed effectively.
   - ☐ Resize performed effectively with each file less than 15K in size.
   - ☐ JPG files saved as instructed with no errors in file names.

ACTIVITY 2 • CHANGING SETTINGS

In this activity, you will become familiar with:

- ■ Resolution
- ■ Scan Speed
- ■ Page Size
- ■ Photo Quality

- Auto Detect
- Page Formatting
- Region Size
- Region Type
- Saving as Images and Text

For this exercise, you will scan the front cover of your textbook or an image within one of your textbooks.

Resolution

1. Click Set Custom Resolution. Change the resolution to 300 dpi by clicking in the box and typing "300." Depending on your use for the scan, most of the time, you will want to scan at 300 dpi. Anything above that will cause a big file size without improving the resolution that much.
2. Click "Save this custom resolution, and use every time."

Resolution

Scan Speed

3. Leave this on Normal Scan Speed. You can scan certain types of images or documents without losing quality.
4. Settings is located on both the Main window and the Viewer window. The Scan Speed can only be changed from the Main window.

Scan Speed

Page Size

5. Click on Set Scaling Percentage. Type "50" in the percent box.
6. You can also choose a Page Size from the drop-down list in choice 2.

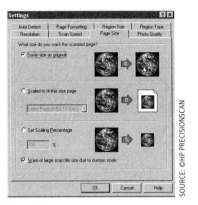

Page Size

Photo Quality

7. The default for this setting is Best.
8. It is best to leave it on Best unless you have limited disk space.

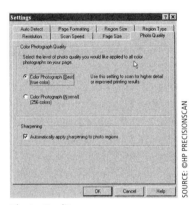

Photo Quality

Auto Detect

9. This setting places a blue outline around regions on your page.
10. This setting also detects page orientation of Portrait or Landscape.

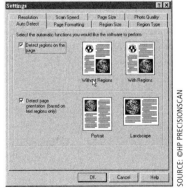

Auto Detect

Page Formatting

11. The default on this setting is Fixed Page Format, which keeps the original layout of the page. It is not as easy to make changes to the document in this format.
12. You can choose Flowed Page Format, which takes out columns and other formatting; this makes it easier to make format changes to the document.

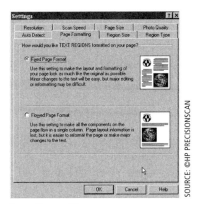

Page Formatting

Region Size

These settings can be changed only from the Viewer window and only when one region is selected.

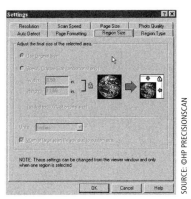

Region Size

Region Type

13. These settings can be changed from the Viewer window only.
14. Leave this setting on Color Drawing, which is the default.

Region Type

15. Scan the cover of your textbook. Click on the drop-down box for Scan To and choose Image and Text File.
16. Adjust other settings as needed.

Saving as Images and Text

17. Once you accept the scan in the Viewer window, notice that the default file type is .rtf (Rich Text Format). This is the default when text is involved in the scan. Save the scan as *Textbook.rtf*. Then save it again as *Textbook.jpg*.

ACTIVITY 2 • MINI-PROJECT

Create Scan of Image and Text for Pet Adoption

1. Using Microsoft Word, create a title in WordArt or a large font with color, type, and size changes. Type the title "Pet of the Week."
2. Insert one of the pet pictures from Activity 1 in your word processing document.
3. Create five bulleted items that describe the pet in the picture. Try to make the items persuasive so that someone would be interested in adopting the pet.
4. Save in the *PetProject* folder as *WeekPet.rtf*.
5. Print the document. Note: Printing is taking place to practice scanning image and text documents. You could actually save this as an RTF document in the word processing software, but for learning purposes you should follow the instructions in this assignment.
6. Before scanning the document, check to see that the scanner is set for 300 dpi, medium speed, and medium quality.
7. Scan the document. Choose the scan type as picture and text. Save in the *PetProject* folder as *PetWeek.rtf*.
8. The following criteria should be met:
   - ☐ Title as instructed with an acceptable font type, size, and color and/or WordArt.
   - ☐ Picture from previous activity inserted appropriately.
   - ☐ Five bulleted items persuasively written.
   - ☐ No errors in the flyer.
   - ☐ Scan is clean and straight.
   - ☐ Proper type of scan selected.

ACTIVITY 3 • SCANNING A DOCUMENT

In this activity, you will become familiar with:

- Scanning Text
- Saving as Text

Scanning Text

1. Using a word processing program, type a list of ten things you have learned so far about using OCR software and scanning in general. Save it as *ScanningTips.doc*. Print the document. (Normally, for most uses of this document, you would not need to scan the document. For learning purposes, use this document to scan in this activity.)
2. Place the document on your scanner. Be sure your glass is clean!
3. Open your OCR software.

4. Change the Scan To so it is Text.
5. Change Scan in Color to No.
6. Go to Settings > Detect Regions and clear the Detect Regions check box.
7. Click Scan.

Saving as Text

8. Click Accept. In this case the default will be .txt.
9. Save as *TopTips.txt*.

ACTIVITY 3 • MINI-PROJECT

Create a Scan of Pet Adoption Guidelines

1. Go to http://jedi.accn.org/~adoptpet/. If the Web site is no longer available, use a search engine to search for "pet adoption guidelines."
2. Using a word processing program, type the title "Pet Adoption Guidelines."
3. Create an enumerated list of eight to ten items that are guidelines for pet adoption either from the Web site given or one you have found in your search.
4. Save the document in your *PetProject* folder as *Adoption.txt*.
5. Print the document.
6. Scan the document.
7. Save the scan in your *PetProject* folder as *Guidelines.txt*.
8. The following criteria should be met:
   ☐ No errors in the title or enumerations in the *Adoption.txt* file.
   ☐ Accurate list of adoption guidelines as found on the Web site.
   ☐ Scan performed as a text scan.
   ☐ Document placed in the scanner properly.
   ☐ Scanned document saved as instructed.

PART 1 • SIMULATION

Using HP PrecisionScan to Prepare to Sell a House

1. Find a photograph of a house. It can be your current house, a previous house, or a friend's house.
2. Scan the photograph. Save it in the *RealEstate* folder as *House.bmp*.
3. Using your image management software, crop and resize the *House.bmp* file appropriately. Save in the *RealEstate* folder as *ForSale.jpg*. File size should be no larger than 15K.
4. Use a word processing program to create a flyer with the image and some bulleted text persuading someone to purchase the house. Save in the *RealEstate* folder as *BuyIt.rtf*. Print the document and scan the document. Save in the *RealEstate* folder as *Selling.rtf*.
5. In a word processing document, create the following in a TXT document. Title the document "Real Estate Addendum."
6. Save in the *RealEstate* folder as *Addendum.txt*.

The parties to the Contract and any broker who signs this addendum agree to negotiate in good faith in an effort to resolve any dispute related to the Contract that may arise between the parties or between a party and a broker.

If the dispute cannot be resolved by negotiation, the parties to the dispute shall submit the dispute to mediation before resorting to litigation.

This Agreement for Mediation will survive closing.

NOTE: Mediation is a voluntary dispute resolution process in which the parties to the dispute meet with an impartial person, called a mediator, who would help to resolve the dispute informally and confidentially. Mediators facilitate the resolution of disputes but cannot impose binding decisions. The parties to the dispute must agree before any settlement is binding.

Date:

Buyer:

Buyer:

Seller:

Seller:

Other Broker:

Listing Broker:

7. Print the document.
8. Scan the document. Save in the *RealEstate* folder as *Mediation.txt*.
9. The following criteria should be met:
   - ☐ Image of house is a clean scan, saved as instructed, and appropriate size.
   - ☐ Image of house cropped and resized appropriately.
   - ☐ Word processing document *BuyIt.rtf* contains all required elements with no errors.
   - ☐ *Selling.rtf* is a clean scan.
   - ☐ TXT file created as instructed with no errors.
   - ☐ Scan of TXT file clean.

ScanSoft PaperPort

Part 2

ScanSoft PaperPort
Publisher: ScanSoft
Visioneer PaperPort is scanning software that comes with many image management features.

ACTIVITY 1 • SETTING PREFERENCES

In this activity, you will become familiar with the following preference tabs:

- General
- Desktop
- Item Names
- Folder
- Link Bar
- Import/Export
- SimpleSearch
- Web Page Capture
- Advanced

Preferences
SOURCE: ©SCANSOFT PAPERPORT

1. Go to the menu bar and choose Edit > Preferences.

General

2. On the General tab, Show Text on Buttons and Show Tooltips are checked as the default. You can also check Maximize Window at Startup. If you close the program maximized, it will open maximized anyway.

Desktop

3. Click on the Desktop tab. You can make a number of changes to the desktop. Experiment with some changes. Click Change Default Desktop Folder. At this time, you may want to change this. Get instructions from your instructor as to what the default folder should be.

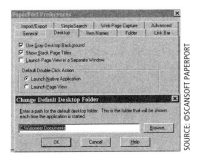

SOURCE: ©SCANSOFT PAPERPORT

Desktop Tab

Item Names Tab

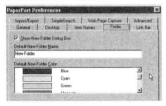

Folder Tab

Link Bar Tab

Import/Export Tab

Web Page Capture Tab

Item Names

4. Click on the Item Names tab. When you create new items in PaperPort, it creates a default header that is a date. You can change the format of this date or you can create a customized header for new items.

Folder

5. Click on the Folder tab. Folders can be customized with a default name as well as a color choice. Choose a color choice.

Link Bar

6. Click on the Link Bar tab. This tab enables you to choose the Link Bar, set size of tools, style of tools, and the way they appear on your desktop. Go to the menu bar and choose Edit > Link Preferences for more choices on the Link Bar.

Link Bar

Import/Export

7. Click on the Import/Export tab. You can change the JPG image quality on this tab by moving the slider to a higher level.

SimpleSearch

8. Click on the SimpleSearch tab. Under this tab, you can change the SimpleSearch to enable background updating as well as change the idle time for the updating to begin. You can also refresh the thumbnails automatically while updating.

Web Page Capture

9. Click on the Web Page Capture tab. This allows Windows to load the Web Page Capture at startup. It also tells you whether it is running and allows you to stop the running of Web Page Capture.

Advanced

10. Click on the Advanced tab. This allows you to change file sizes and compression quality as well as whether the image is inserted as a full-size or thumbnail image.

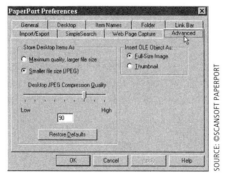

Advanced Tab

ACTIVITY 1 • MINI-PROJECT

Create a Thumbnail Image

1. Your school has decided to scan the ID cards into a database for each student. These scans will be archived at the end of each school year, so it is important that you get the best quality at the smallest file size.
2. Use your ID card with a picture on it; if you do not have one available, use a driver's license.
3. Make some changes to the preferences. Create a customized header with the date in digit format. Using Import/Export, adjust the JPG image quality to a lower quality. Use the Advanced tab to adjust the image to a thumbnail.
4. Scan the ID card.
5. Save in a folder titled *VisioneerActivities* as *IDCard.jpg*. Save all images in this project in the *VisioneerActivities* folder.
6. Make adjustments to increase the JPG quality. Save as *AdjustedJPG.jpg*.
7. Insert both scanned images into a word processing document. Write a short summary of the difference in quality versus file size. Make a decision as to which preference to use for scanning the ID cards.
8. Save the document as *IDPref.doc*.
9. The following criteria should be met:
    - ☐ Preferences changed as instructed for date, image quality, and thumbnail image.
    - ☐ Image saved as instructed with no errors in the file name.
    - ☐ Second scan completed successfully.
    - ☐ Summary well-written and contains no errors. Information in summary is accurate.

ACTIVITY 2 • SCANNING

In this activity, you will become familiar with:

- ◼ TWAIN
    - ○ Command Bar
- ◼ Page and Desktop View
    - ○ Zoom In
    - ○ Zoom Out
    - ○ Actual Size
- ◼ Acquire
- ◼ Save As
- ◼ Import

TWAIN

1. Place a business card, collected by either you or your instructor, on the scanner glass. Be sure the glass is clean.

Command Bar

2. Click on the Twain icon on the Command Bar to access your scanner.

Twain

SOURCE: ©SCANSOFT PAPERPORT

Command Bar

SOURCE: ©SCANSOFT PAPERPORT

3. Scan the image of the business card to PaperPort.

Page and Desktop View

4. The scan default is in Desktop View. Double-click on the image to change to Page View. You can also change to Page View by going to the Command Bar and clicking on the Desktop icon, which will toggle to Page View.

Page View   Desktop View

SOURCE: LEFT AND RIGHT ©SCANSOFT PAPERPORT

Zoom In

SOURCE: ©SCANSOFT PAPERPORT

Zoom In

5. Go to the Command Bar and click on the Zoom In icon.

Zoom Out

6. Go to the Command Bar and click on the Zoom Out icon.

Zoom Out

SOURCE: ©SCANSOFT PAPERPORT

Actual Size

7. Go to the Command Bar and click on the Actual Size icon.

Acquire

8. Using Word, open *ScanningTips.doc* from your CD. Print the document.
9. Go to the menu bar and choose File > Acquire. This begins the scanning process for your scanner.
10. Open the scanned image in Page View.

Actual Size

SOURCE: ©SCANSOFT PAPERPORT

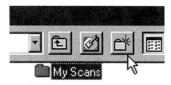

Create Folder

SOURCE: ©SCANSOFT PAPERPORT

Save As

11. Go to the menu bar and choose File > Save As. Create a new folder and name it *MyScans*. Save your document as *ScanningTips.MAX* in the *MyScans* folder.

Import

12. Go to the menu bar and choose File > Import. Browse to your CD and find the *Dog.jpg* image file.
13. Double-click to import into PaperPort.

ACTIVITY 2 • MINI-PROJECT

Create Scan of Schedule

1. Using a word processing program, create a table with your schedule for the week. Begin with Monday and end on Saturday. Make the table as detailed as possible.
2. Save the document in the *VisioneerActivities* folder as *Schedule*. Save all activities in this project in the *VisioneerActivities* folder.
3. Print the document.
4. Scan the document by using Acquire.

5. Save as *Acquired.MAX*.
6. The following criteria should be met:
   - ☐ Detailed word processing document using a table.
   - ☐ Document saved as instructed with no errors in the file name.
   - ☐ Document printed as instructed.
   - ☐ Document scanned straight and clean.
   - ☐ Scanned document saved as instructed.

ACTIVITY 3 • TOOL PALETTE

In this activity, you will become familiar with the following tools:

- ■ Select Rectangular Area
- ■ Erase Image
- ■ Straighten the Page
- ■ Pan Image
- ■ Add Note
- ■ Annotations Editor
- ■ Add Text
- ■ Add Highlighting
- ■ Add Freehand Annotation
- ■ Add Line or Arrow
- ■ Add Picture
- ■ Creating a Stack
   - ○ Go to Page
   - ○ Renaming a Stack

Select Rectangular Area

1. Open your *MyScans* folder, and find the *ScanningTips.MAX* document that you created in the previous activity. Double-click on it to open it in Page View.
2. Go to the Tools Palette and click on Select Rectangular Area. If you hover the mouse pointer over the tools, it will show you the ScreenTip for that tool name. You can also click on the tool, hold your mouse button down, and read the explanation of that tool in the lower left corner of the status bar.
3. Select everything on your scan except for the number 4. Begin at the top left of the document and drag the box around the document. After you have made your selection, right-click and choose Crop.

Erase Image

4. Click on the Erase image tool. Right-click on the tool to choose color and eraser size. In this activity, choose white for the color and choose the second level for the eraser size.
5. Erase any extraneous pixels on the image. (If you need to, decrease the size of the eraser to the smallest size.) Erase the punctuation at the end of the sentences. You can also remove stray dots by going to the menu bar and choosing Page > Remove Stray Dots.

Straighten the Page

6. Click on the Straighten the page tool. This tool can also be used to skew the image if desired. Draw a straight line across the top of your document. The document should straighten or move slightly. Do this on all four sides just to be sure that the document is perfectly straight on the page.

Select Rectangular Area Tool
SOURCE: ©SCANSOFT PAPERPORT

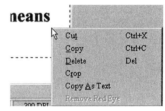

Rectangular Menu
SOURCE: ©SCANSOFT PAPERPORT

Eraser Image Tool
SOURCE: ©SCANSOFT PAPERPORT

Straighten Page Tool
SOURCE: ©SCANSOFT PAPERPORT

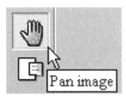

Pan Image Tool

SOURCE: ©SCANSOFT PAPERPORT

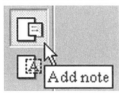

Add Note Tool

SOURCE: ©SCANSOFT PAPERPORT

Edit Annotations Tool

SOURCE: ©SCANSOFT PAPERPORT

Add Text Tool

SOURCE: ©SCANSOFT PAPERPORT

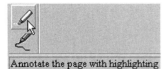

Add Highlighting

SOURCE: ©SCANSOFT PAPERPORT

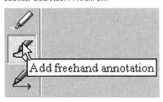

Add Freehand Annotation Tool

SOURCE: ©SCANSOFT PAPERPORT

Add Line or Arrow Tool

SOURCE: ©SCANSOFT PAPERPORT

Pan Image

7. Click on the Pan tool. Click on the Restore button on PaperPort. This should cause scroll bars on your *ScanningTips* document. The Pan tool turns to a hand when hovered in the middle of the document. Hold the mouse button down while the Pan tool is the hand and scroll up and down to move the document. You can also scroll left and right if you cannot see all the document at once.

Add Note

8. Click on the Add note tool.
9. Right-click on the Add note tool and change the font to Size 12 Times New Roman. Be sure the color is black. Right-click on the Add note tool again and change the color of the note to light yellow.
10. Click on the *ScanningTips* document and type in the note "These are only a few tips!"

Annotations Editor

11. Click on the Edit annotations tool. This tool allows you to select, move, and resize annotations such as the Add Note annotation. Drag the selected annotation so it is centered under the title. Resize as appropriate. Save as *Tips.MAX* in the *MyScans* folder.

Add Text

12. Click on the Add text tool. Right-click on the Add text tool to change the font size. Change the font size to 28. Add the punctuation at the end of the sentences back in by clicking in the appropriate places and typing the punctuation. Save.

Add Highlighting

13. Click on the Add highlighting tool. Right-click on the Add highlighting tool and change the color to light yellow. Drag it across the document title "Scanning Tips." Save.

Add Freehand Annotation

14. Click on the Add freehand annotation tool. Right-click on the Add freehand annotation tool and change the color to blue and the Line Width to the middle width. Draw a wavy line underneath the word "bigger" in item 3. Save.

Add Line or Arrow

15. Click on the Add line or arrow tool. Right-click on the Add line or arrow tool. Change color to red, Line Width to the fourth choice, and Line Arrowhead to a double arrowhead. Draw the line under the first tip. Save.

Add Picture

16. Click on the Add Picture tool. Click on a blank spot on the document and choose Important to add it to the document. Save. Click on the Desktop icon.

Creating a Stack

17. Drag *ScanningTips.MAX*, *Tips.MAX*, and *Dog.jpg* on top of each other to create a stack. Right-click on the stack and experiment with Unstack and Reorder. To Unstack you choose Unstack, then click on the first item and drag it off. Continue this until they are all separated.

Go to Page

18. To access Go to Page, click on the Page Navigation bar on the stack. This brings up the menu for switching within your stack. Experiment with the menu.

Renaming the Stack

19. Click on the stack name. This is the name above the current item. It is in bold. Type a new name. In this case, type "My Stack." When the stack is first created, it takes on the name of the first item in the stack until you rename it.

Add Picture Tool
SOURCE: ©SCANSOFT PAPERPORT

Stack
SOURCE: ©SCANSOFT PAPERPORT

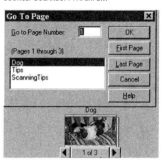

Go To Page
SOURCE: ©SCANSOFT PAPERPORT

ACTIVITY 3 • MINI-PROJECT

Create a Scan from a Newspaper

1. Scan a comic strip from a newspaper.
2. Save in the *VisioneeerActivities* folder as *Newspaper.MAX*. Save all the activities in this project in the *VisioneerActivities* folder.
3. Use the Straighten the page tool to straighten the page. Save as *Straightened.MAX*.
4. Use the Add note tool to add a brief description of your reaction to the comic strip. Save as *Reaction.MAX*.
5. Use the Add highlighting to highlight something in the cartoon strip. Save as *Highlighted.MAX*.
6. Use the Add freehand annotation tool to draw a wavy line underneath a word on the comic strip. Save as *Annotated.MAX*.
7. Scan a coupon from the newspaper. Save as *Coupon.MAX*.
8. Draw an arrow to the discount or bonus amount on the coupon. Save again.
9. Scan a want ad about a dog for sale. Add a picture of a dog to the scan. Save as *Dog.MAX*.
10. Create a stack with all of your images in alphabetical order. Rename the stack *News*.
11. The following criteria should be met:
    - ☐ Scan of the comic strip image was appropriate.
    - ☐ Straightened the page.
    - ☐ Highlighted a word or phrase in the comic strip.
    - ☐ Used freehand annotation appropriately.
    - ☐ Coupon scanned appropriately.
    - ☐ Arrow drawn on the bonus amount on the coupon.
    - ☐ Scan was appropriate of a want ad as instructed.
    - ☐ Stack created in alphabetical order.
    - ☐ No errors in file names.

ACTIVITY 4 • IMAGE TOOLS

In this activity, you will become familiar with the following tools:

- Rotate 90 Degrees Right
- Rotate 90 Degrees Left
- Picture Wizard
- Autofix Picture
- Adjust Picture
- Sharpen Picture
- Crop Page
- Invert Page
- Enhance Lines

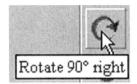

Rotate Right Tool
SOURCE: ©SCANSOFT PAPERPORT

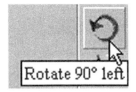

Rotate Left Tool
SOURCE: ©SCANSOFT PAPERPORT

Rotate 90 Degrees Right

1. Scan your school identification card. Double-click the scanned image to go to Page View.
2. Be sure the Image Toolbar is turned on. If it is not showing, go to the menu bar and choose View > Image Toolbar.
3. Click on the Rotate 90 degrees right tool. Save as *RotateRight.MAX* in your *MyScans* folder. Leave it on your screen for the next activity.

Rotate 90 Degrees Left

4. Click on the Rotate 90 degrees left tool until the scanned image is upside down on your screen. Save as *UpsideDown.MAX*. Leave it on your screen for the next activity.

Picture Wizard

5. Click on the Rotate 90 degrees left tool until the image is appropriately rotated.
6. Click on the Picture Wizard on the Image Toolbar. Click Next until you get to the screen with a number of pictures to choose from. Choose the one that looks best, then click Finish.
7. Save as *MyID.MAX*.

Picture Wizard
SOURCE: ©SCANSOFT PAPERPORT

Autofix Picture

8. Import *Soccer.MAX* from your CD.
9. Click Autofix picture from the Image Toolbar. Save as *SoccerFixed.MAX*. Leave it on the screen for the next activity.

Adjust Picture

10. Click on Adjust Picture from the Image Toolbar. Choose the picture that looks best to you and click OK. You can also make adjustments to brightness and contrast, color, and tint. If you are fairly satisfied with the picture, you may want to make less change by sliding the number lower on the slider.

Autofix Picture
SOURCE: ©SCANSOFT PAPERPORT

Adjust Picture
SOURCE: ©SCANSOFT PAPERPORT

Sharpen Picture

11. Click on the Sharpen picture tool and experiment with sharpening the picture.

Crop Page

12. We only need one of the pictures in this image. Click on the Crop page tool and crop one of the images out of the page. Once you have the part selected that you want cropped out, right-click and choose Crop. Save as *SoccerFinished.MAX*.

Invert Page

13. Click on Invert page from the Image Toolbar. Save as *Inverted.MAX*.

Enhance Lines

14. Import *GradeSheet.MAX* from your CD.
15. Change to Page View.
16. Click on Enhance Lines from your Image Toolbar. Use the Rectangular area tool to draw over lines that need straightening or darkening, then click on the Enhance lines tool.
17. Use the Remove stray dots tool and the Eraser tool to make the document look cleaner. Save as *MyGrade.MAX*. Print a copy for your instructor.
18. Create a stack with all the assignments on the grade sheet. Place *RotateRight* first and *Inverted* on top of the stack. Rename the stack *Activity4*.

ACTIVITY 4 • MINI-PROJECT

Create a Scan of News Headlines

1. Cut out three news headlines from a current newspaper. Arrange all three headlines on the glass of a scanner and scan them.
2. Save in the *VisioneerActivities* folder as *Headlines.MAX*. Save all activities in this project in the *VisioneerActivities* folder.
3. Use the Picture Wizard, Autofix Picture, Adjust Picture, and Sharpen Picture to create a better image of your headlines.
4. Save as *FixedHeadlines.MAX*.
5. Crop the image so that only one of the headlines is remaining. Save as *CroppedHeadline.MAX*.
6. Use Enhance lines and the Eraser tool to create a better image. Save as *ImprovedHeadline.MAX*.

   ☐ Original scan of three headlines is clear and somewhat straight.
   ☐ Use of the Picture Wizard, Autofix Picture, Adjust Picture, and Sharpen Picture creates an improved image.
   ☐ Image cropped without cutting off any of the headline or leaving any of the other headlines.
   ☐ Enhance lines and the Eraser tool used effectively.
   ☐ All files saved as instructed with no errors in file names.

Sharpen Picture Tool
SOURCE: ©SCANSOFT PAPERPORT

Crop Page Tool
SOURCE: ©SCANSOFT PAPERPORT

Invert Page
SOURCE: ©SCANSOFT PAPERPORT

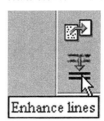

Enhance Lines
SOURCE: ©SCANSOFT PAPERPORT

Using Visioneer PaperPort to Create a Scanned News Article

1. Think of someone that has influenced your life in a positive way. It could be a parent, a friend or neighbor, a sibling, and so on. Obtain a picture of this person to use in this project.
2. Scan the picture of the person in step 1. Save in a folder titled *Mentor* as *01MentorImage.MAX*. All activities in this project will be saved to the *Mentor* folder.
3. Scan the image again, setting the preferences for lower quality, smaller file size, and thumbnail image. Save as *02ThumbnailImage.jpg*.
4. Browse to locate an image that represents this person's interest, his or her job, or something that reminds you of the person. Save as *03RepMentor.jpg*.
5. In a word processing document, write an article on why you chose this person. It should be at least 50 words long. Import *02ThumbnailImage.jpg* and *03RepMentor.jpg* into the document. Use WordArt or other ways of creating a headline to add to the article. Save as *04MentorArticle*.
6. Print a copy of *04MentorArticle*.
7. Scan *04MentorArticle*.
8. Erase any extraneous marks on the scanned image. Straighten the page if necessary. Add a brief note at the bottom of the document of something else you have thought of that has influenced you about this person. It can be one sentence. Save as *05MentorArticle.MAX*.
9. Add highlighting to two words for emphasis. Add a freehand annotation to two other words for emphasis. Save as *06MentorArticle.MAX*.
10. Use some of the adjustment tools to create a better-looking image. Save as *07AdjustedImage.MAX*.
11. Crop the image as needed. Save as *08CroppedImage.MAX*.
12. Use the Eraser tool and Enhance lines tool to make the image look professional. Save as *09ProfessionalImage.MAX*.
13. Create a stack titled *MentorImages* and place all the images in ascending order in the stack.
14. The following criteria should be met:
    - ☐ All activities saved in the folder *Mentor*.
    - ☐ Scanned image for lower quality, smaller file size, and thumbnail image meets specifications.
    - ☐ Image used to represent the person appropriate to what is written in the article.
    - ☐ Article well written, contains no errors, and at least 50 words long.
    - ☐ WordArt or headline and images placed in the document.
    - ☐ Note added to the bottom of the document using the Add text tool.
    - ☐ Two words highlighted for emphasis; two words use a freehand annotation for emphasis.
    - ☐ Adjustment tools for a better image used effectively.
    - ☐ Image cropped appropriately.
    - ☐ Eraser tool and Enhance lines tool used effectively.
    - ☐ Stack created with correct name and in ascending order.
    All images included in the stack.

Microsoft Excel Charts

Part 3

> **Microsoft Excel**
> **Publisher: Microsoft Corporation**
> Excel is a spreadsheet program that can also serve as a database.
> It enables you to create charts and graphs through a wizard.

ACTIVITY 1 • PIE CHARTS

In this activity, you will become familiar with:

- ■ Inputting Spreadsheets
- ■ Creating Pie Charts
- ■ Formatting Pie Charts

Inputting Spreadsheets

1. Open Excel. Input the spreadsheet in the figure to the right. Save it as *PopularColors.xls*.
2. Format the title font to Size 14 Times New Roman.
3. Format the column headings as Size 12 Times New Roman, bold.
4. Select A4:B8.

Creating Pie Charts

1. Click on the Chart Wizard.
2. Because the information about colors is a part of the whole, the best type of chart would be a pie chart. There are six choices of pie charts. Choose the second one in the top row. This is a pie with a 3-D visual effect.

	A	B	C	D
1	**Most Popular Colors**			
2				
3	SUV/Truck/Van	**2000**		
4	White	23%		
5	Silver	14%		
6	Blue	11%		
7	Black	10%		
8	Other	32%		
9				
10	Source: DuPont Herberts Automotive Systems			
11	Troy Michigan, 2000. www.dupont.com.			
12				

Spreadsheet

Chart Wizard
SOURCE: ©MICROSOFT EXCEL

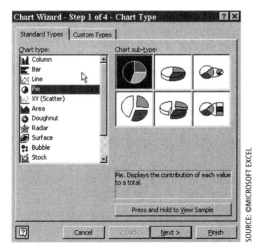

Chart Type

SOURCE: ©MICROSOFT EXCEL

---

3. Click Next twice.
4. Type the title "Most Popular Colors."
5. Click on the Data Labels tab. Click Percentage so that the percent amount shows on the pie slices. Click to turn off the Show leader lines.
6. Click Next.
7. Choose to Place chart As new sheet. Name the worksheet Colors.
8. Click Finish. Save the workbook again.

Place Chart

SOURCE: ©MICROSOFT EXCEL

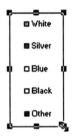

Legend

SOURCE: ©MICROSOFT EXCEL

Formatting Pie Charts

1. Click in the text box with the title in it. Change the font to Size 22 Times New Roman.
2. Click after the last word in the title. Press the Enter key, then type "SUV/Trucks/Van."
3. Press Enter again and type "2000."
4. Select the second and third headings. Change the Size to 20 and turn bold off.
5. Click on the Legend. Increase the size by hovering the mouse pointer over the bottom right corner. When the mouse turns into a diagonal arrow, click and drag to resize.
6. Double-click on a piece of the pie. Be sure you have not selected the entire pie, but only one piece of the pie. Change the color to appropriately match the color that it depicts. For instance, the piece of the pie that represents white as the most popular color should be white. Do this for each piece of the pie.
7. For the other piece of the pie, choose Fill Pattern, then a Preset of Rainbow to represent a variety of different colors.

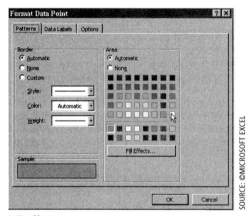

Fill Effects

8. Save as *PopularColors.xls*.

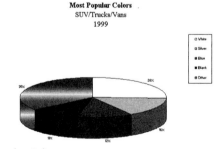

Popular Colors

SOURCE: ©MICROSOFT EXCEL

ACTIVITY 1 • MINI-PROJECT

Create a Pie Chart Showing Use of Time

1. Think about your current schedule and how you use your time on any given school day. In a spreadsheet, type the title "Use of Time" and underneath it the day of the week you are using as an example. Choose the day of the week you think is busiest for you in your use of time. If you have more activities such as practice or lessons on a certain day then choose that day.
2. In Column 1 type "Activity" and in Column 2 type "Amount of Time." List at least six activities in Column 1. The activities could be such things as sleeping, school, football practice, and homework. Estimate, in hours, the amount of time out of 24 hours you spend in that activity.
3. Create a pie chart as an object on the spreadsheet. Format titles, subtitles, and slices of the pie to create an appealing image.
4. Save the spreadsheet and pie chart as *TimeSpent.xls*.
5. Create a different spreadsheet and title it "Proposed Time Spent" with a subtitle of the same day of the week as the first activity.
6. Make adjustments in the amount of time spent on any given activity. These should be realistic changes and perhaps even additions of activities. If you find that by eliminating some time from one activity, you can spend more time doing something on a daily basis that should be done, then add that activity. You may add two activities if you need to for a total of eight activities on this chart. You must make at least one adjustment in your schedule.
7. Create a pie chart as an object on the spreadsheet. Format the pie chart as needed. Save as *ProposedTimeSpent.xls*.
8. The following criteria should be met:
   - ☐ Spreadsheet information accurate and complete.
   - ☐ Chart created as requested and correct according to the spreadsheet information.
   - ☐ Formatting of chart eye-appealing.
   - ☐ Second spreadsheet has at least one adjustment in time and is realistic. It shows some thought given to the time spent on the given activities.
   - ☐ Pie chart in second spreadsheet formatted to create an effective image.

ACTIVITY 2 • COLUMN CHARTS

In this activity, you will become familiar with:

- Creating Column Charts
- Naming the Series
- Formatting Column Charts
- Interpreting Column Charts

Creating Column Charts

1. Open *CintronTechnology.xls* from your CD.
2. Select the part of the spreadsheet needed to create the chart.

Day of Week	2001	2002	2003
Monday	5	4	2
Tuesday	1	5	4
Wednesday	1	8	3
Thursday	6	2	1
Friday	10	9	5

Selection

SOURCE: ©MICROSOFT EXCEL

Column Chart

Series

3. Go to the menu bar and choose Insert > Chart.
4. In the Chart Wizard dialog box, choose the Clustered column with a 3-D visual effect.
5. Hold down the left mouse button to view a sample to be sure you have selected the right amount of text and numbers to place in the chart.

Naming the Series

1. Click Next. This brings you to Step 2 of 4 in the Chart Wizard dialog box. Click on the Series tab. Click in the Name box and type "2000."
2. Click on Series 2 in the Series box and type "2001" in the Name box.
3. Click on Series 3 in the Series box and type "2002" in the Name box.
4. Click Next. This brings you to Step 3 of 4 in the Chart Wizard dialog box.
5. Type the three titles in their respective boxes.
   Chart title—"Cintron Technology Training Center"
   Category (X)—"Day of Week"
   Value (Z)—"Number of employees"

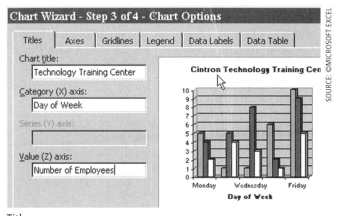

Titles

6. Click Next. This brings you to Step 4 of 4 in the Chart Wizard dialog box.
7. Click As new sheet. Name the worksheet "Cintron Technology."
8. Save the workbook as *CintronTechnology.xls*.

Formatting Column Charts

1. Select the Chart Title and change it to Size 18 Times New Roman.
2. Select the *x*-axis Title to Size 12. Leave it on Arial font.
3. Select the *y*-axis Title to Size 12. Leave it on Arial font. Change the Orientation for the *y*-axis title by double-clicking the text box. In the Format Axis Title dialog box, click on the Orientation tab. Move the Orientation to 90 degrees. Leave it on Context for Text direction.
4. Enlarge the Legend text box.
5. Double-click on Series 2000. In the Format Data Series dialog box, choose Fill Effects.
6. Click on the Texture tab. Choose Denim by double-clicking on it, then clicking OK in the dialog box.

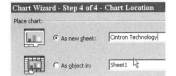

New Sheet

Orientation

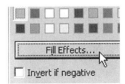

Fill Effects

7. Double-click on "Series 2001." On the Format Data Series dialog box, choose Fill Effects.
   Double-click on "Series 2001" for Bouquet.
8. Double-click on "Series 2002." On the Format Data Series dialog box, choose Fill Effects.
   Double-click on "Series 2002" for Woven Mat.
9. Add a subheading of "Employee Absences" in Size 12 Arial.
10. Save the workbook as *CintronTechnology.xls*.

SOURCE: ©MICROSOFT EXCEL

Textures

Interpreting Column Charts

1. Copy and paste the chart into a word processing document. Do not worry if the chart now looks grayscale. Note that the image itself is now shown on the task pane in the clipboard.
2. Below the image of the chart, explain what these statistics mean by answering the questions. Save as *ColumnChart.doc*.
   Answer the following questions and add four additional facts of your own from the chart:
   a. What day of the week do most absences occur?
   b. Was there a year that had more absences than the other two years?
   c. What day of the week had the least absences in 2000?
   d. What day of the week had the least absences in 2001?

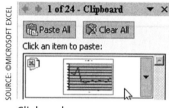

SOURCE: ©MICROSOFT EXCEL

Clipboard

ACTIVITY 2 • MINI-PROJECT

Create Column Charts from Image Information

1. In a team of three or four students, take three digital pictures of items with two each in the picture. For instance, take a picture of two apples, two books, two pencils, and so on.
2. Each student in the team crops each of the images so that only one of the items is in the picture. All team members should crop each of the images on their own.
3. Create an Excel spreadsheet for each image to show information on the image. It should contain four column headings: Name of Image, Size in Bytes, Height, and Width (in pixels).
4. The first crop that you did in step 2 should be recorded on the spreadsheet as Crop 1. Save the image as *Crop1.jpg*.
5. Crop the picture again, leaving out as much as possible except for the object itself. This should be recorded on the worksheet as Crop 2. Save as *Crop2.jpg*.
6. You should then resize the picture at 75% of the size after the second crop. Record this on the worksheet as Resize 75%. Save as *Resize1.jpg*.
7. You should then resize one more time at 50% of the current size. Record this on the worksheet as Resize 50%. Save as *Resize2.jpg*.
8. Create a column chart as an object on the spreadsheet to compare the sizes of the four changed images in kilobytes. Title the bar chart with no series. Be sure to format the color to appropriately display the object in the picture. Insert the object as *Resize2.jpg*.
9. Create another column chart as an object on the spreadsheet to compare the heights of the four changed images. Title the bar chart with no series. Be sure to format the color to appropriately display the object. Insert *Resize2.jpg* onto the bar chart.
10. Save the spreadsheet as *LikeObjects.xls*. The spreadsheets and chart should fit on one page.

11. Meet back with your team. Decide as a team on which object you will use to present to the class. Create two charts as a team. The first chart should be a comparison by team member of their *Crop1.jpg* in kilobytes. The second chart should be a comparison by team member of their *Resize2.jpg* in kilobytes. As a team, write a summary of the comparison that the chart indicates. What does the chart tell you? Why is this important? What did you learn from your other charts? Summarize any other findings from this project with input from each team member. Save as *Summary*.
12. Present your summary to the class.
13. The following criteria should be met:
    - ☐ Digital images are of quality and showed creativity in type of image.
    - ☐ Excel spreadsheet has appropriate data information and column headings as instructed.
    - ☐ Charts inserted on the spreadsheet as instructed with appropriate formatting and image placed appropriately.
    - ☐ Team worked well together.
    - ☐ Team charts inserted on the spreadsheet as instructed with appropriate formatting.
    - ☐ Summary well-written with substantial data in it and no errors.
    - ☐ Presentation to class included participation by all team members.

ACTIVITY 3 • LINE CHARTS

In this activity, you will become familiar with:

- ■ Creating Line Charts
- ■ Interpreting Line Charts
- ■ Creating 3-D Line Charts
  - ○ Selecting Random Cells
  - ○ Title, Category, and Value Names

Creating Line Charts

Chart Titles

1. Open *TaylorAdvertising.xls* from your CD.
2. Create a Line Chart showing the year by month totals. Select B4:M5.
3. Go to the menu bar and choose Insert > Chart.
4. Choose Line for Chart type. Chart sub-type should be Line with markers displayed at each data value. Choose Next.
5. Do not make changes to Data Range or Series. Click Next.
6. Click on the Titles tab.
7. Type in the Chart title "Taylor Advertising."
8. Type in the Category (X) axis title "Months."
9. Type in the Category (Y) axis title "Gross Income."
10. Click on the Legend tab. Clear the Show legend check box.
11. Click Place chart As new sheet and name the worksheet "Taylor."
12. Change formatting of titles to appropriate font sizes and types. Add a subheading of "Internet Sales 2XXX."
13. Save again.

Interpreting Line Charts

14. Copy and paste the chart to a Word document. List at least five facts in interpreting what the chart means.
15. Save the document as *Taylor.doc*.

Creating 3-D Line Charts

Selecting Random Cells

1. Open *TaylorAdvertising.xls*.
2. Click and drag to select cells B10:M10. Hold down the Ctrl key while continuing to select cells B15:M15. You should have selected the total rows for Houston and Dallas Offices.
3. Click on the Chart Wizard.
4. Choose Line Chart on the Standard tab, then choose 3-D line with a 3-D visual effect.
5. Click on the Series tab. Name Series 1 "Houston Office." Name Series 2 "Dallas Office."
6. While still on Step 2 of 4, click in the Category (X) axis labels. Click on the Collapse Dialog Box button. This button collapses the dialog box so you can now select something other than the default. Select the headings January–December.

Collapse
Dialog Box

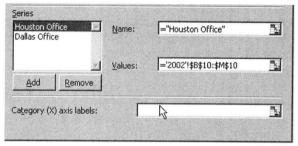

Category Labels

SOURCE: LEFT AND RIGHT ©MICROSOFT EXCEL

7. Click on the Collapse Dialog Box button again to open the dialog box again. Notice on your image in Step 2 of 4, you now have January–December on the *x*-axis instead of 1–10.

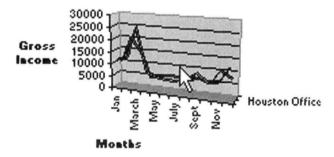

X-Axis

SOURCE: ©MICROSOFT EXCEL

8. Click Next.

Chart Wizard - Step 3 of 4 - C

| Titles | Axes | Gridlines | Leg |

Chart title:
Taylor Advertising

Category (X) axis:
Months

Series (Y) axis:

Value (Z) axis:
Gross Income

SOURCE: ©MICROSOFT EXCEL

3-D Titles

Title, Category, and Value Names

1. Type "Taylor Advertising" in the Chart title.
2. Type "Months" in the Category (X) axis.
3. Type "Gross Income" in the Value (Z) axis.
4. Click Next.
5. In Step 4 of 4, Place chart As new sheet. Name the worksheet "Houston Dallas." Click Finish. Save the workbook again.
6. In the Format Axis dialog box, adjust the scale as needed.
7. Change Fonts for titles, and x- and y-axis labels as appropriate. Add a secondary title of "Comparison of Houston and Dallas Offices."
8. If there are any extra labels in the corners of the 3-D chart, right-click on them and choose Clear.
9. Change the Orientation on any axis label to make it appropriate.
10. Increase the size of the Legend.
11. Copy and paste the chart to a Word document.
12. Answer the following questions:
    a. In what three-month series were the two locations fairly close in gross income?
    b. In what month did the Houston office have the highest gross income over the Dallas office?
    c. In what month did the Dallas office have the highest gross income over the Houston office?
    d. What month had the lowest gross income for the Houston office?
    e. What month had the lowest gross income for the Dallas office?
    f. Brainstorm and write a short paragraph on some possible reasons for these differences in gross income. Include at least three possible reasons in your paragraph.
13. Save the Word document as *HoustonDallasChart.doc*.

ACTIVITY 3 • MINI-PROJECT

Create a Line Chart Showing Salary Trends

1. Go to http://austin.about.com/cs/localstatistics/ or another Web site about the city of Austin, Texas.
2. Locate statistical information that shows a trend that can be used to create a line chart. Create two spreadsheets with line charts as objects on the spreadsheet. Make one of the charts a 3-D chart.
3. Format the charts with a title and subtitle if appropriate. Use color to gain attention on the image.
4. Save the spreadsheets and charts as *01Trend.xls* and *02Trend.xls*.
5. The following criteria should be met:
   ☐ Topic chosen for both charts appropriate to the type of chart.
   ☐ Information for charts has been input into the spreadsheet appropriately and accurately.
   ☐ Formatting on the charts was detailed and eye-catching. There were size, font, and color changes.
   ☐ Charts and spreadsheet named as instructed with no errors in file names.
   ☐ Chart had an appropriate title and subtitle if needed. Title formatted appropriately to gain attention to the image.

ACTIVITY 4 • STOCK CHARTS

In this activity, you will become familiar with:

- Formatting Cells
- Creating Stock Charts
  - ○ Creating a Chart
  - ○ Placing Chart as Object
  - ○ Moving a Chart
  - ○ Resizing a Chart
- Interpreting Stock Charts

Formatting Cells

1. Open *JMC.xls* from your CD.
2. Look at the number data that you will be using for the stock chart. Notice that there is inconsistency in the decimals. It is usually best to change the decimals to two places, for the chart to be easily interpreted.
3. Select B5:D11.
4. Go to the menu bar and choose Format > Cells. In the Format Cells dialog box, choose Number. Leave the formatting on two decimal places and click OK.

Creating Stock Charts

Creating a Chart

1. Select A5:D11.
2. Click on the Chart Wizard.
3. In the Chart Wizard dialog box, choose Stock. Since our information on the spreadsheet includes only High, Low, and Close, we will choose the first Chart sub-type. Click Next.

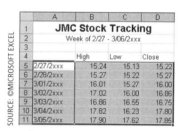

SOURCE: ©MICROSOFT EXCEL

Selection

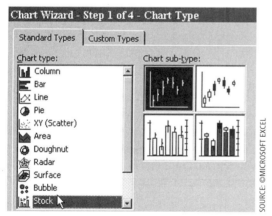

SOURCE: ©MICROSOFT EXCEL

Chart Type

4. On Step 2 of 4, choose Series and name the series. Series 1 is High. Series 2 is Low. Series 3 is Close.
5. In the Category (X) axis labels, select the dates to be placed in Category X. Click Next.
6. On Step 3 of 4, click on the Title tab and type an appropriate title for the chart. Click Next.

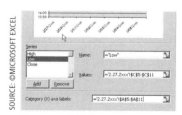

SOURCE: ©MICROSOFT EXCEL

Category X Values

Placing Chart as Object

1. On Step 4 of 4, choose the Place chart As object in. Click Finish.

Moving a Chart

2. Click on your chart and drag it so that it is not covering the spreadsheet.
3. Double-click on the *y*-axis numbers to open the Format Axis dialog box. Click the Scale tab. Adjust the Minimum, Maximum, and Major unit as seen at left.

Resizing a Chart

1. Select the chart. Hover your cursor over the top middle of the edge of the chart until the cursor changes to a black vertical arrow. See below.

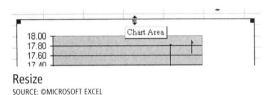

Resize
SOURCE: ©MICROSOFT EXCEL

2. Stretch the spreadsheet upward until the numbers are appropriately spaced vertically. See above.
3. Save the workbook as *JMC.xls*.

Interpreting Stock Charts

1. Copy and paste the chart into a Word document. Write a paragraph interpreting the chart. Answer the following questions:
   a. What day had the smallest amount of fluctuation or change in the stock?
   b. What day had the highest amount of fluctuation or change in the stock?
   c. What type of change was seen overall in the stock this week?

ACTIVITY 4 • MINI-PROJECT

Create a Stock Chart

1. Using the *Wall Street Journal,* choose three companies whose company name begins with the same letter as your last name.
2. Begin a spreadsheet for each company. Post to each of the three spreadsheets daily, using the *Wall Street Journal* for your information. Save as *01WallStreet.xls*, *02WallStreet.xls*, and *03WallStreet.xls*.
3. At the end of the week or a five-day period, create a stock chart for each of the companies from your spreadsheet information. Format the chart appropriately. Create the stock chart on the same document as your spreadsheet.
4. Merge a large block of cells on your spreadsheet. Write an analysis of how your stock did that week.
5. The following criteria should be met:
   - ☐ Appropriate company names chosen.
   - ☐ Spreadsheet information accurate and posted daily.
   - ☐ Spreadsheet files saved appropriately with no errors in file names.
   - ☐ Spreadsheets contain no errors.
   - ☐ Each of the stock charts created correctly. Proper selections made for what should be found on the chart.
   - ☐ Formatting on the stock chart helps users understand the chart numbers.
   - ☐ Cells merged appropriately and a good explanation given on the summary of the stock activity for the given businesses.

Sidebar (left):

Format Axis

| Patterns | Scale | Font | Numb |

Value (Y) axis scale

Auto
- ☐ Mi_n_imum: 15
- ☐ Ma_x_imum: 18
- ☐ Ma_j_or unit: 0.2
- ☑ Mi_n_or unit: 0.04
- ☑ Category (X) axis
  - _C_rosses at: 15

SOURCE: ©MICROSOFT EXCEL

Scale

Using Excel and Charting, Create Charts for a Camp Store

1. With a partner, use the following list of items in a small camp store to create different types of charts. Fill in the wholesale price and retail price by visiting a grocery store or interviewing someone who works in a grocery store. Find out the retail price and deduct 35% to find the wholesale price. Fill in the missing information on the spreadsheet including totals. Format the numbers in the spreadsheet for no decimal places and no dollar signs. There is an asterisk in the cells that require a total. Delete the asterisk, then add the formula for the total.

Grocery Item	Department	Number in Inventory	Wholesale Inventory Cost	Retail Inventory Cost
Eggs	Dairy	4 dozen		
Milk	Dairy	4 gallons		
Yogurt	Dairy	12 ea		
Total Dairy Inventory			*	*
Pork Chops	Meat	4 pkgs.		
Steak	Meat	8 pkgs.		
Total Meat Inventory			*	*
Green Beans	Canned Goods	12 ea		
Corn	Canned Goods	12 ea		
Asparagus	Canned Goods	6 ea		
Total Canned Goods Inventory			*	*
Toothbrush	Cosmetics	12 ea		
Listerine	Cosmetics	6 ea		
Shampoo	Cosmetics	6 ea		
Deodorant	Cosmetics	6 ea		
Total Cosmetics Inventory			*	*
Total Store Inventory			*	*

2. Create a pie chart of the total retail cost of inventory by category. Use the Ctrl key to select lines that are not right next to each other (at random).
3. Format the pie chart with an appropriate title and colors for the pie slices. Format fonts, size, and color on the chart.
4. Save as *01Camp.xls*.
5. Create a bar or column chart. Include in the chart the four wholesale totals from each category.
6. Format the chart and text for size, font, and color. Include a chart title.
7. Save as *02Camp.xls*.
8. The camp management would like to analyze the effectiveness of the camp store. The following information has been obtained from the cash register as far as number of sales over the summer.

Date	Number of Items Sold
06/03/02	24
06/10/02	22
06/17/02	18
06/24/02	27
07/01/02	32
07/08/02	40
07/15/02	38
07/22/02	45
07/29/02	44

9. Create a line chart showing the trend in sales at the camp store. Format the line chart for an effective image.
10. Save as *03CampStore.xls*.
11. The stock in this particular store closed yesterday at 12-1/4. The high was 12-3/4 and the low was 11-3/4. Project the next seven days' high, low, and closing stock amounts. Create a stock chart to demonstrate your projection.
12. Save as *04CampStore.xls*.
13. The following criteria should be met:
    - ☐ Retail prices realistic with a correct value in the wholesale column.
    - ☐ Totals accurate.
    - ☐ Pie chart contains accurate information.
    - ☐ Pie chart formatting demonstrates effort.
    - ☐ Correct amounts in the column or bar chart.
    - ☐ Column or bar chart's formatting demonstrates effort.
    - ☐ Line chart accurate.
    - ☐ Line chart formatting demonstrates effort.
    - ☐ Stock chart accurate and reasonable projections.
    - ☐ Stock chart formatting demonstrates effort.

MapScape.com

MapScape.com
Publisher: Tactician Corporation
Mapscape.com is an online mapping program that allows the use of normal mapping tools such as Pushpins, Pan Tool, and Zoom Tool. Sites can be bookmarked as well as creating thematic maps, emailing maps, and printing maps. It also allows some business applications such as site analysis, configuring trade areas, and reporting.

ACTIVITY 1 • ATLAS

In this activity, you will become familiar with:

- Creating a Login
- Getting Started
- Terms
- Tools
  - Jump
  - Centering the Map
  - Pushpins
  - Pan Tool
  - Zoom Tool
- Bookmarks
- Thematic Map
- Emailing a Map
- Printing a Map

Registration

Creating a Login

1. MapScape is a Web-generated mapping program by Tactician Corporation. The address is http://www.mapscape.com. You must first create a login. Once you have done this, Tactician will send you a PIN (personal identification number) to your email account.

ATLAS
Your personal marketing
bookmark locations and

SITES AND M
Generate a site or area a
report on thousands of c

Atlas
SOURCE: ©MAPSCAPE.COM

Getting Started

2. Choose Atlas to get started.

Terms

3. Follow the links to learn more about the terms associated with mapping and MapScape.

Easy Navigation - Using the Jump, Pan, and Zoom tools, you can navigate your map to anywhere in the country!

Bookmark - Personalize your maps and bookmark them! You can save unlimited bookmarks and retrieve them anytime.

My Map - Turn map overlays on and off to suit your needs! Use color-coded pushpins to plot company and competitor locations; and - new! - print your Atlas map, full-size!

Thematic - Customize your thematic map by selecting the variable, geography and colors that suit your needs!

Flash Report - Use Flash Reports to point-and-click a location on the map and display a mini-demographic report for that location.

SOURCE: ©MAPSCAPE.COM

Terms

Jump To Tool
SOURCE: ©MAPSCAPE.COM

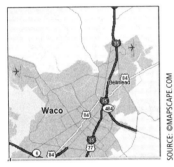

Waco

SOURCE: ©MAPSCAPE.COM

Tools

Jump

4. Click on Jump to get started with a map. Type in the address of one of the sites for Texas State Technical College. It is 3801 Campus Drive, Waco, Texas.

Centering the Map

5. Click the place on the map that you would like to become the center. This will automatically redraw the map.

Pushpins

6. Choose the Pushpin. Drag the Pushpin around until you have it positioned according to the figure to the left. This is the approximate location of Texas State Technical College.

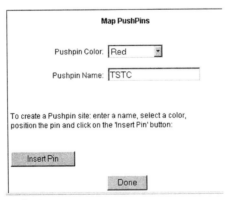

Push Pin

TSTC

SOURCE: LEFT AND RIGHT ©MAPSCAPE.COM

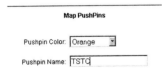

Pushpin Choices
SOURCE: ©MAPSCAPE.COM

7. Once you have made your choices and have the Pushpin positioned, click Insert Pin.

Pan Tool

8. Use the Pan tool to move around on the map. Hover the pointer over the arrow to display "S." Click on the "S" arrow. Notice that this brings the map too far down. Hover the pointer over the arrow to display "N." Click on the "N" arrow

to bring it back up. Continue to experiment with the Pan tool. Bring your map back to where it started each time.

Pan Tool

Zoom Tool

9. Use the Zoom tool to zoom down one level so that some of the street names show on your map. Answer the following questions:
   a. Name a major highway that goes through Waco.
   b. Name at least two other surrounding towns or communities.
   c. What other highways run through Waco?

Bookmarks

10. Create a bookmark by going to the menu bar and choosing Bookmark > Create. Type in "Waco" in the dialog box and click Create.

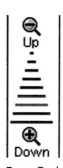

Zoom Tool

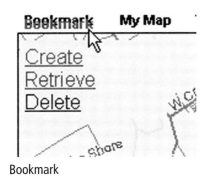

Bookmark

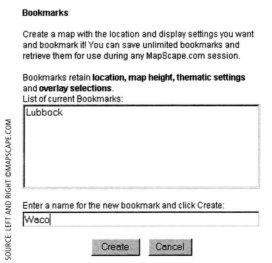

Bookmarks

Create a map with the location and display settings you want and bookmark it! You can save unlimited bookmarks and retrieve them for use during any MapScape.com session.

Bookmarks retain **location, map height, thematic settings** and **overlay selections**.
List of current Bookmarks:

Lubbock

Enter a name for the new bookmark and click Create:

Waco

Create Cancel

Waco Bookmark

Thematic Map

11. Go to the menu bar and choose Thematic > Thematic Map.
12. In the Thematic Mapping dialog box, choose a geography by Zip Code and the Age variable. Change classification to 6 Classes, Equal Class Counts.

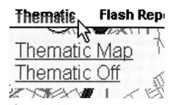

Thematic Map

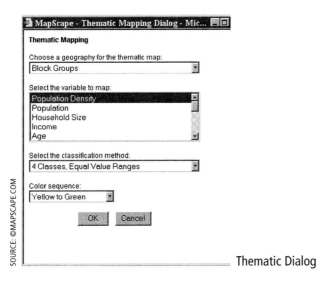

Thematic Dialog

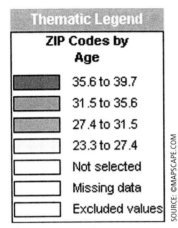

Thematic Legend

Email Tool

13. Look at the Thematic Legend and answer the following questions:
    a. Name at least two streets that have the youngest population in Waco.
    b. In what area do most of the 33-year-olds live?
    c. Name at least two streets that have the oldest population in Waco.
    d. What is the average age of the citizens of Waco?
    e. List two zip codes for the city.

Emailing a Map

14. Email your map to your instructor for assessment. The subject should be "Waco TSTC." Answer the questions in steps 9 and 13 and attach the map. To email in Internet Explorer 6, hover the mouse pointer at the top left corner of the map. You should get a task bar with four icons on it. The third icon from the left is the Email icon. Click on it. Note: If you are unable to complete the email task, get instructions from your instructor as to how to submit the map and questions for assessment.

15. Go to the Internet and search for Texas State Technical College. Find a location other than Waco. Create a map of the alternative location of your choosing.

16. Create a Pushpin on the location within the city.

17. Zoom down so that the street names show on the map.

18. Create a bookmark of your location.

19. Create a thematic map of your location.

Printing a Map

20. Print a copy of the map for your instructor by going to the menu bar and choosing My Map > Print Map.

21. See the figure below (right) to complete the Print dialog box.

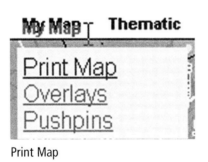

Print Map

Print Map Dialog Box

22. Be sure to sign off when you have completed your work in MapScape. If you do not, the next time you get ready to use it, it will give you a message that you are still signed in from the last session.

Sign Off

ACTIVITY 1 • MINI-PROJECT

Create a Map for Decision-Making

1. Your company is in the business of selling clothing. Your desire is to reach as large a population as possible, with the average age being 35. The city choices for a new clothing company are Seattle, Washington, 98104; Plano, Texas, 75074; and Jacksonville, Florida, 32202.
2. Create a thematic map with geography by Zip Code.
3. Print each of the maps. Bookmark each map, naming it with the city name.
4. Using a word processing document, answer the following questions for each city:
   a. In what area do most of the 35-year-olds (or closest to that age) live?
   b. What is the average age of the citizens of that city?
   c. List two zip codes for the city.
5. Summarize your decision as to which city would work best given the current criteria. In your summary, list some other factors that you believe should be included in the location decision. Save as *Location*.
6. Email the map of the best city to your instructor unless the instructor tells you otherwise.
7. The following criteria should be met:
   - ☐ Thematic maps with geography by Zip Code created for all three cities.
   - ☐ Each map printed.
   - ☐ Each map bookmarked.
   - ☐ Questions answered in the word processing document with a correct decision made, given the information.
   - ☐ Thought went into the list of other factors that should be included in the location decision.
   - ☐ The map was emailed to the instructor.

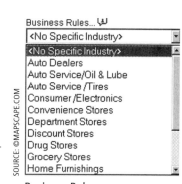

Business Rules

SOURCE: ©MAPSCAPE.COM

ACTIVITY 2 • SITES AND MARKETS

In this activity, you will become familiar with:

- ■ Generating Site Analysis
- ■ Creating a Report

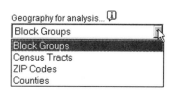

Geography for Analysis

SOURCE: ©MAPSCAPE.COM

Generating Site Analysis

1. Leave Business Rules on <No Specific Industry>.
2. In Geography for analysis, choose ZIP Codes.
3. Click Continue.
4. Click on the Jump tool. Jump to Schulenburg, TX.

Location

SOURCE: ©MAPSCAPE.COM

5. Click on the New Site button. Fill in the New Site dialog box. See the figure below for information to put in the dialog box.

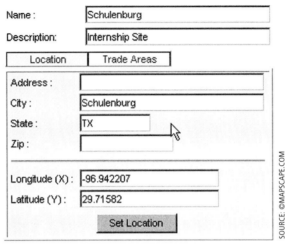

New Site

6. Click Save.
7. Create new sites and save them for Columbus, Texas; Hallettsville, Texas; Weimar, Texas; and Gonzales, Texas.
8. Once you have five sites set up, click on MapIt to create your map.

MapIt

9. Click on Finish to begin generating the report.

Creating a Report

10. Type the Report Title "Schulenburg Internship Sites."
11. Type the Secondary heading "Sumio Iwasaki."
12. Type the date and your name on the Report footer.
13. Choose Workforce/Education (census) since this is for Internship sites.
14. Choose Convenience Stores in Additional Map Display Features.
15. Click on Finish.

Menu

ACTIVITY 2 • MINI-PROJECT

Create a Map of a Business Trip

1. You are planning a business trip from Houston, Texas to Bismarck, North Dakota. You will make three stops before arriving in Bismarck. They are Wichita, Kansas; Lincoln, Nebraska; and Sioux Falls, South Dakota. Create a map of this trip.
2. Title the report "Spring Business Trip" with the secondary heading as "Places to Stop." Use the current date and your name on the Report footer. Decide what other factors to include as additional map display features.
3. Click Finish. Print the report.
4. The following criteria should be met:
   - ☐ The five cities listed on the printed report.
   - ☐ Title and secondary heading of the report as instructed.
   - ☐ Footer contains date and your name.
   - ☐ At least one other map feature displayed.
   - ☐ Map created and printed out in a timely manner.

ACTIVITY 3 • QUICK REPORTS

In this activity, you will become familiar with:

- ■ Choosing Report Locations
- ■ Choosing Trade Areas
- ■ Specifying Types of Reports

Choosing Report Locations

1. Click on Quick Reports.
2. Fill in the information for Step 1 of the Quick Report. In the Name box, type "Bookstore Research."
3. In the Description box, type "researching of possible bookstore locations."
4. Fill in Temple, TX for the City and State.

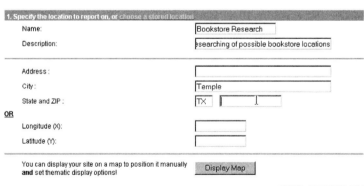

Step 1

SOURCE: ©MAPSCAPE.COM

Choosing Trade Areas

5. In Step 2, type 45 miles for radius in miles of Trade Area 1.

2. Specify up to 3 trade areas for the location		
Trade Area 1 :	45	miles
Trade Area 2 :		miles
Trade Area 3 :		miles

Step 2

6. In Step 3, choose Major Shopping Centers for the report.
7. Choose Counties for the geography for the report.
8. Type "Bookstore Research" for the Report title.
9. Type "Possible Future Locations" for the Report subtitle.
10. Type the date with your name underneath the date for the Report footer.
11. Choose Supermarkets for Additional Map Display Features.
12. Click on Generate Report.

Specifying Types of Reports

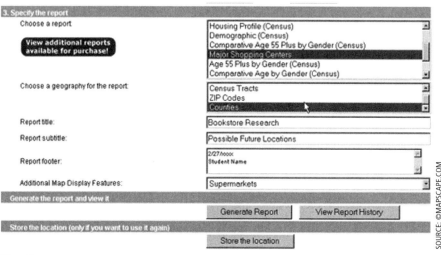

Step 3

13. Right-click on the map. Save as *Bookstores.gif*.
14. Create a word processing document. Insert *Bookstores.gif* as a picture. Using a marker, mark and number three possible locations for a bookstore. Write an analysis of why each one of these locations is a possibility. Give at least two reasons for each of the locations. Save as *BookstoreAnalysis.doc*.

ACTIVITY 3 • MINI-PROJECT

Create a Map and Chart for a Business Decision

1. After doing research, you have learned that fitness centers do best financially in areas where at least 20 percent of the 35 to 44-year-old population earns $25,000 or more.
2. Create a report for your supervisor for Lubbock, Texas, as a potential site for a new fitness center. Select all the criteria that you will need to make the decision and give appropriate titles and secondary headings for the report.

3. Using the report, paste the table of information in an Excel spreadsheet. Delete all columns except those needed for this report. Create an exploded pie chart as an object on the spreadsheet showing the information needed to make the decision. Format the pie chart so that the supervisor can see at a quick glance whether this is a good decision or not.

4. Type a note at the bottom of the spreadsheet with the results. Does Lubbock, Texas, meet the criteria for a site location of the new fitness center? Format the note so that the blocks are merged with a border. Consider font type, size, and color changes for visual appeal. The report should contain the spreadsheet, the pie chart, and the note all on one page.

5. Save as *FitnessCenter.xls*.

6. The following criteria should be met:

   ☐ Report from MapScape set up correctly.

   ☐ Table of information pasted in the spreadsheet with all columns deleted except those needed to make the decision.

   ☐ Exploded pie chart accurate and formatted for a quick decision.

   ☐ Note at the bottom of the spreadsheet appropriately formatted.

   ☐ Note at the bottom of the spreadsheet concisely written with a correct decision made based on the results of the report.

PART 4 • SIMULATION

Using MapScape to Assist in Business Decisions

1. In a team of three or four students, choose three cities to visit. Plan the business trip and print the map.

2. Use those same three cities to create reports on the possibilities of beginning a new game room as a business. Statistically, game rooms do best where the population is the youngest. Choose the city with the youngest population and a medium-level income ($35,000 or more).

3. Create a chart from the reports and print the chart as a separate report from the spreadsheet. Save as *01GameRoom.xls*, *02GameRoom.xls*, and *03GameRoom.xls*.

4. Using word processing software, write a business plan for the game room. Save as *BusinessPlan.doc*. Include in the business plan:
   a. Location (charts should be attached)
   b. Name of game room
   c. What you will need to purchase to get started
   d. Estimate of cost of mall location or other location (call a local mall or game room to get an estimated amount for space)
   e. How many game machines are you planning to install? If you can, find out what these will cost each.
   f. What other activities will you include in your game room?
   g. Will you have a refreshment center?
   h. Will you include other marketing strategies to make the game center a popular place to hang out?

5. Create three logos for your possible game room. It should be one logo created with two variations of the logo. Save as *01Game.jpg*, *02Game.jpg*, and *03Game.jpg*.

6. Create a cover page for your business report with the name of the project, the logo you chose from the three, the date submitted, and the names of the students who worked on the project.

7. Turn the project in to the instructor in a business report folder with the following (in order):
   a. Cover page
   b. Business plan
   c. Chart
   d. Printouts of all maps
   e. Any other supporting material obtained during the project
   f. Sources (MapScape.com, names of people you may have interviewed, names of their businesses, and any other sources you may have used)
8. The following criteria should be met:
   ☐ Map of business trip appropriately set up and printed.
   ☐ Printouts of reports appropriate for the needs of this project.
   ☐ Charts visually appealing as well as easy to read.
   ☐ Logo appropriate for type of business and visually appealing.
   ☐ Cover page contains all information as instructed.
   ☐ Business report covers all points as instructed.
   ☐ Report put together as instructed in an organized manner.
   ☐ Sources include adequate information to support the business plan.
   ☐ Team worked well together, with all members contributing equally.

Microsoft MapPoint

**Microsoft MapPoint
Publisher: Microsoft Corporation**
MapPoint is a high-end mapping program by Microsoft Corporation that enables use of mapping tools and many other features. Some of the features offered are route planning, locating intersections, searching for places, and charting using latitude and longitude. There are many different styles of maps, as well as the ability to look up specific types of restaurants and hotel locations.

ACTIVITY 1 • BASIC MAPPING

In this activity, you will become familiar with:

- Find a Place
- Copy a Map
- Zoom a Map
- Scroll a Map
- Paste a Map
- Route Planner
- Find Nearby Places

Find a Place

1. Open Microsoft MapPoint according to your instructor's directions.
2. Type "Grand Canyon, Arizona" in the Find box. Click Find.

Copy a Map

1. Go to the menu bar and choose Edit > Copy Map.
2. Open Microsoft Word and paste the map.

Zoom a Map

1. Using the Zoom Slide, zoom out until you can see both Arizona and Texas to get an idea of where you are going. If you have a wheel on your mouse, note that you can also zoom in and out with the wheel on your mouse.
2. Click on the Select tool, then draw a box around the area you want to view. Zoom in on that one area. After drawing the box, click in the area to zoom.

Scroll a Map

1. Hover the mouse pointer on the right edge of the map until you see the Move Right arrow, as shown on the following page. Use this arrow to scroll the map

Find
SOURCE: ©MICROSOFT MAPPOINT

Copy Map
SOURCE: ©MICROSOFT MAPPOINT

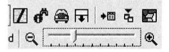

Zoom Slide Tool
SOURCE: ©MICROSOFT MAPPOINT

Select Tool
SOURCE: ©MICROSOFT MAPPOINT

Pan Tool
SOURCE: ©MICROSOFT MAPPOINT

Route Planner Tool
SOURCE: ©MICROSOFT MAPPOINT

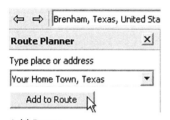
Add Route
SOURCE: ©MICROSOFT MAPPOINT

Get Directions Tool
SOURCE: ©MICROSOFT MAPPOINT

Copy Directions
SOURCE: ©MICROSOFT MAPPOINT

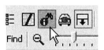
Nearby Places Tool
SOURCE: ©MICROSOFT MAPPOINT

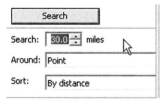
Miles
SOURCE: ©MICROSOFT MAPPOINT

so that it is centered horizontally with Arizona and Texas equally in the map view. Practice using the scroll arrows to move the map around. You can scroll in eight different directions.

Move Right

2. Click on the Pan tool. Your cursor changes to a hand. Click and drag the map. This moves the position of the map a little at a time.

Paste a Map

1. Copy the map and paste it into the Word document with the other map. You now have two different views of the map.
2. Save as *GrandCanyon.doc*.

Route Planner

1. Click on the Route Planner icon, as shown in the figure labeled Route Planner Tool.
2. Type the name of your hometown in the box and click Add to Route.
3. Type "Grand Canyon, Arizona" in the box and click Add to Route.
4. Practice zooming out on the map and using the scroll arrows to position the map best for your trip.
5. Click on the Get Directions icon.
6. Select the directions by clicking and dragging. Go to the menu bar and choose Edit > Copy.
7. Paste into the Word document.
8. Save again.

Find Nearby Places

1. Click on the Find Nearby Places icon, as shown to the left.
2. Change the distance to search for to 30 miles.
3. In a word processing document, answer the following questions:
   a. How far is it from your city to Grand Canyon, Arizona?
   b. How long will it take you to travel that distance?
   c. How much money will it cost you?
   d. What airports are nearby? What is the distance in miles of these airports from the Grand Canyon?
   e. What hotels and motels are nearby? What is the distance in miles of these hotels and motels from the Grand Canyon?
   f. Are there any landmarks near the Grand Canyon? What is the distance in miles from the Grand Canyon to these landmarks?

4. Save as *Activity1.doc*.
5. Right-click on the closest airport. Zoom to that airport.
6. Right-click on the other airport and highlight it. Copy and paste the new map into *GrandCanyon.doc*.
7. Click on Show or Hide Places.
8. Click on the Restaurants tab. Choose BBQ, Mexican, and Pizza Places.
9. Click on the Places tab. Choose Cinemas and Parks and Rides. Clear all of the other check boxes.
10. Click Apply and OK.
11. Click on one of the restaurants and show the address and phone number. Copy the map and paste it into *GrandCanyon.doc*.

ACTIVITY 1 • MINI-PROJECT

Create Maps to Assist in Planning a Trip

1. Search the Internet for Niagara Falls, New York or Canada. Plan a seven-day round trip vacation to both of them from Atlanta, Georgia.
2. Copy maps to a word processing document as needed to include as an attachment to your itinerary. Save as *MapAttachments.doc*.
3. The itinerary should include specifics such as time leaving, stops along the way for sightseeing, lunches in either restaurants or parks, other meals, and where to spend the night. Be sure to leave enough time for the return trip. The itinerary should be in table format in a word processing document. Save as *Itinerary.doc*.
4. The following criteria should be met:
   - ☐ A minimum of two maps copied to use as documentation for the trip.
   - ☐ Itinerary demonstrates use of the Route Planner and Show Places.
   - ☐ Itinerary is detailed and does not leave any gaps in time.
   - ☐ Files saved as instructed with no errors in file names or files.

ACTIVITY 2 • MAP USES

In this activity, you will become familiar with:

- Locating an Intersection
- Searching for Places
- Charting Using Latitude or Longitude
  - ○ Location Sensor
- Measuring Distance
- Map Styles
  - ○ Road Map
  - ○ Road and Data Map
  - ○ Data Map
- Importing Data
- Linking Data

Locating an Intersection

1. Type in the Find box "Texas Avenue & University Avenue." The ampersand between the two street names indicates that an intersection is being searched for. Click Find.
2. In the Find dialog box, add the city and state (College Station, Texas).

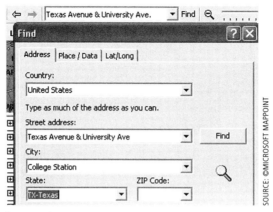

Intersections

3. Use the Select tool and zoom until both streets are easily identified on the map.
4. Use the Pan tool to move the map so that it is centered.
5. Save as *CollegeStation.ptm*.
6. Copy the map and paste into a PowerPoint presentation. Create one blank slide, paste the map into the slide, then resize the map to fit the slide.
7. Save as *CSIntersection.ppt*.

Searching for Places

1. Follow your instructor's directions for answering the questions in this activity.
2. In the Find box, type "Enchanted Rock." Click Find. Choose the address for the Enchanted Rock located in Texas.
   a. Near what city or town is it located?
   b. What is the name of the road on which it is located?
3. In the Find box, type "Garner State Park." Click Find.
   a. Near what city or town is it located?
   b. In what county is it located?
4. In the Find box, type "Longhorn State Park." Click Find.
   a. In what city or town is the park located?
   b. What is the road number on which the park is located?
5. Search for two other points of interest of your choice. State two facts from the map for each of them.

Charting Using Latitude and Longitude

1. Follow your instructor's directions for answering the questions in this activity.
2. Go to the menu bar and choose Edit > Find.
3. Click on the Lat/Long tab.

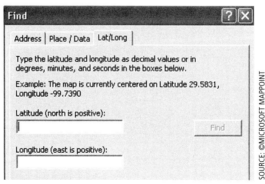

Lat/Long Tab

4. Type in "39.5545" for North and "−106.04293" for East.
    a. What state have you charted?
    b. What city shows on the map?
5. Click on the Legend and Overview icon on the Standard toolbar.
6. Click on the plus sign on Transportation to expand the directory. Note the symbol for Interstate Shield.
7. What interstate highway do you see on the map for latitude 39.5545 and longitude −106.04293?
8. Go to the Find dialog box. Click on the Lat/Long tab. Type in "33.8068" and "−101.8870."
9. Using the Select tool, draw a Zoom box around the pushpin placed by your find. Zoom in.
    a. What city or town is closest to the pushpin?
    b. On what interstate highway is this city or town located?

Location Sensor

1. Turn on the Location Sensor by going to the menu bar and choosing Tools > Location Sensor.

Legend Tool

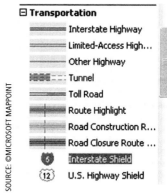

Transportation

Location Sensor

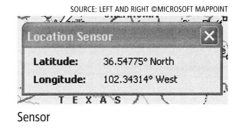

Sensor

2. Look up the following latitude and longitude locations using the Location Sensor.
    a. Los Angeles, California
    b. Tampa, Florida
    c. Jacksonville, Florida
    d. Boston, Massachusetts
    e. Your city or town

Measuring Distance

1. As a senior at Ellison High School in Killeen, Texas, you are considering several universities in the state of Texas to further your education. Measure the distance to each.
    a. Texas A&M University, College Station
    b. Sam Houston State University, Huntsville
    c. University of Texas, Austin
    d. Texas Tech University, Lubbock
2. Start with a new map. Zoom in to Texas. Then zoom in to Killeen and College Station.
3. Go to the menu bar and choose Tools > Measure Distance.
4. Begin from Killeen and trace the road to College Station. When you get to College Station, double-click to end the trace.
5. Save the map as *CollegeStation.ptm.*
6. Repeat this process for the other three schools.

Map Styles

Road Map

1. Start with a new map. Go to the menu bar and choose File > New. Double-click on New North American Map.

New North American Map

2. Click on the Find tool. In the Find dialog box, click on the Address tab. Type "One Dell Way" in the Street address. Type "Round Rock" for the City. Type "Texas" for the State.
3. Click Find and OK.
4. Highlight the Pushpin for this address.
5. This is the address for Dell Computer. The default map style is a Road Map. Click the style box to view the other styles of maps. This type of map has more details and is best used for physical addresses and/or driving directions.
6. Save the map as *DellComputer.ptm*.

Road and Data Map

1. Start with a new map. Go to the menu bar and choose File > New. Double-click on New North American Map.
2. Using the Select tool, click once on the state of Kansas. This selects only that state. Right-click and choose and Zoom to.
3. Save this map as *Kansas.ptm*.
4. Click on the Find tool.
5. Input the address information for Gateway Computers as shown below. Click Find and select Overland Park, Kansas, from the list.

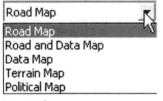

Map Styles

SOURCE: ©MICROSOFT MAPPOINT

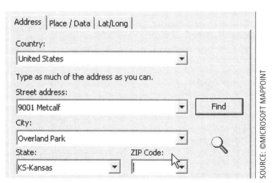

Gateway

6. Click on Route Planner and plan a route from Wichita, Kansas, to Overland Park, Kansas. Zoom out in order to see both cities once they have been added to

the route. Using the Select tool, draw a box around the area you will travel and zoom in to just that area.

7. Change the style of map to Road and Data Map. This map gives you street-level detail as well as provides a nice visual with an evenly colored background.

8. Save as *OverlandParkTrip.ptm*.

Data Map

1. Start with a new map.

2. You have been given the task to create a map showing four states: Wyoming, Nebraska, Colorado, and South Dakota. Using the Selection tool, draw a box around the four states then Zoom to them.

3. Save this map as *FourStates.ptm*.

4. The map also needs to show the following cities: Ten Sleep, Wyoming; Lowell, Wyoming; Thermopolis, Wyoming; Lincoln, Nebraska; Oshkosh, Nebraska; Westminister, Colorado; Aurora, Colorado; Philip, South Dakota; and Platte, South Dakota. Choose Route Planner and add each city as a stop.

5. Click on United States. If the Location and Scale toolbar is not showing, go to the menu bar and choose View > Toolbars > Location and Scale.

6. Using the Select tool, draw a box that includes all nine cities. Double-click within the box to zoom to them. Repeat this until you have zoomed in on the cities as much as you can.

7. This map will be used in the advertisement for the new salesperson. It needs to be uncluttered for the ad, so the style of map should be a Data Map. It may also be used on a PowerPoint show in a kiosk to advertise. Click in the Style box and choose Data.

8. Save as *SalesTerritory.ptm*.

9. Print a copy for the ad. Go to the menu bar and choose File > Print. Take a look at the print options. Leave all options on default and click OK.

Importing Data

1. Data can be imported from a number of file formats, including Access, Excel, and .txt format.

2. Go to the menu bar and choose File > New. Double-click on Import Data Wizard to select it.

3. Choose *StateLocations.xls* from your CD to import into MapPoint.

4. Import from the Arizona worksheet. There are some obvious column headings that MapPoint automatically picks up. City and State are two of those column headings. If MapPoint does not recognize the column heading, then you must use the drop-down box to choose a matched column heading.

5. Click Finish to accept these column headings.

6. The only map type allowed for this type of import is Pushpin, because it contains only geographic locations. Accept the Pushpin map by clicking Next.

7. Change the Pushpin type to red triangle. Click Finish.

Column Headings

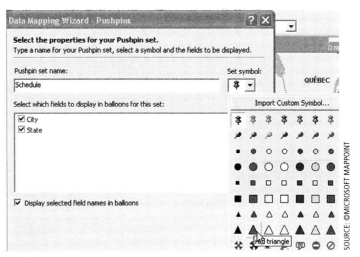

Pushpin Properties

8. Change the Zoom level to Arizona.
9. Save as *Arizona.ptm.*
10. Follow steps 3 through 9 for the Texas and Florida worksheets, importing them from the workbook *StateLocations.xls.* Choose what type of pushpin to use on each one of them. Save as *Texas.ptm* and *Florida.ptm.*

Linking Data

1. Go to the menu bar and choose File > New. Double-click on Link Data Wizard. Click Next.
2. Change the primary key to city. Click Finish.
3. On the Map type, double-click on Pushpin to change the properties. Change properties so only City is displayed in a balloon. Make the pushpin a small yellow triangle.

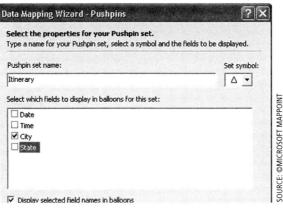

DMW Pushpins

Trip Order

4. Click Finish.
5. Click on Route Planner. Plan the trip in order according to the figure at left.
6. Click Get Directions.
7. Save as *AmarilloToAustin.ptm.*
8. Open *Itinerary.xls* from your CD. Save in your directory as *UpdatedItinerary.xls.*
9. Delete the rows with El Paso and Odessa. Save as *UpdatedItinerary.xls.*
10. Open the map *AmarilloToAustin.ptm.*

11. Go to the menu bar and choose Data > Update Linked Records.
12. Save as *UpdatedMap.ptm*.

ACTIVITY 2 • MINI-PROJECT

Create a Series of Maps and Trips

1. Find the following intersections:
   a. Smith & Longview
      What two states have this intersection?
   b. Smith & Main
      What is the name of the city that comes up first in the list?
   c. Smith & Sanders
      What state is this intersection in that starts with the letter "M"?
   d. 38th & Main
      How many of these intersections are in Texas?
   e. Ocean Blvd. & Smith
      What is the zip code of the intersection that is first in the list?
2. Use the Location Sensor to look up latitude and longitude for the following:
   a. Winnepeg, Canada
   b. Cedar Rapids, Iowa
   c. Kars, Turkey
   d. Hannover, Germany
   e. Dijon, France
3. Create maps and measure distance for the following trips:
   a. San Antonio, Texas, to Baton Rouge, Louisiana
   b. San Diego, Texas, to Belton, Texas
   c. Seattle, Washington, to Salt Lake City, Utah
   d. Houston, Texas, to Orlando, Florida
   e. New Orleans, Louisiana, to Memphis, Tennessee
4. Create the indicated map style for each of the following:
   a. Meridian State Park—Road Map, leave as zoomed in default.
      Save as *Meridian.ptm*.
   b. Garner State Park—Road and Data Map, zoomed to 14 mi.
      Save as *Garner.ptm*.
   c. Mother Neff State Park—Road Map, create a pushpin, zoom to 150 mi.
      Save as *MotherNeff.ptm*.
   d. Tyler State Park—Road and Data Map, zoom to 55 mi. Save as *Tyler.ptm*.
   e. Abilene State Park—Road Map, zoom to 14 mi. Save as *Abilene.ptm*.
5. Create a TXT file with the following information. Use a comma, as shown, between fields as this will be imported into MapPoint.
      Alfred Maclay Gardens State Park, Tallahassee, Florida
      Econfina River State Park, Lamont, Florida
      Florida Caverns State Park, Marianna, Florida
      Tallahassee–St. Mark's Historical Railroad Trail State Park, Tallahassee, Florida
6. Save the file as *HorseParks.txt*.
7. Import the file into MapPoint using the Import Wizard. Use a customized pushpin of your choice to designate the areas. Create a road map zoomed in at 1500 mi.
8. Save as *HorseParks.ptm*.
9. Using the Linking Data Wizard and Route Planner, plan the preceding trip to the Florida state parks that offer horse riding.
10. Save as *HorseRidingTrip.ptm*.

11. The following criteria should be met:
    ☐ Answers in steps 1, 2, and 3 are correct.
    ☐ In step 4, maps are correct type, zoomed as instructed, and saved correctly.
    ☐ In step 5, TXT file was inputted and saved correctly.
    ☐ In step 7, TXT file imported effectively with customized pushpins and correct zoom as instructed.
    ☐ Link Wizard used effectively to plan the trip to the Florida parks that offer horse riding.

ACTIVITY 3 • DRAWING ON A MAP

In this activity, you will become familiar with:

■ Pushpins
■ Highlighter
■ Scribble
■ Lines
■ Text Box
■ Arrows
■ Basic Shapes
■ Radius Circles

Pushpins

Create Pushpin Tool
SOURCE: ©MICROSOFT MAPPOINT

1. Plans are to open three new stores in the Oregon area. The stores will only be opened in minor or major cities.
2. Go to the menu bar and choose File > New. Double-click on New North American Map.
3. Zoom in to Oregon.
4. If the Drawing toolbar is not visible, go to the menu bar and choose Edit > Toolbars > Drawing.
5. Click on the Create Pushpin tool on the Drawing toolbar docked at the bottom of your screen.
6. Find at least three minor or major cities to plot as future store locations. Click on the map on the city symbol, choose blue triangle, and type in the pushpin balloon "Store No. 1" and on the second line of the balloon, type the dummy URL "http://www.ci.nameofthecity.state.us" or find the actual URL for the city's homepage and use that instead. Repeat this process for the other two stores. The second line will create a hyperlink to the city's homepage. You can also create links to email as well as computer files.

Highlighter

Yellow Highlight Tool
SOURCE: ©MICROSOFT MAPPOINT

1. Click on the Yellow Highlight tool on your Drawing toolbar.
2. Highlight the road to the three cities. Do not cover up the Pushpins you created. You can click and drag to highlight or you can click on the beginning point and then click on the ending point. Be sure to double-click to end the highlight.
3 Save as *FutureStores.ptm*.

Scribble

1. Each summer, a Future Business Leaders of America summer leadership course is held in Trinidad, Texas. The president of the organization is from Alvin, Texas, this year. Chart the path that the president will drive to get to Trinidad this summer.

2. Using the Scribble tool, trace the shortest route to get to the training.
3. Save as *LeadershipTraining.ptm*.

Lines

1. The state teachers' conference will be held in Houston at the Galleria this summer. Print a map for the keynote speaker coming from the Dallas area to the conference.
2. Go to the menu bar and choose File > New. Double-click on New North American Map.
3. Click in the Find box and type "Galleria Shopping Center, Houston, Texas."
4. Click on the Route Planner. Add Galleria Shopping Center to the map.
5. Zoom the map in to Texas.
6. Using the Select tool, drag a box around the route to zoom.
7. Use the Line tool to draw a line from Dallas to Houston.
8. Change the line color to Blue. You can also change the line style if you choose.

Text Box

1. Use the Text Box tool to draw a box with a blue border, filled with yellow, with the information shown in the figure below.
2. Drag the text box to center it between Dallas and Houston as shown.
3. Go to the menu bar and choose View > Map Font > Medium.
4. Resize the text box as needed.
5. Use the Fill tool to shade the inside of the text box a light yellow as shown.

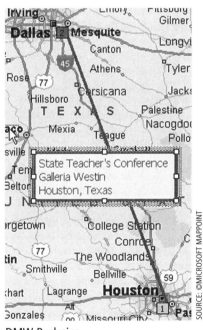

DMW Pushpins

Scribble Tool
SOURCE: ©MICROSOFT MAPPOINT

Line Tool
SOURCE: ©MICROSOFT MAPPOINT

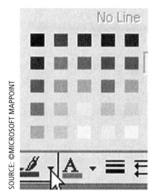

Line Color Options

Text Box Tool
SOURCE: ©MICROSOFT MAPPOINT

Arrows

1. Use the arrow to draw a route from Austin to Houston.
2. Change the color of the arrow to red. Notice that the arrow will appear in the direction you move your mouse. You can also change the arrow style if you choose.
3. Save the map as *DallasHouston.ptm*.

Arrow Tool
SOURCE: ©MICROSOFT MAPPOINT

Basic Shapes Tool
SOURCE: ©MICROSOFT MAPPOINT

Send Back
SOURCE: ©MICROSOFT MAPPOINT

Radius Tool
SOURCE: ©MICROSOFT MAPPOINT

Basic Shapes

1. Go to the menu bar and choose File > New. Double-click on New North American Map.
2. Using the Select tool, click on Kentucky. Zoom in to Kentucky.
3. Click on the Oval Basic Shape. Make the line border red with a light yellow fill to the oval.
4. Draw the oval around Fort Knox, Kentucky.
5. Click on the Draw tool in the far left corner of the Drawing toolbar. Choose Send Behind Roads.
6. Click on the Rectangle Basic Shape.
7. Change the border color to orange and the fill color to light green.
8. Draw a rectangle around Leitchfield.
9. Zoom in to these two places. Be sure you adjust the size of your Basic Shapes and check their placement before saving the map. When zoomed, these shapes will move out of their correct placement.
10. Save as *ShapesMap.ptm*.

Radius Circles

1. Firemen for the city of Los Angeles who work at the central fire station must live within a 10-mile radius.
2. Go to the menu bar and choose File > New. Double-click on New North American Map.
3. Use the Select tool to draw a box around Los Angeles, California, to zoom in on it.
4. Click on the Radius tool.
5. Start drawing a radius, beginning at the center point of Los Angeles. Drag it out for 10 miles. The radius should have a blue line color with yellow fill.
6. Save as *LARadius.ptm*.

ACTIVITY 3 • MINI-PROJECT

Create Maps for Directions to a Conference

1. The Florida Business Technology Education Association (FBTEA) is hosting its fall conference in Orlando, Florida. Create four directional maps to get to the conference. The maps should give directions coming from Tallahassee, Jacksonville, Miami, and Tampa. Save as *Tallahassee.ptm*, *Jacksonville.ptm*, *Miami.ptm*, and *Tampa.ptm*.
2. Use drawing tools to indicate routes and a text box to explain what the route is for. In the text box, type "FBTEA Fall Conference, October 18–21, 2XXX." Use your creativity to demonstrate skill in the use of as many of the drawing tools as possible.
3. Create a 10-mile-radius map of Orlando. Some of the hands-on workshops will be at various high schools, but none of them are more than 10 miles away. Demonstrate this using a radius map.
4. Save as *10Miles.ptm*.
5. The following criteria should be met:
   - ☐ Map from Tallahassee clear and saved as instructed.
   - ☐ Map from Jacksonville clear and saved as instructed.
   - ☐ Map from Miami clear and saved as instructed.
   - ☐ Map from Tampa clear and saved as instructed.

☐ Demonstrates use of Pushpins, Highlighter, Scribble, Lines, and Arrow at least once on the four maps.
☐ Text box formatted for an effective note explaining the reason for the map.
☐ Radius map demonstrates a 10-mile radius of Orlando.

ACTIVITY 4 • MAP TYPES

In this activity, you will become familiar with:

- Shaded Area Maps
- Shaded Circle Maps
- Sized Circle Maps
- Multiple Symbol Maps
- Pie Chart Maps

Shaded Area Maps

1. Go to the menu bar and choose File > New. Double-click on Data Mapping Wizard.

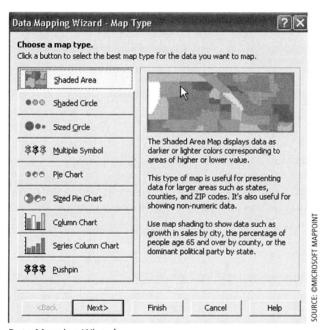

Data Mapping Wizard

2. In the Data Fields Wizard, the data field should be Population, ages 55 and above (projected 2005). Leave None for dividing. Show the data by County.
3. Leave the color at shades of green and click Finish.
4. Zoom in to Dallas. Draw a 20-mile radius around Dallas. The radius should not be filled, because it would distort the demographic statistics. The border of the radius should be blue.
5. Save as *Dallas20mile.ptm*.
6. Repeat this process for Houston. Save as *Houston20mile.ptm*.
7. Compare and contrast the results of your maps for Houston and Dallas.
8. Give at least two specific business applications that would rely on this type of information.

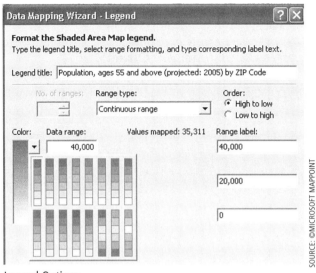

Legend Options

9. Save your analysis in a word processing document as *ShadedAreaMaps.doc*.

Shaded Circle Maps

1. Go to the menu bar and choose File > New. Double-click on Data Mapping Wizard.
2. Choose Shaded Circle. The darker the circle, the more houses built during the time 1950–1959. Click Next.
3. Click Next in the Data Set dialog box.
4. In the Data Fields dialog box, choose Housing Units built between 1950–1959 shown by County, not divided. Click Next.
5. Change the Legend formatting to shades of gray. Click Finish.
6. Zoom to Waco and draw a 50-mile radius around Waco.
7. What two cities or towns had the most houses built during 1950–1959? Draw a text box on the map and type your answer in the text box.
8. Save as *Waco50mile.ptm*.

Sized Circle Maps

1. Go to the menu bar and choose File > New. Double-click on Data Mapping Wizard.
2. Choose Sized Circle Maps. The larger the circles, the higher the average income in this activity.
3. Click Next in the Data Set dialog box.
4. In the Data Fields dialog box, choose the average household income (2000) by City. Click Next.
5. Choose a color for your circles. Click Finish.
6. Zoom in to the United States.
7. Draw a text box and name the state with the highest average income and the amount, and the state with the lowest average income and the amount.
8. Save as *AvgHouseholdIncome.ptm*.

Multiple Symbol Maps

1. Go to the menu bar and choose File > New. Double-click on Data Mapping Wizard.
2. Choose Multiple Symbol.
3. Click Next in the Data Set dialog box.

4. In the Data Fields dialog box, choose the Average Household Size (2000) showed by Census Tract.
5. Leave the Legend formatting the same, except change the white circle to a different color that isn't being used.
6. Draw a text box and name the top Average Household Size in 2000 and the one closest to that one.
7. Save as *AvgHouseholdSize.ptm*.

Pie Chart Maps

1. Go to the menu bar and choose File > New. Double-click on Data Mapping Wizard.
2. Choose Pie Chart.
3. Click Next in the Data Set dialog box.
4. In the Data Fields dialog box, make the choices shown in the figure below. Click Next.

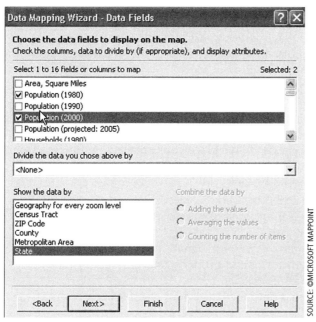

Data Fields Dialog Box

5. Click Finish in the Data Fields dialog box.
6. Zoom in on the United States.
7. Draw a text box on the map and explain which parts of the United States have seen an increase in population over the past 20 years.
8. Save as *PopulationExplosion.ptm*.

ACTIVITY 4 • MINI-PROJECT

Create Maps for Comparison

1. Use the Data Mapping Wizard to create a Shaded Area map. Use Worldwide Demographics to show the area in square kilometers by country/region. Change the color of the shaded area and zoom in to Europe.
2. Save the map as *Europe.ptm*.

3. Find the areas of the following countries in square kilometers:
    a. Iceland
    b. United Kingdom
    c. France
    d. Germany
    e. Spain
4. Use the Data Mapping Wizard to create a Shaded Circle Map. The map should show Worldwide Demographics to show the infant mortality rate in 2000. Save the map as *InfantDeaths.ptm*.
5. Using the world map zoom, answer the following questions from your *InfantDeaths* map:
    a. What is the infant mortality rate in the United Kingdom?
    b. What is the number per 1,000 in Afghanistan?
    c. What is Morocco's infant mortality rate?
    d. What is Egypt's infant mortality rate?
    e. What is Mongolia's infant mortality rate?
6. Create a column chart map showing the usage of personal computers in households. Compare the following countries: United Kingdom, Germany, Sweden, Poland, and Switzerland. Save as *PersonalComputers.ptm*.
7. Use Excel to input the information and create a column chart demonstrating your data.
8. Copy and paste the map onto your page with your column chart.
9. Save as *PCUsage.xls*.
10. If you were considering marketing personal computers internationally, what two countries would you market to? Base your answer on the general information from your map and charts. Why? Place your answers on the Excel spreadsheet in a merged box with a border. Save again.
11. The following criteria should be met:
    ☐ Questions in steps 3 and 5 answered correctly.
    ☐ Map of the countries set up for accurate information and saved as *PersonalComputers.ptm*.
    ☐ Information from *PersonalComputers* map input into an Excel chart accurately. Chart formatted properly to accurately display the statistics.
    ☐ Map copied and pasted onto the Excel chart to effectively support statistics.
    ☐ Analysis of Excel chart accurate and well thought out.

PART 5 • SIMULATION

Using Maps to Target a Market

1. In a team of three or four students, create an overseas map showing number of cellular phones per 1,000 household members. Save as *CellPhones.ptm*.
2. Decide on three places to target a new market for the selling of cellular phones. Use as your criteria less than 10 for each 1,000 household members.
3. Create a map of each of the places you have decided on. Zoom in so that you can see the city and surrounding cities. Add a text box explaining what the results of your data map were for that area. Save as *01CellMarket.ptm*, *02CellMarket.ptm*, and *03CellMarket.ptm*.
4. You will need an office on the East Coast to work the new international market. Choose three cities where your office could be located to submit as a proposal. Plan a trip to visit the three cities from Atlanta, Georgia. Include an itinerary of

places to stay, restaurants, driving time, and distance. Use drawing tools on your map to create a visual of the trip. Save the map as *Proposal.ptm*. Save the itinerary as *EastCoastOffice*.

5. Create three different images to represent each city to use in your proposal at a later date. Save them as *01EastCoast.jpg*, *02EastCoast.jpg*, and *03EastCoast.jpg*.

6. Insert each image into a word processing document along with a short explanation of the advantages of using this city as a place for the global office. Create maps to support any advantages, such as international airports and employment statistics. Copy any supporting maps to your word processing document. Save as *01Office*, *02Office*, and *03Office*.

7. The following criteria should be met:
   - ☐ Team worked well together and each team member participated.
   - ☐ Decision on three new sites for cell phone distribution accurate according to the information on the map.
   - ☐ Itinerary contains all detailed information necessary and uses map skills.
   - ☐ Images create appropriate representation of the city.
   - ☐ Advantages to a global office in each of the cities accurately supported by maps.

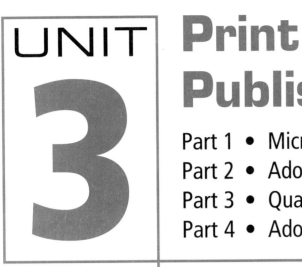

UNIT 3

Print Publishing

Part 1 • Microsoft Publisher
Part 2 • Adobe PageMaker
Part 3 • QuarkXPress
Part 4 • Adobe Acrobat

Desktop publishing has changed rapidly over the last few years, even months. Innovative software such as Publisher, PageMaker, and QuarkXPress have allowed us to produce professional-looking documents. As business and marketing needs merge, software changes could not have come at a better time.

You will learn to use Publisher and the many templates that are available in the software. Its ease of use enables us to create print ready documents without even batting an eye.

You will learn to use PageMaker, which has been a software in the forefront of desktop publishing for many years. It affords many innovative font choices, a font matching system, and color matching systems that help create eye-catching documents.

You will also learn to use QuarkXPress. For those who are in constant need of desktop publishing solutions, this software provides ease of use and yet astonishing results. Although there are no templates, the software lends itself to creating your own templates.

Finally, you will learn to create PDF files that can be used as forms or downloaded, viewed, and printed online. Using Adobe Acrobat to create PDF files allows more flexibility in using your skills to communicate not only through the written word and visuals, but also online. By now you have probably found it convenient to go online and download a form, fill it out, and send it back immediately rather than drive for hours or wait for days for the form to come through the mail. Have you ever lost the manual to an appliance or camera? Go online—more than likely you will find it there as a PDF file.

Desktop publishing no longer requires that you have the talent for designing. It only requires that you think creatively, but mostly it requires having the good sense to use the tools that technology affords you!

Microsoft Publisher
Publisher: Microsoft Corporation
This desktop publishing software assists in creating letterhead
and business cards, brochures, newsletters, flyers, and more.
Many templates are available for quick use.

ACTIVITY 1 • QUICK FLYER

In this activity, you will become familiar with:

- By Publication Type
- Page Orientation
- Changing Text
- Changing Pictures
- Changing Bulleted Text
  - Bulleted Lists
  - Line Spacing
  - Font Size
- Changing a Picture by Wizard
- Resizing a Picture
- Color Schemes
- Font Schemes
- Print Preview
- Quick Zoom
- Saving a Publication

By Publication Type

1. You will start from a design already created by Publisher.
2. The default is By Publication Type, which is the choice you will be using. Click on the triangle next to Flyers to expand the menu.

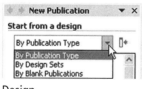

Design

Flyers

SOURCE: LEFT AND RIGHT ©MICROSOFT PUBLISHER

3. Choose Announcement from the expanded menu.
4. Choose the flyer for Lost Pet/Item Flyer by clicking on it once. If you choose the wrong flyer, go to the menu bar and choose File > New to get back to the Publication Type choices and choose the correct one.

SOURCE: ©MICROSOFT PUBLISHER

Lost Pet

Page Orientation

1. Go to the menu bar and choose File > Page Setup.
2. The flyer is in portrait orientation. Click on Landscape to change to landscape orientation. Obviously, this is not the right orientation. Change back to portrait.
3. Page orientation should be changed early in the project if needed.

Changing Text

1. In Publisher, everything must be in a frame. On this flyer there are seven frames. See if you can find all seven.
2. Click in the title frame at the top. Select the text within that frame and replace it by overtyping "Lost Shih Tzu." Note that the font size changes automatically to fit the frame.

Changing Pictures

1. Click on the picture underneath the title frame to select it.
2. Right-click on the picture and choose Change Picture > From File. Browse to the CD to replace it with the picture *ShihTzu.jpg*. You may need to get directions from your instructor as to where the pictures on the CD are located.

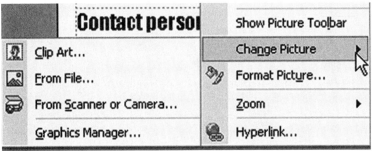

Change Picture

SOURCE: ©MICROSOFT PUBLISHER

Changing Bulleted Text

Bulleted Lists
1. Select the bulleted list to the right of the picture. Replace the bulleted list by overtyping with the following information:
   - Solid white tail
   - Brindle and white with a solid streak of white on her head
   - Name is Gracie
   - Hot pink collar with a red heart-shaped name tag
2. Select the bulleted list.
3. Go to the menu bar and choose Format > Indents and Lists. Change the bullet type. You can use one of the standard bullets or click New Bullet and find another one in a different font.
4. Change the size of the bullet to the same size as the text.

Line Spacing
5. Once you have entered the bulleted list, then select the text. Go to the menu bar and choose Format > Line Spacing. Change the spacing before paragraphs to 6 pt.

Font Size
6. If the text still does not fill up the space, select the text and change the font size to 16. You may need to experiment to get it to fit in the area. (You can also use AutoFit, which you will learn about in another activity.)
7. In the text frame below the picture of the Shih Tzu, type the following paragraph: "Last seen on the corner of Melrose and Main in Houston, Texas. If found, please contact K-9 Kennels immediately."
8. In the bottom left text box, change person to "Ted."
9. Change the phone number to "979-555-4000."

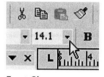

Font Size

SOURCE: ©MICROSOFT PUBLISHER

Changing a Picture by Wizard

1. Click on the picture wizard. In Apply a design, choose Starburst Cutout.
2. Select the text within the text box and type "$500 Reward."

Wizard

SOURCE: ©MICROSOFT PUBLISHER

Resizing a Picture

1. Resize the starburst cutout by hovering the mouse pointer over the top right edge until you get the Resize cursor.
2. Click and drag to resize the shape to fit the area. Keep the image proportionate by holding down the Shift key while dragging to resize.

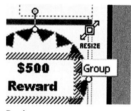

Resize

SOURCE: ©MICROSOFT PUBLISHER

Color Schemes

1. On the task pane, go to Color Schemes. If Color Schemes is not available, click the Back button on the task pane.
2. Choose Mulberry by clicking on the Mulberry image.

Font Schemes

1. Click Font Schemes.
2. Change to Binary with the Major font as Verdana and Minor font as Georgia. See the bottom right figure.

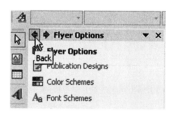

Back Task Pane

SOURCE: ©MICROSOFT PUBLISHER

Font Schemes

SOURCE: ©MICROSOFT PUBLISHER

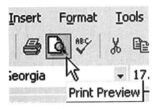

Print Preview

SOURCE: ©MICROSOFT PUBLISHER

Print Preview

1. Print Preview the flyer. This should always be used to check for placement of text boxes and pictures. Using Print Preview will help to avoid overprinting by finding errors before printing.
2. Close Print Preview.

Quick Zoom

1. Press F9 to proofread each text block. The F9 key zooms in to Actual Size.
2. You can also use Zoom on the standard toolbar by clicking in the Zoom box and typing in a new percentage or using the drop-down menu.

Saving a Publication

1. Go to the menu bar and choose File > Save as.
2. Choose the directory in which to save the file and save it as *ShihTzu.pub*.

ACTIVITY 1 • MINI-PROJECT

Create a Flyer for a School Board Election

1. One of your parents, a friend, or a relative has decided to run for the school board and has asked you to help him or her create a flyer that will be placed in various locations in your city. Use a flyer template from Publisher to create three different designs to use. You may want to sit down with the person running for the board and get some input into qualifications and a possible slogan to use for the flyer. Save your flyers as *01SBElection.pub*, *02SBElection.pub*, and *03SBElection.pub*.
2. Meet with your team to discuss what you like about each person's design. On the back of each flyer, write down one positive remark made about the flyer. Then write down two constructive changes that were suggested. Place the flyer that you and your team decide is your best to turn in to your instructor.
3. The following criteria should be met:
   - ☐ Digital or scanned picture of good quality, appropriate size, and placement.
   - ☐ Bulleted list of qualifications is brief, but effective.
   - ☐ Appropriate slogan.
   - ☐ Eye-catching heading.
   - ☐ Appropriate font schemes applied.
   - ☐ Appropriate color schemes applied.
   - ☐ Fonts appropriate size.
   - ☐ Change of bullet type.
   - ☐ Use of one attention-getting-design with a text box over it.
   - ☐ Entire flyer and paragraph spacing adjusted to balance white space.
   - ☐ No spelling or grammar errors.
   - ☐ Demonstration of some creativity.
   - ☐ Organization of information in flyer.

ACTIVITY 2 • BROCHURE

In this activity, you will become familiar with:

- ■ Inserting and Deleting Pages
- ■ Ungrouping Objects
- ■ AutoFit

- Search for Clip Art
- Align Text
- Tab Set
- Delete Frames

Inserting and Deleting Pages

1. On the task pane, choose By Publication Type > Brochures > Price List > Bubbles Price List Brochure.
2. Use the Page Navigation tool in the status bar to click on page 2.
3. Go to the menu bar and choose Edit > Delete Page. You will get a warning message that you are deleting everything off that page. Click OK. Just for practice, go to the menu bar and choose Insert > Page. You can insert a page before or after the current page. Note the choices on the dialog box. Leave them as the default.

Ungrouping Objects

1. Click on the text frame in the far upper right.
2. Hover the mouse pointer over the frame and note the Ungroup Objects icon, as shown in the figure to the right.

AutoFit

1. Click on the Ungroup Objects icon. The icon now becomes Group Objects. Click on it again. For this exercise you do not need to ungroup the object, but you may need to in another exercise.
2. Select the text in the text box and type "Bloom College." Go to the menu bar and choose Format > AutoFit Text > Best Fit.

Search for Clip Art

1. Click on the picture of the computer. Right-click on the picture and choose Change Picture > Clip Art.
2. Search for "College" as shown in the figure to the right.
3. Find the picture shown below (right) or a similar image of a college campus. Click on the arrow to the right of the picture and choose Insert. Resize the picture to fit the area.

Align Text

1. Click in the text box below the picture of the college and type "University Interscholastic League Region 2 Competition." While the text is selected, click the Align Right button. Use AutoFit Text.
2. In the box for your business tagline, type "Lifelong Learners." Center the text. Use AutoFit Text.
3. In the bottom text box, delete the text and overtype with "979/555-4402." Use AutoFit Text.
4. In the Back Panel Heading, select the text and type "Schedule." Center the text. Use AutoFit Text.

Tab Set

1. Select the text in the large text box below "Schedule." Set a right tab, as shown on the following page.

Brochure

SOURCE: ©MICROSOFT PUBLISHER

Delete Page

SOURCE: ©MICROSOFT PUBLISHER

Ungroup Objects

SOURCE: ©MICROSOFT PUBLISHER

Search Clip Art

College

SOURCE: ©MICROSOFT PUBLISHER

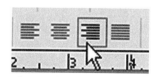

Align Right

SOURCE: ©MICROSOFT PUBLISHER

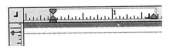

Right Tab

SOURCE: ©MICROSOFT PUBLISHER

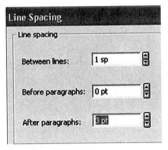

Line Spacing

SOURCE: ©MICROSOFT PUBLISHER

Insert Picture

SOURCE: ©MICROSOFT PUBLISHER

Move

SOURCE: ©MICROSOFT PUBLISHER

Trophies

SOURCE: ©MICROSOFT PUBLISHER

Logo Picture

SOURCE: ©MICROSOFT PUBLISHER

2. With the text still selected, change the line spacing as shown to the left.
3. Input the following information with the first column at the left margin and the second column at the tab that was set in step 1.

Accounting	8:00
Calculations	2:00
Comp. Appli.	10:00
Comp. Science	11:00
Cross Ex Debate	8:00
Fiction Writing	2:00
Literary Crit.	10:00
Number Sense	9:00
Poetry Inter.	2:00
Ready Writing	1:00

4. Press Enter twice below the last line. Go to the menu bar and choose Insert > Picture > Clip Art. Search for Lines. Find one similar to the figure to the left. Click the arrow and choose Insert. Resize the line to fit within the margins of the text box.
5. Click on the line to select it. Click and drag to move the line as needed.
6. Below the line, type the following information:

Orientation	8:00
Grade Meeting	9:00
Assembly	3:00
Celebration	5:00

7. Change the telephone picture to a trophy. Search for "Trophies." Use the trophy as shown to the left or one similar.
8. Type the following caption in the text box underneath the picture of the trophy: "Trophies awarded to places 1, 2, and 3. Ribbons will be awarded to places 4, 5, and 6."

Delete Frames

1. Click on the logo picture as shown in the bottom, left figure. Press the Delete key to remove this picture.
2. Type "Bloom College" in the text box. Use AutoFit Text.
3. In the next text box, type "902 College Avenue, Bloom, TX 77833."
4. In the last text box, type "Phone: 979-555-4402, Fax: 979-555-1102, Email: college@Bloom.org."
5. Click on page 2. Go to the menu bar and choose Insert > Picture > From File. Browse to the CD to insert *BloomCollege.gif*. Resize the image to fit across all three columns.
6. Save as *BloomCollege.pub*.

ACTIVITY 2 • MINI-PROJECT

Create a Brochure for a Career Fair

1. If your school is planning a career fair, offer to create a brochure advertising it. If there is no career fair at your school, then create a brochure for one that will give them some ideas to begin an annual career fair.
2. In a team of three or four students, make a plan for the brochure. Each team member should create his or her own brochure using the plans from the team.

The evaluation of the brochure could be done by an advisory board or panel of instructors to determine the best brochure in the class.

3. In organizing your brochure, you will need to determine when and where the career fair will be held. You will also need to make a list of vendor participants such as colleges or universities, employers, and armed services recruiters in your area. Brainstorm in your team to determine other information that you can put on the brochure to make it appealing. Save the brochure as *CareerFair.pub*.

4. The following criteria should be met:
   - ☐ Appropriate template chosen.
   - ☐ Information on front of brochure is attention-getting and informative.
   - ☐ Image on front of brochure is of good quality and appropriate size and creates an appropriate image for the career fair.
   - ☐ Extra page inserted.
   - ☐ Table of information in brochure demonstrates ability to set tabs.
   - ☐ Minimum of three images in the brochure, one of which is either scanned or digital.
   - ☐ Information throughout the brochure is appropriate and thorough; no important details omitted.
   - ☐ Brochure is error-free.
   - ☐ Overall image of brochure creates a desire to attend the career fair.

ACTIVITY 3 • NEWSLETTER

In this activity, you will become familiar with:

- ■ Two-Sided Printing and Multiple Pages
- ■ Deleting Pages
- ■ Inserting a Date
- ■ Inserting Text Files
- ■ Drop Cap
- ■ Recoloring Pictures
- ■ AutoFlow
- ■ Character Spacing
  - ○ Scaling
  - ○ Tracking
  - ○ Kerning
- ■ Page Navigation
- ■ Deleting Objects
- ■ Moving Objects
- ■ Creating a Hyperlink
- ■ Customizing Color Schemes
- ■ Inserting and Formatting WordArt
- ■ Inserting Objects
- ■ Inserting and Formatting Page Numbers
- ■ Tables
- ■ Formatting Bullets

Two-Sided Printing and Multiple Pages

1. On the task pane, go to By Publication Type > Newsletters > Tipped Title Newsletter.
2. This newsletter is four pages long and is set for two-sided printing. You are going to create a two-page newsletter.
3. Note that pages 2 and 3 are connected, since the newsletter is set for two-sided printing. Click on these two pages, as shown to the right.

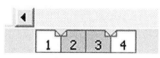

Connected Pages
SOURCE: ©MICROSOFT PUBLISHER

Both Pages

One-Sided Printing

Deleting Pages

1. Go to the menu bar and choose Edit > Delete Page.
2. You will get a dialog box asking if you want to delete Both pages, Left page only, or Right page only. Leave it on the default of Both pages and click OK.
3. You will get a question as to whether you want to delete this page and a warning. Click OK.
4. Change this publication to one-sided printing by clicking on the 1, as shown to the left.
5. Save the newsletter as *DPNewsletter.pub*. Since you have already made several changes to the newsletter, it is a good idea to save it now so you don't lose anything. Save often by clicking on the Save tool on the standard toolbar or using the shortcut Ctrl + S.
6. Click on the newsletter title and overtype with "Desktop Publishing."

Inserting a Date

1. Click in the text box that has the date in it. Select the text in the box, then go to the menu bar and choose Insert > Date. Choose the style shown in the figure below.
2. Choose to Update automatically by selecting the check box.

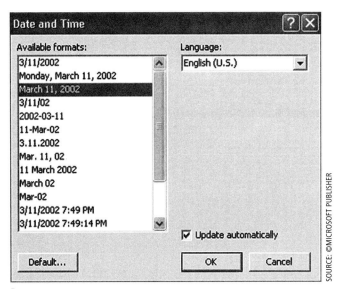

Date

Inserting Text Files

1. Use a digital camera to take a picture of your school. Right-click on the top left picture and select Change Picture > From File. (Sometimes when you use the right mouse button, the correct menu may not pop up the first time. If this happens, try it again.) Browse to where you have placed your digital picture of your school and insert the picture.
2. In the text box below the picture of your school, type your school name. Click the Center icon to center it horizontally. Use AutoFit Text.
3. Click in the Lead Story Headline text box. Overtype the text with "A Defining History."
4. Click in the text box below the Lead Story Headline. With the text selected, go to the menu bar and choose Insert > Text File. Browse to the CD and insert the file *History.txt*. You will notice that the text did not completely fill that text box. Use AutoFit Text. Sometimes you may end up with a font size that is a decimal, as shown to the left.

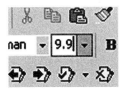

Font Sizes

Drop Cap

1. Add a drop cap to the first letter of the Headline Story. Select the letter D in "Desktop Publishing."
2. Go to the menu bar and choose Format > Drop Cap.
3. Click on the Custom Drop Cap tab. Leave it as a Dropped Cap. Change Size of letters to 2 lines high. Clear the Use current color check box and change the font color to an appropriate accent color.
4. Click Apply, then OK.

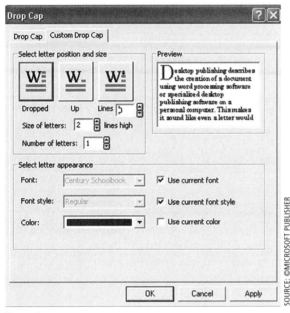

Drop Cap

Recoloring Pictures

1. Click on the picture in the Headline Story. Right-click on the picture and choose Change Picture > ClipArt.
2. Search for a piece of clip art with "History" as the key word.
3. Choose the computer as shown; if it is not available, find another picture to use.
4. Click on the Headline Picture. If the Picture toolbar does not pop up, right-click and choose Show Picture Toolbar.
5. Click on the Format Picture button on the Picture toolbar.
6. Click on the Color and Lines tab.
7. Change the fill color to Accent 3 and the line color to Accent 1.

Headline Picture

SOURCE: ©MICROSOFT PUBLISHER

Picture Toolbar

SOURCE: ©MICROSOFT PUBLISHER

AutoFlow

1. Overtype the information in the text box below the Headline Picture with "Learning desktop publishing is easier with today's technology!"
2. Click in the Secondary Story Headline text box and overtype with "Typography."

3. Click in the text box for the Secondary Story. Go to the menu bar and choose Insert > Text File. Browse the CD for the file *Typography.txt.*
4. The autoflow message will pop up on your screen. See below. Click No. Use AutoFit Text.

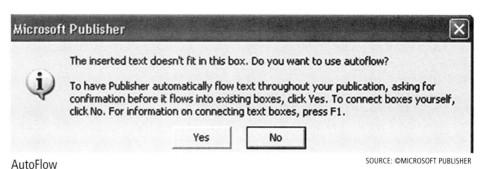

AutoFlow

5. If you have not saved recently, this would be a good time to click the Save icon on the standard toolbar.

Character Spacing

Scaling
1. Select the title in the Secondary Story Headline, "Typography."
2. Go to the menu bar and choose Format > Character Spacing. In the Scaling box, change the number to 120%. Click Apply, then OK.
3. This will stretch the word *Typography* out a little more.
4. To shrink, choose a number below 100%.

Tracking
1. This will stretch a text block out to better fit an area.
2. Find a text block in one of the stories that does not take up the entire space in the column. Select the block of text.
3. In the Tracking drop-down list, choose Loose. Click Apply, then OK.
4. Look at the block of text. If it looks okay, leave it. Experiment with customizing the tracking on the text block.

Kerning
1. Sometimes in proportional print, letters seem too close to each other. Kerning spreads them apart so they are more evenly spaced.
2. Select the *i* and the *s* in *History* in the Headline Story.
3. Go to the menu bar and choose Format > Character Spacing. Choose Normal by two spaces. Click Apply, then OK.
4. You can click in the box to turn on Automatic Pair Kerning at 14 pt. If you still want to kern the pair of letters more, you can.

Page Navigation

1. Go to page 2 by clicking on the 2 in Page Navigation.
2. Click in the top left text box. Type your school's initials in all caps. Use AutoFit Text.
3. In the next two text boxes, overtype the information with your school's information. See the figure to the left for an example.

Page Navigation

Harker Heights High School
703 Ann Blvd.
Harker Heights, MS 82531

Phone: 915-555-7729
Fax: 915-555-0192
Email: student@hhhs.org

School Info

Deleting Objects

1. Click on the text box with "Your business tag line here."
2. Right-click on the box and choose Delete Object.

Delete Object

SOURCE: ©MICROSOFT PUBLISHER

Moving Objects

1. Click on the black oval with the text box.
2. Hover the mouse pointer over the black oval until you get the Move cursor. See the figure to the right.
3. Hold down the left mouse button and drag the black oval up a little to take up some of the space of the object you deleted in the previous step.

Move

SOURCE: ©MICROSOFT PUBLISHER

Creating a Hyperlink

1. Click inside the text box overlaying the oval and overtype the name of your school's Web Site.
2. Triple-click the Web site address to select it quickly. Click on the Insert Hyperlink tool.
3. Type in the address of your school's Web site. See below.

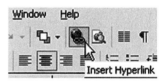

Insert Hyperlink

Hyperlink Tool

SOURCE: ©MICROSOFT PUBLISHER

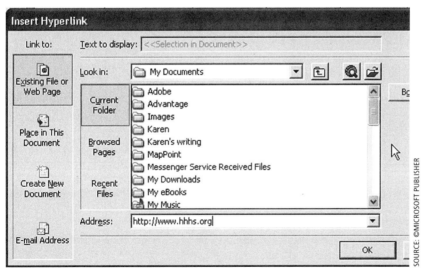

Insert Hyperlink

Customizing Color Schemes

1. The font color does not show up with the black on the oval now that it is a hyperlink. Go to the menu bar and choose Format > Color Schemes. At the bottom of the task pane, choose Custom color scheme.

2. In the Color Schemes dialog box, click the drop-down arrow next to Hyperlink and choose White. Click OK.

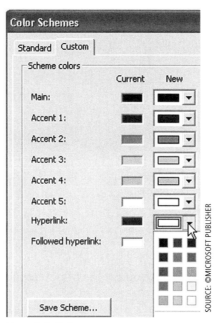

Hyperlink Color

3. Click in the Organization Logo and overtype with your course name.
4. Click in the large text box to the right. With the text selected, go to the menu bar and choose Insert > Text File. Browse to the CD and insert *Facts.doc*. Click No to using autoflow. Resize the text box so the text fits.

Inserting and Formatting WordArt

1. Click on the Back Page Story Headline. Press Delete to remove the text.
2. Go to the menu bar and choose Insert > Picture > WordArt. Choose the second one in the second row. See below.

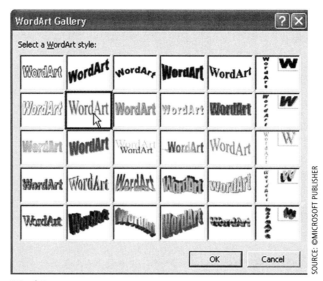

Word Art

3. Type "Fonts" for the title. Click OK.
4. Resize "Fonts" to fit in the text box where the title was located. Place the new title as shown to the right.
5. Click on the WordArt you just created. If the WordArt toolbar does not appear, go to the menu bar and choose View > Toolbars > WordArt.

Fonts

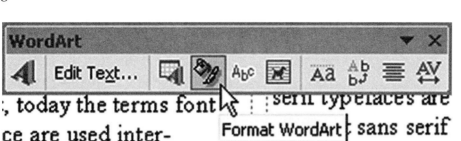

WordArt Toolbar

6. Click on the Format WordArt tool on the toolbar. See above.
7. Click on the Colors and Lines tab. Change the Fill Color to Accent 1 and the Line Color to Accent 3.
8. Click on the WordArt shape tool on the WordArt toolbar. Choose Deflate.
9. Click on the WordArt Same Letter Heights tool on the toolbar. This adjusts the letters so they are proportionate in height.
10. Click on the WordArt Character Spacing tool on the WordArt toolbar and choose Loose.
11. Deselect the title to close the WordArt toolbar.

Inserting Objects

1. With your cursor in the text box with "Fonts," go to the menu bar and choose Insert > Picture. Search for Lines. Choose the Line shown below and resize as needed.

Resized Line

2. Click in the last text box. Go to the menu bar and choose Insert > Text File. Browse to your CD to insert the file *Fonts.doc*. Click No to using autoflow.
3. Click in the text box. Use AutoFit Text.
4. Save.

Inserting and Formatting Page Numbers

1. Go to the menu bar and choose Insert > Page Numbers.
2. In the Page Numbers dialog box, change the Position to Bottom of page (Footer) and the Alignment to Center. Leave the page number on the first page.

Tables

1. Click in the table titled "Inside this issue." Type the following information in the table:

Special Terms	2
Fonts	2
Web Address	2
Contact Information	2

2. Select the rows that you do not use. Go to the menu bar and choose Table > Delete Rows.

Formatting Bullets

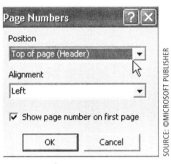

Page Numbers

1. Click in the area titled "Special points of interest." Type the following:
   - A look back at desktop publishing
   - Definition of desktop publishing
   - Typography
   - Fonts
   - Specialized desktop publishing terms
2. Select the bulleted items. Go to the menu bar and choose Format > Indents and Lists. In the dialog box, choose New Font. In the font drop-down list, choose Wingdings. Find any star to use as the new bullet. Increase the font size to 12.

ACTIVITY 3 • MINI-PROJECT

Create a School Organization's Newsletter

1. Create a newsletter for a school club or organization of which you are a member. If you do not belong to an organization, write the newsletter for an organization you belonged to at one time or write the newsletter for your friends.
2. Brainstorm what you will put in your newsletter:
   a. What pictures can you put in the newsletter? Think of at least three.
   b. Visualize what you want your masthead to look like.
   c. What short announcements can you put in the newsletter? Think of at least three.
   d. What short story can you put in the newsletter? Think of at least two.
   e. What longer story (two columns or more) can you put in the newsletter? Think of at least one.
3. Once you have planned your newsletter, use word processing software to write the stories. You will save these documents as text files, so formatting is not important. They should be typed single-spaced. Save as *01SchoolNewsletter.txt*, *02SchoolNewsletter.txt*, and *03SchoolNewsletter.txt*.
4. Submit a printed copy of your stories to your instructor. You should have at least two short stories and one longer story.
5. Correct the edited stories returned by your instructor. Save again.
6. Use a Publisher template for newsletters to create your newsletter. Save as *SchoolNewsletter.pub*.
7. The following criteria should be met:
   - ☐ Appropriate template chosen.
   - ☐ Masthead is eye-catching and contains appropriate information.
   - ☐ Minimum of three images; appropriate in type and size.
   - ☐ Minimum of two pages.
   - ☐ Drop cap used effectively.
   - ☐ One picture recolored.
   - ☐ Autoflow used properly.
   - ☐ AutoFit used effectively.
   - ☐ Minimum of one hyperlink to a Web site.
   - ☐ Color scheme is appealing and appropriate.
   - ☐ Minimum of one WordArt used effectively.
   - ☐ Page numbering in proper format.
   - ☐ Minimum of one bulleted list with customization.
   - ☐ Articles well-written with no errors.

- ☐ Announcements in eye-catching format.
- ☐ Overall appearance of newsletter demonstrates creativity and mastery of skills.

ACTIVITY 4 • CREATING SETS

In this activity, you will become familiar with:

- ■ By Design Sets
- ■ Business Card Options
- ■ Letterhead Options
- ■ Fax Cover Sheet Options

By Design Sets

By Design Sets

1. Use your image management software to create a logo that can be used on a business card, letterhead, and fax cover sheet. Save as *TechLogo.gif*.
2. Create a business card. On the task pane, click on By Design Sets.
3. Choose Accent Bar Business Card.

Business Card Options

1. In Business Card Options, choose Include for the logo. Change the logo to the one you saved. Choose Multiple for copies per sheet.
2. Input the information for the business cards. Increase font sizes as needed. See below.

Info

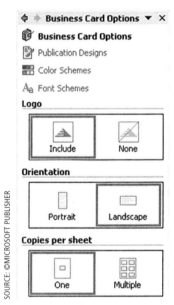

Business Card Options

3. Click on Color Schemes. Choose Iris.
4. Click on Font Schemes. Choose Capital.
5. Save as *BusinessCard.pub*.

Letterhead Options

1. Create a letterhead. On the task pane, click on By Design Sets.
2. Choose Accent Bar Letterhead.
3. Click Include for the logo. Change the logo to the one you created.
4. Input the information using the same information as the business card. Increase font sizes as needed.
5. Click on Color Schemes. Choose Iris.
6. Click on Font Schemes. Choose Capital.
7. Save as *Letterhead.pub*.

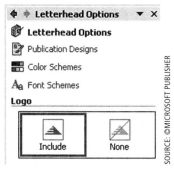

Letterhead Options

Fax Cover Sheet

Fax Cover Sheet Options

1. Create a fax cover sheet. On the task pane, click on By Design Sets.
2. Choose Accent Bar Fax Transmittal Sheet.
3. Click Include for the logo.
4. Input the information using the same information as the business card and letterhead. Increase font sizes and resize text boxes as needed.
5. Click on Color Schemes. Choose Iris.
6. Click on Font Schemes. Choose Capital.

ACTIVITY 4 • MINI-PROJECT

Create a Business Set for an American Stock Exchange Business

1. Go to http://www.amex.com. Read about the five most active companies in the American Stock Exchange for that day. Click on each link and read the background on the company. If there is a link to its Web site, follow it to read further about the company.
2. Choose one of the companies and create a new set of designs for its business stationery. Create a business card, a letterhead, and a fax cover sheet. Save them as *ASEBusinessCard.doc*, *ASELetterhead.doc*, and *ASEFaxCover.doc*.
3. The following criteria should be met:
   - ☐ Logo should be reflective of the type of business. It should be a sharp, clean look that will work well on all stationery.
   - ☐ White space balanced.
   - ☐ Font is an appropriate size and type is eye-catching and readable.
   - ☐ Logo placed and sized appropriately.
   - ☐ Information on letterhead is on top two inches.
   - ☐ Some creativity evident.
   - ☐ No errors and phone numbers were all verified.

ACTIVITY 5 • INVITATION

In this activity, you will become familiar with:

- By Blank Publications
- Objects Toolbar
- Boundaries and Guides
- Drawing a Text Box
- Clip Organizer Frame
- Publication Designs
- Nonbreaking Spaces
- Viewing Special Characters
- Text Effects
- Copying and Pasting a Picture
- Design Gallery Objects
- Grouping and Ungrouping Objects
- AutoShapes
- Spell Checking

By Blank Publications

1. On the task pane, choose By Blank Publications.
2. Choose Side Fold Card. A Microsoft Publisher dialog box will pop up on your screen asking if you want to automatically insert pages. Click Yes.

Blank Publications

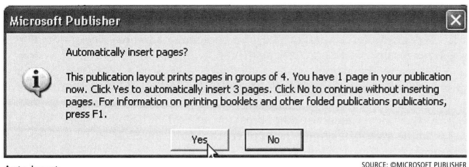

Auto Insert

SOURCE: ©MICROSOFT PUBLISHER

Objects Toolbar

1. Be sure you are on page 1 of the publication. Click on the Text Box icon on the Objects toolbar docked at the left.
2. If the Objects toolbar is not showing, go to the menu bar and choose View > Toolbars > Objects.

Text Box

SOURCE: ©MICROSOFT PUBLISHER

Boundaries and Guides

1. Go to the menu bar and choose View > Boundaries and Guides. Notice that the blue and pink boundaries and guides disappear. These are used to snap your objects in place. They help guide the placement of these objects so that they are centered or placed appropriately in your publication.
2. Turn the Boundaries and Guides back on by going to the menu bar and choosing View > Boundaries and Guides.

Drawing a Text Box

1. Draw a text box beginning with the top left blue guide. Click on the text box tool. When you move the mouse pointer to the work area, it will turn into a crosshair. Click and hold down the left mouse button. Drag the text box vertically to the 2-inch mark. Drag it horizontally to the right blue guide. The text box should snap to the guide when you release the mouse button.
2. On the task pane, click on Font Schemes. Choose a font scheme for your publication.
3. Click in the text box. Type "Grand Opening." Use AutoFit Text. Center the text horizontally.

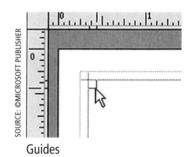

Guides

Clip Organizer Frame

1. On the Objects toolbar, click on the Clip Organizer Frame.
2. In the Search box, type "Optometrist." Choose a piece of clip art to place at the bottom half of the publication.

Publication Designs

1. On the task pane, click on Publication Designs. Apply a design that is appropriate for a business invitation. This is the grand opening for an optometrist's office.

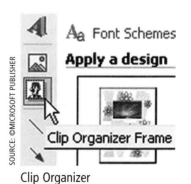

Clip Organizer

2. On the task pane, click on Color Schemes. Apply a color scheme that goes with your clip art. Don't forget that you can recolor your clip art if necessary.
3. Select the "Grand Opening" text and choose the font color to accent your other colors.

Nonbreaking Spaces

1. Insert a text box on the upper half of page 3.
2. Look on a calendar and set the grand opening date three weeks from now on a Wednesday from 2–4 P.M. Type the following information in the text box:
      Wednesday
      Your Date
      2–4 P.M.
   To type the hyphen, use a nonbreaking space. Do this by pressing Shift + Ctrl and the spacebar, typing the hyphen, then pressing Shift +Ctrl and the spacebar again.

Viewing Special Characters

1. You can show special editing characters such as space, paragraph marks, and special hyphens. Go to the menu bar and choose View > Special Characters.
2. See if you can find the three types of special characters in the text box you created in steps 1 and 2 under "Nonbreaking Spaces." What is the special character for a hard return? What is the special character for a hard space? What is the special character for a nonbreaking space?
3. You can turn the special characters off by going to the menu bar and choosing View > Special Characters, or by clicking the Special Characters tool on the standard toolbar.

Text Effects

1. Format the text in step 2 under Nonbreaking Spaces with an Accent color and an Effect.
2. Click on the Clip Organizer Frame tool in the Objects toolbar. Search for Lines. Find a line that would look good above "Wednesday" and below the attention getter on page 3. Resize the line to fit within the guides. Snap it to the guide.
3. Right-click on the line and choose Format Picture. Change the fill and line color to match the colors throughout the invitation.

Copying and Pasting a Picture

1. Right-click on the line and choose Copy. Right-click anywhere on the page and choose Paste.
2. Move the second line so it is at the top of the page within the guides.

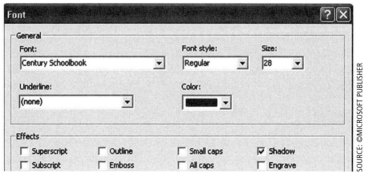

Font Effects

Design Gallery Objects

1. On the Objects toolbar, click on the Design Gallery Objects tool. Click on the Category Attention Getters. Choose Shadowed Slant Attention Getter by double-clicking on it.
2. Resize the attention getter to fill the bottom space. Move the attention getter if necessary.

Design Gallery Object
SOURCE: ©MICROSOFT PUBLISHER

Grouping and Ungrouping Objects

1. Right-click on the attention getter to Ungroup. There are two AutoShapes and one text box. Format each AutoShape with fill and line colors and styles.
2. Regroup the attention getter when you are finished formatting. To do this, click on one of the objects and then press the Shift key while clicking on the other two objects. When all three are selected, the Group Objects tool will appear in the lower right corner. Click on it once to group the objects. See the figure labeled Group Objects.
3. Type in the text box in the attention getter "Drawings for Discounts." Choose a font color.
4. If available, use MapPoint to create a map of the location of Shinoda Eye Care. It can be in any location in the United States. Zoom in on the map enough to see the names of the streets for directions to the grand opening. On the map, create a text box with the following information in it:
   Shinoda Eye Care
   Yuki and Jun Shinoda
   Street Address
   City, State ZIP
   Phone Number
   Use an arrow on the map to draw a direction from the text box to the street on the map where the office is located. Copy the map and paste it into page 2 of your invitation.

Format AutoShapes

Group Objects
SOURCE: ©MICROSOFT PUBLISHER

AutoShapes

1. Go to page 4 of your invitation. Click on the AutoShape tool. Choose Basic Shapes > Oval. Use click and drag to draw an oval on page 4 of the invitation.
2. Click on the Text Box tool. Draw a text box within the oval AutoShape.
3. Type in the oval:
   Yuki and Jun
   Shinoda
   Optometrists
4. Center the text and resize the AutoShape and text box as needed.
5. Format the text for size, color, and effects.
6. Format the AutoShape with a fill color and for line color, style, and weight.

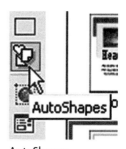

AutoShapes
SOURCE: ©MICROSOFT PUBLISHER

Spell Checking

1. On the standard toolbar, click on the spelling and grammar tool. This should not replace proofreading your finished invitation!
2. If the Spelling tool is dimmed, click inside a story to begin the spelling and grammar check. Replace, change, or ignore words as appropriate.

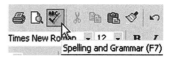

Spelling
SOURCE: ©MICROSOFT PUBLISHER

Create an Invitation to an Open House at the Retirement Home

1. You are the activities director at the local retirement home. Each year you host an open house the third Saturday in March. Prepare an invitation for your residents to give to their friends and relatives. You can look up the name and address of a retirement home or nursing home in your community either on a Web site or in the phone book.

2. Be sure the following questions are answered on the invitation:
    a. What day (including day of the week) will the open house take place?
    b. What type of dress is appropriate for the open house?
    c. Where will the open house take place?
    d. What time is the open house? When will it end?
    e. Will there be refreshments and/or dinner?
    f. Will there be entertainment? A guest speaker? Tours?
    g. Is there any other information that the person attending will need to know?

3. Save as *RetirementHome.pub*.

4. The following criteria should be met:
    ☐ All details included on the invitation are easy to read.
    ☐ No errors on the invitation.
    ☐ Font scheme is appropriate for the overall theme of the invitation.
    ☐ Clip art appropriate in size and type.
    ☐ Appropriate design applied for the invitation.
    ☐ Minimum of one text effect used.
    ☐ Minimum of one line clip art used.
    ☐ Minimum of one attention getter from the Design Gallery used.
    ☐ Minimum of one set of grouped objects.
    ☐ Minimum of one AutoShape used.
    ☐ Invitation uses at least the front and the inside.

ACTIVITY 6 • DESIGNING A NEWSLETTER

In this activity, you will become familiar with:

■ Insert Masthead
■ Arranging Layout Guides
■ Connecting Frames
■ Using Overflow
■ Hyphenation
■ Find and Replace
■ Creating Tables
■ Rotating Text and Objects
■ Watermarks
■ Headers and Footers
■ Design Checker

Insert Masthead

1. Go to the menu bar and choose File > New. On the task pane, choose Blank Publication or click on the New tool on the standard toolbar.
2. Go to the menu bar and choose Insert > Page. Insert two pages. Choose After the current page.

3. Go to the menu bar and choose Insert > Design Gallery Object > Masthead. Choose any masthead. Resize the object to snap to the grids at the top of page 1.
4. Go to the menu bar and choose Format > Color Schemes. Choose a color scheme for your newsletter. This is a newsletter that you will create as the volunteer secretary for the homeowners association in your subdivision. Consider the image you want when choosing colors. Close the color scheme on the task pane.
5. Overtype the information in the masthead. It should include the name "RiverEnd Homeowners Association." Depending on the style of masthead you chose, you can include the address of the secretary. "3005 RiverEnd Road, Noblesville, Indiana 46060."
6. Insert the current date on the masthead. It should be set to update automatically.
7. Go to page 2 using the Page Navigation tool in the status bar.

Arranging Layout Guides

1. Go to the menu bar and choose Arrange > Layout Guides. Change the Grid Guides to three columns.

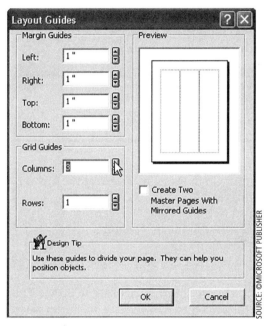

Layout Guides

2. Use the Text Box tool to create a text box that is 1-1/2 inches vertically and stretches from left to right margin horizontally (within the blue lines).
3. Click on the Text Box tool and draw another text box under the horizontal text box. This text box should go the length of the page, staying within the layout guides of the first column.
4. Select the text box you created. Go to the menu bar and choose Edit > Copy.
5. Go to the menu bar and choose Edit > Paste. Move the new text box to the second column so that it snaps in place.
6. Go to the menu bar and choose Edit > Paste. Move the new text box to the third column so that it snaps in place.
7. Save as *RiverEnd.pub*. Continue to save throughout the activity.

Text Box Link

SOURCE: ©MICROSOFT PUBLISHER

Text

Picture

SOURCE: ©MICROSOFT PUBLISHER

Previous Frame

SOURCE: ©MICROSOFT PUBLISHER

OverFlow

SOURCE: ©MICROSOFT PUBLISHER

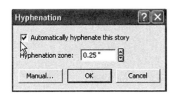

Hyphenation

SOURCE: ©MICROSOFT PUBLISHER

Connecting Frames

1. Click in the text box in the first column to select it. On the Connect Frames toolbar, click on the Create Text Box Link tool.
2. While the cursor is a pitcher in a pour position, click on the text box you want to connect to. See the figure to the left. Repeat this to connect the second column to the third column.
3. Click on the text box in the second column. Note that the Text Box Link is dimmed, but the opposite of it, Break Forward Link, is ready to be used. Select it. Practice this with the three columns. Be sure to leave the three columns connected when you are finished.
4. Click in the first column. Go to the menu bar and choose Insert > Text File.
5. Browse to your CD and double-click on *OakWilt.doc*.

Using Overflow

1. A Microsoft Publisher dialog box appears, telling that the text does not fit. Do you want to use autoflow? Click No. See below.

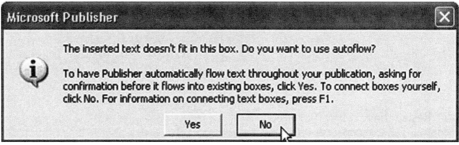

AutoFlow

SOURCE: ©MICROSOFT PUBLISHER

2. Practice using Go to Next Frame and Go to Previous Frame at the top and bottom of each of the connected text boxes.
3. Place the mouse pointer in the third column. Note the Overflow icon.
4. Go to page 3 and create a 2-inch text box in the first column.
5. Go to page 2 and click on Create Text Box Link.
6. Go to page 3 and click in the 2-inch text box you created. The rest of the article should flow into that text box.
7. On page 2, go to the menu bar and choose Insert > Picture > ClipArt. Drag the clip art to the middle of column 2. You can recolor the clip art if necessary. For a more professional look, you may want to take a digital picture of a tree at your school or scan a picture of a tree.
8. Right-click on the clip art and choose Format Picture. In the Format Picture dialog box, click on the Layout tab. Be sure that Square is chosen for the Wrapping Style.
9. Go to page 3. Look at the Connect icon at the bottom of your text box in column 1. It should be the overflow icon, indicating that there is more text. Resize the text box until all text is showing in that article.

Hyphenation

1. Click in any of the four text boxes where the Oak Wilt article resides.
2. Go to the menu bar and choose Tools > Language > Hyphenation.
3. Clear the "Automatically hyphenate this story" check box. Click OK.
4. Look at your story to see that hyphenation was turned off. You can also choose to go through each word that is hyphenated by clicking Manual.

Find and Replace

1. Place the mouse pointer in the text box at the beginning of the story. Go to the menu bar and choose Edit > Replace. In the Replace dialog box, type "oake" in the Find what box and "oak" in the Replace with box. It is best to click Find Next and replace each one individually unless you know there are no instances of words similar to oak in the story.
2. In the blank text box on page 2, insert a WordArt with the title "Oak Wilt." Format the WordArt and the text box. Include customized border art around the text box.
3. Add a customized drop cap to the beginning of the story.
4. In the first column, create a 3-inch text box. Format the text box with a fill color so it will attract attention. Type the following information in the text box:

Replace

Annual Family Picnic	
WHEN:	June 1, 2XXX
WHERE:	RiverEnd Pavilion
WHO:	Entire Family
	Kids Welcome!
BBQ:	Provided by Sam's
RSVP:	Karin Hite by May 23, 2XXX
Phone:	915-555-7401

Use the following text enhancements: bold, italic, at least two different font colors, size, types, one font effect, horizontal alignment changes.

5. Resize the text box if needed.

Creating Tables

1. Go to the Objects toolbar and click on the Insert Table tool.
2. Draw a table at the bottom half of page 1 across both columns. In the Create Table dialog box, change the number of rows to 10, the number of columns to 3, and the table format to List with Title 1. If you need more rows, you can always go to the menu bar and choose Table > Insert Rows Above or Below.

Insert Table

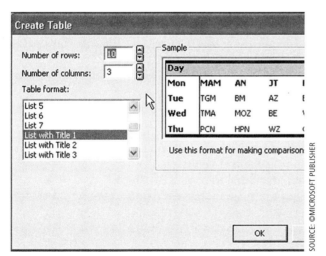

Create Table

3. Type the title in the gray area. The first line of the title is "Treasurer's Report." The second line of the title is "Submitted by Ted Thompson."

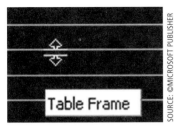

Table Frame

Increase Indent

Dues

Text

Rotate

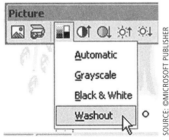

Washout

4. Increase the width of the first column of the table and decrease the width of the second and third columns. The last two columns should be approximately one inch wide. The first column's width will take up the rest of the space.
5. Select all rows of the table and decrease the height of the rows by hovering the mouse pointer on the line until your cursor looks like the one to the left and the Table Frame screen tip pops up.
6. To increase or decrease an indent within a table cell, use the Increase or Decrease Indent tool on the Formatting toolbar.
   Input the following information:

Column 1	Column 2	Column 3
Revenue:		
Annual Dues (75 members × $50)		$3,750.00
Expenses:		
Annual Picnic	$ 500.00	
Miscellaneous	38.25	
Postage	24.00	
Lawn Care	836.00	
Repairs on Sprinkler System	235.00	
Utilities	625.00	
Total Expenses	$2,258.25	
Revenue Remaining		$1,491.75

7. To underline with a double line, go to the menu bar and choose Format > Font. Change Underline Style to Double in the drop-down box.
8. On page 1 in the top right column, add an AutoShape with a text box and a picture. See the figure to the left for the information to put in the text box.
9. Group the objects.

Rotating Text and Objects

1. The text should be rotated in some way. You can do this by hovering the mouse pointer on the green button at the top of the text box until the cursor turns into the Rotate tool. See the figure to the left.
2. You can also rotate a text box by going to the menu bar and choosing Arrange > Rotate or Flip.

Watermarks

1. Go to page 3. Insert a picture. Drag the picture to the middle of the page. Resize it so it is in all three columns. It should not take up the entire page.
2. Click on the picture. If the Picture toolbar does not appear, go to the menu bar and choose View > Toolbars > Picture Toolbar.
3. Go to the Color tool as shown at left and choose Washout.
4. With the picture selected, go to the menu bar and choose Arrange > Order > Bring to Back.

Headers and Footers

1. Go to the menu bar and choose View > Headers and Footers. The Header and Footer floating toolbar should appear.

2. In the Header box, click the Align Center icon, then click the Insert Page Number icon on the Header and Footer toolbar.
3. Click on the Show Header/Footer icon to move to the footer.
4. Type your name at the left margin.
5. Note that in place of the page numbers in the status bar you now have the letter
R. This indicates that you are on the Master Page. When you are in Headers and
Footers, it will put the information on every page as it does a Master Page.
When you close the Header and Footer toolbar, it automatically takes you out
of the Master Page, or you can go to the menu bar and choose View > Master
Page.

Header and Footer
SOURCE: ©MICROSOFT PUBLISHER

Design Checker

1. Finish the other two columns by adding an article on landscaping. Research the
Internet for the information to put in your article. Be sure to reference the article.
2. Go to the menu bar and choose Tools > Design Checker. Check all pages and
make any necessary changes.
3. Save your work.

ACTIVITY 6 • MINI-PROJECT

Create a Newsletter on Interviewing Skills

1. Go to http://www.google.com. Search for job tips, job interviews, and interviews. Read articles and take notes. Write a short article (one column or less)
and one long article (two or more columns) on the information you have read
that you think is most important. Use word processing software and save the
articles. Make a note of several tips that are important that can be placed as an
eye-catcher on the newsletter.
2. Go to http://www.collegegrad.com/video/index.shtml and watch the videos
on interviewing success, or watch a video on interviewing that is available in
your classroom. Write a short article on the information you learned in the
video. Make a note of any tips that can be used as lists or in other attention-
getting ways.
3. Print the articles you have written. With a partner, edit the articles that each of
you have written. The partner's name should be on the printouts as the editor.
Turn these in to your instructor for approval.
4. Begin creating your newsletter using a blank publication.
5. Save the newsletter as *InterviewingSkills.pub*.
6. The following criteria should be met:
   - [ ] Articles are well-written and thorough, and use appropriate topics with
     no errors.
   - [ ] Masthead has correct information and is eye-catching
   - [ ] Newsletter contains two or three columns.
   - [ ] At least one text box is linked with autoflow used.
   - [ ] Minimum of three images used. One piece of clip art in the middle of an
     article, demonstrating correct wrapping. Images are professional-looking
     and properly sized.
   - [ ] Minimum of one text box filled.
   - [ ] Minimum of one table with at least two columns and four rows inserted in
     the newsletter.
   - [ ] Minimum of one text box rotated.
   - [ ] Minimum of one watermark used.

☐ Master Page used to place page numbers as headers on each page.
☐ Hyphenation turned off.
☐ Drop cap used effectively.
☐ Used Design Checker and made changes suggested.

PART 1 • SIMULATION

Using Publisher to Create a Campaign

1. You have decided to run for president of your state FBLA (Future Business Leaders of America). You will need to create the following items to be used during and/or after your campaign:
    a. Flyer, 8-1/2 by 11 inches. Save as *CampaignFlyer.pub*.
    b. Poster, tabloid size (11 by 17 inches). Save as *CampaignPoster.pub*.
    c. Business cards. Save as *FBLABusCards.pub*.
    d. Letterhead. Save as *FBLALetterhead.pub*.
    e. Fax cover sheet. Save as *FBLAFAX.pub*.
    f. Brochure. The brochure is a marketing tool to promote you for this officer position. It should include a digital or scanned picture of you on the front. Your logo and slogan should be in the brochure. It should also list your qualifications for the job such as other offices held, organization memberships, and character attributes that would make you the right choice for this officer position. You should have some goals for FBLA on the brochure. Be sure to include local as well as state goals. Save as *FBLABrochure.pub*.
    g. Newsletter. The newsletter can be an extension of the brochure. You can create a type of autobiography of your life in your newsletter. Write articles about some unique experiences you may have had in your life or about your family in general. You can include several scanned or digital pictures of yourself. Save as *FBLANewsletter.pub*.
    h. Invitation (to celebrate your victory). Save as *FBLAInvitation.pub*.
    i. At least one other creative item to use in the campaign. Save as *CreativeItem.pub*.
2. Decide on a slogan and logo for your campaign. Design those so that you have a continuity of theme throughout your designs.
3. If you have not been a member of FBLA, you may need to read some about the organization and their goals at http://www.fbla-pbl.org.
4. The following criteria should be met:
    ☐ Minimum of nine pieces to the simulation.
    ☐ Desktop publishing items are error-free.
    ☐ Creativity demonstrated on most projects.
    ☐ Clip art and images appropriate, varied by type and properly sized and placed.
    ☐ Color schemes appropriate.
    ☐ Font schemes appropriate.
    ☐ Enhancements for fonts such as color, shading, text effects, size, bold, and underline used.
    ☐ Extra effort evident in the use of skills learned such as: drop caps, tables, watermarks, headers and footers, frames and shading, appropriate masthead, and so on. Project displays mastery of the skills learned in Publisher.

Adobe PageMaker

Adobe PageMaker
Publisher: Adobe Systems Incorporated
PageMaker is desktop publishing software used extensively in the publishing industry. This software has many templates available for quick use in creating flyers, brochures, newsletters, and other marketing or business documents.

ACTIVITY 1 • FLYER

In this activity, you will become familiar with:

- Document Setup
- Publication Window
  - Document
  - Rulers
  - Status Bar
  - Pasteboard
- Toolbox
- Pointer Tool
- Rectangular Frame Tool
- Text Tool
- Undo
- Color Palette
- Fill and Stroke
- Text Alignment
- Placing a Picture
- Bullets
- Paragraph Spacing
- Indents and Tabs
- Hanging Indent
- Hyphenation
- Text Box
- Viewing
- Circle Frame Tool
- Arrange
- Hexagon Frame Tool

Document Setup

1. Go to the menu bar and choose File > New. The Document Setup dialog box appears.

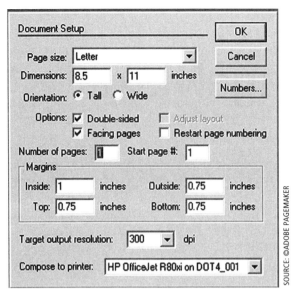

Document Setup

2. The following choices are available in the Document Setup dialog box: page size, orientation, double-sided, facing pages, page numbering, margins, output resolution, and printer choice.
3. Clear the Double-sided check box. Note that when you do so, Facing pages also turns off and the Inside and Outside margins become Left and Right margins.
4. Leave all the other choices in the Document Setup dialog box at the defaults.
5. Click OK.

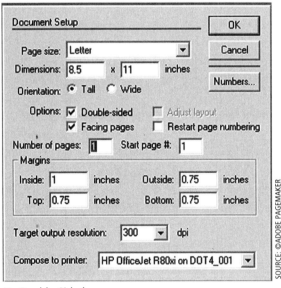

No Double-Sided

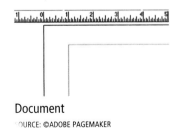

Document

Publication Window

Document

1. The document opens in view size Fit in Window. The purple and pink box around the inside of the document is the guides that represent the margins.
2. These can be toggled off by going to the menu bar and choosing View > Hide Guides. Toggle them back on by choosing View > Show Guides.

Rulers

1. Note in the Document figure on the previous page that the rulers are also on. These can be toggled off by going to the menu bar and choosing View > Hide Rulers. Toggle them back on by choosing View > Show Rulers.
2. Click in the area where the Horizontal and Vertical Rulers intersect.
3. Hold down the mouse button until the intersection turns black. Continue to hold down the mouse button while dragging out of the intersecting area. The pointer should turn into a crosshair. Drag the vertical and horizontal rulers so that the rulers are set on zero at the margin guides (purple and pink box). Sometimes when using the rulers to align objects, it helps to start at zero.

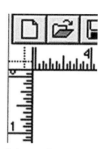

Intersection

SOURCE: ©ADOBE PAGEMAKER

Status Bar

1. Note in the figure to the right, the page icons L and R in the status bar, representing the left and right master pages. This figure is a document set up as double-sided, facing pages. The number 1 represents the page number. There is only one page in this document.
2. In the figure to the right, the status bar shows only an R because this document was not set up for double-sided. It shows only one page. This figure should look like the one you have set up on your screen.

Status Bar

SOURCE: ©ADOBE PAGEMAKER

Single Page

SOURCE: ©ADOBE PAGEMAKER

Pasteboard

1. This is the area outside the document. It is used to store unused objects temporarily.
2. If you know you will not use the object then you will delete it. But if you think there is a chance you are going to use it in your publication, you can slide it off the document into the pasteboard area so it will be available for later use.
3. The entire pasteboard can be viewed by going to the menu bar and choosing View > Entire Pasteboard. This may become necessary if you cannot find one of your objects that you have stored on the pasteboard.
4. To return to Fit in Window view, go to the menu bar and choose View > Fit in Window.

Toolbox

1. Many of the tools you will use are in the toolbox shown to the right.
2. Go to the menu bar and choose Help > Help Topics.
3. Click on Search and type in the search box "Toolbox."
4. Click on the third word down, "Toolbox." This should open up a diagram of the toolbox with shortcuts and labels for each tool. Right-click on the right side of the screen where the diagram is pictured and choose Print. This is the diagram for PageMaker for Windows. You can use your printout as a reference. You may also want to print out the "Using the Toolbox" diagram as it gives more information on the use of each tool.

Toolbox

SOURCE: ©ADOBE PAGEMAKER

Pointer Tool

1. Click on the Pointer tool.
2. The Pointer tool is used to select, move, and resize text objects and images.

Pointer Tool

SOURCE: ©ADOBE PAGEMAKER

Rectangular Frame Tool

1. The Rectangular frame tool is used to create a placeholder for objects or type.
2. Click on the Rectangular frame tool and draw a frame from the left to the right margin. Drag the frame 2 inches vertically.

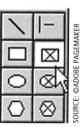

Rectangular Frame Tool

SOURCE: ©ADOBE PAGEMAKER

Text Tool

Text Tool

1. The Text tool is used to type, select, and edit text.
2. Click on the Text tool.
3. Go to the menu bar and choose Type > Size > 72.
4. Click in the rectangular frame that you have drawn on your document. Type "Join the Fun!" in the rectangular frame.
5. With the Text tool still selected, drag across the text to select it. Go to the menu bar and choose Type > Font. Choose a font that is bold and could grab someone's attention.

Undo

1. Go to the menu bar and choose Edit > Undo. Notice that it is grayed out, which means it can not be used right now.
2. Select the text and delete the text.
3. Go to the menu bar and choose Edit > Undo to undo your edit. If you have made other changes since pressing Delete, you will not be able to undo that action. Undo only works on the last action taken.
4. PageMaker remembers your last action and lets you reverse it.
5. The Undo command cannot undo all actions. It cannot reverse changes made using the Styles and Colors Palettes, and it cannot undo most commands from the File menu or the Type menu.

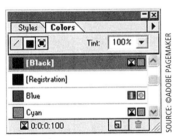
Color Palette

Color Palette

1. With the text still selected, go to the Color Palette and choose Blue for the font. If the Palette is not on your screen, go to the menu bar and choose Window > Show Colors.
2. Experiment with changing the font color. Leave it on Blue before going to the next step.
3. Save the flyer as *FreePizza.pmd*.

Fill and Stroke

1. With the Pointer tool and the Rectangular frame selected, go to the menu bar and choose Element > Fill and Stroke.

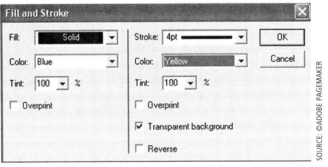
Fill and Stroke

2. In the Fill and Stroke dialog box, click on the down arrow next to the Fill box. Change the None to Solid. Choose Cyan tinted at 10% for the Color. See the figure labeled Fill and Stroke.
3. On the Stroke side, choose 4 pt. for the stroke with Cyan as the Color.

Text Alignment

1. Click anywhere in the text.
2. Go to the menu bar and choose Type > Alignment > Align Center.

Placing a Picture

1. Go to the menu bar and choose Window > Plug-in Palettes > Show Picture Palette. If the Picture Palette is not loaded on your hard drive, you may need the CD. Ask your instructor for directions.
2. In the Category drop-down box, choose Food & Dining.
3. Click on the binoculars at the bottom of the Pictures dialog box.
4. In the Search Pictures dialog box, type "pizza" in the Search for Keywords box.
5. Click Search.
6. Double-click on the picture you would like to place on your flyer.
7. With your cursor changed into "PS," click on the left area under the title of the flyer.
8. Click on the Pointer tool and resize the image of the pizza as needed.
9. Click on the Text tool and type "Free Pizza" above the picture.
10. The text is placed in a text box. Click on the Pointer tool. Resize the text box as needed by placing the mouse pointer on the bottom right handle and dragging to the appropriate size.
11. Use your judgment to change the font type, size, and color and appropriately place the text for "Free Pizza."
12. Click on the Rectangular frame tool.
13. Begin drawing a Rectangle at 3 inches on the horizontal ruler and drag down to 6 inches on the vertical ruler.
14. Click on the Text tool.
15. Go to the menu bar and choose Type > Size > Other and type "20."
16. Type the following, pressing Enter after each line:
    Presentations Available:
    Financial Aid Information
    Students in Free Enterprise (SIFE)
    Plan Your Future
    Keys to College Success
17. Select the text you typed. Be sure you have clicked on the Text tool before selecting text.
18. Go to the menu bar and choose Type > Font > Comic Sans MS.
19. Select the Rectangle with the Pointer tool. On the Color Palette, click on the Fill icon. Choose Yellow tinted at 10%.
20. Click on the Save icon on the standard toolbar to save the flyer again.

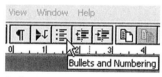

Bullets

SOURCE: ©ADOBE PAGEMAKER

Bullets

1. Click on the Bullets and Numbering icon on the toolbar. See above, right.
2. In the Bullets dialog box, click on the circle bullet.

Paragraph Spacing

1. With the text selected, go to the menu bar and choose Type > Paragraph.
2. Type ".25" in Before paragraph spacing.

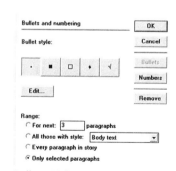

Bullets Dialog Box

SOURCE: ©ADOBE PAGEMAKER

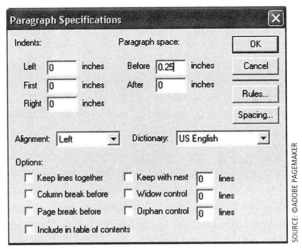

Paragraph

Indents and Tabs

1. With the text still selected, go to the menu bar and choose Type > Indents/Tabs.
2. Set a tab at .25 spaces over from the bullet.

Hanging Indent

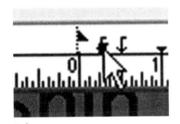

Tabs

SOURCE: ©ADOBE PAGEMAKER

1. While holding down the Shift key, drag the bottom triangle over to the .25 tab. This sets a hanging indent.
2. You can also set the hanging indent by going to the menu bar and choosing Type > Paragraph. In the Left Indent box, type ".25." In the First Indent box, type "−.25."

Hyphenation

1. Hyphenating words in a bulleted list in this small an area decreases the readability of the text.
2. With your Text tool chosen and your cursor placed in the Rectangular frame, go to the menu bar and choose Type > Hyphenation.
3. In the Hyphenation dialog box, click the Off radio button.
4. Resize the Rectangular frame as needed.
5. Remember to save your work frequently. Save your *FreePizza.pmd* document again now.

Text Box

1. Click on the Text tool. Click below the image of the pizza and type the following:
   March 26, 2XXX
   7 PM
   Balora High School
   Balora, Texas
   Student Center
   Bring a Friend!
2. With the Text tool selected, press Ctrl + A to select all the text.
3. Format the text as size 22, Arial Black, and cyan.
4. With the Text selected, go to the menu bar and choose Type > Alignment > Align Center.
5. With the Pointer tool, drag the text box to center it on the left side in the area below the pizza.

Viewing

1. When inputting or proofreading text, it may be necessary to zoom in. You can do this several different ways.
   a. Click on the Zoom In or Zoom Out icon on the standard toolbar.
   b. Go to the menu bar and choose View > Zoom In or Out.
   c. Use the Zoom tool in the toolbox to zoom in and use the Hand tool to move the flyer around in the viewing space on your work area.
   d. Right-click in the document and choose a view.
2. Use Ctrl + 0 (zero) for a shortcut to Fit in Window.

Zoom

SOURCE: ©ADOBE PAGEMAKER

Circle Frame Tool

1. Click on the Circle Frame tool.
2. Draw a circle or ellipsis on the bottom right empty space. Snap it to the right margin.
3. Fill it with cyan tinted at 50%.

Zoom Tool

SOURCE: ©ADOBE PAGEMAKER

Arrange

1. Go to the menu bar and choose Element > Arrange > Send to Back.
2. By doing this you will be able to place another object on top of this object.

Hand Tool

SOURCE: ©ADOBE PAGEMAKER

Hexagon Frame Tool

1. Click on the Hexagon Frame tool and draw a shape inside the circle. Fill it with cyan color tinted at 100%.
2. With the Text tool, type inside the Hexagon Frame "Door Prizes."
3. Stroke the Hexagon frame with a Yellow dotted line.
4. Use your judgment to make additional changes to fonts, paragraph spacing, and alignments.
5. Save your flyer again.

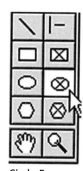

Circle Frame

SOURCE: ©ADOBE PAGEMAKER

ACTIVITY 1 • MINI-PROJECT

Create a Flyer for TechForce

You are an employee of TechForce. TechForce provides PC support for local businesses. One of your duties is to use PageMaker and provide desktop publishing services to the business.

You will create three flyers as assigned by your supervisor.

1. In a team of three or four students, write a dress code policy for the business. The policy should include five rules.
2. Flyer 1: Create a flyer outlining the dress code policy written by your team. Each team member creates his or her own flyer. Save as *DressCode.pmd*.
3. In a team of three or four students, plan a company picnic for the first Saturday in May. Look on the calendar for a specific date for the current year. Plan details such as where, when, what to bring, and who is invited. You may want to schedule it at a local place where there will be swimming or other activities available.
4. Flyer 2: Create a flyer to announce the company picnic. Each team member creates his or her own flyer. Save as *CompanyPicnic.pmd*.
5. Flyer 3: Each month the company selects an Employee of the Month. These employees are rated on performance, attendance, punctuality, and ability to get along with the staff and customers. Create a flyer announcing a one-week paid Hawaiian vacation for two for the Employee of the Year. Decide on how the

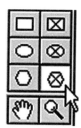

Hexagon Frame

SOURCE: ©ADOBE PAGEMAKER

company will select the Employee of the Year. You may or may not want to include the selection process on the flyer. They will submit the request to you. Save your flyer as *HawaiiVacation.pmd*.

6. The following criteria should be met:
   - ☐ Colors and fonts appropriate.
   - ☐ Flyers are thorough with all important information on them.
   - ☐ Flyers have no errors.
   - ☐ Fill and Stroke used effectively.
   - ☐ Minimum of one appropriate piece of clip art on each flyer. Clip art sized and placed appropriately.
   - ☐ Bullets used on one flyer with hanging indents.
   - ☐ Paragraph spacing and indents and tabs used to balance white space.
   - ☐ Hyphenation appropriate for a flyer.
   - ☐ Minimum of one picture or text frame other than rectangular frame.
   - ☐ Minimum of one stacked picture or text frame with Arrange used.
   - ☐ Team worked well together with equal input and distribution of tasks.

ACTIVITY 2 • BROCHURE

In this activity, you will become familiar with:

- ■ Using a Brochure Template
- ■ Removing a Page
- ■ Inserting a Page
- ■ Editing and Moving Text Boxes
- ■ Placing Images
- ■ Type Style
- ■ Copying Frames

Using a Brochure Template

1. Open PageMaker.
2. With the Templates dialog box on the screen, click in the Category drop-down box and choose Brochures.
3. Double-click on the template *1000327.PMT*. This template is not on your CD; rather it is a template that comes with PageMaker.
4. In the Panose Font Matching Results dialog box, make any substitutions suggested. Click OK.
5. Using your Pointer tool, click on the template information in the upper right corner of page 1.
6. If you accidentally choose the incorrect template, go to the menu bar and choose Window > Plug in Palettes > Show Template Palette.

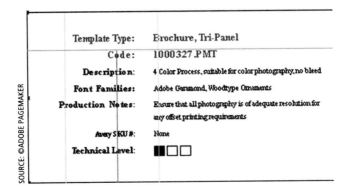

SOURCE: ©ADOBE PAGEMAKER

Template Type:	Brochure, Tri-Panel
Code:	1000327.PMT
Description:	4 Color Process, suitable for color photography, no bleed
Font Families:	Adobe Garamond, Woodtype Ornaments
Production Notes:	Ensure that all photography is of adequate resolution for any offset printing requirements
Avery SKU #:	None
Technical Level:	■☐☐

Template Info

7. Right-click on the template information and choose Actual Size. Read the template information.
8. Press Delete to remove the template information from your document area. You can also turn the tips off by going to the Layers Palette and clicking on the Eye icon to remove it from the layers.
9. If the Layers Palette is not showing, go to the menu bar and choose Window > Show Layers.

Removing a Page

1. Click on page 2 in the status bar.
2. Go to the menu bar and choose Layout > Remove Pages.
3. In the Remove Pages dialog box, leave the default on Remove page(s) 2 through 2 and click OK.
4. Confirm removal of the pages and all their contents by clicking OK.

Page 2
SOURCE: ©ADOBE PAGEMAKER

Inserting a Page

1. Go to the menu bar and choose Layout > Insert Pages.
2. In the Insert Pages dialog box, leave the default as shown in Figure 22 and click Insert.

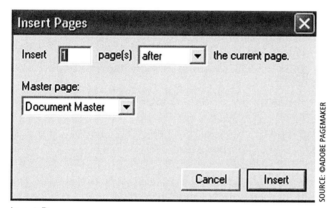

Insert Pages

3. Click on page 1 of the brochure.

Editing and Moving Text Boxes

1. With the Pointer tool, click on the right side of the brochure in the first text box. Remove the text box by pressing the Delete key.
2. Click on the text box with "Auto Insurance" in it. Drag the text box up so that it is underneath the border where the other text box was that you deleted.
3. Click on the Text tool. Select the text "Auto Insurance." Overtype with "Cole Farms, Inc."
4. Resize the text box to font size 24.

Placing Images

1. Using the Pointer tool, click in the rectangular box. Press Delete to remove the rectangular placeholder.
2. Go to the menu bar and choose File > Place. Browse to your CD and double-click on *Beefmaster.jpg*.
3. With the Place tool, click in the area where the rectangular box was to place the image.
4. Resize and move the image as needed.

Place Cursor
SOURCE: ©ADOBE PAGEMAKER

Type Style

1. If it is not already selected, select the text "Cole Farms, Inc."
2. Go to the menu bar and choose Type > Type Style > Bold.
3. Type in the Rectangular frame below the picture of the heifer:
   Producers of Beefmaster Cattle
   Phone: (915) 555-0561
   Fax: (925) 555-8808
   www.colefarms.com
4. Use the Type menu to make changes to the text in font, font size, and alignment. Choose a color for the font. Make other appropriate changes to the rectangular frame and text.

Copying Frames

1. Use image editing software to browse to the CD and open the image *CF_Logo.gif*. The image needs to be resized and made transparent before it can be used. Save the changes you made to the image as *CF_Logoresized.gif*.
2. Use the Pointer tool to click on the logo image and the text box below to delete them.
3. Go to the menu bar and choose File > Place. Browse to where you saved your edited CF Logo. Double-click the image.
4. Your cursor will change to the symbol shown on the previous page. Click on the brochure in the place where you want the image to be located. Resize as needed.
5. Save the brochure as *ColeFarms.pmd*.
6. In the middle of the brochure, click each of the rectangular frames and delete them.
7. Click on the rectangular frame on the bottom of the front of the brochure and copy the frame.
8. Paste the rectangular frame on the bottom of the middle of the brochure. Add the following information above the phone numbers:
   4200 Cattleway Drive
   Fort Worth, TX 76109
9. In the space above the edited rectangular frame, place the image *Heifers.jpg*, which you will find on your CD. Resize as appropriate.
10. On the left side of the trifold, place the Cole Farms logo at the top.
11. In the rectangular frame below, input the following text:
    Cole Farms has been in the business of raising Beefmaster Cattle since 1983. The family invites you to come by the ranch for Open House any Wednesday afternoon. Come see the heifers, including the Grand Champion 4-H Heifer for 2XXX.
    For more information on Beefmaster Cattle, visit http://www.beefmaster.com on the Web.
12. Format the text as Courier, 11 pt. size, and italic.
13. Center the text.
14. Change the paragraph spacing to .2 Before.
15. Place an image below the rectangular box. See left. Find an image similar in shape to the one shown. You can search for an image of barbed wire on the Internet, create your own using image management software, or locate another appropriate image.
16. Use MapPoint or some other mapping software to create a map of Texas with Fort Worth labeled on the map.
17. Use the mapping tools to draw a text box. In the text box, type "Cole Farms, Inc." and the address and phone number.
18. Use the mapping tools to draw an arrow from the text box to Fort Worth.

TriFold

SOURCE: ©ADOBE PAGEMAKER

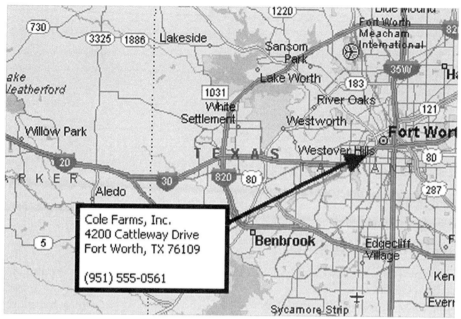

Fort Worth Map

19. Copy and paste the map on page 2 of the brochure. Resize as needed.
20. Save as *ColeFarms.pmd*.

ACTIVITY 2 • MINI-PROJECT

Create a Brochure for a Travel Site

1. Go to http://www.google.com and search for a place to visit of your choice. For instance, you might search for "Paris, France" or "Little Rock, Arkansas."
2. The following is a list of suggested items to include in the brochure. You are not restricted to these alone.
   a. Facts of the place you would like to visit. Include at least 20 facts.
   b. Places and sites to see while you are there.
   c. Restaurants and hotels that may be of interest. You may use the Internet or MapPoint to locate these.
   d. Bar chart of the weather.
   e. Local politics.
   f. Airline schedules. Go to http://www.expedia.com or a similar site to include a table of airline schedules and prices.
3. Save as *TravelBrochure.pmd*.
4. The following criteria should be met:
   ☐ Minimum of three images with clarity and appropriate type and size. These can be a map image, clip art, digital or scanned pictures, or pictures from the Internet.
   ☐ Thorough and appropriate information included in the brochure.
   ☐ Type is appropriate size, color, and style.
   ☐ Effective use of a brochure template.
   ☐ Appropriate use of text boxes.
   ☐ Creativity demonstrated.
   ☐ No errors on brochure.
   ☐ Use of color was appropriate and visually appealing.

ACTIVITY 3 • NEWSLETTER

In this activity, you will become familiar with:

- Newsletter Templates
- Styles
- Select All
- Default Type Menu
- Placing Text Documents
- Changing Case
- Links Manager
- Placing Inline and Wrapped Images
- Drop Cap
- Embellishment Logo

Newsletter Templates

1. In the Templates dialog box, click the drop-down box in Categories and choose Newsletter.
2. Browse the templates and choose *1000397.PMT* by clicking on the template and clicking the Create Publication button.
3. Click OK to substitute any necessary fonts.
4. Click on pages 2 and 3 in the status bar.
5. Go to the menu bar and choose Layout > Remove Pages.
6. Click on page 1.
7. Save the newsletter as *PrintGraphics.pmd*.

Styles

1. Look at the first page of the newsletter. There are four rectangular frames. Click on the one that you think is the masthead.
2. Click on the text tool in the toolbox.
3. Go to the menu bar and choose Type > Style to see if you were correct. Check the style on each of the other rectangular frames. The other styles used are Body-front, Sub-head, and Embellishment-Logo. Check the styles to see if you know which style is used for each rectangular frame.
4. Click on the Text tool.

Select All

1. Go to the menu bar and choose Edit > Select All.
2. Overtype the text with "Print Graphics."
3. Go to the menu bar and choose Type > Font. Choose Arial.
4. Go to the menu bar and choose Type > Size. Choose 72.
5. Go to the menu bar and choose Type > Leading. Choose Auto.

Default Type Menu

1. Sometimes in using templates, the default type for font, size, and leading may be changed.
2. To check and/or correct this, click on the Pointer tool. Click in the pasteboard area to be sure nothing is selected.
3. Go to the menu bar and choose Type > Font > Arial.
4. Go to the menu bar and choose Type > Size > 12.
5. Go to the menu bar and choose Type > Leading > Auto.
6. Go to the menu bar and choose Type > Type Style > Normal.
7. Save the newsletter again by clicking the Save icon on the standard toolbar or pressing Ctrl + S.

Placing Text Documents

1. Click on the text tool.
2. Click in the Sub-head.
3. Using the shortcut Ctrl + A, select all the text.
4. Press Delete to remove the text from the rectangular frame.
5. Go to the menu bar and choose File > Place.
6. Browse to your CD and double-click the *graphics.txt* file.
7. The Text Import Options dialog box will appear. Check that the settings are the same as shown below.

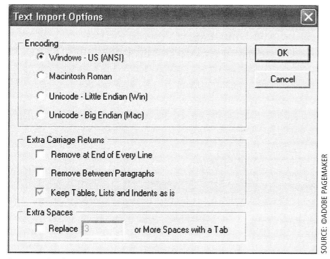

Import Options

8. With the Place tool, click inside the Sub-heading Rectangular frame to copy the text into the Sub-heading. If you want to place the text independent of the Rectangular frame, click outside the frame and drag the text block to the frame.
9. Select all the text in the frame. Change the font color to black.
10. Go to the menu bar and choose Type > Type Style > Italics.

Changing Case

1. With the Text tool, select Desktop Publishing in the Sub-head text.
2. Go to the menu bar and choose Utilities > Plug-ins > Change Case.
3. In the Change Case dialog box, click on UPPER CASE, then Apply and OK.
4. Save the newsletter again.

Links Manager

1. Go to the menu bar and choose File > Links Manager.
2. In the Links Manager dialog box, click on the Options button.
3. In the Link Options: Defaults dialog box, select the Update automatically check box.
4. Using the Pointer tool, click inside the Body-front Rectangular frame.
5. Click on the drop cap and press Delete to remove it.
6. Click inside the Body-front Rectangular frame with the text tool.
7. Go to the menu bar and choose File > Place.
8. Browse to your CD and double-click on *ClipArt.txt*.
9. With the Place tool, click in the Sub-head Rectangular frame to place the text.
10. If your text is centered, go to the menu bar and choose Type > Alignment > Align Left.

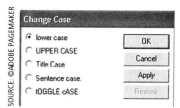

Change Case

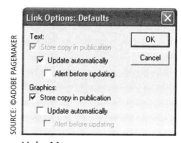

Links Manager

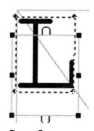

Drop Cap

SOURCE: ©ADOBE PAGEMAKER

11. Open up a word processing program. Browse to your CD and open *ClipArt.txt.*
12. Add at the bottom of the document "Susan Lake, Author."
13. Save and close the word processing document.
14. Go to the menu bar and choose File > Links Manager.
15. In the Links Manager dialog box, click on *ClipArt.txt* and Update.
16. Save and close the document.

Placing Inline and Wrapped Images

1. Click on the Text tool.
2. Click on the Body-front after the first enumeration and text (before number 2).
3. Go to the menu bar and choose File > Place. Browse to the CD and double-click on *Inline.jpg.*
4. Click on the Pointer tool and select the image.
5. Drag the image you just placed to different areas of the document. Notice that you can move it up and down but not from side to side. This has been placed as an inline image and cannot be text-wrapped.
6. Click on the Pointer tool.
7. Go to the menu bar and choose File > Place. Browse to the CD and double-click on *Elephant.jpg.*
8. Click in front of enumeration 3.
9 Using the Pointer tool, click on *Elephant.jpg.*
10. Right-click on the image. Select Text Wrap and choose the second Text Wrap.
11. Drag the Elephant image to the middle of the Body-front article. Resize the image as needed.
12. Click on the inline image and press Delete.
13. Save the newsletter again.

Drop Cap

1. Click on the Text tool.
2. Go to the menu bar and choose Utilities > Plug-ins > Drop Cap.
3. In the Drop cap dialog box, change Size to 2 lines. Click on Apply, then OK.

Drop Cap Dialog Box

SOURCE: ©ADOBE PAGEMAKER

4. If you get the error message that Leading is Top of Caps, this will need to be changed to Proportional. If you did not get the error message, then your paragraph specifications are already set to Proportional and you can skip steps 5–9.

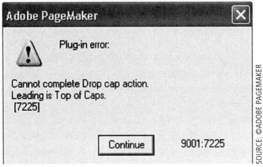

Error Messages

5. With the Text tool, select all text.
6. Go to the menu bar and choose Type > Paragraph. In the Paragraph Specifications dialog box, click on the Spacing button.
7. In the Spacing Attributes dialog box, change Leading method to Proportional.

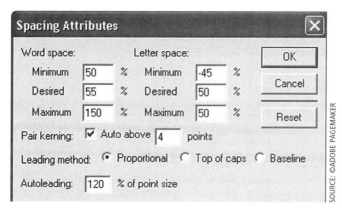

Spacing Attributes

8. Click OK to close the Spacing Attributes dialog box and OK to close the Paragraph Specifications dialog box.
9. Repeat steps 2 and 3 to create the drop cap.
10. Go to the menu bar and choose View > Fit in Window if you are not in that view. Check to see if all the content in the Front-body is showing, including the author's name.
11. Save the newsletter again.

Embellishment Logo

1. Use the Pointer tool to click on the Embellishment Logo.
2. Press Delete.
3. Using image management software, open *pglogo.gif*.
4. The publisher of Print Graphics newsletter wants the logo to be replaced. Create three different versions of the old logo, leaving "pg" in each one of them. The initials can be moved, rotated, resized, changed to a different font, and so on, as long as they are still seen in the logo. Use the new business colors that are used in the newsletter.
5. In the *PrintGraphics.pmd* newsletter, click on the Pointer tool.
6. Go to the menu bar and choose File > Place. Browse to the logos you created. Choose the one you think is the best.
7. Place it where the original Embellishment Logo was on the newsletter.
8. Save the newsletter.

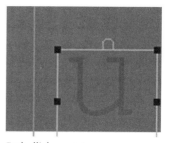

Embellishment Logo
SOURCE: ©ADOBE PAGEMAKER

ACTIVITY 3 • MINI-PROJECT

Create a Newsletter from the School Newspaper

1. Keeping up with school news is important. Get the last newsletter from your school. Read the articles to learn more about what is going on in your school. Summarize the articles and announcements in a shorter version of the newspaper. Do not plagiarize!
2. Attempt to create some continuity of image from the newspaper to the newsletter. This could be the use of a logo or similar masthead.
3. Take digital pictures to include from around the school that are appropriate to the topic.

4. The following criteria should be followed:
   - ☐ Masthead and logo have similar theme to newspaper.
   - ☐ Articles summarized effectively with appropriate announcements in newsletter.
   - ☐ Accurate information as far as articles, dates and meeting places, and so on.
   - ☐ Images taken with digital camera clear, appropriate size, and type. Images wrapped properly.
   - ☐ Colors used in newsletter are eye-catching.
   - ☐ No errors in the newsletter.
   - ☐ Appropriate template used.
   - ☐ Text boxes linked appropriately.
   - ☐ Creation and use of embellishment logo is appropriate.

ACTIVITY 4 • BUSINESS SETS

In this activity, you will become familiar with:

- Logos for Sets
- Business Card Template
- Letterhead Template
- Fax Transmittal Template

Logos for Sets

1. Use image management software to create three logos to submit to the owner for possible use in the business sets.
2. In your team assigned by your instructor, evaluate the logos using the following criteria:

Criteria	Excellent + 5 pts.	Good + 3 or 4 pts.	Needs Improvement + 1 or 2 pts.
Crispness			
Use of color			
Use of design elements			
Originality			
Logo sends appropriate message			
Size			
Balance and contrast			
Totals			

3. Each team member evaluates each logo on the criteria in step 2.
4. The logo with the highest total points from the team's evaluation is the logo that should be used.

Business Card Template

1. Open PageMaker.
2. In the Template dialog box, choose Business Cards from the drop-down Category list.
3. If the Template dialog box is not open, go to the menu bar and choose Window > Plug-in Palettes > Show Template Palette.

4. Click on the Template Information Rectangular frame and press Delete.
5. Using the information in the figure below, overtype the information on the first business card.

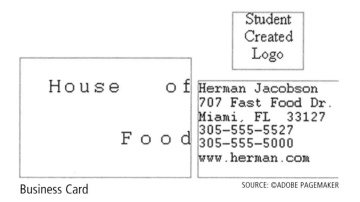

Business Card

SOURCE: ©ADOBE PAGEMAKER

6. In the "House of Food" rectangular frame, change the size of the type so that it fits as shown above.
7. In the rectangular frame with the business owner's name and address information, overtype Herman Jacobson's information. Resize the rectangular frame so that the lines do not wrap.
8. Insert your created logo for the business sets from your team project.
9. Use the Text tool to click inside the rectangular frame with the name of the fast-food restaurant.
10. Press Ctrl + A to select all the text in the frame. Press Ctrl + C or go to the menu bar and choose Edit > Copy to copy the text.
11. Go to the second business card in the top row.
12. Use the Text tool to click on the name of the fast-food restaurant.
13. Select all the text by pressing Ctrl + A.
14. Press Ctrl + V to paste the new text in the rectangular frame or go to the menu bar and choose Edit > Paste.
15. Go to each of the remaining business cards. Click inside the rectangular frame for the restaurant and paste in the new name.
16. Save as *HouseofFood.pmd*.
17. Repeat this procedure for the rectangular frame for the name and address information and the logo.
18. Save again.

Letterhead Template

1. Open PageMaker.
2. In the Template dialog box, choose Business Sets from the drop-down Category list.
3. Double-click on *2000702.PMT* to create the letterhead.
4. Using the Text tool, click on the Rectangular frame with the Company Name. Drag the top rectangular frame off to expose the shadowed Company Name underneath.
5. Go to the menu bar and choose Type > Define Styles.
6. In the Define Styles dialog box, scroll down to select Company Name—shadowed.
7. Click OK.
8. These were already done for you in the template, but you should be aware of the steps they took to create the shadow.
9. Select the shadowed text with the Text tool and overtype it with "House of Food."

10. Repeat the overtyping for the layer on top that is not shadowed.
11. Use the Pointer tool to click on the logo in the upper left corner and press Delete.
12. Click on the shadowed logo and press Delete.
13. Go to the menu bar and choose File > Place.
14. Browse to where you have saved your logo for this business and double-click to choose it.
15. Click on the area of the letterhead where you want to place the logo.
16. Use the Pointer tool to click on the rectangular frame with the address information in it. It is located in the footer area of the letterhead.
17. Go to the menu bar and choose View > Actual Size.
18. Click on the Text tool and overtype the information with the contact information for House of Food.
19. Save as *Letterhead.pmd*.

Fax Transmittal Template

1. Open PageMaker.
2. In the Template dialog box, choose Business Sets from the drop-down Category list.
3. Using the Pointer tool, click on *1000651.PMT* to create the fax transmittal.
4. Click on the logo and press Delete to remove it.
5. Go to the menu bar and choose File > Place. Browse to locate the logo you created.
6. Place it where the template logo was located.
7. Using the Text tool, click on the rectangular frame below the logo.
8. Select all the text and overtype the text with contact information for House of Food.
9. Save as *FaxTemplate.pmd*.

ACTIVITY 4 • MINI-PROJECT

Create a Business Set for a Job Interest

1. Go to http://www.monster.com. Find a company that you might be interested in working for. Follow the links to research the company. Write a summary of your research, answering such questions as:
   a. What is the purpose of the company?
   b. What are their goals?
   c. What is the history of the company?
   d. What is it about the company that gives you a positive image?
   Save the summary as *Monster.doc*.
2. Create a new logo for the company, using the information you have learned about the company as well as the original logo.
3. Use the logo you have created in creating business sets for this company.
4. Create a business card with your name as the person working for the company. Use the job title from the http://www.monster.com site.
   Save as *MyBusinessCard.pmd*.
5. Create a letterhead with your name as the person working for the company.
   Save as *MyLetterhead.pmd*.
6. Create a fax cover sheet with your name as the person working for the company.
   Save as *MyFax.pmd*.
7. The following criteria should be met:
   ☐ Logo reflects the type of business, with a sharp, clean look that will work well on all stationery.
   ☐ White space balanced.

☐ Font is appropriate size and type is eye-catching and readable.
☐ Logo placed and sized appropriately.
☐ Information on letterhead is on top 2 inches.
☐ Some creativity evident.
☐ No errors and verification of all phone numbers.

ACTIVITY 5 • CERTIFICATE

In this activity, you will become familiar with:

- Tall or Wide Publications
- Margins
- Acquire
- Rotate Tool
- Control Palette
- Paragraph Rules
- Rounded Corners
- Frame Options

Tall or Wide Publications

1. Open PageMaker.
2. In the Template dialog box, choose Certificates from the drop-down Category list.
3. Using the Pointer tool, click on *1000502.PMT* to create a certificate.
4. Go to the menu bar and choose File > Document Setup.
5. Change the document to Tall.
6. Click OK.
7. You will notice on your screen that this publication should not be Tall.
8. Go to the menu bar and choose File > Document Setup and change the publication back to Wide.

Margins

1. Go to the menu bar and choose File > Document Setup.
2. Change the margins to 1 inch all the way around (Left, Right, Top, Bottom).

Acquire

1. Locate a picture of your school mascot.
2. Place the picture on the scanner. (If you are using a stand-alone scanner, follow instructions given by your instructor to do the scanning.)
3. Go to the menu bar and choose File > Acquire > Select Source.
4. In the Select Source dialog box, choose the scanner you will use. Scan and save the image.
5. Resize the image to fit the area.

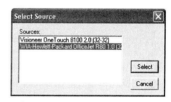

Select Source

SOURCE: ©ADOBE PAGEMAKER

Rotate Tool

1. Click on the Rotate tool.
2. The pointer turns into a starburst when hovered over the image. Click on the top right handle. Drag it out straight to form a handle to use to rotate.

Rotate Tool

SOURCE: ©ADOBE PAGEMAKER

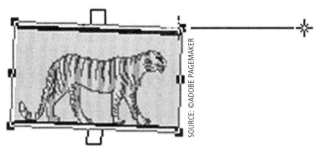
SOURCE: ©ADOBE PAGEMAKER

Starburst

3. Rotate the tiger image (or your school mascot image) slightly as shown above to form an uneven effect.
4. Click on the Pointer tool.
5. Go to the menu bar and choose Edit > Copy.
6. Go to the menu bar and choose Edit > Paste.
7. Drag the pasted image to the opposite side of the certificate.

Control Palette

1. Using the Pointer tool, click on the rectangular frame at the top of the certificate.
2. Select all the text and delete it.
3. If your Control Palette is not on the desktop, go to the menu bar and choose Window > Show Control Palette.
4. In the Control Palette, click on the "T" as shown below.
5. Change the font in the drop-down box to Bell MT.

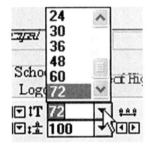

Font Size

SOURCE: ©ADOBE PAGEMAKER

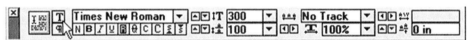

Control Palette

SOURCE: ©ADOBE PAGEMAKER

6. Change the size of the font to 72.
7. In the Color Control Palette, change the color tint to 100%.
8. Type "Desktop Publishing" in the rectangular frame.

Paragraph Rules

1. Using the Text tool, select "Desktop Publishing."
2. Go to the menu bar and choose Type > Paragraph.
3. In the Paragraph Specifications dialog box, click on the Rules icon.

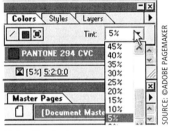

Color Control

SOURCE: ©ADOBE PAGEMAKER

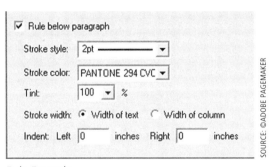

Rule Example

SOURCE: ©ADOBE PAGEMAKER

4. Select the "Rule below paragraph" check box and input the changes shown below.

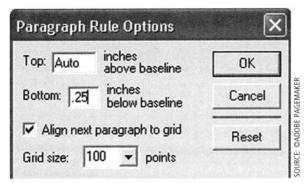

Rule Options

5. Click on the Options icon.
6. In the Paragraph Rule Options dialog box, type ".25" in the Bottom box.
7. Click OK in each of the three dialog boxes to close them.
8. In the rectangular frame beneath "Desktop Publishing," overtype with "Certificate."
9. In the rectangular frame beneath "Certificate," overtype with "of Achievement."

Rounded Corners

1. With the Pointer tool, click on the rectangular frame in the middle (it should have images on either side of it).
2. Go to the menu bar and choose Element > Rounded Corners.
3. In the Rounded Corners dialog box, choose the last choice in the second row.

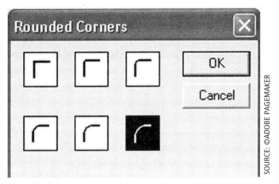

Rounded Corners.

4. Click OK.

Frame Options

1. Use the Pointer tool to click on the rectangular frame with the date in it.
2. Go to the menu bar and choose Element > Frame > Frame Options.
3. In the Frame Options dialog box, click in the Vertical alignment drop-down box, and select Center.
4. On the left signature block, overtype the text with the name of your principal.
5. On the right signature block, overtype the text with the name of your instructor.
6. Place the school logo below the signature blocks with the name of your high school in the rectangular frame next to the logo.

7. Save as *DPCertificate.pmd*.

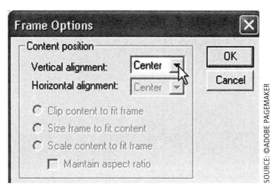

Frame Options

ACTIVITY 5 • MINI-PROJECT

Create a Certificate for Emotional Awareness Training

1. The company you are working for is hosting an Emotional Awareness workshop next Monday. The chief executive officer, Xavier Ramos, will sign the certificate, and so will the workshop presenter, Jenny Sanford.
2. Create and submit a certificate with your name as a participant to turn in to your supervisor for approval.
3. If paper is available, print the certificate on special paper before submitting to your supervisor (instructor) for approval.
4. Save the certificate as *EmotionalAwareness.pmd*.
5. The following criteria should be met:
   - ☐ Appropriate certificate template used.
   - ☐ Accurate information placed on the certificate.
   - ☐ Margins set appropriately to enhance the certificate.
   - ☐ Rotation tool used effectively.
   - ☐ Font size, type, color, and style are appropriate to produce a professional image.
   - ☐ Signature blocks contain the correct names with no errors.
   - ☐ No errors on the certificate.
   - ☐ Acquired picture is appropriate to the document. Minimum of one picture used.
   - ☐ Use of paragraph rules at least once.
   - ☐ Rounded Corner option on the rectangular frame used at least once.
   - ☐ Color and quality of paper professional.

ACTIVITY 6 • DESIGNING A NEWSLETTER

In this activity, you will become familiar with:

- ■ Rectangle Tool
- ■ Importing Colors
- ■ Color Libraries
- ■ Reverse Type
- ■ Column Guides
- ■ Insert Object
- ■ Polygon Settings

- Master Pages
- Text Flow
- Story Editor
- Table

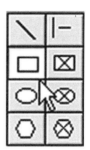

Rectangle Tool
SOURCE: ©ADOBE PAGEMAKER

Rectangle Tool

1. Open PageMaker. Accept all defaults in the Document Setup window by clicking OK.
2. Go to the menu bar and choose Layout > Insert Pages. Insert two pages after the current page.
3. In the toolbox, click on the Rectangle tool. This tool is used to draw rectangles when text is not needed within the rectangle.
4. Draw a rectangle across the entire horizontal margin width and down to 2 inches on the vertical ruler.

Importing Colors

1. Go to the menu bar and choose Window > Show Colors.
2. Click the right triangle as shown at right to access the Palette menu.
3. Choose Import Colors from the Palette menu.
4. Browse to your directory and double-click the *FreePizza.pmd* file.

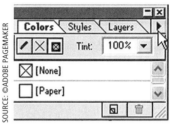

Palette Menu
SOURCE: ©ADOBE PAGEMAKER

Color Libraries

1. In the Color Palette, click the new color option to access the color libraries.
2. In the Color Options dialog box, click on the Libraries drop-down box and choose a library of colors to choose from. Scroll through the libraries and choose a library with a color you desire for your rectangle. Click OK.

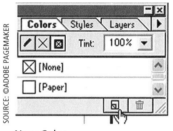

New Color
SOURCE: ©ADOBE PAGEMAKER

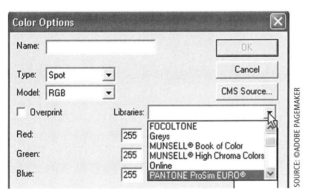

Color Options

SOURCE: ©ADOBE PAGEMAKER

3. In the Color Picker dialog box, choose a color for the rectangle by clicking on the color.
4. Click OK in both dialog boxes to get back to your newsletter.
5. Scroll down in the Color Palette window to select the color from the library and apply it by clicking on it.
6. Click on the Rectangular frame tool. Draw a rectangle overlapping the other rectangle. Begin at 1-1/2 inches on the horizontal ruler and snap to the right margin. Drag down to about 2-1/2 inches on the vertical ruler.
7. Click on Paper on the Color Palette to change the newly drawn rectangle to White.
8. Click on the text tool. Type "The Communicator" in the rectangular frame.
9. In the Control Palette, click on the Paragraph Specifications button.

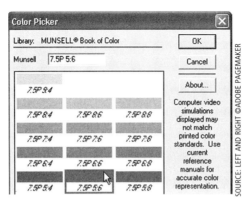

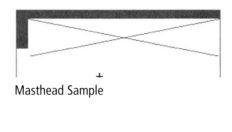

Masthead Sample

Color Picker

10. Click on the Style drop-down list and choose Headline.
11. Using the Text tool, select the text.
12. In the Color Palette, go to the Palette menu and select Color Options.
13. Choose a library and select a color to apply to the Heading.
14. Go to the menu bar and choose Type > Paragraph. Click on the Rules icon.
15. Select the "Rules below paragraph" check box and create a rule below. You decide on the Stroke style, Stroke color, and Tint.
16. Click OK for both dialog boxes to get back to your newsletter.
17. Save the newsletter as *TheCommunicator.pmd*.

Reverse Type

1. Use the Pointer tool to select the rectangular frame.
2. Fill it with a color.
3. Use the Text tool to select the text. In the Control Palette, click on the Reverse icon.
4. Use the text tool to determine a good place to type the other information for the masthead.
   a. Volume 1, Issue 1
   b. Current Date including Day of Week

Column Guides

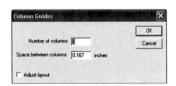

Column Guides

SOURCE: ©ADOBE PAGEMAKER

1. Go to the menu bar and choose Layout > Column Guides.
2. In the Column Guides dialog box, type 2 in the Number of columns box.
3. Use the Text tool to click at the top of the left column.
4. In the Control Palette, click on Paragraph Specifications.
5. In the drop-down list, change the style to Subheading 1.
6. Type "Logo Mania" for the subheading.
7. Use the Pointer tool to resize the text box as needed and drag it to an appropriate position.
8. Select the text and apply a color to the text.
9. Use the text tool to click below the subheading.
10. Click on Paragraph Specifications in the Control Palette and choose Body Text for the style.
11. Go to the menu bar and choose File > Place. Browse to your CD and double-click *Logo.doc*.
12. Place the text below the subheading.
13. Use the Text tool to click in front of the first letter of the body text.
14. Go to the menu bar and choose Utilities > Plug-ins > Drop cap.
15. In the Drop cap dialog box, click on Apply, then Close.
16. Use the Text tool to select the second paragraph only.

17. Go to the menu bar and choose Type > Indents/Tabs. Set a tab for .25. After applying the tab, press Tab to tab the first line.
18. Go to the menu bar and choose Type > Paragraph. Type ".1" in the Before box under Paragraph Spacing.
19. Using image management software and Microsoft Word, create WordArt for the title "Color Theory." Save it as a *ColorTheory.gif*.
20. On page 2 of the newsletter, draw a rectangular shape at the top 2 inches. Decide if you want to fill or stroke the shape and what colors to use.
21. Place the *ColorTheory.gif* image you created in the rectangular shape.

Insert Object

1. Go to the menu bar and choose Edit > Insert Object.
2. In the Insert Object dialog box, click Create from File and browse to your CD.

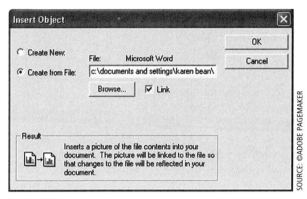

Insert Object

3. Select the Link check box in the Insert Object dialog box.
4. Double-click the file *ColorTheory.doc*.
5. Place the file underneath the title "Color Theory."
6. Using the Pointer tool, click and drag the object so that it is appropriately placed on the page.
7. Place at least one picture from the Picture Palette that sends a message about the article.
8. Save the newsletter again.

Polygon Settings

1. Go to the menu bar and choose Element > Polygon Settings.

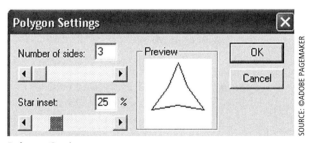

Polygon Settings

2. In the Polygon Settings dialog box, change the Number of sides to 3 and the Star inset to 25%.
3. Click in the Polygon tool in the toolbox and draw a polygon below the article about Logo Mania.
4. Using the Pointer tool, select the polygon.

5. Go to the menu bar and choose Element > Stroke > 8pt.
6. In the Color Palette, choose one of the colors used in the newsletter.
7. Using the Text tool, type above the polygon: "Logos can be as simple as an odd shape. The important thing is that they send out a positive message."
8. Choose a font type, size, and color for the text.
9. Using the Pointer tool, place the shape and the text box appropriately below the story about Logo Mania.

Master Pages

1. Click on the Master Pages icon in the status bar.
2. Using the text tool, click on the bottom of the first page.
3. Type "Page" and then press Ctrl + Alt + P. This inserts the page number command.
4. Select the text and use the Control Palette to format it. Change the text to Size 10 and centered.
5. Repeat this process on the Right Master page.

Text Flow

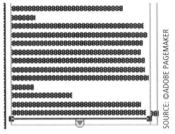

More Text

SOURCE: ©ADOBE PAGEMAKER

1. Click on the Pointer tool then click on the pasteboard.
2. Go to the menu bar and choose Type > Font > Arial.
3. Go to the menu bar and choose Type > Size > 12.
4. Go to the menu bar and choose Type > Type Style > Normal.
5. Go to the menu bar and choose File > Place. Browse to your CD, locate *CommunicationTypes.txt*, and double-click on it to open the file.
6. Place the file on the left column. Notice that the bottom of the column has a Red icon, indicating that there is more text.
7. Click on the Red icon at the bottom of the column to pick up more text.
8. Place the text at the top of the next column. Repeat this procedure until there is no more text remaining to place.
9. You can also turn on autoflow if you know you want to place the text from one column to the next without skipping columns. Go to the menu bar and choose Layout > Autoflow to turn on autoflow.

Story Editor

1. Click on the last page of the story.
2. Go to the menu bar and choose Edit > Edit Story.
3. Delete the last four lines of the story that have question marks in front of them.
4. Close the Story Editor by clicking on the X in the top right corner. This saves the story and takes you back to your newsletter.
5. Go through the story and make formatting changes as needed. These changes would include bold, italic, tabs or indents, and paragraph spacing.
6. Save the newsletter again.
7. On the first page, the second column needs a story about logos.
8. Go to the Internet and search for logos of some of your favorite businesses.
9. Write an article describing these logos and the message that they send to you. You may include information on slogans or mission statements if you wish. Include at least one image that has text wrapped around it within the article.

Table

1. Open Adobe Table 3.0.
2. In the New Table dialog box, create a table with 5 rows and 3 columns.
3. Click OK.
4. Place the mouse pointer on the vertical line between columns.

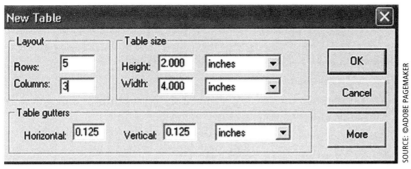

New Table

5. Click and drag to resize the columns. The last two columns should be 1 inch wide and the right margin should be at 5 inches.
6. Input the table information from the figure below.

Criteria	Points Possible	Points Earned
Colors are appropriate.	20	
Text formatting is appropriate.	20	
Images and graphics are appropriate and sized and placed in a way that enhances the newsletter.	20	
Article on logos is thorough and contains all required elements.	20	
Article wrtten by student is free of grammatical and spelling errors.	20	

Table Info

7. In the Text Attributes Palette, format the first row for bold and centered horizontally.
8. Save the table as *Rubric.tbl.*
9. Close the table.
10. Open Adobe PageMaker.
11. With your pointer on the last page of the newsletter, go to the menu bar and choose Edit > Insert Object.
12. Click Create from File and link. Browse to your saved *Rubric.tbl* file and double-click the file.
13. Using the pointer tool, resize the table across both columns right above the page number on page 4.
14. Add a title of "Rubric for the Newsletter."
15. Add an image from the Picture Palette to fill the space on this page. Be sure it is appropriate for the page content.
16. Save the newsletter again.

ACTIVITY 6 • MINI-PROJECT

Create a Newsletter for Another Course

1. Ask one of your teachers in another discipline (Art, History, Science, Math) for lecture notes on an upcoming unit. Organize the lecture notes into newsletter format for a handout to students. If the teacher has a timeline for due dates on activities, tests, or other reminders that they would like to include then place those in the newsletter as well. If not, use important facts, terms, and so on to enhance the newsletter. You may scan pictures from the textbook, but only for learning purposes in preparing this newsletter.

2. An alternative to this newsletter would be to plan the teaching of a chapter on your own. Choose one of your courses, pick a chapter from the book, and summarize the material in the chapter in newsletter format.

3. You can choose to input the text for your articles directly into the newsletter or in word processing software and import them. If you use word processing software, you should decide on the file names when you save them. However, you should demonstrate the ability to use the Story Editor in PageMaker at least once.

4. The following criteria should be met:
   - ☐ Imported colors appropriate for the newsletter topic.
   - ☐ Use of rectangle frames and enhancement of the frames is appropriate.
   - ☐ Minimum of two columns.
   - ☐ Effective use of Polygon tool.
   - ☐ Page numbers inserted into Master Pages appropriately.
   - ☐ Text flow from one column to another is appropriate.
   - ☐ Minimum use of Story Editor one time.
   - ☐ Minimum use of Adobe Table 3.0 one time.
   - ☐ Newsletter contained no errors.
   - ☐ Images were appropriate type, size, and placement.
   - ☐ Masthead contains required information and is eye-catching.

PART 2 • SIMULATION

Using PageMaker to Create Marketing Solutions for Hotel Services

1. With a partner, create marketing solutions for the following hotel:
   Razma Hotel Suites, Inc.
   12 Hotel Lane
   Dallas, TX 76541
   214/555-1078
   214/555-1079 (fax)
   www.razma.com
   email: Hank@razma.com

2. Your job as the multimedia specialist for the hotel includes marketing hotel services.

3. Your current task is to prepare all documents and handouts that guests will find in their room. You may want to visit the Web sites of some hotels to get ideas on what can go in the room or request some samples from a local hotel.

4. Create a folder titled *Razma*. Include the following saved items in the folder:
   a. Hotel stationery. Save as *Stationery.pmd*.
   b. Menu and price list for room service. Save as *Menu.pmd*.
   c. Item and price list for courtesy items (bottled water, candy bars, sodas). Save as *CourtesyItems.pmd*.
   d. Design for notepad and pen. Save as *Designs.pmd*.
   e. Information about using phone and phone numbers. Save as *Phones.pmd*.
   f. Brochure advertising the hotel. (Pick a hotel in your area and use its Web site for the project. Continue to use the name, address, and phone numbers for the hotel in this project.) Save as *Brochure.pmd*.
   g. Newsletter about the area. This hotel is located near the Galleria in Dallas, Texas. Research using the Internet to compile information about the area, sites to see, weather conditions, and so on. Save as *Newsletter.pmd*.
   h. Flyer for the back of the door with the rules of the hotel, check-in time, and check-out time. Your team should create at least six rules. Save as *Rules.pmd*.
   i. Flyer advertising the business center's services. (copying, printing from a disk, faxing, typing services). Include the prices for the services. Save as *BusinessCenter.pmd*.
   j. Flyer advertising other amenities such as swimming pool, spa, and exercise room. Include hours of operation. Save as *Recreation.pmd*.
5. The following criteria should be met:
   - [ ] Flyers display a professional image of the hotel.
   - [ ] Prices and menu items are logical and well thought out for the menu and the courtesy list.
   - [ ] Design for notepad, pen, and hotel stationery give a positive image.
   - [ ] Information about using phone and phone numbers is accurate.
   - [ ] Brochure is colorful, eye-catching, informative, and arranged in an organized way.
   - [ ] Newsletter contains interesting articles and appropriate images.
   - [ ] No errors on any of the documents.
   - [ ] Partners worked well together. Evidence that work was completed equally.

Part 3

QuarkXPress

> **QuarkXPress**
> **Publisher: Quark Technology Partnership**
> QuarkXPress is high-end desktop publishing software used extensively for publishing books and other documents in the publishing industry.

ACTIVITY 1 • FLYER

In this activity, you will become familiar with:

- Document Setup for Flyers
- Publication Window
  - Document
  - Rulers
- Preferences
- Tools Palette
- Item Tool
- Content Tool
- Text Box Tool
- Styling Text
- Resizing Text Boxes
- Background Color
- Moving Text Boxes
- Zoom Tool
- Undo
- Frame
- Picture Box Tool
- Rotation Tool
- Color Palette
- Character Attributes
- Setting Formats
- Hyperlinking
- Changing Shapes

Document Setup for Flyers

1. Go to the menu bar and choose File > New > Document.
2. In the New Document dialog box, you can adjust the page size and orientation, column guides, and margin guides. For this activity, accept the defaults by clicking OK.
3. Go to the menu bar and choose File > Document Setup. Note that in the Document Setup dialog box, you can change some of the same things as in the New Document dialog box. Click Cancel to make no changes.

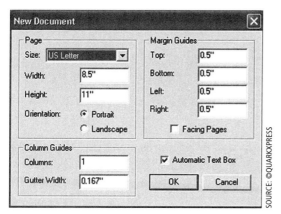

New Document

Publication Window

Document
1. The document opens in Actual Size view. Go to the menu bar and choose View > Fit in Window.
2. The blue box around the inside of the document is the guides that represent the margins. These can be toggled off by going to the menu bar and choosing View > Hide Guides. Toggle them back on by choosing View > Show Guides.

Rulers
1. Go to the menu bar and choose View > Hide Rulers. You can toggle them back on by choosing View > Show Rulers.
2. Click in the Ruler Origin box. This is the area where the horizontal and vertical rulers intersect.
3. Hold down the left mouse button and drag the crosshairs so that the vertical and horizontal rulers are set on zero at the margin guides.

Preferences

1. Go to the menu bar and choose Edit > Preferences > Preferences.
2. Note that there are Application and Document Preferences.
3. In the Preferences dialog box, click on Display under Application Preferences.
4. Change the guide colors for the margin, ruler, and grid. Adjust these colors to your personal preferences.
5. Choose View > Show Baseline Grids. Note that the color is your choice.
6. Choose View > Hide Baseline Grids.

Tools Palette

1. The Tools palette should be on your document window. If it is not, go to the menu bar and choose View > Show Tools. You can also press F8 to toggle the Tools palette on and off.
2. The Tools palette shown to the right is vertical. If you want to change the orientation of the Tools palette to horizontal, press the Ctrl key and double-click the title bar of the palette.
3. Go to the menu bar and choose Help > Help Topics.
4. Click on the Index tab. Type "Tools palette" in the box. Double-click Tool overview.
5. Read the overview of all the tools in the palette.

Document Setup

Ruler Origin Box

SOURCE: ©QUARKXPRESS

Tools Palette

SOURCE: ©QUARKXPRESS

Item Tool

SOURCE: ©QUARKXPRESS

Content Tool

SOURCE: ©QUARKXPRESS

Item Tool

1. Click on the Item tool.
2. The Item tool is used to select, move, resize, and reshape items such as boxes, lines, text paths, and groups.

Content Tool

1. Click on the Content tool.
2. The Content tool imports and edits text and pictures, and repeats some of the same tasks as the Item tool.

Text Box Tool

1. Click on the Text Box tool. Hold down the mouse button on the icon to see all the choices.

SOURCE: ©QUARKXPRESS

Text Box Tools

2. The Text Box tool creates rectangular text boxes as well as other shapes of text boxes.
3. Click on the Text Box tool and use the default rectangle shape.
4. Click on the upper left corner of the margin guides. Drag to draw a rectangular box across the entire horizontal margin and down to 2 inches on the vertical ruler.
5. Click on the Content tool.
6. Type "SAT Prep Classes." You may want to go to the menu bar and choose View > 75% so you can see the letters.
7. Use the Content tool to select the text.

Styling Text

1. Go to the menu bar and choose Style > Size > 60.
2. Go to the menu bar and choose Style > Font. Choose an appropriate font to get someone's attention.
3. Go to the menu bar and choose Style > Alignment > Centered.
4. Go to the menu bar and choose Style > Color > Red.

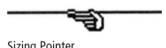

Sizing Pointer

SOURCE: ©QUARKXPRESS

Resizing Text Boxes

1. Click on the Content tool or the Item tool.
2. Hover the mouse pointer on one of the handles of the text box. The Sizing pointer appears.
3. Hold down the mouse button and drag the box up to resize it appropriately for the text inside.

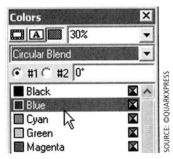

Color Palette

Background Color

1. With the text box selected, click on Blue on the Color palette.
2. Click on the Shading drop-down box and choose 30%.
3. Click on the Color Blend drop-down box and choose Circular Blend.

4. Note that in the Color Blend Box, you can choose a second color. Choose a second color. Leave the Color Blend angle at 0 degrees.

Moving Text Boxes

1. Click on the Item tool then click on the text box.
2. Drag the text box down to the middle of the document.
3. Resize the text box so that the text is on two different lines.
4. Resize the text box back to fit horizontally across the entire document.
5. Move the text box back to the top of the document, snapping it to the top margin.
6. The text box should now be back in its original position and size.

Zoom Tool

1. Click on the Zoom tool.
2. The Zoom tool magnifies your document in 25% increments each time you click on the document.
3. You can also zoom in or out by going to the menu bar and choosing View. The first six options on the menu are for changing the view size of your document.
4. You can also change the view by clicking on the percentage in the status bar at the lower left corner of your screen.
5. Change the zoom in tool to zoom out by holding down the Alt key while clicking the zoom tool.

Zoom Tool
SOURCE: ©QUARKXPRESS

Undo

1. Go to the menu bar and choose Edit > Undo.
2. This action will undo the last action taken.
3. Go to the menu bar and choose Edit > Redo.
4. Redo only remembers your last action.

Frame

1. Use the Item or Content tool to click on the rectangular box.
2. Go to the menu bar and choose Item > Frame.
3. In the Modify dialog box, click on the drop-down box for Width and choose 4 pt.

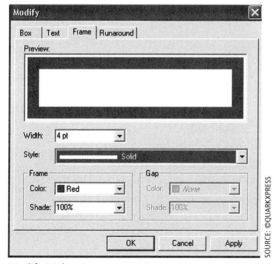

Modify Dialog Box

4. In the Frame section in the Modify dialog box, click the drop-down Color box and choose Red. Click on Apply and OK.
5. Go to the menu bar and choose File > Save As. Name the file *SATPrepFlyer.qxd*.

Picture Box Tool

1. Click on the Picture Box tool. Hold down the mouse button on the icon to see all the choices. Select the beveled-corner Picture Box tool.

SOURCE: ©QUARKXPRESS

Picture Box Tools

Sample Picture Box
SOURCE: ©QUARKXPRESS

2. Click on the document underneath the rectangle with the title in it. Drag the mouse pointer out to 4 inches on the horizontal ruler and 4 inches down on the vertical ruler.
3. Go to the menu bar and choose File > Get Picture.
4. Browse in your collection of clip art and select a picture of food.
5. Use the Content tool to move the picture up toward the top left side of the picture box to make room for a text box. See the Sample Picture Box.
6. Click on the Text Box tool and choose the rounded-corner Text Box tool.
7. Use the Content tool to type "Lunch Served at Noon."
8. Go to the menu bar and choose Style > Size. Change the size to an appropriate size for the area.
9. Go to the menu bar and choose Style > Type Style > Bold.
10. Go to the menu bar and choose Style > Alignment > Centered.

Rotation Tool
SOURCE: ©QUARKXPRESS

Rotation Tool

1. Click on the Rotation tool.
2. The Rotation tool rotates items manually.
3. Hold the Rotation tool down in the middle of the text box. When it turns into the cursor seen in the figure to the left, drag the box to the angle you desire.

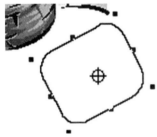

Rotation Cursor
SOURCE: ©QUARKXPRESS

Color Palette

1. Click on the Background Color icon in the Color palette.
2. Choose Red for the background color.
3. Click on the Text Color icon in the Color palette.
4. Change the text color to White.
5. Draw a rectangular text box on the right side of the picture box. Fill the area left on the right side with the box.
6. Type the following in the rectangular text box:
   Saturday
   February 23, 2XXX
   8 A.M. to 4 P.M.
   Cost: $20.00

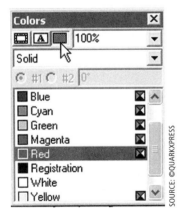

Background Color

Character Attributes

1. Use the Content tool to select the text you typed in the rectangular text box.
2. Go to the menu bar and choose Style > Character. Note that "Character" has an ellipsis after the word, which means that a dialog box will be available to make

changes. You can make these changes individually on the Style menu, but by opening the Character Attributes dialog box, you can make several changes to fonts at one time.

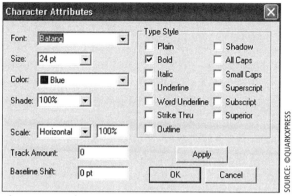

Character Attributes

3. Change the font to Batang, the size to 24 pt. and the color to Blue.
4. Change the type style to Bold. Click on Apply and OK.
5. Go to the menu bar and choose Style > Alignment > Centered.
6. Go to the menu bar and choose Item > Frame.
7. In the Modify dialog box, change the width to 2 pt and the frame color to Red.
8. Click on Apply and OK.

Setting Formats

1. Click on the Text Box tool and choose Rectangle.
2. Draw a rectangular text box from the left to the right margin and from 4 inches to 7 inches vertically.
3. Type the following in the rectangular text box:
   NOTES:
   Get plenty of rest before the class.
   Eat a good breakfast.
   Bring pens, highlighters, and paper.
   Dress comfortably.
4. Select the text and change the size to 28 pt. and the color to Blue.
5. Go to the menu bar and choose Style > Tabs.
6. In the Paragraph Attributes dialog box, choose the Left tab, type ".5" for Position, and click on Set. Click on Apply and OK.
7. With the Content tool, select the NOTES line and the first enumeration.

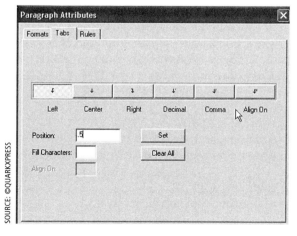

Paragraph Attributes

8. Go to the menu bar and choose Style > Formats. In the Space Before box, type ".25."
9. Click on Apply and OK.
10. In the Color palette, click on Background Color.
11. Choose Red at 10% shading.

Hyperlinking

1. At the left below the rectangular text box with the Notes in it, draw a rounded-corner text box. It should snap to the bottom margin and be drawn to 4-1/2 inches on the horizontal ruler.
2. Type the following information in the box:
   Your High School Name
   City, State Zip
   Your School Phone Number, including Zip Code
   For More Information:
   www.kaplan.com
3. Use the Content tool to select the text.
4. Go to the menu bar and choose Style > Character. Choose Comic Sans MS, Size 24, 70% shaded Blue. Click on Apply and OK.
5. Go to the menu bar and choose Style > Alignment > Centered.
6. Select the word "Information," including the colon. Change the font color to Red.
7. Select the Web address for Kaplan Test Prep.
8. Go to the menu bar and choose Style > Hyperlink > New.
9. In the New Hyperlink dialog box, type in the following URL: http://www.kaplan.com.

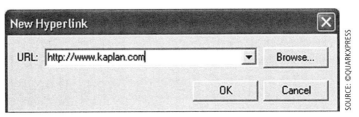

New Hyperlink

10. Go to the menu bar and choose Item > Frame. Change the frame to 2 pt. with Red as the color.
11. Move the text box as needed within the area.

Changing Shapes

1. Click on the text box tool.
2. Draw a rectangular text box in the area in the lower right.
3. Use the Item tool to click on the text box. Go to the menu bar and choose Item > Shape > Concave-Corner Text Box. This is how you can change the shape of the picture or text box after it is already drawn.
4. Type the following in the box:
   Presented by
   Kaplan Inc.
5. Decide on an appropriate font, font size, and style of font.
6. With the text selected, go to the menu bar and choose Style > Alignment > Centered.
7. Determine a frame width and color and apply it.
8. Make any formatting changes to improve the look of the flyer.
9. Save the document.

ACTIVITY 1 • MINI-PROJECT

Create a Flyer for a Newspaper Advertisement

1. Use the skills you learned in creating a flyer to create a flyer that can be used in a newspaper advertisement.
2. Go to http://www.graphicsetc.net. Click on Flyer Samples. There are six examples of excellent flyers used in advertising situations. Choose one of the flyers. Print it out to use the information on the flyer. Re-create the flyer. It does not have to be exact, but it should be close. Use your own images from clip art or the Internet, or use scanned or digital images. If the Web site is no longer available, go to a search engine and search for "Sample Flyers." Get the flyer approved by your instructor before beginning.
3. Save the flyer as *Advertisement.qxd*.
4. The following criteria should be met:
   - ☐ Replication of sample flyer demonstrated attention to detail.
   - ☐ No errors on flyer.
   - ☐ Colors are close or follow design rules.
   - ☐ Font choices create a similar image to the original flyer and are sized appropriately.
   - ☐ Images of good quality with correct size and type.
   - ☐ Effort demonstrated on the flyer.
   - ☐ Flyer effects a positive image.

ACTIVITY 2 • BROCHURE

In this activity, you will become familiar with:

- Document Setup for Brochures
- Inserting Pages
- Deleting Pages
- Resizing Pictures
- Get Text
- Drop Cap
- Line Tool
- Bring Forward
- Changing Pages
- Line Text-Path Tool

Document Setup for Brochures

1. Go to the menu bar and choose File > New > Document.
2. In the New Document dialog box, change Orientation to Landscape and Column Guides to 3.
3. Click on Facing Pages.
4. Clear the Automatic Text Box check box. This box can be used to fill the entire page with color if desired, but you will not be using it. You can easily delete this box using the Item tool if you decide after the Document Setup that you do not need it.
5. Click OK.
6. Go to the menu bar and choose View > Fit in Window.

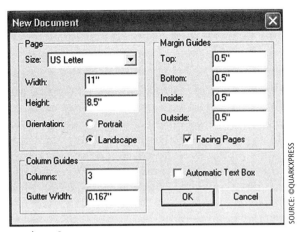

Brochure Specs

Inserting Pages

1. Go to the menu bar and choose Page > Insert.
2. In the Insert Pages dialog box, type "2" in the box for the number of pages to insert.

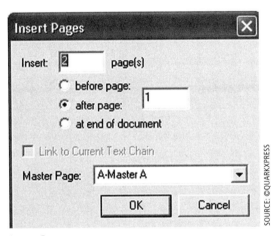

Insert Pages

3. Do not make any other changes to the other defaults. Click OK.

Deleting Pages

1. Go to the menu bar and choose Page > Delete.
2. In the Delete Pages dialog box, type "3" in the box for the page number to delete.

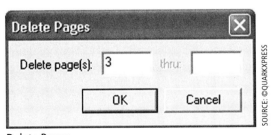

Delete Pages.

3. Click OK.

Resizing Pictures

1. Click in the Ruler Origin area and drag the crosshairs so that the horizontal and vertical rulers are both on 0 at the top and left margin guides.
2. Click on the Picture Box tool.
3. At the top half of the third column, draw a picture box.
4. Begin at 7-1/2 inches on the horizontal ruler and drag over to approximately 9-1/2 inches. On the vertical ruler, begin at 1 inch and drag down to approximately 2-1/2 inches.
5. Go to the menu bar and choose File > Get Picture.
6. Browse to the CD and double-click on *WaterLily.jpg*.
7. Go to the menu bar and choose Style > Center Picture.
8. Go to the menu bar and choose Style > Fit Picture to Box.
9. Drag on the bottom right handle to decrease the size of the box. Notice that the image does not resize with the box. Click Undo.
10. Hover the mouse pointer over the bottom right handle. Hold down the Ctrl key. Drag to increase the size of the picture box. Notice that holding down the Ctrl key also increases the size of the picture with the box.
11. Resize the picture box appropriately for the area at the top of the front page of the brochure.
12. Use the Item tool to reposition. Reminder: The Item tool moves the box, whereas the Content tool moves the picture inside the box.
13. With the picture box selected, go to the menu bar and choose Item > Shape. Select the circular shape.
14. Save the brochure as *Quark.qxd*.
15. Create a text box with the text "Quark, Inc." inside it.
16. Fill the text box with yellow, Linear Blend.
17. Change the font size, color, and type.
18. Change the alignment to Centered for the text.
19. Rotate the text box and place it on the right edge of the water lily image.
20. Add a text frame to the text box that is the same color as the text.

Get Text

1. Use the Rectangular text box tool to draw a text box beginning at 4 inches on the vertical ruler. Snap the text box to the bottom margin.
2. Use the Content tool to click inside the box.
3. Go to the menu bar and choose File > Get Text.
4. Browse to your CD to get *WaterLily.doc*.
5. Select the text that you imported.
6. Change the font type.

Drop Cap

1. Go to the menu bar and choose Style > Formats.
2. In the Paragraph Attributes dialog box, click on drop caps.
3. Leave the Character Count at 1. Change the Line Count to 2.
4. Go to the Internet and search for articles on water lilies. Add two more sentences to the article on water lilies that tie in with the positive image this company has created.
5. You can add another image of a water lily from your available clip art or the Internet if appropriate.

Line Tool

1. Draw a rectangular text box in the first column. Snap the rectangular box to all the margins.

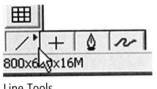

Line Tools

2. Fill the entire text box with Yellow, shaded at 20%.
3. Type "History" at the top of the rectangular box. Format "History" in Size 36 font.
4. Change the font color to Pink.
5. Change the alignment to Centered.
6. Click on the Line tool.
7. Draw a line below the title from the left margin to the right margin.
8. With the line still selected, go to the menu bar and choose Style > Line Style. Change the line style to Thin-Thick.
9. Go to the menu bar and choose Style > Line Style. Change the width to 4 pt.
10. Go to the menu bar and choose Style > Color > Magenta.

Bring Forward

1. With the line selected, go to the menu bar and choose Item > Bring Forward.
2. Use the Content tool to click in the area below the line.
3. Go to the menu bar and choose File > Get Text. Browse to your CD and locate *History.txt*.
4. Change the font color to Blue and the font size to 12 and choose a font type.
5. Select all the text and change the after paragraph spacing to .125 and the first line indent to .25.
6. Save the file.

Changing Pages

1. On the status bar at the bottom left of the Quark screen, click on the right arrow next to the page number box.
2. You should see three pages. The left page with the "A" on it represents the Master Page. Click on the page with the number 2 on it.

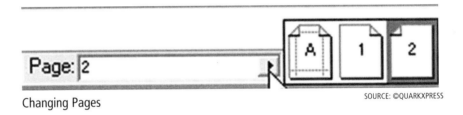

Changing Pages

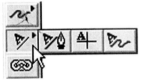

Line Text-Path Tools

Line Text-Path Tool

1. Click on the Line Text-Path tool.
2. Draw a line at an angle across the middle column at the bottom half of the column.
3. Type "Be a Star!" on the line.
4. Format the text size, color, and font type.
5. Go to the menu bar and choose Style > Width. Change the width to 4 pt.
6. Go to the menu bar and choose Style > Color. Change the color of the line.
7. Draw a picture box near the angled line.
8. Get the picture *Star.gif* from your CD.
9. With the picture selected, go to the menu bar and choose Style > Fit Picture to Box.
10. Use the Line Text-Path tool to add a straight line below the picture. Hold down the Shift key while drawing the line to get a perfectly straight line.
11. Type the text "Join the Quark Team!" on the line.
12. Format the text as appropriate.

Star

13. In the left column, draw a text box and type the title "Getting Hired." Format the font appropriately for color, size, and type. Center the title horizontally.
14. Draw a text box down to 5 inches on the vertical ruler. Snap the text box to the right margin of the column.
15. Go to the Quark Web site at http://www.quark.com. Write an article in the text box answering these questions:

    What are the hiring policies of Quark?
    What does it take to advance at Quark?
16. At the bottom of this column, add a digital picture of someone at your school working.
17. In the middle column, add a text box and title it "Dress Code Policy." Write an article explaining the Quark dress code policy.
18. In the third column, draw a text box in the entire column. Title the article "Building a Work Team."
19. Write an article explaining the following:

    Name at least three things that Quark believes are important to building a successful team.
    Describe some other company policies that help to build the team.
    Hint: These specifically revolve around food.
20. Change font types, color, and size as appropriate. Use alignment, fill color, and box color to enhance the brochure.
21. Save the document.

ACTIVITY 2 • MINI-PROJECT

Create a Brochure to Sell a Multimedia Book

1. You are an employee of South-Western Publishing Company, the publisher of your textbook. Create a brochure to assist in selling the textbook to teachers. Plan the brochure before beginning. Include as a minimum the following details:
   a. Name of textbook
   b. Authors
   c. Publication date
   d. Listing of units covered
   e. Special features in the textbook
   f. Overall mission statement of what the book is attempting to accomplish
2. Include scanned pictures from the textbook.
3. Save as *MultimediaText.qxd*.
4. The following criteria should be met:

   ☐ Minimum details required are included.
   ☐ Information displayed on the brochure in an organized manner.
   ☐ Colors appropriate and used effectively.
   ☐ Images appropriate size and type and of good quality.
   ☐ Fonts varied and appropriate type, size, and color.
   ☐ Minimum of one stacked text box and/or picture box with use of Bring Forward.
   ☐ Minimum of one use of Line tool.
   ☐ Minimum of one use of Line Text-Path tool.
   ☐ No errors on the brochure.

ACTIVITY 3 • NEWSLETTER

In this activity, you will become familiar with:

- Document Setup for Newsletters
- Creating Style Sheets
- Scissors Tool
- Tabs
- New Colors
- Linking Text Boxes
- Freehand Line Tool
- Rules
- Cutting and Pasting Text
- Runaround
- Anchor
- Spelling
- H&Js
- Master Pages
- Tables
- Bullets

Document Setup for Newsletters

1. Go to the menu bar and choose File > New.
2. In the New Document dialog box, change to portrait orientation, clear the Facing Pages check box, select the Automatic Text Box check box, and type 2 in the number of columns box.
3. Click OK.
4. Go to the menu bar and choose View > Fit in Window.
5. Drag the Ruler Origin crosshairs to 0.
6. Save the document as *XPert Publishing.qxd*.

Creating Style Sheets

1. Go to the menu bar and choose Edit > Style Sheets.
2. In the Style Sheets for *XPert Publishing.qxd* dialog box, click on New, then Character.

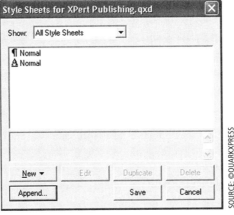

Style Sheets

SOURCE: ©QUARKXPRESS

Font: Bauhaus 93
Size: 60 pt
Color: Cyan

Masthead
SOURCE: ©QUARKXPRESS

3. Make the changes in character style seen in the figure to the left. Name the style "Masthead." You do not need to type anything in Keyboard Equivalent.

4. Click on Save.
5. Use the Rounded-Corner Text Box tool to draw a Text Box across the top margin from left to right and down to 1-1/4 inches on the vertical ruler.
6. Type "XPert Publishing" in the text box.
7. Use the Content tool to select the text.
8. Go to the menu bar and choose Style > Character Style Sheet > Masthead.

Scissors Tool

1. Click on the Scissors tool.
2. Use the Scissors tool to click on the top left corner of the rectangular text box. You will get the warning seen below.

Scissors Tool

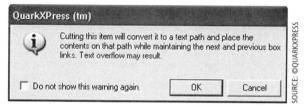

Scissors Warning

3. Click OK.
4. Use the Item tool to click on the bottom part of the rectangular text box and press Delete to remove it. See below for an example of your finished masthead. It does not have to look exactly like the figure.

XPert Masthead

5. Format the line for 2 pt width, cyan color.

Tabs

1. Use the Rounded Rectangular Text Box tool to draw a rounded-corner picture box about 1/2-inch long. The width should extend from the left to the right margin.
2. Use the Content tool to click within the rounded-corner picture box.
3. Go to the menu bar and choose Style > Tabs.
4. In the Paragraph Attributes dialog box, click on Right and type in the position 7.0.

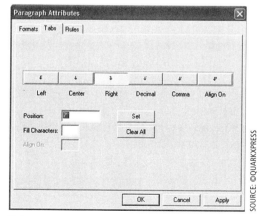

Tabs

5. Click on Set.
6. In the rounded-corner picture box, type at the left margin "Volume 1, Issue 1."
7. Press the Tab key once. Type the current date.
8. Use the Content tool to select the text you typed and change the font to Batang or a similar font.

New Colors

1. Go to the menu bar and choose Item > Frame.
2. Change the width to 2 pt.
3. Click in the Color drop-down list and choose Other.
4. In the New Color dialog box, type "Purple" for the name and choose a purple color from the color wheel.

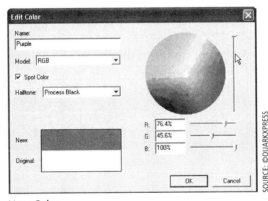

New Color

5. Click OK.
6. Draw a rounded-rectangle text box to place behind the company name.
7. Use the new color Purple for the background at 30% shading.
8. Add a 2 pt cyan border to the rounded-rectangle text box.
9. Go to the menu bar and choose Item > Send Backward.
10. Save the document.

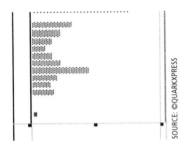

More Text

Linking Text Boxes

1. Use the Rectangular Text Box tool to draw a text box in the first column. Draw a second text Box in the second column.
2. Click on the Content tool.
3. Choose File > Get Text.
4. Browse to your CD and double-click on *Typefaces.doc*.
5. Note that at the bottom of the first column, the red box appears indicating more text that did not fit in that column. See the figure labeled More Text.
6. Click on the Linking tool.
7. Click anywhere in the first column to establish the beginning link.
8. Click anywhere in the second column to link to the first column.
9. Click in front of Typeface and type a title. Use your creativity to come up with a title for the first four paragraphs of this article.
10. Change the font to a sans serif font, Size 18. Center the text horizontally. Change the color to one of the two colors used in the masthead.

Linking Tool

Freehand Line Tool

1. Click on the Freehand Line tool.
2. Draw a squiggly line from the left to right margin underneath the title you created.

Free Hand Line Tool

3. Choose Style > Color and choose one of the two colors that were used in the masthead.
4. Use the Content tool to click in front of the "T" in "Typeface."
5. Go to the menu bar and choose Style > Formats. Set a drop cap for the first paragraph.
6. Select the "T" in "Typefaces" and change the font to a fancy font.
7. Use the Content tool to click in front of "Size of your font . . . "
8. Use your creativity to come up with a title for the rest of the paragraphs in the article.
9. Change the font to a sans serif font, Size 18. Use a color to offset the colors already used on the page.

Rules

1. With your cursor at the end of the title you created, go to the menu bar and choose Style > Rules.
2. Click on Rule Below.
3. Change the width to 2 pt. and choose a color.

Cutting and Pasting Text

1. Select the third paragraph of the article.
2. Go to the menu bar and choose Edit > Cut.
3. Click on the Concave-Corner Text Box tool.
4. Draw a concave-corner text box from the right margin to the left margin, about 2 inches high.
5. With the Content tool inside the text box, go to the menu bar and choose Edit > Paste.
6. Resize the text box as needed.
7. Change the style of the frame to All Dots, 4 pt. width.
8. Decide on a fill color. Shade to 30%.

Runaround

1. Go to the menu bar and choose Item > Runaround.
2. In the Modify dialog box, click the Runaround tab.

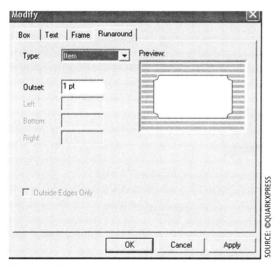

Runaround

3. In this case, the runaround has defaulted to wrapping the text around the box. Even though you have made no changes, click OK.

Anchor

1. Use the Item tool to click on the freehand line you drew in column 1.
2. Go to the menu bar and choose Style > Anchor.
3. Click on New.

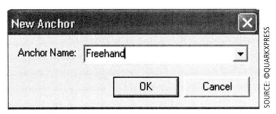

New Anchor

4. In the New Anchor dialog box, type in the name "Freehand" and click OK.
5. Change the first line indent on all paragraphs to .25.

Spelling

1. Go to the menu bar and choose Utilities > Check Spelling > Document.

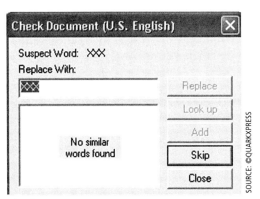

Check Document

2. In the Check Document dialog box, verify any words that were suspect. Make changes as needed.

H&Js

1. Go to the menu bar and choose Edit > H&Js. (Hyphenation and Justification)
2. In the H&Js dialog box, double-click on Standard.

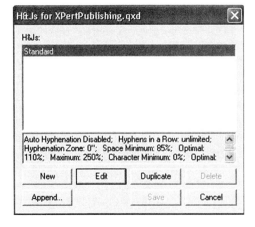

H&Js

SOURCE: ©QUARKXPRESS

3. In the Edit Hyphenation dialog box, clear the Auto Hyphenation check box. Note the other choices in the dialog box for future use.

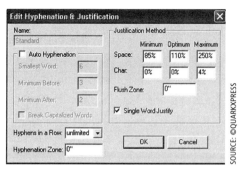

Edit Hyphenation

4. Click OK.
5. In the H&Js dialog box, click on Save to make the hyphenation change to your document.
6. Save the document.

Master Pages

1. Use the Item tool to select the rounded-corner rectangle text box with the volume, issue, and date information in it.
2. Copy the rectangular text box.
3. Click on the Master Pages by going to the status bar and clicking on the drop-down arrow next to the page number.
4. Paste the rectangle on the Master Page, then drag the rectangle to snap it to the top margin.
5. You may need to delete the automatic text boxes before pasting.
6. Go to page 2 of the document. Note that the element you placed on the Master Page is now on page 2 of the document. It will also appear on any subsequent pages you add. Add a page to try it. Delete the extra page.

Tables

1. Go to page 2 of the document.
2. Click on the Tables tool.
3. Draw a table that almost touches the left and the right margin and goes down 2 inches vertically.
4. In the Table Properties dialog box, type "6" for Rows and "6" for Columns.
5. Click OK.
6. Select the entire table by clicking and dragging the mouse.
7. Change alignment to Centered and size of the font to 18.
8. With Caps Lock on, type the following letters one per table cell:

   F O N T S P
   A G A E D O
   C O L O R I
   E X T P O N
   S A N S P T
   S E R I F X

Tables Tool
SOURCE: ©QUARKXPRESS

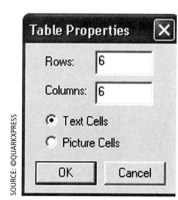

Table Properties

Bullets

1. Create a rectangular text box below the table you created.
2. Type in the text box: "Find the following words in the word search above:"

3. Go to the menu bar and choose Style > Tabs.
4. In the Paragraph Attributes dialog box, click in the Position box and type ".25," then click on Set. Be sure the Left button is clicked so that you are setting a Left Tab.
5. Type "1.75" in the Position box and click on Set.
6. Type "2.0" in the Position box and click on Set.
7. To create a bullet, hold down the Alt and Shift keys and press 8. Press Tab before typing "Fonts."
8. Press Tab again to 1.75. Hold down the Alt and Shift keys and press 8. Tab again to 2.0. Type "Color."
9. Hold down the Alt and Shift keys and press 8. Type "Serif." Tab to 1.75. Hold down the Alt and Shift keys and press 8. Tab to 2.0. Type "Faces."
10. Repeat this process to add "Sans" and "Point" with bullets in front of them.
11. Create a table with picture cells. The table should have one row and three columns.
12. Place a digital picture of yourself and two friends in each of the cells in the top row.
13. Below the table, draw another table that is the same size and specifications. This one should be for text.
14. Type the student names in the new table. Format the student names as needed.
15. Underneath the table, draw a line text path across from the left to the right margin.
16. Type on the text path: "Desktop Publishing Team."
17. Format the text, making effective choices for a headline.
18. Go to the Internet and search for "QuarkXPress tips" or "desktop publishing tips."
19. Complete the second column of the newsletter with articles or lists of tips. The following elements should be met:
    ☐ Headline in correct font and size with appropriate color.
    ☐ Minimum of two text boxes, appropriately placed and sized, one shaded in color.
    ☐ Minimum of two picture boxes; appropriate images, size, and placement.
    ☐ Bulleted list.
    ☐ Drop cap with fancy font.
    ☐ Minimum of one rule, either above or below.
    ☐ Minimum of one color change with appropriate color.
    ☐ Error-free.
    ☐ Design pleasing to the eye.
    ☐ No hyphenation.
    ☐ Freehand Line tool used with change in line width and color.

ACTIVITY 3 • MINI-PROJECT

Create a Newsletter on the Smithsonian Institution

1. Visit the Smithsonian Institution Web site at http://www.si.edu. Peruse the Web site, taking notes on announcements. You could also use an electronic encyclopedia to do research on the Smithsonian or visit a library. Organize your notes on 3 × 5 or 4 × 6 index cards that will be turned in to your instructor as part of the project. Decide on a longer article that can be written and two short articles. Be sure to explore the links to gather your information.
2. Use the Smithsonian logo on the newsletter. You may need to save the file from the Internet, then open it in your image management software and use your image management skills to make it appropriate for placement on your newsletter. Save as *SmithsonionLogo.gif*.

3. Study the image that the Web site has created for the Smithsonian Institution. Attempt to create a similar image for continuity.
4. Save as *SmithsonianNews.qxd*.
5. The following criteria should be met:
   - ☐ Index cards are organized and demonstrate evidence of note-taking that was used in the creation of the newsletter.
   - ☐ Colors appropriate for the topic.
   - ☐ Fonts appropriate in size, type, and color.
   - ☐ Images of quality and appropriate in size and type.
   - ☐ Logo altered effectively for this newsletter.
   - ☐ Creation of a style sheet.
   - ☐ Minimum of one use of Scissors tool.
   - ☐ New color added from color wheel.
   - ☐ Minimum of one use of linked text box.
   - ☐ Minimum of one use of Freehand Line tool.
   - ☐ Minimum of one use of rule above or below paragraph.
   - ☐ Minimum of one use of runaround.
   - ☐ Minimum of one use of bullets.
   - ☐ Minimum of one use of table.
   - ☐ No errors on newsletter.

ACTIVITY 4 • BUSINESS SETS

In this activity, you will become familiar with:

- ■ Document Setup for Letterhead Templates
- ■ Show Invisibles
- ■ Color Wheel
- ■ Grouping
- ■ Fit to Print Area
- ■ Document Setup for Fax Transmittal Templates
- ■ All Caps

Document Setup for Letterhead Templates

1. Create a new document with the following attributes: portrait orientation, one column, non-facing pages, and no automatic text box. All other elements in the New Document dialog box should not be changed.
2. Drag the Ruler Origin crosshairs to 0 inches.
3. Draw a rectangular text box from the left to the right margin and down vertically to 1 inch.
4. Draw a rectangular picture box in the left corner of the rectangular text box. It should be approximately 1-1/4 inches wide.
5. Go to the menu bar and choose File > Get Picture. Browse to your CD and double-click *MAC.gif*.
6. Resize the picture box to fit the logo.
7. While holding down the Ctrl key, resize the text box to fit the rectangular text box vertically and horizontally. It should be approximately 1-1/2 inches.
8. Go to the menu bar and choose Item > Frame.
9. In the Modify dialog box, on the Frame tab, change the width to 4 pt. and choose a frame color of Cyan.
10. Beginning at 1-1/2 inches horizontally, draw a rectangular text box almost to the right margin. Snap to the bottom margin.

Show Invisibles

1. Go to the menu bar and choose View > Show Invisibles. It sometimes helps to see the hard returns and tab codes. In the figure below, can you identify the paragraph code? The tab code?
2. Input the information for the first three lines (company name; street address; city, state, and zip) into the rectangular text box from the figure below.

512.555.1200→   Medical·Administration·Corporation¶
                 1200·Medical·Way¶
                 San·Antonio,·TX··79737¶
                 512.555.2100·(fax)→   www.mac.com¶

Invisibles

SOURCE: ©QUARKXPRESS

3. Select the three lines and go to the menu bar and choose Style > Alignment > Centered.
4. For the fourth line (telephone numbers and Web address), go to the menu bar and choose Style > Tabs.
5. On the tab ruler in the rectangular text box, set a center tab and a right tab. Determine the best place to set the center tab. Set the right tab as close to the right end of the ruler as possible.
6. Input the fourth line of the company information.
7. Select the four lines of text and change the font size to 12 and the color to Cyan.
8. With the rectangular text box selected, go to Item > Frame. Change the width to 4 pt. and choose Other for the color.

Color Wheel

1. Use the color wheel to select a color that is close to the fuchsia color on the logo.
2. Drag the slider until you get a close color match to your document.

Grouping

1. Click on the first text box, hold down the Shift key, and click on the picture box. Continue holding down the Shift key while selecting the other text box. When all three are selected, go to the menu bar and choose Item > Group.
2. Drag the entire group above the right margin. The top of the group should begin at approximately .75 on the vertical ruler.
3. Go to the bottom of the document.
4. Draw a rectangular text box at the bottom margin. It should go from the left to the right margin horizontally and about 1/2-inch on the vertical ruler.
5. Set a center tab and a right tab at the right margin.
6. Type the following names. Begin at the left margin but tab after each name.
   Madison Matilla, M.D.
   Ivan Abercrombie, Ph.D.
   Carlos Collier, M.D.
7. Select the three names. Change the color to cyan and italicize the font.
8. Use the Line Text-Path tool to draw a line from the left to the right margin above the names.
9. Change the line width to 4 pt. and the color to the new color you chose from the color wheel.
10. Group the text box and the line.
11. Drag the entire group down below the bottom margin. The line should snap to the bottom margin guide.

12. Go to the menu bar and chose File > Save As. In the Save as dialog box, click in the drop-down box for Save as type and choose Template (.qxt).

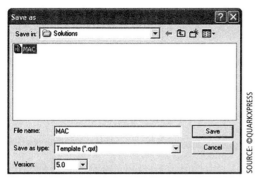

Save As Template

13. In the File name box, type "MAC."
14. Click on Save.

Fit to Print Area

1. Go to the menu bar and choose File > Print.
2. In the Print dialog box, on the Setup tab, select the Fit in Print Area check box.

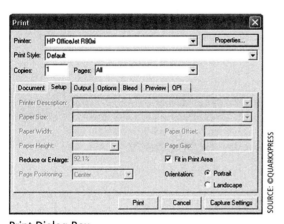

Print Dialog Box

3. Get printing instructions from your instructor.

Document Setup for Fax Transmittal Templates

1. Open *MAC.qxt*.
2. Save it as *FAX.qxd*.
3. Draw a rectangular text box below the heading on the template. The text box should be approximately 1/4-inch from all margins.
4. Type "FAX" at the top left corner in the rectangular text box.
5. Select the word "FAX" and change the font to Berlin Sans, Size 60.
6. Immediately after the "X" in "FAX," change the font size to 14 and press Enter.
7. Type "To:" Use an underscore to type a line to approximately 3-1/2 inches on the ruler.
8. Tab so that there is at least one space between the underscore and the next word.
9. Type "From:" Type the underscore to the margin. Be sure it does not scroll to the next line. Erase any characters that scroll to the next line.

10. Repeat this process for the next line, typing the words "Fax:" and "Pages (including cover)."
11. Repeat this process on the third line, typing the words "Fax Number" and "Date."
12. Select the three lines. Go to the menu bar and choose Style > Formats.
13. On the Formats tab in the Paragraph dialog box, type ".1" in the Space Before and Space After blanks.
14. On the next line, type "Confidentiality Notice." Bold, italicize, and center the text.
15. Type the following paragraph in italic but not bold:

The information contained in this fax may be confidential or privileged. This fax is intended to be reviewed initially only by the individual named above. If the reader of this transmittal page is not the intended recipient or a representative of the intended recipient, you are hereby notified that any review, dissemination, or copying of this fax or the information contained herein is prohibited. If you have received this fax in error, please immediately notify the sender by telephone and return this fax to the sender at the above address. Thank you.

16. Type the word "Comments" a double space below the end of the preceding paragraph.
17. Select the rectangular text box and add a 2 pt. thick-thin-thick frame to it.
18. Go to the menu bar and choose Utilities > Check Spelling > Document. Replace any misspelled words. Verify all names.
19. Select the word "To:"

All Caps

1. Go to the menu bar and choose Styles > Type Style > All Caps. Repeat this process for the next five captions.
2. Save the document as *FAX.qxt*.

ACTIVITY 4 • MINI-PROJECT

Create a Template for School Stationery

1. Visit with your instructor or principal to get the following information:
   a. Official school logo
   b. Mission statement or slogan
   c. Copy of official school letterhead and fax cover sheet
   d. Address, phone number, fax number, Web address, and email address for the school. Find out what the principal wants included on his or her business card.
2. Design a business card for the principal using the school logo and all other information necessary for a business card. Save as *Principal.qxd*.
3. Design school letterhead. Save as *SchoolLetter.qxt*. Notice that it is being saved as a template.
4. Design a fax cover sheet. Save as *SchoolFax.qxt*. Notice that it is being saved as a template.
5. The three designed pieces in a set should include the following criteria:
   ☐ Continuity of logo, slogan, and theme on all designs.
   ☐ No errors on any design.
   ☐ Images appropriate in type, size, and placement.
   ☐ Color appropriate to school colors.
   ☐ Fonts appropriate in size, type, and color.
   ☐ Creativity demonstrated in creation of letterhead.
   ☐ Fax cover sheet is realistic in terms of cost and expense of printing.
   ☐ White space balanced on all designed pieces.

ACTIVITY 5 • CREATING A BOOK

In this activity, you will become familiar with:

- Setting Up a Document for a Book
- Page Numbering
- Find/Change
- New Book
- Add Chapter
- Book Palette
- Synchronizing Styles

Setting Up a Document for a Book

1. Go to the menu bar and choose File > New > Document.
2. In the New Document dialog box, set up the document for portrait orientation, one column, facing pages, and automatic text box. Click OK.
3. Go to the status bar and click in the drop-down box. Choose the Master Document. You can also view the Master Document by going to the menu bar and choosing Page > Display > Master Document.
4. Create a rectangular text box in the top left corner. Type "Good Attitudes."
5. Go back to the document by going to the status bar and clicking on the drop-down arrow. Choose page 1.
6. Click inside the automatic text box on page 1. Use the shortcut Ctrl + Shift + C to center the line.
7. Type "Chapter 1."
8. Change the font to Size 16. Choose a sans serif font.
9. Before returning to the next line, change the font size to 14.
10. Press Enter twice. Type "Perseverance."
11. Press Enter twice. Use Ctrl + L to place your cursor at the left margin.
12. Go to the menu bar and choose File > Get Text.
13. Browse to your CD and double-click *Perseverance.doc*.

Page Numbering

1. Go to the menu bar and choose Page > Section.
2. In the Section dialog box, accept the default. You can also change the numbering to start on each section by clicking on Section Start check box.
3. Click OK.

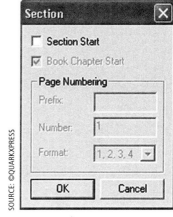

Page Numbering

Find/Change

1. Go to the top of your document by pressing Ctrl + Home.
2. Go to the menu bar and choose Edit > Find/Change.
3. In the Find/Change dialog box, click in the Find What box and type "replace."

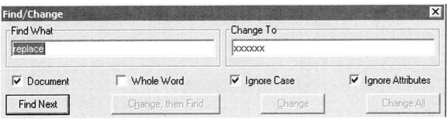

Find/Change

4. Click in the Change To box and type "xxxxxxx."
5. Click the Find Next button.

6. The cursor should stop on the first occurrence, allowing you to Change, then Find; Change, or Change All.
7. Choose Change then Find to check each occurrence.
8. When you have reached the end of the document, click on the document, then press Ctrl + Home to return to the top of the document.
9. In the Find What box, type "Find." Do not make a change in the Change To box.
10. Click on Find Next and change each occurrence as necessary in the document.
11. Save the document as *Chapter1.qxd*.

New Book

1. Go to the menu bar and choose File > New > Book.
2. In the New Book dialog box, type "Good Attitudes." Click on Create.

Add Chapter

Add Chapter

SOURCE: ©QUARKXPRESS

1. In the Good Attitudes dialog box, click on the Add Chapter icon.
2. Browse to your CD to find Chapter 1 and double-click on it. The first chapter always has an M beside it, as it is considered the Master Chapter.
3. Go to the menu bar and choose File > New > Document. Click OK to accept the defaults.
4. Click inside the automatic text box.
5. Type "Chapter 2" in Size 16 aligned at the center.
6. Press Enter twice. Type "Enjoy Life" in size 14 aligned at the center.
7. Press Enter twice. Go to the menu bar and choose File > Get Text.

Book Palette

1. Browse to your CD and double-click *EnjoyLife.doc*.
2. At this point, the Book palette should still be floating in your document window. If it is not, it means the book is closed. Closing the Book palette will also close all open documents that have been added to the book.
3. Follow steps 3 through 7 in the "Add Chapter" section, and replace Chapter Numbers and Chapter Names with the following:

Chapter3 *BeAccountable.doc*
Chapter4 *HelpOthers.doc*
Chapter5 Think of your own good attitude for this chapter.
          Insert the file *Think.doc*.
Chapter6 Think of one more good attitude for this last chapter.
          Insert the file *OneMore.doc*.

When you have finished, you should have six chapters added to the Book palette. See below.

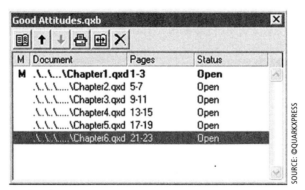

Book Palette

4. Once you have named the book, the book will automatically save changes.
5. Go to the menu bar and choose Edit > Style Sheets.
6. In the Style Sheets dialog box, click on New. Choose Paragraph Style Sheet on the pop-up menu.
7. In the Edit Paragraph Style Sheet dialog box, click on the General tab.
8. Name the style sheet Book, based on Normal.
9. In the Edit Paragraph Style Sheet dialog box, in the Character Attributes section, click on New.
10. In the Edit Character Style Sheet dialog box, name the style sheet "Book." Change the font to Times New Roman, 11 pt. See below.

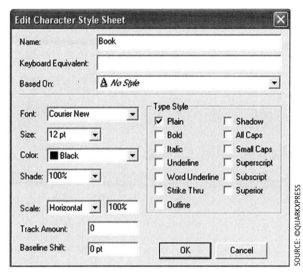

Style Sheet

11. Click OK.
12. In the Edit Paragraph Style Sheet dialog box, click on the Formats tab.

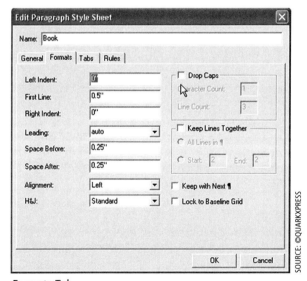

Formats Tab

13. Change the First Line indent to .5 inches.
14. Change the Space Before and Space After to .25 inches. Be sure the Alignment is on Left.
15. Click OK in the Edit Paragraph Style Sheet dialog box.
16. Click Save.

Synchronizing Styles

Synchronize

SOURCE: ©QUARKXPRESS

1. On your Book palette, click on Chapter 1. Hold down the Shift key and click on Chapter 6. This should highlight (select) all the units in the book.
2. Click on the Synchronize button on the Book palette. In the Synchronize Selected Chapters dialog box, click on Title and Subtitle.
3. Click on the right arrow for each of them to move them to the right pane.
4. Click OK.
5. Save the changes to your document by going to the menu bar and choosing File > Save.

ACTIVITY 5 • MINI-PROJECT

Create a Literary Magazine as a Class Project

1. Divide into four teams. If the class is larger than 20, you can add a fifth team. Decide on another section in the literary magazine for the fifth team.
   a. Poetry
   b. Short Stories
   c. Songs
   d. Art
2. In your team, brainstorm and submit a name to your instructor for the literary magazine. Submit the name with an appropriate font in a word processing program or image management software. Be creative! Save as *MagazineName* in the software you chose. The final name can be voted on by the class. As a class, decide on colors to use.
3. In your team, create a logo to use on the front cover of the literary magazine. Submit to your instructor. Create the logo in image management software and save as *MagazineLogo*. The logo can be evaluated by an advisory board, principals, or other group of school employees to determine which one will be used on the cover.
4. Within your team, each team member should be responsible for bringing to class five original pieces of art in the team's assigned area. For instance, the Poetry team will bring in five pieces of poetry. The poetry can be written by the student or a friend or relative. If students wish to, they can work with their English instructor to get some from an English class. It is recommended that the Short Story team bring in only two short stories each, depending on their length.
5. The team should create a division cover and save it as *DivisionCover.qxd*.
6. Each team will elect a leader from their team to report to the class and instructor on their progress and activities.
7. The team should create a Productivity Form that will keep a record of the date, assigned task, and team member completing the task. Each team should save their part of the book as the chapter number. Chapter 1 is Poetry; Chapter 2 is Short Stories; Chapter 3 is Songs; Chapter 4 is Art.
8. Each team will obtain the other chapters from the other teams. They will build the book with all four chapters in it and an index with a title page and cover pages for each chapter. Each team should be responsible for creating five copies of the book and binding it.

9. Save the final copy of the literary magazine as *ClassProject.qxd*.
10. The following criteria should be met:
   - ☐ Teams worked productively with all members contributing.
   - ☐ No errors on the copy of the magazine.
   - ☐ Work finished in a timely manner.
   - ☐ Appropriate colors used.
   - ☐ Appropriate fonts in style, size, and type used.
   - ☐ Images appropriate in size, color, and type.
   - ☐ Final product was put together correctly, organized, and bound.

PART 3 • SIMULATION

Using Quark to Market an Aquarium Business

1. John Wally is opening an aquarium business next month. It will be located at 3005 Aquarium Blvd., Corpus Christi, TX 78404. The phone number is 512/555-7708 and the fax number is 512/555-8077. They do not currently have a Web site, but there are plans for one in the immediate future. The Aquarium Center, Inc., will sell fish and tanks as well as all the accessories.

2. You decide to apply for a job as the marketing director and get the job. Your first assignment is to complete the following tasks:

   a. Create a flyer announcing the grand opening. It is the first Saturday in June. Mr. Wally has given you a $100 budget to offer door prizes or free give-aways. You need to decide on what you will do with the $100. Create a folder titled *Aquarium*. Save the grand opening flyer in the *Aquarium* folder as *GrandOpening.qxd*.

   b. Create a brochure to assist in marketing the new business. You may want to visit a fish store before beginning the brochure to get some prices and types of equipment and fish you will keep in your store. Some of the information you can get from the Internet by searching for goldfish, tropical fish, aquar-iums, and so on. Use a variety of sources for your information on the brochure. Interview or email someone who is in the business. Prepare a list of questions prior to the interview about how this person has marketed his or her business. Obtain a copy of anything he or she has used to develop a business image. Save the brochure in the *Aquarium* folder as *Brochure.qxd*.

   c. Create a business card, letterhead, and fax cover sheet. Design a logo to place on these business sets. Save in the *Aquarium* folder as *BusinessCard.qxd*, *Letterhead.qxt*, and *FaxCover.qxt*.

   d. Create a newsletter full of fun facts about fish. Research on the Internet, in an electronic encyclopedia, or at your library to obtain facts. You can also include some interesting fish stories. This newsletter should be geared toward the younger population as they will frequent the store. Include at least one word search puzzle created in a table with different names of fish. Save in the *Aquarium* folder as *FunFacts.qxd*.

   e. Build a book of at least four chapters and ten pages in length. The chapters can include Diseases of Fish, Types of Fish, Filtration Systems, and Tropical Fish Aquariums. You are not limited to these four; they are only sugges-tions for your chapters. You could also research four different types of fish and write a chapter on each type of fish you researched. Save the book in the *Aquarium* folder as *Book.qxd*.

   f. Create a tabloid-size poster to place on the door advertising some specials. Save in the *Aquarium* folder as *Specials.qxd*.

g. Create an advertisement for the local newspaper announcing the grand opening as well as some specials. Save in the *Aquarium* folder as *Ad.qxd*.
3. The following criteria should be met:
   ☐ All nine items saved correctly in the *Aquarium* folder.
   ☐ An effective business image created throughout the simulation.
   ☐ Colors appropriate and used throughout the simulation.
   ☐ Appropriate fonts in size, type, and style applied to all documents.
   ☐ Images creative and taken from a variety of sources.
   ☐ White space balanced and effectively used on all documents.
   ☐ Projects show some initiative and effective use of most tools learned in Quark.
   ☐ Documents are error-free.
   ☐ Information on aquariums is accurate and shows evidence of research.

Adobe Acrobat

Adobe Acrobat
Publisher: Adobe Systems Incorporated
Adobe Acrobat converts documents created in many popular applications to PDF files so that they can be read on any workstation, even though that workstation may not have the software used to create the original document. These documents can be uploaded to a Web site and retain the look of the original document. PDF documents can be used interactively and sent electronically.

ACTIVITY 1 • SCANNING

In this activity, you will become familiar with:

- Importing as a Scan
- Cropping the Image
- Saving a PDF File

Importing as a Scan

1. Open Adobe Acrobat.
2. Open Word. Browse to your CD and double-click *OutstandingTeacher.doc*.
3. Print the *OutstandingTeacher.doc* file.
4. Place the hard copy of *OutstandingTeacher.doc* on your scanner. Be sure the glass is clean.
5. Go to your menu bar and choose File > Import > Scan.
6. In the Acrobat Scan Plug-in dialog box, be sure that the device you are using is in the drop-down box and the format is single-sided.

SOURCE: ©ADOBE ACROBAT

Acrobat Scan

7. Click on Scan.

8. In the Scan dialog box, choose the paper source you are using from the drop-down box.

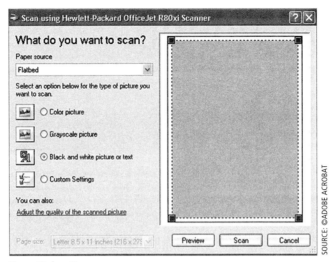

Scan Dialog Box

9. Click the radio button for Black and white picture or text.
10. Click on Scan.
11. There is only one page, so in the Acrobat Scan Plug-in dialog box, click on Done.

Done

Cropping the Image

1. Click on the Crop Tool.
2. Drag the mouse pointer carefully around the words on the page to crop out any excess white paper. Crop off the last paragraph of the scan by right-clicking on the document after having selected the part you want left in.
3. Click on the Crop Tool again and click OK in the dialog box.
4. In the Crop Pages dialog box, accept all the defaults and click OK.

Crop Tool

SOURCE: ©ADOBE ACROBAT

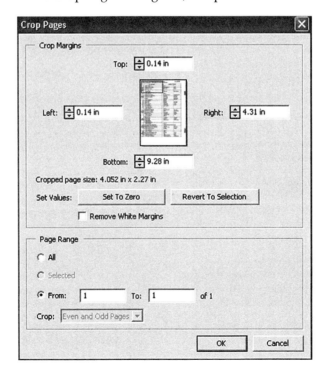

Crop Pages

SOURCE: ©ADOBE ACROBAT

Saving a PDF File

1. Go to the menu bar and choose File > Save As.
2. In the Save as dialog box, name the file *TBTEA.pdf*. The file type should already be PDF.

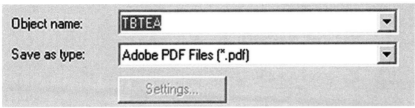

Save As

SOURCE: ©ADOBE ACROBAT

ACTIVITY 1 • MINI-PROJECT

Create a Scanned Certificate in PDF Format

1. Print a copy of *EmotionalAwareness.pmd*.
2. Scan the certificate using Adobe Acrobat. The certificate may later be used as part of an online portfolio.
3. Save as *ScannedCertificate.pdf*.
4. The following criteria should be met:
   - ☐ Glass was clean on the scanner. Certificate was straight when placed on glass in scanner.
   - ☐ Proper procedures evident in scanning the certificate.
   - ☐ Quality of scanned certificate is excellent.
   - ☐ Scanned certificate cropped as needed.
   - ☐ Certificate saved with name requested and no spelling errors.

ACTIVITY 2 • CREATING PDF DOCUMENTS FROM WORD

In this activity, you will become familiar with:

- Creating and Saving as PDF
- Opening in Adobe Acrobat
- Note Tool
- Stamp Tool
- Document Summary

Create PDF
SOURCE: ©ADOBE ACROBAT

Creating and Saving as PDF

1. Open Word then go to the menu bar and choose File > Open. Browse to your CD and double-click *Typefaces.doc*.
2. Click on the Create Adobe PDF icon.
3. In the Save PDF file As dialog box, choose a folder to save the file in. (You may want to create a folder for PDF files.)
4. In the File name box, type "Typefaces." Notice that the Save as type is PDF files.
5. Click on Save.

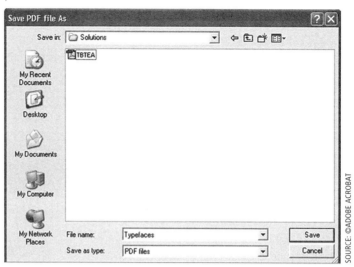

PDF Word

Opening in Adobe Acrobat

1. Open Adobe Acrobat.
2. Go to the menu bar and choose File > Open. Browse to your folder and double-click on *Typefaces.pdf*.

Note Tool

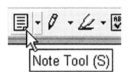

Note Tool

SOURCE: ©ADOBE ACROBAT

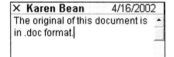

Note

SOURCE: ©ADOBE ACROBAT

1. Click on the Note Tool.
2. Click in front of the first word of the document with your Note Tool cursor.
3. In the Note pop-up, type "The original of this document is in .doc format."
   See the figure labeled Note.
4. Collapse the note by clicking on the X on the left side of the title bar.
   An icon appears acting as a place marker for the note.
5. Double-click on the icon to open the note. Collapse the note again.
6. If you want to remove the note from the document, click on the icon once to select it and press Delete.
7. Resize the note window to fit the text by clicking and dragging the note from the right corner.
8. Save again.

Stamp Tool

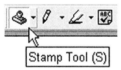

Stamp Tool

SOURCE: ©ADOBE ACROBAT

1. Click on the arrow next to the Note Tool icon on your toolbar.
2. Choose Stamp Tool.
3. Click your Stamp cursor in the middle of the document.
4. Right-click on the "Approved" stamp and choose Properties. See the bottom left figure.
5. Scroll down the list and choose Departmental.

Stamp Properties

SOURCE: ©ADOBE ACROBAT

Document Summary

1. Choose File > Document Properties > Summary.
2. Check out the file size.

ACTIVITY 2 • MINI-PROJECT

Create a PDF File on Facts about Adobe Acrobat

1. Open Word (or other word processing software) and create an enumerated list of facts you know about Adobe Acrobat. Prepare the list in proper format with a title. There should be six facts. If you need more facts, go to http://www.adobe .com and follow the links to Adobe Acrobat. Save as *AcrobatFacts.doc*.
2. Create a PDF file from the *AcrobatFacts.doc*.
3. Use the Note Tool to create a note next to the fact that you think is the most important. In the note, type "Most Important Fact."
4. Use the Stamp Tool to place an appropriate stamp on the document.
5. Save the file as *FactsAcrobat.pdf*.
6. The following criteria should be met:
   ☐ Facts list accurate and thorough.
   ☐ Facts list prepared in proper format for enumerations.
   ☐ Facts list has no errors.
   ☐ Document saved with correct name and no errors in file name.
   ☐ Note Tool used as instructed.
   ☐ Stamp Tool used as instructed.
   ☐ Final PDF file is a good, clean copy cropped as needed and saved with no errors in the file name.

ACTIVITY 3 • CREATING PDF DOCUMENTS FROM PUBLISHER

In this activity, you will become familiar with:

- Converting to PDF
- Zooming In or Out
- TouchUp Text Tool
- Square Tool
- Highlight Tool
- Save As

Converting to PDF

1. Open Publisher.
2. Go to the files on your CD and open *RiverEnd.pub*.
3. Go to the menu bar and choose File > Print.

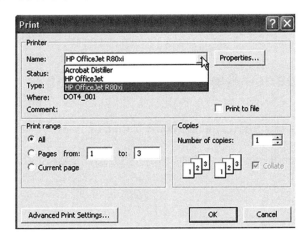

Print

SOURCE: ©ADOBE ACROBAT

4. In the Print dialog box, click the arrow next to the Name box and choose Acrobat Distiller.
5. Click OK.
6. The file will automatically open on your screen in Adobe Acrobat for editing and/or saving.

Zooming In or Out

1. On the standard toolbar, there are several options for changing View size. See below.

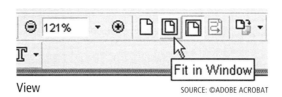

View

SOURCE: ©ADOBE ACROBAT

2. Click on Fit in Window. Note that you can also change the view size by clicking on the Zoom In or Out icon or typing in the percentage you want.
3. Change the view back to Actual Size.

TouchUp Text Tool

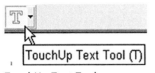

TouchUp Text Tool

SOURCE: ©ADOBE ACROBAT

1. Click on the TouchUp Text Tool.
2. Within the masthead, click on the line with the current date.
3. Change the month to the next month. For instance, if it is April on the masthead, then change it to May.

Square Tool

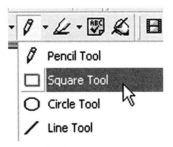

Square Tool

SOURCE: ©ADOBE ACROBAT

1. Click on the arrow next to the Pencil Tool and select the Square Tool.
2. Draw a square around the volume, issue, and date information in the masthead.

Highlight Tool

1. Click on the Highlight Tool.
2. Click inside the square you drew and drag to highlight the text.

Highlight Tool

SOURCE: ©ADOBE ACROBAT

Save As

1. Go to the menu bar and choose File > Save as.
2. Be sure you are saving in the correct folder.
3. Name the object *RiverEnd.pdf*.

ACTIVITY 3 • MINI-PROJECT

Create a Business Expense Report in PDF Format Using Publisher

1. Open Publisher and create a business expense report from a template. You may choose which template to use.
2. Change all necessary information on the template to the following company:
   Richlawn Medical Services
   2323 Oaklawn Drive

Odessa, TX 79761
915/555-1110
915/555-1000 (fax)

3. Save the file as *Richlawn.pub*.
4. Create a PDF file from *Richlawn.pub*. Save it as *Lawnrich.pdf*.
5. On the PDF file, use the TouchUp Text Tool to change the street address name to 2424 Lawnoak Drive.
6. Use the Square Tool and Highlight Tool to highlight the company name in one place on the business form.
7. Save the file as *EditedLawnrich.pdf*.
8. The following criteria should be met:
   - ☐ Appropriate template used.
   - ☐ All information in template changed that needed to be changed.
   - ☐ Document saved with appropriate file name and no errors in the file name.
   - ☐ TouchUp Text Tool used as requested.
   - ☐ Square Tool and Highlight Tool used as requested.
   - ☐ Saved both PDF files as requested with no spelling errors in the file names.
   - ☐ Final edited copy of PDF file was a clean copy with necessary cropping.

ACTIVITY 4 • CREATING PDF DOCUMENTS FROM PAGEMAKER

In this activity, you will become familiar with:

■ Exporting to PDF
■ Digital Signatures

Exporting to PDF

1. Open PageMaker.
2. Browse to your CD and double-click *DPCertificate.pmd*.
3. Go to the menu bar and choose File > Export > Adobe PDF.
4. In the PDF dialog box, click on Export. Note all the options available in this dialog box.

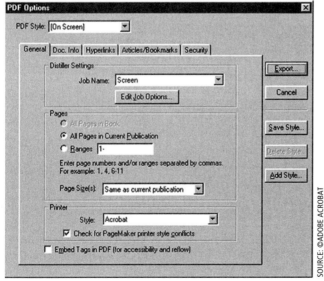

PDF Options

5. In the Export PDF As dialog box, click on the drop-down arrow in the Save in box. Browse to the folder to place your document in the folder.

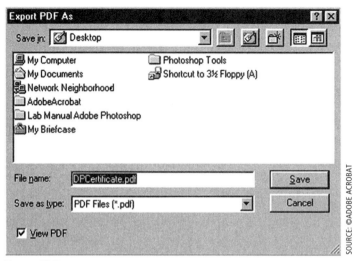

Export PDF

6. Leave the file name as *DPCertificate.pdf* and click on Save.

Digital Signatures

1. The document should be open in Acrobat. If it is not, open Acrobat and open *DPCertificate.pdf*.
2. Go to the menu bar and choose Tools > Digital Signatures > Sign Document.
3. In the Digital Signatures—Alert dialog box, read the message, then click OK.

Digital Signatures—Alert

4. Click and drag in the space for your instructor's signature. Enter his or her name and use "school" as the password.
5. Click OK.
6. Click on the check mark on the signature to verify that the signature is valid.
7. Close the document.

ACTIVITY 4 • MINI-PROJECT

Create a For Sale Sign in PDF Format Using PageMaker

1. Think of something you own that you might want to sell. If you don't have anything you want to sell, pretend you are selling a stereo or other item you own and place a price on it. Consider an image that you could use to make it appealing. You could bring a digital image from home or a picture that you can scan. You can also use clip art galleries or images from the Web.

2. Go to the category signs and choose a template to use for your sign.
3. Using the FreeText Tool, create a text box somewhere on the flyer to use for a digital signature.
4. Save as *MySale.pmd*.
5. Create a PDF file from *MySale.pmd*.
6. Crop and edit as needed. Include your digital signature in the text box you created for that purpose.
7. Save as *SaleMy.pdf*.
8. The following criteria should be met:
    - ☐ Appropriate template used.
    - ☐ Personal information for sale item included on flyer.
    - ☐ Image appropriate in type and size.
    - ☐ Digital signature included.
    - ☐ File saved as requested with no error in file name.
    - ☐ PDF file clean and edited as needed.

ACTIVITY 5 • CREATING PDF DOCUMENTS FROM EXCEL

In this activity, you will become familiar with:

- ■ Converting to PDF
- ■ Rotate View Clockwise Tool
- ■ Find
- ■ Linking
- ■ Hand Tool

Converting to PDF

1. Open Excel.
2. Go to the files on your CD and open *CreatingPDF.xls*.
3. Click on the Convert to PDF icon.
4. In the Save as dialog box, accept the suggested name of *CreatingPDF.pdf* by clicking on Save.
5. Open Adobe Acrobat.
6. Open *CreatingPDF.pdf*.

Rotate View Clockwise Tool

1. Click on the Rotate View Clockwise icon.
2. Click on the PDF image until it is back to the original position.

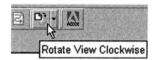

Rotate Tool
SOURCE: ©ADOBE ACROBAT

Find

1. Click on the Find Tool.
2. In the Find dialog box, click in the Find What box. Type "Format."

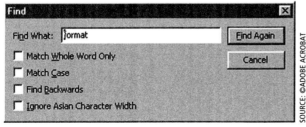

Find

3. Click Find Next until you find all occurrences of "Format."

Linking

1. Click on the Link Tool.
2. Use the mouse pointer to draw the rectangle around the title "Creating PDF Files."
3. In the Link Properties dialog box, change the color to red.

Link Tool

SOURCE: ©ADOBE ACROBAT

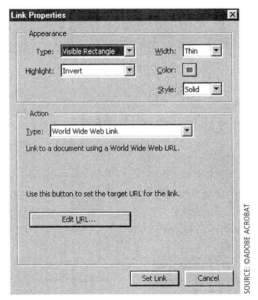

Link Properties

4. In the Type drop-down box, select World Wide Web Link.
5. Click on Edit URL.
6. In the Edit URL dialog box, type http://www.microsoft.com. Click OK.

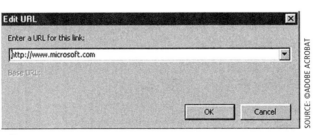

Edit URL

7. Click on Set Link.

Hand Tool

1. Click on the Hand Tool.
2. Select the link you created.
3. Choose to view in Adobe Acrobat or your browser.

Hand Tool

SOURCE: ©ADOBE ACROBAT

ACTIVITY 5 • MINI-PROJECT

Create a Budget Chart in PDF Format Using Excel

1. Use Excel to input the spreadsheet. Be sure to include your name in the title and the current date on the second line. Save as *StudentBudget.xls*.

Budget for *Student Name*

Week of

Revenue:		
Part-time job		$120.00
Expenses:		
Movie	12.00	
Gas	20.00	
CD	14.00	
Clothing	50.00	
Magazine	5.00	
Savings	19.00	
Total Expenses		$120.00

2. Create a pie chart of the expenses on your spreadsheet. It should be created as an object on the current spreadsheet. Be sure that both the spreadsheet and the pie chart are showing on one page. Include a title on the pie chart. Save again.
3. Create a PDF file of the spreadsheet and the chart.
4. Use the Link Tool to draw a rectangle around the title on the chart. Set the Action Type to Open a File. Choose the original Excel file you created and click on Set Link.
5. Save as *BudgetStudent.pdf*.
6. The following criteria should be met:
   - ☐ Spreadsheet input accurately with name and current date, no errors, and proper formatting as shown.
   - ☐ Pie chart created as instructed.
   - ☐ Link set correctly to the original Excel file.
   - ☐ PDF file edited properly and saved with no errors in the file name.

ACTIVITY 6 • CREATING PDF FORMS

In this activity, you will become familiar with:

- ■ Form Tool
- ■ Check Box
- ■ List Box
- ■ Radio Button

Form Tool

1. Open Adobe Acrobat.
2. Browse to your CD and double-click on *OnlineScholarship.pdf*.
3. Click on the Form Tool icon.

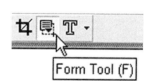

Form Tool

SOURCE: ©ADOBE ACROBAT

4. Click and drag to draw a rectangular box. The box should be approximately the height of the words next to it and even horizontally with the heavy line below "GPA."

5. In the Field Properties dialog box, type "Name" in the Name box. Leave all other properties at the default. Click OK.

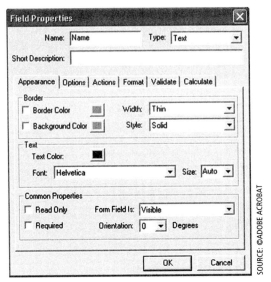

Field Properties

6. Draw a rectangular box next to "Street Address." In the Field Properties dialog box, type "StreetAddress." Click OK.

7. Continue drawing rectangular boxes for each field. The GPA box can be smaller. The names of the fields should be "CityStateZIP," "HighSchool," "University," and "GPA."

Check Box

1. In the next section, "Other information concerning your needs," draw 1-inch boxes.

2. In the Field Properties dialog box, set the fields up as follows:

Field Name: Dorm	Type: Check Box	Check Style: Check
Field Name: Siblings	Type: Check Box	Check Style: Star
Field Name: Scholarships	Type: Check Box	Check Style: Cross

   Note: To access Check Style, you will need to click on the Options tab in the Field Properties dialog box.

List Box

1. For the next item, "How many scholarships have you received?," draw a 2-inch rectangular box. In the Field Properties dialog box, the Type should be List Box. Click on the Options tab. In Item, type "1." Then, click on Add. In Item, type "2." Then, click on Add. Repeat this to add the numbers 3, 4, 5, and more than 5 in the list. Click OK.

2. If you make a mistake on any rectangular form, you can make changes to the properties by right-clicking on the box and selecting Properties. This will bring the Field Properties dialog box back up on your screen.

3. Save the form.

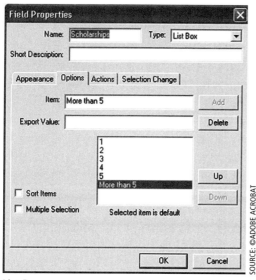

Field Properties

Name: Scholarships Type: List Box

Short Description:

Appearance | **Options** | Actions | Selection Change

Item: More than 5 [Add]

Export Value: [Delete]

1
2
3
4
5
More than 5 [Up]

☐ Sort Items

☐ Multiple Selection Selected item is default [Down]

[OK] [Cancel]

SOURCE: ©ADOBE ACROBAT

List Box

Radio Button

1. In the last question about your major, use the Form Tool to draw a 1-inch box.
2. In the Field Properties dialog box, name the field "Major." Choose Radio Button from the drop-down menu for Type. Click OK.
3. You have eight more 1-inch boxes to draw. In this question, you want the person filling out the form to select only one of the radio buttons. Each of the nine fields must be named the same name for this to happen. Therefore, all nine fields will have the name "Major."
4. It will be easier to make your rectangular boxes uniform if you use Copy and Paste. This will also prevent having to type the same field name eight times. With your cursor on the first rectangular box you drew, go to the menu bar and choose Edit > Copy. Then go to the menu bar again and choose Edit > Paste. Drag the box to place it next to "Business." Continue going to the menu bar and choosing Edit > Paste and placing the boxes until you have all nine boxes in place.
5. Save the form.
6. It would be a good idea to fill in the form to try it before you consider it finished. Click on the Hand Tool to practice filling in the form. Do not save the changes when you fill in the form.

ACTIVITY 6 • MINI-PROJECT

Create a PDF Form for Student Information

1. You are requested to create a form for a college instructor's use. Each student is required to fill in an online information sheet.
2. Create a document similar to the one shown below using word processing software. Save as *StudentInfo.txt*. Note that there are no lines drawn for fill-ins. It is best to leave these off if you know you are creating a PDF form. Be sure to leave enough space between fields for drawing the form fill-in. You may want to adjust the spacing from what you see in the sample.

Student Information Sheet
Richard Rollandelli, Instructor

Date

Student Name

Address

Phone Number

Email

Web site

Major

GPA

Organization Memberships

Where do you live? dorm apartment at home

Do you consider yourself an independent learner? Yes No

Do you have PowerPoint and a computer available? Yes No

Do you procrastinate or
complete assignments early? Procrastinate Complete Early

3. Create a PDF form from the word processing document. Save it as *InfoStudent.pdf*. Use the Forms Tool to create fill-ins.
4. The following criteria should be met:
   ☐ All information in the word processing document with no errors.
   ☐ Document saved as requested with no errors in file name.
   ☐ Form fill-ins are appropriate type.
   ☐ Form fill-ins drawn uniformly and appropriate in size.
   ☐ Student Information Sheet saved in PDF format with no errors in file name.
   ☐ PDF file edited as needed.

PART 4 • SIMULATION

Using Adobe Acrobat to Create Forms about BPA

1. As a member of your local BPA (Business Professionals of America), you have been elected Webmaster. One of your biggest tasks this year will be to create applications and forms in PDF to add to the local Web site. Create a folder entitled *BPA* and save all documents in that folder.
2. Research the BPA Website at http://www.bpa.org to assist with creating the following:
   a. Use Publisher to create a flyer with the mission statement. Enhance the flyer to create a positive image for the organization. Save as *MissionFlyer.pub*. Convert to PDF and save as *FlyerMission.pdf*.
   b. Use Excel to create a spreadsheet of Future NLC (National Leadership Conference) dates. Save as *NLCFuture.xls*. Convert to PDF and save as *FutureNLC.pdf*.
   c. Create a document in any program with a logo and mission statement on it. Enhance the document so that it can be used for programs and other document covers. Save as *CoverSheet.doc*. Print the program cover. Scan the program cover using Adobe Acrobat and save as *SheetCover.pdf*.
   d. Follow the link "Driving Your Future Program." Read about the program. Write a summary of the program in a word processing document and save as *DrivingFuture.doc*. Create a PDF file from the word processing docu-

ment and save as *FutureDriving.pdf*. If this program is no longer available, follow the links to other programs and summarize a different program offered by BPA.

e. Use PageMaker to create a brochure marketing BPA. On the Web site, follow the link "Organization Information" and summarize the organization in brochure format. Save as *OrganizationInfo.pmd*. Convert the brochure to PDF and save as *InfoOrganization.pdf*.

f. Create a membership form for your local chapter using word processing software. Read the information on the Web site for dues amount. The form should include: name of student, address, phone number, email, parents' names, classification, memberships in other organizations, GPA, list of at least 10 different competitions they can enter so on the form they can check which one they are interested in, dues amount, amount paid for dues, and check number. Enhance the form with a logo from the organization, borders, and at least one different font type and size. Save the form as *MembershipForm.doc*. Convert the form to PDF and save as *FormMembership.pdf*.

3. The following criteria should be met:

☐ *MissionFlyer.pdf* includes details of mission and is a clean PDF file.

☐ *NLCFuture.xls* and *FutureNLC.pdf* include correct information.

☐ *SheetCover.pdf* properly scanned and cropped as needed.

☐ *SheetCover.pdf* creates a positive image of the organization.

☐ *FutureDriving.pdf* is a well-written summary of the program and a clean PDF file.

☐ *InfoOrganization.pdf* brochure organized in a way that elicits a positive impression of the organization.

☐ Information in the brochure is detailed and appropriate for a brochure.

☐ *FormMembership.pdf* includes all details requested and the appropriate fill-ins for the type of information.

☐ Use of some special tools on the PDF files, such as Note Tool, Stamp Tool, TouchUp Text Tool, Square Tool, Highlight Tool, Digital Signatures, Linking, and Form Tool. At least seven of the nine tools were used.

☐ All documents error-free.

Unit 4

Presentation Strategies

Part 1 • Microsoft Sound Recorder
Part 2 • Macromedia Flash
Part 3 • Adobe LiveMotion
Part 4 • Jasc Animation Shop
Part 5 • Microsoft PowerPoint

Unit 4 is multimedia-intensive. In this unit, you will learn to create and use sound and animation for presentations and Web pages.

You will begin by learning how to create narratives using the Sound Recorder. Many times we associate particular events or products with music, which makes the ability to record part of a track off a particular CD an effective marketing tool.

Using Flash and LiveMotion, you will learn to create animated text, images, and objects to create interest in your business. You will learn about SWF files and find that your creativity will be utilized more than ever in learning how much you can do with animation. Put your imagination in your book bag because you will need it in these activities.

Animation Shop, part of Paint Shop Pro, gives you a unique opportunity to create animated banners and images with a few simple clicks. Transition, text, and image effects give you even more flexibility in creating animated GIFs that will add interest to your presentations and Web pages.

Finally, you will use your skills in adding sound and animation to your presentations. PowerPoint enables you to create simple to complex presentations for business, school, and personal use. Unleash the power in this software and you will be amazed at how easy it is to speak effectively, whether it is to sell, teach, or inform.

Microsoft
Sound Recorder

Microsoft Sound Recorder
Publisher: Microsoft
Sound Recorder is a Windows program that allows the user to create and play digital sound files.

ACTIVITY 1 • USING THE MICROPHONE

In this activity, you will become familiar with:

- Setup
- Recording Control
- Volume Control
- Recording Sound
- Saving

Setup

1. You will need to follow your instructor's directions for getting started. These instructions will depend on a number of factors, including the type of computer lab you have, the configurations in that lab, and the type of microphone system.
2. For a standalone computer or if you want to try this at home, install your microphone by plugging it into the microphone port in the back of your computer. Many computers are now color-coded so that you can easily get the microphone in the correct port. Some computers now have built-in microphones, in which case you will not need to install a microphone.
3. If you choose to use a headset, the headset will come with a speaker and microphone plug in a split. Be sure to unplug your speakers and use the plugs that come with the headset.

Recording Control

1. Go to Start > Programs > Accessories > Entertainment > Volume Control.
2. In the Volume Control dialog box, choose Options > Properties. Click on the Recording radio button. This dialog box now becomes a Recording Control dialog box.
3. In the Recording Control dialog box, select the Microphone and CD-ROM check boxes. Click OK. See the top left figure on the following page.
4. In the Recording Control dialog box, select the Select check box under Microphone and adjust the balance as shown in the top right figure on the following page. (You may need to make other adjustments to the volume, depending on your equipment.)

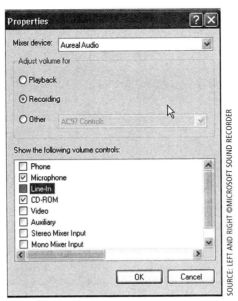

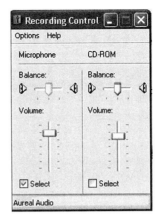

Recording Control

Recording Properties

Volume Control

1. Go to Start > Programs > Accessories > Entertainment > Volume Control.
2. In the Volume Control dialog box, go to the menu bar and choose Options > Properties. Select the Volume Control, Microphone, and CD-ROM check boxes. Click OK.

Properties

3. In the Volume Control dialog box, select the Microphone Mute check box, as shown below. If you do not do this, you may get distortion or feedback in your recording. You should not have anything else muted in Volume Control.

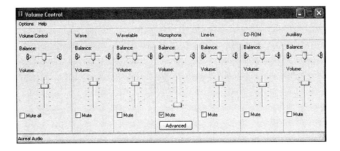

Volume Control

Recording Sound

1. Open the Sound Recorder by going to Start > Programs > Accessories > Entertainment > Sound Recorder.
2. With the microphone in hand or nearby or your headset on, click on the red recording button in the Sound Recorder dialog box and begin speaking. You should see the green line change as you talk.
3. Speak clearly into the microphone or headset. Experiment with how close to the microphone you need to be. Say something like "This is a test to see if my Sound Recorder works in Windows XP." If it is recording, you will see the green line change, similar to the figure labeled Recording.
4. Click on the Stop button.
5. Click on the Rewind button.
6. Click on the Playback button.
7. In a word processing document, write an introduction of yourself ("Good morning [or afternoon], I'm _____") and a brief explanation of how to record a WAV file. Use your own words from what you have learned in this activity. Save as *WrittenSummary.wav*.
8. Record what you have written. Play back what you have recorded. Assess the recording for volume, voice speed, and clarity of speaking.

Saving

1. When you are satisfied with the recording, go to the menu bar and choose File > Save As.
2. In the Save As dialog box, click on the Change button.
3. In the Sound Selection dialog box, click in the Name drop-down box. Since this is a voice recording, choose Telephone Quality. This will create a smaller file size than CD or Radio Quality.
4. Browse to the appropriate directory and save the file as *Summary.wav*.

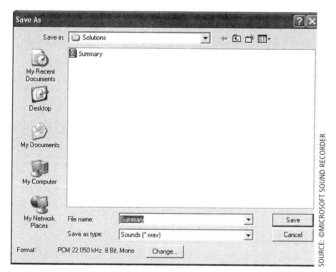

Save As

SOURCE: ©MICROSOFT SOUND RECORDER

Record Button

SOURCE: ©MICROSOFT SOUND RECORDER

Recording

SOURCE: ©MICROSOFT SOUND RECORDER

Stop Button

SOURCE: ©MICROSOFT SOUND RECORDER

Rewind Button

SOURCE: ©MICROSOFT SOUND RECORDER

Playback Button

SOURCE: ©MICROSOFT SOUND RECORDER

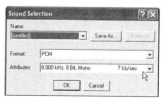

Sound Selection

SOURCE: ©MICROSOFT SOUND RECORDER

ACTIVITY 1 • MINI-PROJECT

Create an Introduction

1. Your friend is running for a state office in one of the Career and Technology Student Organizations (CTSO). He or she has asked you to act as campaign manager, which means you need to give an introduction when the candidate delivers his or her campaign speech at the state conference.
2. Use word processing software to write a short introduction for your friend. Be sure to include your name, your friend's name, a campaign slogan, what office your friend is running for, and what makes him or her qualified for that office. The speech can be only five minutes long, which includes your introduction, so your introduction should be no more than 60 seconds but at least 30 seconds long. Save as *Manager*.
3. The other student does not necessarily have to be in this class, but you should get together with that person to get a list of qualifications and discuss a campaign slogan.
4. Practice the speech using the Sound Recorder.
5. Save as *Campaign.wav* using Telephone Quality.
6. The following criteria should be met:
   - ☐ Introduction well-written with excellent examples of why the student is the best person for that office.
   - ☐ Introduction includes all requested elements.
   - ☐ Introduction within the 30- to 60-second time limit.
   - ☐ Introduction demonstrates an effort to persuade students that this is the right person for the office by the words and/or enthusiasm in speech.
   - ☐ Student did not stumble over words in sound recording.
   - ☐ Student spoke with clarity and slowly enough to be understood.
   - ☐ File saved as instructed with no errors in file name.

ACTIVITY 2 • RECORDING MUSIC

In this activity, you will become familiar with:

- ■ Setup
- ■ Recording
- ■ Mixing Sounds

Setup

1. Go to Start > Programs > Accessories > Entertainment > Volume Control.
2. In the Volume Control dialog box, choose Options > Properties.
3. Click on the Recording Radio button.
4. Select the Microphone and CD-ROM check boxes. Click OK.
5. If CD-ROM is on Mute, clear the Mute check box.
6. Go to Start > Programs > Accessories > Entertainment > Volume Control to open a second instance of Volume Control.
7. In the Volume Control dialog box, select the Select check box under Microphone and adjust the balance.
8. In the Volume Control dialog box, click on Advanced under the Microphone section.
9. In the Advanced Controls for Microphone dialog box, select the 1 Microphone Gain (+20dB) check box. Click on Close.

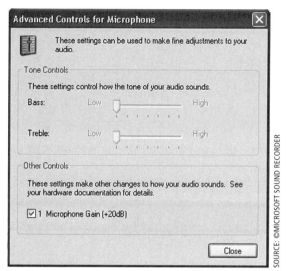

Advanced Controls

10. Open the Sound Recorder by going to Start > Programs > Accessories > Entertainment > Sound Recorder.

Recording

1. Place a music compact disk (of your instructor's choice) in your CD-ROM player.
2. Go to Start > Programs > Accessories > Entertainment > Windows Media Player.
3. You should now have opened Recording Control, Volume Control, Sound Recorder, and Windows Media Player.
4. Select the track you want to play.

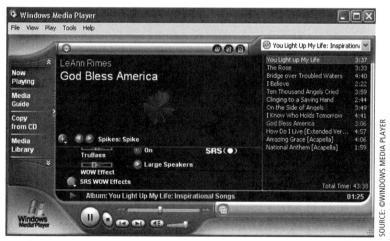

Windows Media Player

5. Click on the red record button on the Sound Recorder. The green line will change size and shape if it is recording.
6. Record only 30 seconds of the song. (Fair use allows 30-second clips of songs only.)
7. Listen to your recording. Select New and record again if necessary to get the clip in a good starting and stopping point so it sounds as natural as possible. You want the clip to start smoothly and not stop as if it were in the middle of something if at all possible.

8. When you are satisfied with the quality, go to Save As in the Sound Recorder dialog box.
9. Click the Change button. In the Name drop-down box, choose CD Quality.
10. Save as *01Music.wav* in CD Quality.
11. Create clips of two other songs.
12. Save as *02Music.wav* and *03Music.wav* in CD Quality.

Mixing Sounds

1. Open *01Music.wav*. This is the first file you recorded in the previous activity.
2. Click on the left double-sided arrows to move to the beginning of the recording.
3. In the Sound Recorder dialog box, choose Edit > Mix with File.

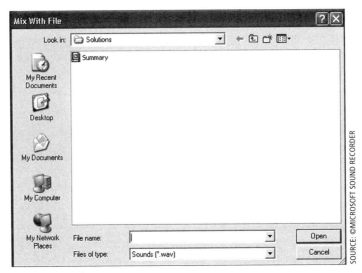

Mix With File

4. Select *Summary.wav* from your previously recorded introduction.
5. Play the new sound and notice that your voice is superimposed over the music.
6. Save as *Mix.wav* in CD Quality.

ACTIVITY 2 • MINI-PROJECT

Create a Product Association

1. You have probably experienced a time where a certain song reminds you of an event or a person. In business, many times that association is used to create a business or corporate identity.
2. Think of at least three products you use on a daily basis that you may be able to associate with a part of a song. Write a short explanation of the association on an index card. Locate the song on a CD.
3. Record an appropriate clip (30 seconds or less) for each product.
4. Save as *01Clip.wav*, *02Clip.wav*, and *03Clip.wav* in CD Quality.
5. Record a separate recording of your voice explaining each association with the product and song. Save as *01Ex.wav*, *02Ex.wav*, and *03Ex.wav*.
6. Mix the *01Clip.wav* and *01Ex.wav*. Save as *01Mix.wav*.
7. Mix the *02Clip.wav* and *02Ex.wav*. Save as *02Mix.wav*.
8. Mix the *03Clip.wav* and *03Ex.wav*. Save as *03Mix.wav*.

9. The following criteria should be met:
   - ☐ Products chosen are appropriate.
   - ☐ Explanation of association is appropriate and well thought out with a good recording.
   - ☐ Clip is 30 seconds or less.
   - ☐ Clip is of quality in volume and clarity.
   - ☐ Clip starts and stops at a point that sounds natural.
   - ☐ Clips saved as instructed.
   - ☐ Mixed files mixed with the proper song and saved as instructed.

PART 1 • SIMULATION

Using Sound Recorder to Create an Identity

1. You are a new employee with Urkl WebDesign, Inc. This business designs Web sites for other businesses. Each of the employees has a Web page that serves as a resume for clients to peruse. In this activity, you will not create the Web site, but you will prepare an image of yourself, a recording of yourself giving your name and a very brief explanation of your experience or training with Web design, and a song that you believe associates you and your goals.

2. Dress for success one of the days during this activity. Get another student to take a digital image of you. Be sure to consider the type of background for the image. Crop the image as necessary. Save as *Me.jpg*.

3. On an index card, prepare a written introduction. Include your name, any experience you have had with Web design and any training you have had. Include software names. Project the introduction to the future end of the class. In other words, include the software you will learn in this class for Web design.

4. Record your introduction. Save as *MyIntro.wav* in Telephone Quality.

5. Locate and record a song clip that you believe can serve as an identifier with your goals. It should leave a positive impression. Save as *Goals.wav* in CD Quality.

6. Mix *MyIntro.wav* and *Goals.wav*. Save as *MyId.wav* CD Quality.

7. The following criteria should be met:
   - ☐ Self image was a quality photograph. Student dressed for success and the background was appropriate for the use of the photograph.
   - ☐ Introduction was clear, well thought out, and a quality recording.
   - ☐ Song clip was of quality and appropriate to the goals.
   - ☐ Mixed file recorded properly.
   - ☐ All files saved as instructed.

Part 2 | Macromedia Flash

> **Macromedia Flash**
> **Publisher: Macromedia**
> Flash is the industry standard for interactive vector graphics and Web animation. It contains a number of tools for drawing and animating graphics, designing interactive elements, and generating HTML code.

ACTIVITY 1 • DRAWING AND PAINTING

In this activity, you will become familiar with:

- Setting the Stage
- Line Tool
- Arrow Tool
- Stroke Color
- Rotate Modifier
- Scale Modifier
- Segmenting or Grouping
- Lasso Tool
- Formatting Line Segments
- Ovals and Rectangles
- Fill Color
- Moving Borders and Shapes
- Ink Bottle Tool
- Copy and Paste
- Zoom In and Out
- Brush Tool
- Pencil Tool
- Eraser Tool
- Paint Bucket Tool
- Dropper Tool
- Pen Tool

Setting the Stage

1. Open Flash. Flash automatically opens a new movie.
2. Go to the menu bar and choose View > Rulers to toggle on your rulers. You can also right-click anywhere in the stage area and choose Rulers.
3. Go to the menu bar and choose Modify > Movie. This opens the Movie Properties dialog box. You can change the movie size to match the printer or the contents or you can customize the size of the stage. The background color of the stage can also be changed. If your ruler units are not in inches, change that in

the drop-down box. Click on Save Default and OK. You can also right-click your mouse button anywhere in the stage area and choose Movie Properties.

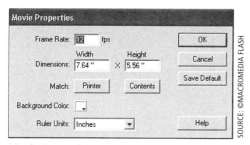
Movie Properties

Line Tool
SOURCE: ©MACROMEDIA FLASH

Line Tool

1. Go to the Tools palette and click on the Line Tool.
2. Beginning at 2 inches both vertically and horizontally, draw a 2-inch line. Hold down the Shift key while drawing the line to make the line straight.

Arrow Tool
SOURCE: ©MACROMEDIA FLASH

Arrow Tool

1. Click on the Arrow Tool.
2. Select the line by clicking on the line with the Arrow Tool. Be sure to note the difference between a selected line and an unselected line. Click it on and off several times to see the difference.
3. Selecting the line with the Arrow Tool opens the modifiers and enables you to change the stroke color.

Stroke Color
SOURCE: ©MACROMEDIA FLASH

Stroke Color

1. Click on the Stroke Color box and select green (#00FF00).
2. Click on the Stroke Color box again. Open the Color dialog box by clicking on the color wheel in the top right corner.
3. Drag the slider so that Red and Green are both on 14. You can also type 14 in the Red and Green boxes.

Rotate Modifier
SOURCE: ©MACROMEDIA FLASH

Rotate Modifier

1. Click on the Rotate Modifier.
2. Note the change to your line. It now has circles on each end and a circle in the middle. Hover the mouse pointer over the circle on the right end. Hold down the left mouse button and drag the line to 3-1/2 inches on the ruler.

Rotate Image
SOURCE: ©MACROMEDIA FLASH

Scale Modifier
SOURCE: ©MACROMEDIA FLASH

Scale Modifier

1. Click on the Scale Modifier.
2. Note the changes in the line. It has eight handles around it. Hover the mouse pointer on the bottom right handle. Hold down the left mouse button and drag toward the top left handle to resize in proportion. You can also hold down the Shift key while dragging to keep the proportion. Practice resizing the image using some of the other handles. Keep the size small enough so that it is within the viewable stage area.

Scale Image
SOURCE: ©MACROMEDIA FLASH

Segmenting or Grouping

1. With the line selected, go to the menu bar and choose Edit > Copy.
2. Click off the line.
3. Go to the menu bar and choose Edit > Paste.
4. Use the Arrow Tool to click on the new line. Click on the Rotate Modifier and rotate the line until it looks like an X crossed over the first line.
5. The line is now four segments. Hover the mouse pointer over the intersection of the X. Notice that the pointer changes to a corner angle. Hover the mouse pointer over the middle of one of the lines. Notice that the pointer changes to an angle. Experiment with bending the segments.
6. If you select a segment and then release, hold down the left mouse button down and drag, you can break the segments away from the group. If you hold down the left mouse button and drag without releasing, you can bend and stretch the segments to different shapes.
7. Leave this line segment in the shape of a K.

Lasso Tool

Tools

Lasso Tool

1. Click on the Lasso Tool.
2. Drag the pointer, which now looks like a lasso, around the object. In this case, the object is the letter K.
3. Go to the menu bar and choose Edit > Copy. Click off the object.
4. Go to the menu bar and choose Edit > Paste.
5. Select the second K with the Lasso Tool and apply a red color stroke to it.
6. Right-click on the stage and choose Movie Properties. Change the background to Yellow and click on the Contents button to fit the stage to the image.
7. Save as *K.fla*.
8. Go to the menu bar and choose File > New. Draw two circles the same color and approximate size. Use the Arrow Tool to double-click on one of the circles. Drag it so that it overlaps the other circle.
9. Click off the circles to deselect the circles. Notice that doing so segmented them and made them a group. Double-click on the circle you moved and drag it away. Part of the first circle is now gone.
10. Draw two more circles the same color and approximate size. Use the Arrow Tool to select one of the circles.
11. Go to the menu bar and choose Modify > Group. This places a blue box around the circle. Double-click and drag it so that it overlaps the other circle. Click off it to deselect it.
12. Use the Arrow Tool to select the circle again. Drag it by itself so it is not overlapping the other circle. Because it was grouped first, it is its own object.
13. Double-click on the grouped object and notice that the stage dims. You can format the circle to a different shape and color. Try this, then double-click anywhere in the stage area when you are finished.
14. Draw two circles that are different colors. Use the Arrow Tool to select one of the circles. Go to the menu bar and choose Modify > Group.
15. Drag it over to overlap the other circle. Notice that it moves as a group.
16. Drag it off the other circle. Notice that it does not take a segment from the other circle.
17. Save as *CircleFun.fla*.

Formatting Line Segments

1. In a new Flash movie, draw five lines, approximately 2 inches each. Leave at least 1/2-inch between each line vertically.
2. Click on the Arrow Tool.

3. Go to the menu bar and choose Window > Panels > Stroke.
4. On the Stroke panel, you can choose line styles, thickness, and color.

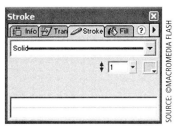

Stroke Panel

5. Click on the right arrow underneath the Close button on the Stroke panel. Choose Custom.

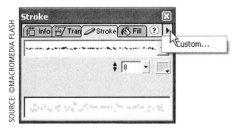

Custom Line

6. Choose a Line Style. Depending on the Line Style chosen, additional customizing features may open.

Custom Line

7. Experiment with customizing all five lines so that no two lines look the same.
8. Change the stage size to the contents.
9. Save as *CustomLines.fla*.

Ovals and Rectangles

1. Go to the menu bar and choose File > New. Click on the Oval Tool. Note the Rectangle Tool next to it.
2. Click on the stage area and draw a circle. Draw another circle, except this time hold down the Shift key while dragging to draw the circle. This makes it easier to create a circle.
3. Draw another shape, except this time shape the circle like an egg.
4. Click on the Rectangle Tool.
5. Draw a square. Draw another square, except this time hold down the Shift key while dragging to draw the square. This makes it easier to create a square.
6. Draw a rectangle. Click on the Rectangle Radius Modifier.
7. Type "10" in the Rectangle Settings dialog box and click OK.

Oval Tool
SOURCE: ©MACROMEDIA FLASH

Round Radius Modifier
SOURCE: ©MACROMEDIA FLASH

Rectangle Settings
SOURCE: ©MACROMEDIA FLASH

Fill Color

Fill Color

1. Using the Arrow Tool, click on one of the circles to select it.
2. Click on the Fill Color box and choose a color.
3. Add a gradient fill to one of the circles. After adding the gradient, right-click on the circle and choose Panels > Transform. You can also click on the Show Info button in the bottom right tray area. These buttons are a quick way to open the panels.

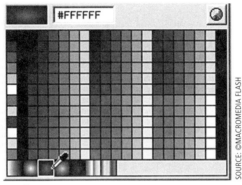

Gradients

4. On the Transform panel, click on the Fill tab. Click on the Fill Style drop-down box and choose either Radial or Linear.
5. Click on the color marker you would like to change. Click on the Color palette button and choose a color.
6. You can adjust the color intensity of the gradient by dragging the Color Markers.
7. Add other Color Markers to the effect by clicking below the Gradient bar.
8. Click on the Save button (disk icon) to save the gradient and add it to the Color palette. The new gradient will show as a swatch in the Color palette.
9. Add Fill Color and Stroke Color to the other circles.
10. Save as *Shapes.fla*.

Moving Borders and Shapes

1. Go to the menu bar and choose File > New. Draw two rectangles any size or color. Place them in a vertical column, one below the other.
2. Use the Arrow Tool to click and drag one of them to the side. Notice that the fill moves separately from the border.
3. Use the Arrow Tool to double-click and drag the other rectangle. Notice that when it is double-clicked to select it, the fill and border move together.
4. Modify the movie to the size of the contents.
5. Save as *MovingRectangles.fla*.

Ink Bottle Tool

1. Go to the menu bar and choose File > New. Use the Arrow Tool to select one of the circles.
2. On the Stroke panel, change the line style, thickness, and color to complement the circle's fill color.
3. Click on the Ink Bottle Tool.
4. Click on the outer edge of the image to apply the stroke attributes to that image.
5. Continue Steps 2–4 until all the ovals and rectangles have a customized stroke.
6. Save as *CustomStrokes.tif*.

Ink Bottle Tool

Copy and Paste

1. Go to the menu bar and choose Help > Samples > Eggplant. This will open *Eggplant.fla* as the current movie on your stage.
2. Use the Lasso Tool to select the eggplant.
3. Go to the menu bar and choose Edit > Copy.
4. Choose File > New.
5. On the new stage, go to the menu bar and choose Edit > Paste.

Zoom In and Out

1. In the status area, click in the Zoom box and type "75" (percent).
2. If you still can't see all of the eggplant on your stage area, reduce the size again.
3. Click on the Zoom Tool.
4. When the Zoom Tool is selected, you have modifiers of Enlarge and Reduce. You can also use these tools to assist in changing the view size of the eggplant on your stage.

Brush Tool

1. Click on the Brush Tool.
2. Click on Brush Mode. Choose the Paint Normal modifier. This modifier paints over anything on the stage.
3. Click on the Brush Size and change to a small brush.
4. Click on the Brush Shape drop-down box and change to an oval, elongated shape.
5. Change the fill color to white.
6. Paint one of the hands on the eggplant. Notice that everything is painted, including lines.
7. Go to the menu bar and choose Edit > Undo. (The shortcut for Undo is Ctrl + Z; for Redo, it is Ctrl + Y.)
8. Click on Brush Mode. Change to the Paint Fills modifier.
9. Paint both hands with the white. Notice that with the Paint Fills modifier selected, the inside of the hand is painted, but the lines are left.
10. Change the fill color to light yellow.
11. Change the Brush Modifier to Paint Behind. Paint all over the shoes on the eggplant. Notice that when you release the mouse button, you have painted only behind the shoes.
12. Use the Arrow Tool to select only the top part of the stem of the eggplant.
13. Click on the Brush Tool and change to a light green. (It must be a lighter shade than the current color of the stem.)
14. Change the Brush Modifier to Paint Selection. Paint the area selected. Notice that when you release the mouse button, the stem is now two shades of green.
15. Change the Brush Modifier to Paint Inside. Paint Inside begins a brush stroke inside a fill area without affecting any lines.
16. Change to a fill color of brown. Paint an outline of brown inside the body of the eggplant. In other words, you do not need to paint the entire body of the eggplant brown. Paint only the inside edge.
17. Save as *MyEggplant.fla*.

Zoom Tool

Brush Tool

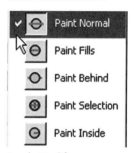

Brush Modifiers

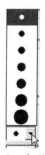

Brush Size

Brush Shape

Pencil Tool

SOURCE: ©MACROMEDIA FLASH

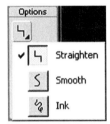

Pencil Modifiers

SOURCE: ©MACROMEDIA FLASH

Eraser Tool

SOURCE: ©MACROMEDIA FLASH

Eraser Shape

SOURCE: ©MACROMEDIA FLASH

Paint Bucket Tool

SOURCE: ©MACROMEDIA FLASH

Dropper Tool

SOURCE: ©MACROMEDIA FLASH

Pen Tool

SOURCE: ©MACROMEDIA FLASH

Pencil Tool

1. Go to the menu bar and choose File > New. Click on the Pencil Tool.
2. Click on the Pencil Mode modifier. Choose Straighten.
3. Draw three clouds on your screen, changing the shape of each a little. Notice what Straighten does to the clouds. Depending on how you drew the clouds, you may even have ended up with a perfect oval.
4. Change the Pencil Modifier to Smooth. Draw three more clouds.
5. Change the Pencil Modifier to Ink. Draw three more clouds.

Eraser Tool

1. Click on the Eraser Tool.
2. Choose an Eraser shape.
3. Click on Eraser Modes. Notice that the modifiers are the same as for the Paint Brush. Leave it on Erase Normal for now.
4. Click on the Faucet Modifier for a quick erase of entire lines and fills. Since our clouds are only lines, click on the outer edge of one of the clouds that you don't intend to use. This should erase the entire image.
5. Erase all but three of the clouds. Leave your best clouds. Experiment with the different Eraser Modifiers as you did with the eggplant.

Paint Bucket Tool

1. Using the Arrow Tool, click on one of the clouds to select it.
2. Click on the Paint Bucket Tool.
3. Choose Close Large Gaps on the Gap Size Modifier in case you have left some gaps in drawing with the pencil.
4. Change the fill color to a light blue. Fill the other clouds with a varying shade of blue.

Dropper Tool

1. Use the Arrow Tool to select one of the clouds.
2. Use the Ink Bottle Tool to add a dark blue stroke to the cloud.
3. Click on the Dropper Tool.
4. Click the Dropper Tool on the cloud with the dark blue Stroke. The pointer turns into the Ink Bottle Tool.
5. Click on the edge of each of the other clouds to add the dark blue stroke.
6. Save as *Clouds.fla*.

Pen Tool

1. Go to the menu bar and choose File > New. Click on the Pen Tool.
2. Move the pointer to the stage area and begin dragging to start the curve. When the curve bar appears, you can rotate the curve bar by dragging to bend the line and change the line length. Start dragging and release the mouse button when you have the curve you want.
3. Straight lines can be drawn by clicking on a beginning point on the stage and clicking on an ending point.
4. Experiment with using the pen for drawing. Work with a partner to attempt to achieve the same drawing. Share techniques you learned in achieving the results you desired. Some things you can draw (but are not limited to): music notes, letters of the alphabet, shapes, school acronyms.
5. Choose three of your best drawings. Erase the other drawings with the Eraser Tool. Modify the stage to fit the contents.
6. Save as *Best.fla*.

7. Use word processing software to create a "Tips List." In enumerated format, list at least five tips you learned about using the Pen Tool.
8. Save as *PenTips.fla*.

ACTIVITY 1 • MINI-PROJECT

Create an Array of Buttons

Kyong Kim, Webmaster, has asked you to assist in redesigning the Web site. She has not decided on a theme yet, but just wants you to come up with some ideas for usable buttons. You may want to reinforce your skill using the tools for drawing and painting by going to the menu bar and choosing Help > Lessons > 02 Drawing.

1. Use an Excel spreadsheet. In Column A, type the following list of tools you will use in this mini-project:

   Line Tool, Arrow Tool, Stroke Color, Rotate Modifier, Scale Modifier, Segmenting or Grouping, Lasso Tool, Formatting Line Segments, Oval Tool, Rectangle Tool, Round Rectangle Radius, Fill Color, Ink Bottle Tool, Brush Tool, Brush Modifiers, Pencil Tool, Pencil Modifiers, Eraser Tool, Eraser Modifiers, Paint Bucket Tool, Dropper Tool, Pen Tool

2. As you are completing steps 3 through 7, type "01," "02," "03," "04," and "05" in Column B to indicate which file (look below) the tool was used in at least once. Save as *ToolCheck.xls*.
3. Use the Oval Tool to draw five unique buttons. Save as *01Buttons.fla*.
4. Use the Rectangle Tool to draw five unique buttons. Save as *02Buttons.fla*.
5. Use the Pencil Tool to draw five unique buttons. Save as *03Buttons.fla*.
6. Use the Pen Tool to draw five unique buttons. Save as *04Buttons.fla*.
7. Use the Brush Tool to draw five unique buttons. Save as *05Buttons.fla*.
8. The following criteria should be met:
   - ☐ Excel spreadsheet set up as instructed, with no errors, and accurate as far as use of tools.
   - ☐ Each group of buttons graded on usefulness, uniqueness, visual appeal, and use of available tools.

ACTIVITY 2 • CREATING TEXT

In this activity, you will become familiar with:

- Text Tool
- Text Formatting
- Setting Margins and Indents
- Moving Text Boxes

Text Tool

1. Go to the menu bar and choose File > New. Click on the Text Tool.
2. To add a Label text box, click in the stage area and then type your high school name. When you type text in the Label text box, the text does not wrap. The width of the box expands as you type. Note that the top right corner of the text label box is a circle.
3. To add a Block text box, click the Text Tool, then click and drag to the width you desire. Type in the box "Bellville High School Senior Class invites you to graduation ceremonies Friday, June 1, 2XXX." Note that the text wraps to the next line within the Block text box.

Text Tool
SOURCE: ©MACROMEDIA FLASH

Character Dialog Box

Text Formatting

1. Click on the A icon, as shown at left. This opens the Character dialog box.
2. Highlight the text in the Label text box.
3. Click on the Character tab in the Character dialog box.
4. In the Font drop-down box, choose Batang, or a similar font if it is not available.
5. Click in the size box and change to Size 24 by either sliding or typing "24" in the box.
6. Change the color to one of your school colors by clicking on the Color box and selecting the color.
7. Click on the Block text box and select the text.
8. Change the text type to Verdana, or a similar font if it is not available.
9. Click on the Color box to change the color to red.
10. Change the text size to 24.
11. Click on the Paragraph tab in the Character dialog box. Click on the Center Justify icon.
12. To add character spacing between the text, click on the Character tab on the Character dialog box. In the AV drop-down box, change the character spacing to 2.
13. Resize the Block text box by hovering the mouse pointer over the top right square of the text box and dragging to the right until the text takes up only four lines.
14. Save as *TextChanges.fla*.

Setting Margins and Indents

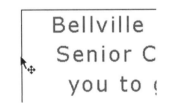

Paragraph Controls

1. Open *TextChanges.fla*. This is the file you created in Text Formatting. Using the Arrow Tool, click on the Bellville High School text box to select it.
2. Click on the Paragraph tab in the Character dialog box.
3. In the Left margin box, type ".25." Press tab twice.
4. In the Right margin box, type ".25."
5. Note the Indention box. We will not use it for this activity, but be aware that it is there for your use in other activities.
6. In the Line spacing box, type "4," then Enter.
7. Save again.

Moving Text Boxes

1. Open *TextChanges.fla*. This is the file you created in "Text Formatting."
2. Double-click on one of the text boxes.
3. Hover the mouse pointer over the text box until it changes to the pointer shown at left.
4. Hold down the left mouse button and drag the box to a new location on the screen. Release the button.
5. Save again.

Move Cursor

ACTIVITY 2 • MINI-PROJECT

Create Text That Gets Attention

1. Create three Label text boxes with local Internet providers' names and URL in them. The information within the box should not wrap. Format each Label text box with a different font type, size, and color.
2. Create three Block text boxes that contain short motivational quotes. Go to http://www.google.com or your favorite search engine and search for "motivational quotes."

3. Quotes should wrap within the Block text box.
4. Format the Block text boxes so each one has a different font type, size, and color.
5. Change the left and right margins to .25 and the spacing to .4.
6. If needed, resize and move the Label text boxes to arrange them in an organized manner on the stage.
7. Modify the size of the stage for the contents.
8. Save as *TextQuotes.fla*.
9. The following criteria should be met:

   ☐ Three Label text boxes has accurate information for local Internet providers.
   ☐ Information in Label text boxes formatted in a different font type, size, and color.
   ☐ Quotes demonstrate evidence of research and are appropriate.
   ☐ Quotes formatted for a different font type, size, and color.
   ☐ Quotes formatted for left and right margins and spacing as instructed.
   ☐ Quotes arranged in an organized manner on the stage.

ACTIVITY 3 • LAYERS

In this activity, you will become familiar with:

- Naming Layers
- Adding Layers
- Deleting Layers
- Setting Layer Properties
- Stacking Layers
- Adding Guide Layers
- Adding Mask Layers
- Creating a Mask

Naming Layers

1. Go to the menu bar and choose Help > Samples > Eggplant.
2. Use the Lasso Tool to select the eggplant.
3. Right-click and choose Edit > Copy.
4. Choose File > New.
5. Right-click your mouse button and choose Edit > Paste.
6. Click on the Zoom Tool and choose the Reduce Modifier. Click once on the stage area or click until you can see the entire eggplant on the stage.
7. On the Layer palette, double-click on Layer 1. See below.

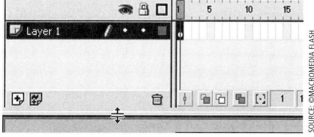

Layer 1

8. Type "Eggplant" to rename Layer 1.

Adding Layers

1. Click on the Arrow Tool. Select the eggplant. If it is not all selected, press Ctrl + A to select all.
2. Use the Scale Modifier to resize the eggplant to approximately half of its current size.
3. Move the eggplant to the middle of the stage area.
4. Save as *LayeredScene.fla*.
5. Choose Window > Eggplant. Click on the sunflower. Copy the sunflower to your clipboard.
6. On your Layer palette, click on Insert Layer. Note the pencil icon next to the Layer name. This indicates that it is the current layer being edited. See the Insert Layer figure to the left.
7. Paste the sunflower into Layer 2. Rename Layer 2 "Sunflower."
8. Move the sunflower to the right of the eggplant.
9. Save again.

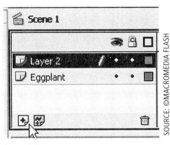

Insert Layer

Deleting Layers

1. On the Layer palette, click on Insert Layer.
2. Rename it "Sunflower 2."
3. Click on the Sunflower layer and choose Edit > Copy.
4. Click on the Sunflower 2 layer and choose Edit > Paste.
5. Add a "Sunflower 3" layer and paste one of the other sunflower layers into it.
6. You decide you only want two sunflowers, so click on the Sunflower 3 layer. Be sure the pencil is next to the layer so you know you are deleting the correct layer. Click on the trash can icon to delete the layer. See the Delete Layer figure to the left.
7. Save again.

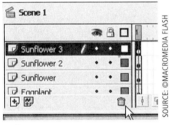

Delete Layer

Setting Layer Properties

1. On the Layer palette, many of the properties can be set.
2. Click below the eye icon next to Sunflower 1. This removes the layer from being visible on the stage area.
3. Click below the lock icon next to Eggplant. This locks the layer from any changes, although it is still visible on the stage area.
4. Click on the Color box underneath the Show All Layers as Outlines icon next to Sunflower 2. This changes the layer to outline only. You can also click the icons themselves and apply Lock, Outline, and/or Show/Hide Layers to all layers at one time.
5. Click all locks, eyes, and outlines to remove them from the layers.
6. Go to the menu bar and choose Modify > Layer.

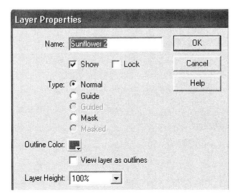

Layer Properties

SOURCE: ©MACROMEDIA FLASH

7. Click on the Sunflower layer to make it the current layer being edited.
8. Notice that you can lock, hide, and rename layers in this dialog box. You can also specify what type of layer. Leave this at Normal.
9. Change the Outline Color by clicking in the Outline Color box. Change the color to black.
10. Leave the Layer Height at 100 percent, but note that you can change this if necessary.
11. Click OK to return to your stage area.
12. Insert a new layer. Rename the layer "Sun." Use the appropriate drawing tools to draw a sun on the layer.
13. Click on the sunflower to add to that layer. Draw a grass landscape on the bottom half of the stage area. It does not have to look exactly like the figure to the right. This is only to be used as a reference.
14. Insert a new layer. Rename the layer "Tree." Use the appropriate drawing tools to draw a tree with a brown trunk, green for the branch area, and red apples. While doing this, it may be a good idea to hide all the other layers.
15. Show the other layers to check for placement. It is easier to move the tree only if the other layers are hidden. Hide the other layers to adjust the placement of the tree if necessary.
16. Save again.

Landscape

Stacking Layers

1. Click on the Eggplant layer in the Layer palette. Hold down the left mouse button and drag the layer to the top of the list. Restack the rest of the layers in alphabetical order.
2. Look at your stage area. The tree is probably covered by the landscape. In order for the tree to be placed in front of the landscape, the stack will need to be rearranged. The landscape is in the Sunflower layer. The tree will need to be moved above the Sunflower layer in order for the landscape to fall behind it on the stage area.
3. Hold down the left mouse button and drag the tree up one level.
4. Choose Window > Eggplant. Select a hat, eyes, and mouth to place on your *LayeredScene.fla*. This is the file you created in "Adding Layers." You can make more than one selection at a time by holding down the Shift key while selecting the object.
5. Insert a new layer named "Accessories" and paste the objects in the new layer.
6. Scale the objects as needed. Rearrange the objects.
7. Restack the layers if needed.
8. Draw a cloud with a gradient fill in the top right corner to finish the scene. Place it on its own layer and name the layer "Cloud." Rotate the cloud to place it at an angle.
9. Save again.

Stacked Layers

Adding Guide Layers

1. Choose File > New if you do not already have a new stage area on your screen.
2. On the Layer palette, right-click on Layer 1 and choose Guide. A guide layer helps you position objects. You can have a plain guide layer or a motion guide layer. The plain guide layer does not appear in your final movie. Double-click on the layer and name it "Guide."
3. On the Layer palette, click on Insert Layer. Double-click on the layer and name it "Circle."
4. Draw a circle with a stroke of 3-1/2 and a line drawn with a pencil attached to the right of the circle. Stroke the line the same color as the stroke on the circle and at 3-1/2.

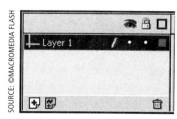

Guide Layers

5. On the Layer palette, click on Insert Layer. .Double-click on the layer and name it "Square."
6. Draw a square with similar attributes to the circle, except different colors. Draw a pencil line to the right of the square.
7. On the Layer palette, click on Insert Layer. Double-click on the layer and name it "Triangle."
8. Use the Pencil Tool to draw a triangle with similar attributes to the circle and square.
9. Save as *GuideLayer.fla*.
10. Motion guide layers are linked to layers with objects that you want to animate along a path. The motion guide layer always appears directly above the layer or layers to which it is linked.
11. Open *GuideLayer.fla* if it is not already open.
12. Click on the layer that you want to link to a motion guide layer. Click on Triangle in this case.
13. Click on the Add Guide Layer icon, as shown at left.
14. Save as *MotionGuide.fla*.

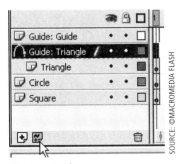

Motion Guides

SOURCE: ©MACROMEDIA FLASH

Adding Mask Layers

1. You can hide objects on underlying elements using a mask layer. They are linked to other layers.
2. On the timeline, click on the layer that you want to add a mask to.
3. Click on the Insert Layer icon.
4. Hold down the right mouse button and choose Mask. Doing this will mark the layer as a mask layer. Lock it so it cannot be changed, and link it to the layer below it.
5. Click on the layer that is unmasked. Draw a large square and fill it with a gradient. Customize the gradient for varying shades of yellows and blues with at least six color markers. Fill the square.
6. Click on the Text Tool. Create a Label text box and type "Midnight Madness Sale." Copy and paste the Label text box eleven times so that there are twelve Label text boxes. Format each of the boxes. Use at least three shades of blue for color. Use at least three different fonts and font sizes.
7. Rotate some of the boxes to create a kind of helter-skelter effect.
8. Save as *MidnightMadness.fla*.

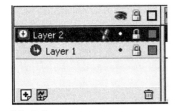

Mask Layer

SOURCE: ©MACROMEDIA FLASH

Creating a Mask

1. Unlock the mask layer.
2. Draw a fill shape on the stage over the area you want to view in the layer below. Fill it with light yellow and use a light yellow stroke.
3. Lock the mask layer and view the masking effect. Both layers should be locked.
4. Save again.

ACTIVITY 3 • MINI-PROJECT

Create Layers of all Types

1. Go to http://www.davidrobey.com or a Web site using Flash. Create similar navigation rectangles, each in a separate layer.
2. Create a plain guide layer. You will have nine rectangles when you are finished with ten layers. The tenth layer is the guide layer.
3. Create the rectangles as close to the font and color in your example as possible.
4. Save as *Example.fla*.

5. Create a new movie. Use the Rectangle Tool with a Rounded Radius Modifier to draw a sack. Use the Eraser Tool, Stroke, and any other tools to make the sack look realistic.
6. Name the layer "Sack."
7. Add five more layers. Name them "Red," "Blue," "Green," "Yellow," and "Orange." In the Red layer, draw three circles, varying the size on all three. They should all be red. Stroke them white so it looks like they have no border. Follow this procedure for the rest of the layers.
8. Create each of the layers with the colored circles as motion guide layers underneath the Sack layer.
9. Save as *Sack.fla*.
10. Create a new movie.
11. Go to the menu bar and choose File > Import. Browse to your CD and locate *Flower1.jpg*. Double-click on the file.
12. Go to the menu bar and choose Modify > Movie.
13. In the Movie Properties dialog box, choose a peach color for the background.
14. In the timeline, double-click and name the layer "Rose."
15. Insert a new layer. Name it "Mask."
16. Use the Oval Tool to draw an oval over the main rose in the picture. Add at least three other ovals over varying places in the picture that you think are the best parts to the picture.
17. With the mouse pointer on the mask layer in the timeline, right-click and choose Mask. This should lock both of the layers and show the part of the bottom layer that you want shown.
18. Save as *MaskFlower.fla*.
19. Press Ctrl + Enter to activate the Flash Player and see what the finished movie looks like.
20. The following criteria should be met:
    - ☐ Rectangles chosen are a replication of the samples viewed.
    - ☐ Layers and guide layer set up appropriately.
    - ☐ Motion layers set up appropriately.
    - ☐ *Sack.fla* follows instructions in color and proportions and uses a variety of tools in creating the sack.
    - ☐ Image imported correctly.
    - ☐ Ovals placed effectively.
    - ☐ Layer set up properly for a mask.

ACTIVITY 4 • SYMBOLS

In this activity, you will become familiar with:

- Working with Bitmaps
- Using Images as Fills
- The Library
- Creating Symbols
- Inserting Instances
- Modifying Instances
- Editing Symbols

Working with Bitmaps

1. Go to the menu bar and choose File > Import.
2. Browse to your CD to locate *Bitmap.bmp*. Double-click on the file.
3. Use the Arrow Tool to select the bitmap image.

4. Go to the menu bar and choose Modify > Trace Bitmap. This turns the BMP image into a vector graphic.
5. Save as *Vector.fla*.

Using Images as Fills

1. Go to the menu bar and choose File > Import.
2. Browse to your CD to locate *Bitmap.bmp*. Double-click the file.
3. Use the Arrow Tool to select the bitmap image. Go to the menu bar and choose Modify > Break Apart.
4. Select the Oval Tool. On a new layer, draw a large circle.
5. Click on the Dropper Tool, then click on the bitmap image that you broke apart.
6. Click on the circle you drew to fill the image.
7. Save as *BitmapFill.fla*.

The Library

Library

1. Click on the Library icon in the lower right corner of your screen.
2. This opens the Library, which should show your bitmap in it. It automatically adds images that you are using in the project.

Creating Symbols

1. Open *BitmapFill.fla*. This is the file you created in Using Images as Fills.
2. Use the Arrow Tool to click on the filled circle.
3. Go to the menu bar and choose Insert > Convert to Symbol.
4. In the Symbol Properties dialog box, type "Picture" in the Name box. Change the Behavior to Graphic by clicking the radio button in front of Graphic.

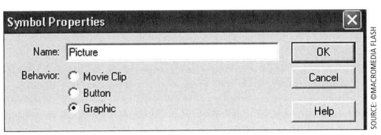

Symbol Properties

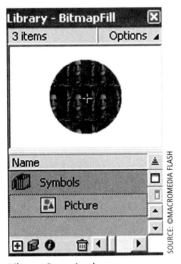

Library Organized

5. Click OK.
6. Organize the Library by clicking on the New Folder button (orange). Name the folder "Symbols."
7. Drag the Picture symbol that you created into the Symbol folder.

Inserting Instances

1. To use an instance from the Library, click on the file in the Library and drag it to the stage. Place at least three of the instances you created on your screen.
2. Use Scale on one of the instances and use Rotate on one of the other instances.
3. Save as *Instances.fla*.

Modifying Instances

Show Instance

1. Click on one of the instances on your stage.
2. If the Instance panel does not open, click on the Show Instance icon in the lower right corner of your screen.

3. On the Instance panel, click on the Effect tab. Click on Brightness and slide the Brightness to 15 percent.
4. Choose Advanced from the drop-down menu and change red and green to 75 percent.

Editing Symbols

1. Use the Arrow Tool to select the symbol you want to edit.
2. On the Instance panel, click on Edit Symbol.
3. At this point, only one of the instances should be showing on your stage.
4. Use the Arrow Tool to select the instance. Add a blue stroke around the circle. Use the Stroke panel to make changes in thickness and style of stroke. Use the Ink Bottle Tool to apply the stroke.
5. To leave editing, click on Scene above the timeline.
6. Save as *EditedInstance.fla*.

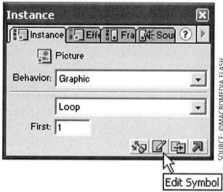

Edit Symbol

ACTIVITY 4 • MINI-PROJECT

Create an Edited Symbol for Special Holidays

Bernice Watson of Cookies Galore, Inc., has asked you to take her current logo and create several versions of it for holiday use with Flash creations.

1. Browse to your CD and open *Cookies.bmp*.
2. Convert to a vector graphic.
3. Convert to a symbol graphic for use in Flash movies.
4. Insert three instances of the symbol from your Library.
5. Modify one instance for a washed-out look to use as a watermark.
6. Save as *01CookiesGalore.fla*.
7. Create a *Cookies Galore* folder and organize your Library. Drag the symbol to the Library.
8. Edit the symbol for two different holidays. Make at least two changes each time. This could include painting behind the current symbol with an appropriate color for that holiday and importing another object to effectively place on the symbol.
9. Save as *02CookiesGalore.fla* and *03CookiesGalore.fla*.
10. The following criteria should be met:
    - ☐ Converted to vector graphic.
    - ☐ Converted to a symbol with appropriate name and type.
    - ☐ One instance modified for a washed-out look.
    - ☐ Folder created in Library and Library is organized.
    - ☐ Symbol edited for two different holidays with at least two changes.

☐ Creativity demonstrated in editing the symbols for holiday use with appropriate images created for each holiday.
☐ Files saved as instructed with no errors in file names.

ACTIVITY 5 • ANIMATION

In this activity, you will become familiar with:

- Setting Up the Movie
- Adding Frames
- Adding Keyframes
- Onion-Skinning
- Adding Blank Keyframes
- Removing Frames
- Creating Scenes
- Creating Motion Tweens
- Rotating a Symbol
- Spinning a Symbol
- Changing Symbol Size for Animation
- Morphing into Shapes
- Saving as a Movie Clip

Setting Up the Movie

1. Go to the menu bar and choose File > New to begin a new movie.
2. Go to the menu bar and choose Modify > Movie.
3. In the Movie Properties dialog box, type "6" in the Frame Rate text box. In most cases, the default of 12 fps should work. You can set it as high as 24 fps, but many computers cannot handle that speed.
4. Leave the width and height at the default.

Adding Frames

1. Click on Frame 60 on the timeline.
2. Go to the menu bar and choose Insert > Frame. This inserts regular frames between the last regular frame or keyframe up to 60 (where you clicked in step 1).

Adding Keyframes

1. Click on frame 5. Go to the menu bar and choose Insert > Keyframe.
2. Draw a small red ball in the lower left corner of the stage.

Onion-Skinning

1. Turn on Onion-Skinning. Onion-Skinning does not show in your movie. It shows only in the stage area so you can see where to place the next object. The objects in the other frames will appear dimmed, or you can choose to have them shown in outline. Click on the Onion-Skin icon in the timeline. In the timeline area, drag the Onion-Skin out so that it covers all the frames in this activity.

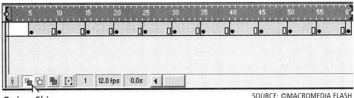

Onion Skin

SOURCE: ©MACROMEDIA FLASH

2. Click on frame 5. Go to the menu bar and choose Insert > Keyframe.
3. Click on frame 10. Press F6 to quickly add a keyframe to frame 10. This should add the red ball to the frame, since it was not a blank keyframe. Drag the red ball up and to the right about 1/2-inch.
4. Click on frame 15. Press F6 to quickly add a keyframe on frame 15. Drag the red ball up and to the right about 1/2-inch.
5. Repeat these instructions, adding keyframes every five frames. Once you have moved the red ball so many times that it has reached the top of the stage, start dragging it to the right and down toward the right bottom corner.
6. Stop the movie at frame 60.
7. Save the movie as *Bouncing.fla*.
8. Play the movie by clicking on the first frame and pressing Enter, or by pressing Ctrl + Enter. To stop the preview, press Enter. You can also preview by going to the menu bar and choosing Control > Test Movie. Return to the Flash Editor window by clicking the Windows Close button if you opened the Flash Player.

Adding Blank Keyframes

1. Go to the menu bar and choose File > New.
2. Choose File > Import. Browse to clip art that is available to you and locate a butterfly, fly, bee, bird, or other similar creature. Anything that flies will work for this activity. If the object is too large, click on the object and scale the object. It should be a fairly small object.
3. Use the Arrow Tool to click on the clip art you imported.
4. Go to the menu bar and choose Insert > Convert to Symbol.
5. Click on the Show Library icon at the bottom right corner of your screen if the Library is not on the stage.
6. On your timeline, click on frame 60. Go to the menu bar and choose Insert > Frame. This allows your movie to work continuously.
7. Click on frame 5. Go to the menu bar and choose Insert > Blank Keyframe.
8. Use the Library to drag your symbol to the stage area. Randomize your symbol on the stage area two or three instances.
9. Click on frame 10. Use the shortcut to insert a blank keyframe by pressing F7.
10. The frames can also be labeled. Go to the menu bar and choose Modify > Frames. On the Frames panel, type "Random" in the Label box.
11. Drag several instances of your symbol from the Library at random to the stage area.
12. Repeat these instructions for Frames 15, 20, 25, 30, 35, 40, 45, 50, and 55.
13. Save as *Flying.fla*.
14. Press Ctrl + Enter to activate the Flash Player.
15. You can adjust the speed of the movie by adding frames between the other frames or modifying the movie properties and changing the frames per second.

Removing Frames

1. Go to the menu bar and choose File > New.
2. Click on frame 10 and go to the menu bar and choose Insert > Frame. This inserts continuous frames up to that point.
3. Click on frame 8. Go to the menu bar and choose Insert > Remove Frames. You can also remove frames by pressing Delete. This removes the frame and moves all other frames one place to the left—so if you had ten frames, you now have nine frames.
4. Close the file without saving.

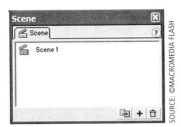

Scene Panel

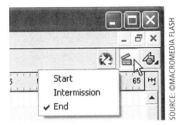

Switch Scenes

Creating Scenes

1. Go to the menu bar and choose Window > Panels > Scene.
2. Click on the Add Scene icon to add a scene. Add two scenes so that there are now three scenes.
3. Rename the scenes by double-clicking on them. Name them "Start," "Intermission," and "End."
4. Click on Edit Scene up at the top right corner of your screen (below the Windows Close button) to switch between scenes. See the figure labeled Switch Scenes.
5. Save as *Scenes.fla*.

Creating Motion Tweens

1. Go to the menu bar and choose File > New.
2. At the far right of the stage, draw a silver cylinder. Use the Brush Tool and Stroke to create what looks like an opening on the left end of the cylinder. Name this layer "Cylinder."
3. On a new layer, create a ball on the left side of the stage. Name the layer "Ball."

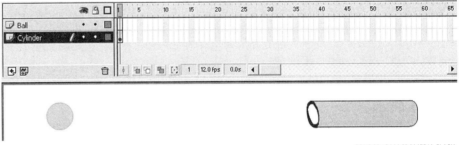

Begin Tween

4. Insert a keyframe where you want to start the motion tween.

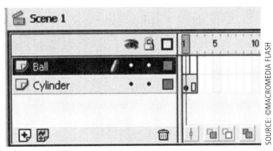

Insert Keyframe

5. Click on the last frame you want to include in the motion tween. This will be frame 10 in the example. Insert a keyframe.
6. Move the symbol to the ending position. This should be where you want it after the animation.
7. Click between the two keyframes that make up your motion tween to select the frames.
8. Click on Show the Instance panel in the bottom right corner of your screen.
9. On the Instance panel, click on the Frame tab.
10. Click on the Tweening drop-down box. Choose Motion.
11. A motion tween arrow should be added from the first keyframe in the tween effect to the last keyframe in the tween effect.

12. To preview your movie, click in the first frame of the motion tween and press Enter.
13. Save as *Tweening.fla*.

Rotating a Symbol

1. Go to the menu bar and choose File > New.
2. Import an image of something circular from the clip art you have available.
3. Zoom out so that you can see the entire image on your stage.
4. Use the Arrow Tool to select the image. Go to the menu bar and choose Modify > Group.
5. Scale the image so that it is approximately 2 inches × 2 inches.
6. Go to the menu bar and choose Insert > Symbol.
7. In the Symbol Properties dialog box, name the image "Arrows" and click the Graphic radio button.
8. On the timeline, click on frame 1.
9. Go to the menu bar and choose Insert > Keyframe.
10. Drag an instance of the symbol from the Library to the stage area.
11. Click on frame 5. Go to the menu bar and choose Insert > Keyframe.
12. Click on the Rotate icon on the main toolbar.
13. Rotate the image about one-quarter of the circle.
14. Click between frames 1 and 5 to select the frames.
15. On the Frame panel, click in the Tweening drop-down box and choose Motion.
16. Click on frame 10. Go to the menu bar and choose Insert > Keyframe.
17. Click on the Rotate icon and rotate the image another quarter of a circle.
18. Click between frames 5 and 10 to select the frames.
19. On the Frame panel, click in the Tweening drop-down box and choose Motion.
20. Repeat steps 16 through 19 for Frames 11 through 15 and 16 through 20.
21. Click on frame 1. Press Ctrl + Enter to preview your movie.
22. Save as *Rotating.fla*.

Rotate

SOURCE: ©MACROMEDIA FLASH

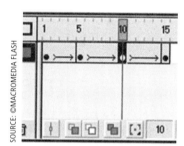

SOURCE: ©MACROMEDIA FLASH

Rotate Tweening

Spinning a Symbol

1. Create a new Flash movie. Import an image to use in this spinning activity and convert it to a symbol.
2. Insert a keyframe in frame 1 to begin the movie.
3. Insert an instance of your symbol in frame 1.
4. Click on frame 20 to end the movie. Insert a keyframe in frame 20.
5. Click in the middle of the frames to select all of the frames. The pointer will turn into a hand if you are clicking in the right place.
6. On the Frame panel, click in the Tweening drop-down box and choose Motion. In the Rotate box, select cw. Type "4" for number of times to rotate.
7. Preview the spinning symbol by pressing Ctrl + Enter. If the movie is too fast, right-click on the stage, choose Movie Properties, and change the frames per second to 6 or less.
8. Add another layer to the stage. Import an appropriate image into the layer.
9. Save as *Spinning.fla*.

Changing Symbol Size for Animation

1. Go to the menu bar and choose File > New.
2. Click in frame 1 and insert a keyframe.
3. Import the *Rose.jpg* graphic from your CD.
4. Scale the rose so that it is very small.
5. Click on frame 20. Insert a keyframe. Resize the rose to about 2 × 2 inches.
6. Click between frames 1 to 20.

7. On the Frame panel, click in the Tweening drop-down box and select Motion. Be sure Scale is checked.
8. Save as *Roses.jpg*.

Morphing into Shapes

1. Go to the menu bar and choose File > New.
2. Click on frame 1. Insert a keyframe.
3. Use the Pencil Tool to draw a shape similar to the one shown to the left. Choose the color and line style.
4. Click on frame 20. Insert a blank keyframe. Use the Pencil Tool to draw a triangle as the final result of the shape.
5. Click between frames 1 and 20. On the Frame panel, click in the Tweening drop-down box and select Shape.
6. Preview by pressing Ctrl + Enter.
7. Save as *Shapes.fla*.

Shapes

SOURCE: ©MACROMEDIA FLASH

Saving as a Movie Clip

1. Open *Spinning.fla*. This is the file you created in "Spinning a Symbol."
2. Select all the frames in the animation.
3. Go to the menu bar and choose Edit > Copy Frames.
4. Go to the menu bar and choose Insert > New Symbol.
5. In the Symbol Properties dialog box, type "Spinning." Choose Movie Clip for the behavior type.
6. Click OK.
7. Select frame 1.
8. Go to the menu bar and choose Edit > Paste Frames.
9. If the Library is not showing, click on the Show Library icon in the bottom right corner. Note that the movie clip you just created is in the Library.
10. Save as *SpinClip.fla*.

ACTIVITY 5 • MINI-PROJECT

Create Eye-Catching Business Names

Portia Sanford of Summer Camp University has asked you to create four proposed animations for use on their Web site and with PowerPoint for marketing.

1. Create four animations with the business initials (SCU) or business name. You may use other image management software to assist in creating the initial image if desired.
2. Create one each that demonstrates rotation, spinning, changing symbol size, and morphing into shapes.
3. Save as *01SCU.fla*, *02SCU.fla*, *03SCU.fla*, and *04SCU.fla*.
4. Save one animation as a movie clip.
5. The following criteria should be met:
   ☐ Rotation animation demonstrates business name or initials effectively.
   ☐ Rotation animation is eye-catching and demonstrates creativity.
   ☐ Spinning animation demonstrates business name or initials effectively.
   ☐ Spinning animation is eye-catching and demonstrates creativity.
   ☐ Changing symbol size animation demonstrates business name or initials effectively.
   ☐ Changing symbol size animation is eye-catching and demonstrates creativity.

☐ Morphing into shapes animation demonstrates business name or initials effectively.

☐ Morphing into shapes animation is eye-catching and demonstrates creativity.

ACTIVITY 6 • INTERACTIVE BUTTONS

In this activity, you will become familiar with:

- Creating a Button Symbol
- Creating Shape-Changing Buttons
- Creating an Animated Button
- Assigning Button Actions

Creating a Button Symbol

1. Go to the menu bar and choose File > New.
2. Go to the menu bar and choose Insert > New Symbol.
3. In the Symbol Properties dialog box, type "Home" for the name of the new button. Click on Button for Behavior type.
4. Click OK.
5. Symbols must have four frames. They are Up, Over, Down, and Hit. Notice in the figure to the right that Up has been selected. The Up frame displays what the interactive button looks like. The Over frame displays what the button looks like when the mouse pointer moves or "rolls" over the button. The Down frame displays what the button looks like when the button is clicked. The Hit frame defines the button area. The contents of this frame is not seen by the user.
6. Go to the menu bar and choose File > Import. Browse to the clip art that is available to you and double-click on an object.
7. Scale and group the object if needed.
8. In the timeline, click on the Over frame. Insert a keyframe.
9. In the timeline, click on the Down frame. Insert a keyframe.
10. In the timeline, click on the Hit frame. Insert a keyframe.
11. Open the Library if it is not open.
12. Click on scene 1 to leave Edit Symbol mode.
13. Drag an instance of the button onto the stage.
14. Preview the button by pressing Ctrl + Enter. You can also check out possible rollover effects by pressing Ctrl + Alt + B.
15. Save as *Create.fla*.

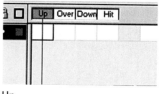

Up

SOURCE: ©MACROMEDIA FLASH

Creating Shape-Changing Buttons

1. Go to the menu bar and choose File > New.
2. Go to the menu bar and choose Insert > New Symbol.
3. In the Symbol Properties dialog box, name the symbol "Yellow Square" and click on Button. Click OK.
4. The stage area automatically goes into Symbol Edit mode when you create a new symbol.
5. Click the Up frame in the timeline.
6. Go to the menu bar and choose Insert > Blank Keyframe.
7. Click on the Over frame to select it. Insert a blank keyframe.
8. Insert blank keyframes in the Down and Hit frames on the timeline.
9. Click on the Up frame to select it.
10. Draw a square with a light yellow fill.

11. Click on the Over frame on the timeline. Click on Onion Skin. Draw a circle with a dark yellow fill.
12. Click on the Down frame on the timeline. Draw a blue square.
13. Click on the Hit frame on the timeline. The symbol in this frame is used to define the Hit frame area. It should be larger than all the other symbols.
14. Click on the Up frame and press Enter to try your buttons. You may want to slow the movie down by going to Movie Properties and changing fps.
15. Save as *ChangingButtons.fla*.

Creating an Animated Button

1. Go to the menu bar and choose File > New.
2. Go to the menu bar and choose Insert > New Symbol. In the Symbol Properties dialog box, type "Fish Bowl" in the Name box. Choose Button as the behavior type.
3. Check to see that you are in Symbol Edit mode. On the timeline, you should see the Up, Over, Down, and Hit frames. Draw a fish bowl.
4. This automatically creates a keyframe in the Up frame. Go to the Over, Down, and Hit frames. Insert keyframes in each of them. Your timeline should look like the one to the left.
5. Click on scene 1 to leave Symbol Editing mode.
6. Open the Library. Drag an instance of the fish bowl to your stage area.
7. Using the Arrow Tool, double-click on the fish bowl to return to Symbol Editing mode. You will see a small plus sign in the middle of the stage area. This means that there is a symbol on the stage. You cannot place a symbol inside itself, so this is a reminder that you have a symbol on the stage already.
8. Click on the Over frame in the timeline. Notice the fish bowl.
9. Go to the menu bar and choose Window > Common Libraries > Movie Clips.
10. On the Library Movie Clips panel, double-click on Supporting Graphic Files. Click and drag Fish Graphic to the stage.
11. Turn the Onion-Skin on in order to see where to place the fish. Scale the fish as needed.
12. Click on the Down frame.
13. Drag an instance of the Fish Movie Clip to the fish bowl.
14. Go to the menu bar and choose Control > Test Movie. Hover the mouse pointer over the fish bowl. The nonmoving fish should appear. Click on the fish bowl. The fish should start swimming around.
15. Save as *AnimatedButton.fla*.

Assigning Button Actions

1. Go to the menu bar and choose File > New.
2. Go the menu bar and choose File > Import. Browse to your CD and double-click on *Texas.jpg*.
3. Go to the menu bar and choose Insert > Convert to Symbol.
4. Click on the Show Library icon in the bottom right corner of your screen. This will open the Object Actions panel.
5. Click on Basic Actions, then double-click on Get URL to apply this action to the button.
6. On the Object Actions panel, click in URL and type "http://www.texas.org."
7. Go to the Movie Properties dialog box and change the size of the stage to Contents.
8. Test the animation by pressing Ctrl + Enter.
9. Save as *Texas.fla*.

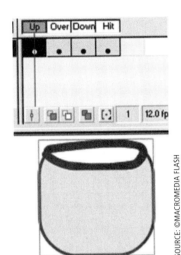

Fish Bowl

SOURCE: ©MACROMEDIA FLASH

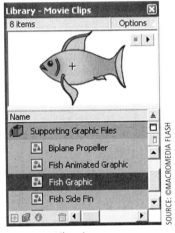

Common Libraries

SOURCE: ©MACROMEDIA FLASH

Show Actions

SOURCE: ©MACROMEDIA FLASH

ACTIVITY 6 • MINI-PROJECT

Create Buttons for Web Sites

1. Josh McKelva, owner of Sun and Fun, Inc., has asked you to create some buttons for use on the new Web site.
2. Create four button symbols that would represent the business name effectively. The buttons can be imported from other clip art as well as drawn with tools available in Flash. You may also create the image in an image management software and import the image into Flash to create as a button. Save as *01Sun.fla*, *02Sun.fla*, *03Sun.fla*, and *04Sun.fla*.
3. Use at least two of the buttons you created to create shape-changing buttons. You can add other images to the movie as long as the original image is in the movie at least once. Save as *05Sun.fla* and *06 Sun.fla*.
4. Create at least two animated buttons using some of the original buttons. You can use other images as long as one of the original images is in the movie at least once. Save as *07Sun.fla* and *08Sun.fla*.
5. The following criteria should be met:
   - ☐ Button symbols represent the business name in either color, shape, or texture.
   - ☐ Button symbols demonstrate creativity.
   - ☐ Shape-changing buttons demonstrate creativity.
   - ☐ Shape-changing buttons work properly, and effectively represent the business name.
   - ☐ Animated buttons demonstrate creativity.
   - ☐ Animated buttons work properly, and effectively represent the business name.
   - ☐ All buttons named as instructed with no errors in file names.

ACTIVITY 7 • SOUND

In this activity, you will become familiar with:

- ■ Adding Sound
- ■ Assigning Sound
- ■ Creating Event Sounds
- ■ Assigning Start and Stop Sounds
- ■ Assigning Streaming Sounds
- ■ Looping Sounds
- ■ Editing Sounds

Adding Sound

1. All sounds in Flash are either event-driven or streamed. Event-driven means they are activated by an action in your movie and must be downloaded completely before playing. Streamed sounds are downloaded as they are needed and start playing even if the rest of the clip is not loaded yet.
2. Go to the menu bar and choose File > New.
3. Draw a black rectangle. Add yellow text to it and type "Summary."
4. Click on Add Layer on the timeline to add a layer above the layer you created in step 3.
5. Name the layer "Sound."
6. Click on frame 1 on the Sound layer you created.
7. Go to the menu bar and choose File > Import. Browse to your files to locate the *Summary.wav* file you created, or create a sound file introducing yourself to use for this activity.

Library Sound

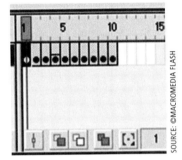

Finished Timeline

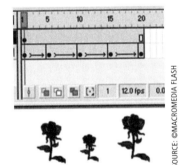

Sized Flowers

SOURCE: ©MACROMEDIA FLASH

8. Click on the Show Library icon in the bottom right corner of your screen.
9. Click and drag the Summary sound to your stage area.
10. Preview the Sound by pressing Enter.
11. Save as *SoundSum.fla*.

Assigning Sound

1. Go to the menu bar and choose File > New.
2. On the timeline, click on Layer 1. Insert a keyframe and draw a rectangle in the shape of the body of a car.
3. Click on frame 2, insert a keyframe, and draw two black wheels.
4. Click on frame 3, insert a keyframe, and draw the hood or top of the car.
5. Click on frame 4, insert a keyframe, and draw a yellow headlight.
6. Insert a keyframe in frames 5 through 10.
7. Click on frame 4. Go to the menu bar and choose Window > Common Libraries > Sound.
8. Drag the sound Beam Scan to the stage area. See the figure at left for what the finished timeline should look like.
9. Click on frame 1. Preview the animation with sound by pressing Enter.
10. Save as *Car.fla*.

Creating Event Sounds

1. Go to the menu bar and choose File > New.
2. Click on frame 1. Insert a keyframe.
3. Go to the menu bar and choose File > Import. Browse to the clip art you have available and select a flower.
4. Scale the flower so that it is small on your stage. Go to the menu bar and choose Edit > Convert to Symbol.
5. Click on frame 5. Insert a blank keyframe. Scale the image again. You may want to turn on Onion-Skin to see where to place the new image.
6. Repeat this in frames 10, 15, and 20. The image should be scaled larger in each frame.
7. Add motion tweening between all 20 frames and turn off Onion-Skinning.
8. Add a layer. Name Layer 1 "Flower" and Layer 2 "Flower 1."
9. On Layer 2, click on frame 1 and insert a keyframe. Use the Library panel to drag two instances of the flower to the stage. A flower should be on either side of the flower in Layer 1. Scale them so they are each a little different size, but not much bigger.
10. Click on frame 20 in Layer 2 and insert a keyframe.
11. Click on Layer 1, frame 20. Choose Window > Common Libraries > Sound. Drag an instance of Camera Shutter 35mm SLR to the stage area.
12. On the Instance panel, click on the Sound tab. Click on the drop-down arrow in the Sync box and select Event.
13. Preview the event sound by pressing Enter.
14. Save as *Flower.fla*.

Assigning Start and Stop Sounds

1. Go to the menu bar and choose File > New.
2. Click on frame 1. Draw the beginning shape of a heart. Do not draw much of the shape.
3. Click on frame 20. Insert a blank keyframe. Draw a heart.
4. Click between frames 1 and 20. On the Instance panel, click the Frame tab. In the Tweening drop-down box, choose Shape.
5. Click on frame 25. Insert a keyframe. Fill the heart with a color.

6. Click between frames 20 and 25. On the Instances panel, click the Frame tab. In the Tweening drop-down box, choose Motion.
7. Save as *Heart.fla*.
8. Insert a layer. Name the new layer "Sound." Name the other layer "Heart."
9. Click on frame 1 of the Sound layer. Go to the menu bar and choose File > Import. Locate a clip of a song, either as a sample or one that you have copied from a CD or downloaded from the Internet.
10. On the Instance panel, click on the Sound tab. Choose the sound you want to use. Click in the Sync box and choose Start.
11. Click on frame 25. On the Instance panel, click on the Sound tab. Choose the sound you want to stop. Click in the Sync box and choose Stop.
12. Click between frames 1 and 25. Go to the Instances panel and choose the song. Click in the Sync box and choose effect.
13. Save again.

Assigning Streaming Sounds

1. Start a new file.
2. Insert a keyframe in frame 1.
3. Drag or import a sound to the stage area.
4. Open the Instance panel. Click the Sound tab. Choose the sound you want.
5. Click on the down arrow in the Sync box and choose Stream.
6. Click on frame 20. Insert a keyframe. Leave this frame on Stream if you do not want continuous play. If you want continuous play, change it to Event.
7. Preview by pressing the Enter key.
8. Save as *Stream.fla*.

Looping Sounds

1. Open *Stream.fla*. This is the file you created in Assigning Streaming Sounds.
2. Click the frame containing the sound you want to loop. Looping means that you can play the sound over and over as many times as you like. The last frame with the sound in it cannot be on Stream to loop the sound.
3. On the Instance panel, click on the Sound tab. Select the sound you want to loop in the Sound drop-down box.
4. Click inside the Loops text box and type the number of times you want the sound to loop.
5. Press Enter to play the movie.
6. Save as *Looping.fla*.

Editing Sounds

1. Start a new file.
2. Use a customized brown gradient fill and the Rectangle Tool to draw three poles, similar to the bottom figure on the previous page. Name the layer "Walls."
3. Add a new layer. Name it "Balls."
4. Insert a keyframe in frame 1 and draw a red ball just inside the left wall at the bottom.
5. Insert a blank keyframe in frame 5 and draw a red ball below the horizontal pole.
6. Insert a blank keyframe in frame 10 and draw a red ball against the right pole at the bottom.
7. Click on frame 1. Open the Common Libraries and choose a sound.
8. Drag the sound to the stage area.
9. On the Sound panel, choose the Sound you placed on the stage area. Click in the Sync drop-down box and choose Event. Click on Edit.
10. In the Edit Envelope dialog box, click in the Effect drop-down box and choose Fade in. Click OK.

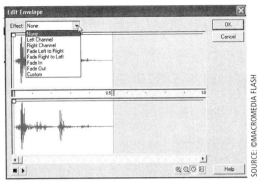

Edit Envelope

11. Click on Frame 5. Drag a sound to the stage area from the Common Libraries.
12. On the Sound panel, choose the Sound you placed on the stage area. Click in the Sync drop-down box and choose Event. Click Edit.
13. On the Edit Envelope dialog box, click in the Effect drop-down box and choose Fade out. Click OK.
14. Click in Frame 15. Open the Common Libraries and choose a sound.
15. Drag the sound to the stage area.
16. On the Sound panel, choose the Sound you placed on the stage area. Click in the Sync drop-down box and choose Event. Click Edit.
17. On the Edit Envelope dialog box, click in the Effect drop-down box and choose an effect of your choice. Click OK.

Editing Sound

18. Click on frame 1. Press Enter to preview the animation.
19. Save as *EditedSounds.fla*.

ACTIVITY 7 • MINI-PROJECT

Create Sounds for Images

1. Use the Sound Recorder to create a recording telling about your favorite part of Flash. Save as *FavFlash.wav*. Create a new movie or use a movie previously created and add this recording to the movie. The movie should be an example of your favorite part of Flash. Save as *AboutFlash.fla*.
2. Create a logo advertising Flash. Add something new to the logo on each of frames 5, 10, and 15. Add a sound from the library and edit the sound. Save as *FlashLogo.fla*.

3. Create a movie of an image for the business Flash Creation, Inc. This movie should be more than a logo. It should contain at least three layers. Add a song as a streaming sound to the movie. It can either be a WAV clip you create with the Sound Recorder or an MP3 file. Save as *FlashCreation.fla*.

4. The following criteria should be met:

☐ Recording is appropriate material and a quality recording.

☐ Movie about favorite part of Flash works and demonstrates capabilities of Flash.

☐ Flash logo appropriate with new elements added in frames 5, 10, and 15.

☐ Appropriate sound added to the Flash logo.

☐ Sound used in the Flash logo was edited appropriately.

☐ Image of Flash demonstrates creativity.

☐ Image of Flash contains all the required elements.

PART 2 • SIMULATION

Using Flash to Create Attention-Getters

1. Go to http://www.flashkit.com. Download a few examples of FLA files to get some ideas. Study them carefully for new ideas or recognition of skills learned.

2. Create a sample image-filled symbol for each of the following companies:
   Southern Lawn Care, Inc.
   Wallush Construction Company

3. Create the following animations:
   Rotating
   Spinning
   Symbol Size
   Morphing

   You can choose which type of animation you create for each of the following companies:
   Sanders Beauty Shop
   Johansen Shoes International
   Rollando Gas and Oil Productions, Inc.
   Sew-Right Corporation

4. Create an interactive button for each the following companies:
   Sollari Educational Institution
   Lee & Lee Law Office

5. The scenes created in this activity may be used by the business on its Web site as a splash page or in a PowerPoint presentation. Both uses would be as a method of getting attention and focusing on the type of company. Choose from one of the following companies:
   Ricardo Pet Shoppe, Inc.
   SuperSale Electronics

   The scenes should have as a minimum:
   Three layers
   One layer with motion
   Keyframes and blank keyframes
   Drawing and painting
   Imported image
   Text
   Symbol animation
   Sound

6. The following criteria should be met:
   - ☐ Southern Lawn, Inc. image-filled symbol appropriate to the type of company. The size, color, texture, and fill pattern is appropriate.
   - ☐ Wallush Construction Company image-filled symbol appropriate to the type of company. The size, color, texture, and fill pattern is appropriate.
   - ☐ Animation created for Sanders Beauty Shop works properly and is appropriate to the type of company. Skill level in creating the animation appropriate.
   - ☐ Animation created for Johansen Shoes International works properly and is appropriate to the type of company. Skill level in creating the animation appropriate.
   - ☐ Animation created for Rollando Gas and Oil Productions, Inc., works properly and is appropriate to the type of company. Skill level in creating the animation appropriate.
   - ☐ Animation created for Sew-Right Corporation works properly and is appropriate to the type of company. Skill level in creating the animation appropriate.
   - ☐ Interactive button for Sollari Educational Institution appropriate to the type of business and works properly.
   - ☐ Interactive button for Lee & Lee Law Office appropriate to the type of business and works properly.
   - ☐ Scene appropriate to the company, works properly, and contains all required elements.

Adobe LiveMotion

> **Adobe LiveMotion**
> **Publisher: Adobe Systems Incorporated**
> LiveMotion is graphical design software used to construct animations, rollovers, navigation devices, backgrounds, and decorative elements for Web pages and presentations.

ACTIVITY 1 • OBJECTS

In this activity, you will become familiar with:

- Composition Setup
- Rectangle Tool
- Undo
- Selection Tool
- Properties Palette
- Color Palette
- 3D Palette
- Object Layers Palette
- Rollover Button
- Previewing Rollovers in a Browser
- Polygon Tool
- Drawing Lines
- Transform Palette
- Pen Tool
- Uniting Objects
- Pen Selection Tool
- Placing Objects
- Library Palette
- Using Mattes
- Crop Tool

Composition Settings
SOURCE: ©ADOBE LIVEMOTION

Composition Setup

1. Go to the menu bar and choose File > New.
2. In the Composition Settings dialog box, click OK to accept the default size and frame rate. This can be changed later if needed by going to the menu bar and choosing Edit > Composition Settings. The width and height are set for the pixel dimensions of the most common monitor, allowing for some space for the toolbar.

Rectangle Tool

1. Click on the Rectangle Tool or press M.
2. Draw several rectangles on your composition. Hold down the Shift key and drag to draw a square. Leave the square selected.

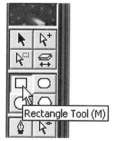

Rectangle Tool
SOURCE: ©ADOBE LIVEMOTION

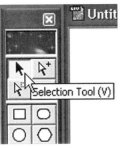

Selection Tool

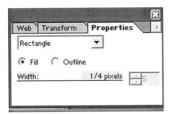

Properties

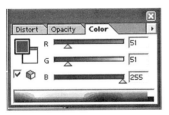

Color Palette

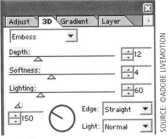

3D Palette

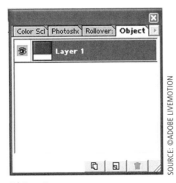

Object Layers

Undo

1. Go to the menu bar and choose Edit > Undo. This is the first choice under Edit. Note that it also gives you the specific name of the last action. You can also use Ctrl + Z to undo one action at a time.
2. Go to the menu bar and choose Edit > Undo. This command gives you a list of the last actions to choose from, so you can undo more than one at a time.
3. Go to the menu bar and choose Edit > Redo. This enables you to redo the last action.

Selection Tool

1. Click on the Selection Tool or press V.
2. If you accidentally deselect the square, use the Selection Tool to drag a marquee around the square to select it.

Properties Palette

1. Go to the menu bar and choose Window > Properties to open the Properties palette.
2. On the Properties palette you can adjust the shape of the square. Click in the drop-down box and change to Rounded Rectangle.
3. You can change from Fill to Outline. Change to Outline by clicking the radio button.
4. Change the width to 35 and the radius to 50.

Color Palette

1. Click on the Color palette. If the Color palette is not visible, go to the menu bar and choose Window > Color.
2. Click on the right arrow at the top left of the Color palette. Be sure you are on RGB.
3. Click on the cube for Web Safe Colors to turn it on. Experiment with changing colors on your composition. Select a different rectangle and experiment using the Properties palette and the Color palette.
4. Go to the menu bar and choose File > Save as. Save the file as *Rectangles.liv*.

3D Palette

1. Create a new composition with the default settings.
2. Draw a rectangle approximately 100 × 75 pixels. You can turn on the ruler by going to the menu bar and choosing View > Show Rulers.
3. Go to the menu bar and choose Window > 3D.
4. Choose Emboss from the drop-down box. See the figure to the left and create the same settings.

Object Layers Palette

1. Object layers belong to each object that you create. They do not belong to the entire composition. Go to the menu bar and choose Window > Object Layers.
2. Click on the New Layer button at the bottom of the Object Layers palette.
3. Double-click on the New Layer Name and name it "Button Settings."
4. On the Layer palette, experiment with the settings to create a Shadow effect. Click on the Color palette to select a color for your shadow.
5. Save as *ShadowButton.liv*.

Rollover Button

1. Create a new 100 × 100 pixel composition.
2. Draw a small circle.
3. Go to the menu bar and choose Window > Rollovers.
4. With the circle selected, click on the New Rollover State on the Rollover palette.
5. Leave the new Rollover layer on Over and change the color.
6. Click on the Preview Mode Tool to preview the rollover button.
7. Save as *Rollover.liv*.

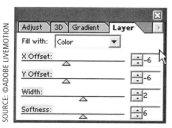

Layer Palette

Previewing Rollovers in a Browser

1. To preview the rollover, go to the menu bar and choose Window > Export. Check the Preview box.
2. Go to the menu bar and choose Edit > Composition Settings. In the Export box, choose Entire Composition. Be sure the Make HTML check box is selected, then click OK.
3. Go to the menu bar and choose File > Preview In. Choose the browser. Once you have chosen the browser, if it is not the active window on your screen, click on it on the taskbar.
4. Hover the mouse pointer over the button to preview. If the rollover has a Down state, click on the rollover.
5. Close the browser.
6. Open *Rollover.liv*. This is the file you created in "Rollover Button." Click on the New Rollover Button on the Rollover palette. This time the Down is in the drop-down box.
7. Go to the 3D palette. Choose Ripple from the drop-down box. Adjust the depth and lighting.
8. Save as *RippleRollover.liv*.
9. Click on the Preview Mode Tool to preview the Rollover Button.

Rollover

Polygon Tool

1. Create a new 200 × 200 pixel composition.
2. Double-click on the Polygon Tool.
3. Choose the number of sides for the polygon. Create a hexagon for this activity. You can use either the Sides slider or the Properties palette.
4. Hold down the Shift key while dragging to create a symmetrical polygon.
5. Apply blue color to the hexagon. Add a 3D effect to the button.
6. Make the button a rollover. Apply green color to the Over position and apply red color to the Down position.
7. Save as *Hexagon.liv*.

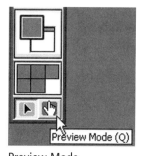

Preview Mode

SOURCE: ©ADOBE LIVEMOTION

Drawing Lines

1. LiveMotion does not have a Line Tool. You use the Rectangle Tool and make changes.
2. Create a new composition with the default settings.
3. Draw a long skinny horizontal line. Begin at 100 on the vertical ruler and 0 on the horizontal ruler. Draw across until you have made it the width of the screen, 500.

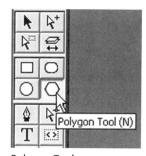

Polygon Tool

SOURCE: ©ADOBE LIVEMOTION

Transform Palette

1. Go to the menu bar and choose Window > Transform if the Transform palette is not on your screen. Change the height to 1.

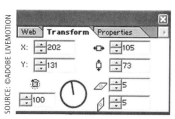

Transform Palette

2. Draw another line beginning at 100 on the horizontal ruler. Begin at 0 on the vertical ruler and drag to draw to the bottom of the screen at 550.
3. Go to the Transform palette and change the width to 1.
4. Use the Rounded Rectangle Tool to draw a rectangle on the composition.
5. Use the Transform palette to change the position to X = 202 and Y = 131. Change the width to 105 and the height to 73. Leave the rotation on 100. Change the skews to 5 and 5.
6. Save as *Transformed.liv*.

Pen Tool

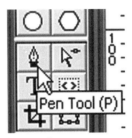

Pen Tool

SOURCE: ©ADOBE LIVEMOTION

1. Use a word processing program to open *PenTips.txt*.
2. Read the seven tips given for using pens. Add three of your own once you have finished the next few activities. Save as *MyPenTips.txt*.
3. Create a new composition with the default settings.
4. Click on the Pen Tool or press P.
5. Change to a green color. Draw three triangles of varying sizes. Click on the screen. Click at the top at an angle to form the beginning of a triangle. Click down at the bottom to end the triangle. Doing this should fill in the triangle. If it does not, go to the Properties palette and be sure Fill is selected.
6. To close the path, click inside the small circle at the beginning point of the path. The small circle should be hollow, but clicking in it fills the circle. See the figure at left.
7. Draw two more triangles.
8. Save as *ClosedPaths.liv*.

Closed Path

SOURCE: ©ADOBE LIVEMOTION

Uniting Objects

Pen Images

SOURCE: ©ADOBE LIVEMOTION

1. Create a new composition with the default settings.
2. Use the Pen Tool to draw the six images in at left. They should all be on the same composition.
3. Begin by drawing the flag. The Properties palette should be on Fill. Red should be selected in the Color palette.
4. Click four corners (without dragging). Close the path by clicking inside the small circle on the first corner you placed.
5. Change the color to black on the Color palette.
6. On the Properties palette, change to Outline and adjust the width to 15.
7. Click two points to create the flagpole.
8. Use the Selection Tool to drag around the image to select the entire image.
9. Go to the menu bar and choose Object > Combine > Unite in Color.
10. Save as *PenImages.liv*.

Pen Selection Tool

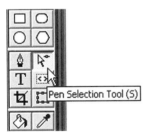

Pen Selection Tool

SOURCE: ©ADOBE LIVEMOTION

1. Open *PenImages.liv*. This is the file you created in "Uniting Objects."
2. Draw the baby buggy. Select black on the Color palette. Click on four corners. Close the path.
3. Click on the Pen Selection Tool or press S. Add points around the bottom, left, and right sides of the square. Click the points and drag to reshape.
4. Click on the Pen Tool. Close the path.
5. Use a similar method to draw the top part of the baby buggy. If you need to, select the top with the Selection Tool and drag it to move it. It does not have to look exactly like the figure.
6. Use the Ellipse Tool to draw the wheels.
7. Use the Selection Tool to draw a marquee around the image.
8. Go to the menu bar and choose Object > Combine > Unite in Color. (If the image is all one color, select Unite.)

9. Save again.
10. Continue to draw the other images using similar steps. If you mess up on an image and want to start over, use the Selection Tool to draw a marquee around it and press Delete.
11. Save again after each image.
12. Use a word processing program to open *PenTips.txt*. Add three more tips to the list if you haven't already. Save as *MyPenTips.txt*.

Placing Objects

1. Create a new composition with the default settings.
2. Go to the menu bar and choose File > Place. Browse to your CD and double-click *Veggies.jpg*.
3. Hover the mouse pointer over the bottom right corner until you see the Resize pointer, shown at right. Click and drag the object to resize. Hold down the Shift key while resizing to keep the proportion, or drag from bottom right to top left. Resize the object to approximately 250 × 150 pixels.
4. Hover the mouse pointer over the top right corner until you see the Rotate Cursor, shown at right. Click and drag to the left to rotate so that the object is at an angle.

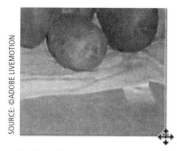

Resize Cursor

Library Palette

1. If the Library palette is not visible, go to the menu bar and choose Window > Library. Be sure that View LiveMotion Objects is clicked on the Library palette.
2. You can add your Veggies object to the Library by clicking on the object and dragging and dropping onto the Library palette.
3. On the Color palette, click on red. Drag an instance of the heart to a blank space on the composition.
4. Scale the heart so that it is approximately 1/2-inch in size.
5. With the heart selected, go to the menu bar and choose Edit > Copy then Edit > Paste.
6. Drag the hearts to the Veggies object to place in opposite corners.
7. Drag an instance of a tree to an empty place on the composition. Be sure your color is green.
8. Drag an instance of an apple to an empty place on the composition. Be sure your color is red. Scale the apple to proportionately fit on the tree. Copy and paste five apples and drag them onto the tree.
9. Save as *FruitsandVeggies.liv*.

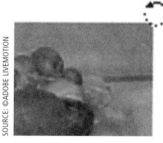

Rotate Cursor

Using Mattes

1. Create a new composition with the default settings.
2. Go to the menu bar and choose File > Place. Browse to your CD and double-click on *Veggies.jpg*.
3. Scale the object so that it is approximately 250 × 150 pixels.
4. Select the Veggies object. Click on the Library palette.
5. Click on a heart shape in the Library.
6. Click on Make Active Matte. See below right.
7. Save as *Matte.liv*.

Library Palette

Crop Tool

1. Create a new composition with the default settings.
2. Go to the menu bar and choose File > Place. Browse to your CD and double-click on *Dog.jpg*.
3. Click on the Crop Tool or press C.

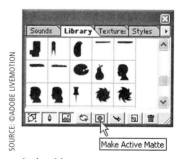

Active Matte

4. Hover the mouse pointer over the middle of the image. Click and drag inward to crop the dog. Your final object should be 200 × 200 pixels with the head centered in the picture.
5. To uncrop an object, drag a selection area to expose the hidden areas.
6. Save as *CroppedDog.liv*.
7. Create a new composition with the default settings.
8. Go to the menu bar and choose File > Place. Browse to your CD and double-click *Flowers.jpg*.
9. Crop the object so that there are only red and yellow flowers.
10. Save as *RedandYellow.liv*.
11. Create a new composition with the default settings.
12. Place *Flowers.jpg* on the composition.
13. Crop the object so that there are only yellow and orange flowers.
14. Save as *YellowandOrange.liv*.

ACTIVITY 1 • MINI-PROJECT

Create a Variety of Buttons

1. Create a variety of buttons for your presentation team to choose from. They should be organized in three different files with six buttons in each file. Save as *01Red.liv*, *02Blue.liv*, and *03Yellow.liv*.
2. The following criteria should be met for each color:
   - ☐ One button drawn with the Rectangle Tool.
   - ☐ One button drawn with the Polygon Tool.
   - ☐ One button shape created with the Pen Tool.
   - ☐ Several varieties of the color family used on the buttons.
   - ☐ One shape from the Library used and colored.
   - ☐ One image placed from another source.
   - ☐ One button created using an active matte.
   - ☐ One button includes use of the 3D palette.
   - ☐ One button includes use of the Transform palette.
   - ☐ One button has rollover effects applied for Over and Down.

ACTIVITY 2 • STYLES

In this activity, you will become familiar with:

- Styles Palette
- Applying a Style
- Eyedropper Tool
- Adding Styles
- Editing Styles
- Removing Styles

Styles Palette

1. Create a new composition with the default settings.
2. On the Styles palette, click on the right arrow next to the word styles to select a display mode.
3. Swatches View is used to display styles as swatch thumbnails. Preview View is used to display a list of names and a large thumbnail only for the currently highlighted style. Name View is used to display small thumbnails and names for all the styles.

Applying a Style

1. Draw a square on the composition.
2. Use the Selection Tool to select the square.
3. Go to the menu bar and choose Window > Styles.
4. Double-click a style swatch or drag a style swatch to your object.
5. Draw a second square.
6. Drag a style to the second square.

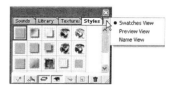

Styles Palette

SOURCE: ©ADOBE LIVEMOTION

Eyedropper Tool

1. Click on the second square.
2. Go to the menu bar and choose Edit > Copy.
3. Select the first square.
4. Click on the Eyedropper Tool or press I.
5. Shift-click on the second square to copy this style to the first square.
6. Save as *SquareStyles.liv*.

Adding Styles

1. Create a new composition with the default settings.
2. Draw a four-sided polygon.
3. Go to the menu bar and choose Window > Styles.
4. Drag the Broach style to the polygon.
5. Go to the menu bar and choose Window > Distort.
6. Click on the drop-down arrow in the Distort palette and choose Twirl. Make adjustments on the sliders to get the best effect.
7. Drag your four-sided polygon to the Styles palette.
8. The Name dialog box will appear. Type "MyBroach" in the Name box and clear the "Ignore color of first layer" check box.
9. Draw a rectangle and a circle.
10. Drag the MyBroach style onto the rectangle and circle.
11. Save as *MyBroach.liv*.

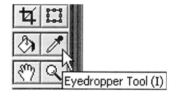

Eyedropper Tool

SOURCE: ©ADOBE LIVEMOTION

Editing Styles

1. Create a new composition with the default settings.
2. Draw an octagon.
3. Change the color on the octagon to purple. Add Drop Shadow 3 style to it and Emboss. Change the Object Opacity to 77 and the Object Layer Opacity to 90.
4. Drag the style to the Styles palette and name it "PurDropEm."
5. Go to the Styles palette and drag Plain Style to the object.
6. Drag the object to the Styles palette.
7. In the Name dialog box, type "PurDropEm" again. It will ask you if you want to replace the existing style. Click on Yes.
8. Save as *DropStyle.liv*.

Removing Styles

1. Create a new composition with the default settings.
2. Draw a circle. Drag the Sphere style to the circle.
3. Copy and paste a second instance of the Sphere.
4. Click on the second instance to select it, and then double-click on Plain Style in the Styles palette.
5. Save as *RemoveSphere.liv*.

New Style

ACTIVITY 2 • MINI-PROJECT

Create a Variety of Rules

1. Create a variety of rules for your presentation team to choose from. They should be organized in three different files with five rules in each file. Save as *01RedRules.liv*, *02BlueRules.liv*, and *03YellowRules.liv*.
2. The following criteria should be met for each color:
   - [ ] All rules 550 pixels wide, with varied height.
   - [ ] Use of texture fits within the color family.
   - [ ] Styles that were edited have at least three changes on them.
   - [ ] Distort palette used on at least one rule in each color family.
   - [ ] Changes made using the Opacity palette.

ACTIVITY 3 • TEXT

In this activity, you will become familiar with:

- Adding Type
- Resizing Type
- Copying and Pasting Type
- Editing Type

Adding Type

1. Create a new composition with the default settings.
2. Draw a 100 × 50 pixel rectangle. Add the Sphere style to it.
3. Click on the Type Tool.
4. Click on the composition.
5. In the Type Tool dialog box, type "Home." Change the font to Magneto or a similar font.

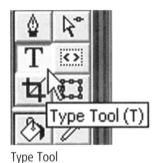

Type Tool
SOURCE: ©ADOBE LIVEMOTION

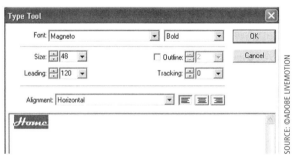

Type Dialog Box

6. Select a color for the font that will easily show up on the button.

Resizing Type

1. Resize the type you created so that it will fit on the rectangle. Hold down the Shift key on the keyboard to keep the proportion. Hover the mouse pointer over any of the edges except the top right until the pointer changes to a four-headed arrow.
2. Drag the type you created to the Sphere rectangle.
3. Use the Selection Tool to select the rectangle and the type by drawing a marquee around them.

4. Go to the menu bar and choose Object > Combine > Unite with Color.
5. Click on the rectangle to select both it and the Type.

Copying and Pasting Type

1. Go to the menu bar and choose Edit > Copy.
2. Go to the menu bar and choose Edit > Paste.
3. The second instance of the button will be pasted on top of the first one.

Editing Type

1. Drag the second instance of the button off the first one so that the button is by itself.
2. Double-click the type to open the Type dialog box.
3. Type "Family."
4. Paste two more buttons. Change the type to "Career" and "Hobbies."
5. Save as *Buttons.liv*.

ACTIVITY 3 • MINI-PROJECT

Create a Personal Identity Button

1. In a team of three or four students, create a button for each of your team members. Each button should represent the person's likes, dislikes, and/or personality.
2. Begin by meeting as a team and writing down at least five things about each of the members of your team.
3. The button can represent the person via shape, style, color, font type, and so on. Be creative in your use of the Library, Distort palette, 3D palette, and other tools learned in this software.
4. Include the person's first name on his or her button.
5. Use word processing software to write an explanation of each of your buttons. Save as *ButtonExp*.
6. Save the buttons as *PersonalID.liv*.
7. The following criteria should be met:
   - ☐ Students worked well together as a team.
   - ☐ Use of tools available.
   - ☐ Success in creating a good representation of the person.
   - ☐ Creative text with text united as a part of the button.
   - ☐ Explanation well thought out and accurate.

ACTIVITY 4 • COLOR

In this activity, you will become familiar with:

- Paint Bucket Tool
- Color Scheme Palette
- Gradient Palette
- Textures Palette
- Adjust Palette
- Photoshop Filters

Paint Bucket Tool

1. Create a new composition with the default settings.
2. Use drawing tools to draw four different-shaped objects.

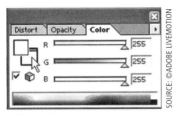

Color Palette

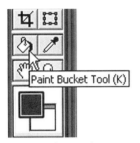

Paint Bucket Tool

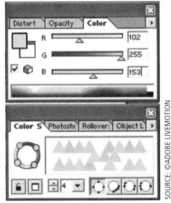

Color Scheme

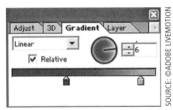

Gradient Palette

3. On the Color palette, click the Foreground color square. If the Color palette is not visible, go to the menu bar and choose Window > Color.
4. Choose a color by clicking on the color bar. Notice that the pointer turns into the Eyedropper Tool to pick up the color.
5. Click on the Paint Bucket Tool.
6. Click on the object that you want to apply the paint to. With the object selected, you can also fill the object with paint without using the Paint Bucket Tool. With the Paint Bucket Tool, you do not have to select the object.
7. Repeat this procedure for the other three objects, painting each one a different color.
8. Click on the background with black to paint the background for the entire composition.
9. Save as *ColoringObjects.liv*.

Color Scheme Palette

1. Create a new composition with the default settings.
2. Use the Library palette to drag three different-shaped stars to the composition.
3. On the Color Scheme palette, be sure the Lock button is not down.
4. If the Color Scheme palette is not visible, go to the menu bar and choose Window > Color Scheme.
5. To establish a color scheme, click on the Color palette to choose a color. Notice that colors begin to start showing up on the Color Scheme palette. Choose a different color to see what happens.
6. Type the exact RGB numbers as seen in the figure at left for this activity.
7. Change the number of colors you want the palette to display to 4.
8. Drag a different color in the color scheme to each of the star shapes.
9. Save as *Stars.liv*.

Gradient Palette

1. Create a new composition with the default settings.
2. Drag three splat shapes from the Library.
3. Click on one of the splat shapes.
4. Click on the Gradient palette. If it is not visible, go to the menu bar and choose Window > Gradient.
5. Choose the Linear gradient type from the drop-down box.
6. Click on the start marker and choose a color from the Color palette.
7. Click on the end marker and choose a color from the Color palette.
8. Slide each of the markers horizontally to create the Gradient you desire.
9. If you decide to rotate the object and do not want the Gradient to rotate, go to the menu bar and choose Object > Transform > Shape Transforms, then clear the Relative check box on the Gradient palette.
10. Apply different Gradient types and colors to the other Splat shapes.
11. Save as *Splat.liv*.
12. Draw another splat shape.
13. Click on the Color Scheme palette and be sure the Lock button is not down. Change the number of colors to show to 2.
14. Click on the start marker and choose a color. Doing so will automatically choose another color that is in that Color Scheme. Click on the end marker and select the other color in the scheme for that color.
15. Apply the Color Scheme to the splat shape.
16. Save again.

Textures Palette

1. Create a new composition with the default settings.
2. If the Textures palette is not visible, go to the menu bar and choose Window > Textures.
3. Click on the Background Color button on the Color palette.
4. Choose Colorwave from the Textures palette and drag it to the composition.
5. Save as *Colorwave.liv*.
6. Create a new composition with the default settings.
7. Draw a shape on your screen.
8. If the Textures palette is not on your screen, go to the menu bar and choose Window > Textures.
9. Drag the Droplets texture to the shape.
10. If the 3D palette is not visible, go to the menu bar and choose Window > 3D.
11. Choose Bevel from the drop-down box and make adjustments to get the effect you desire.
12. Save as *Droplets.liv*.

Adjust Palette

1. Create a new composition with the default settings.
2. You have been asked to create four rules to submit for possible use on the company Web site. They should be as wide as the composition and about 1/2-inch high. They should be in various shades of blue with a lighter adjustment.
3. Use the Rectangle Tool to draw the rules.
4. Apply textures or gradients to each one.
5. If the Adjust palette is not visible, go to the menu bar and choose Window > Adjust.
6. Drag the sliders on the Adjust palette until you have a rule effect that you think will be acceptable.
7. Save as *AdjustedRules.liv*.

Adjust Palette

Photoshop Filters

1. Create a new composition with the default settings.
2. Go to the menu bar and choose File > Place. Browse to your CD and double-click *OrangeBlossoms.bmp*.
3. With the image selected, go to the menu bar and choose Object > Filters > Artistic > Sponge.
4. Adjust the options for Brush Size, Definition, and Smoothness until you have the best effect. If you decide to make more adjustments later, you can double-click the Sponge filter name listed on the Photoshop Filters palette. Click OK.
5. Save as *Sponge.liv*.
6. Apply filters to the following BMP images: *Blue.bmp*, *GreenFish.bmp*, and *FishGreen.bmp*.
7. Choose the Photoshop filter that creates the best effect.
8. Save as *Blue.liv*, *GreenFish.liv*, and *FishGreen.liv*.

Photoshop Filters

ACTIVITY 4 • MINI-PROJECT

Create a Matched Design Set

1. Use a digital camera to take at least five pictures of objects in your classroom, at home, or outdoors. Try to focus on certain colors. Save as *01Obj.jpg*, *02Obj.jpg*, *03Obj.jpg*, *04Obj.jpg*, and *05Obj.jpg*.

2. Place each image in a LiveMotion composition. Apply a Photoshop filter to each one. Create rollovers with each image.
3. Create a background with either the Paint Bucket or the Texture palette.
4. Add some shapes using a color scheme that is appropriate for the colors in the images. Use the Adjust palette to vary the shadings in colors.
5. The following criteria should be met.
   - ☐ Images taken with the digital camera were clear and creative.
   - ☐ An appropriate Photoshop filter used on each image to effectively create an eye-catching rollover.
   - ☐ Background appropriate in color and texture to complement the image colors.
   - ☐ Color schemes complemented backgrounds and images placed in composition.
   - ☐ Adjust palette and Gradient palette effectively used to vary colors and yet complementary to the set.

ACTIVITY 5 • MORE ON ROLLOVERS AND BACKGROUNDS

In this activity, you will become familiar with:

- Using an Image in Rollovers
- Using Two Images in Rollovers
- Hiding an Image in Rollovers
- Creating a Remote Rollover
- Targeting a Remote Rollover
- Creating Moving Gradients
- Adding Sound to a Rollover
- Creating Two-Color Tile Backgrounds
- Using Dimmed Images for Backgrounds

Using an Image in Rollovers

1. Create a new composition with the default settings.
2. Go to the menu bar and choose File > Place. Browse to your CD and double-click on *FishGreen.bmp*.
3. Using the Selection Tool, resize the image to approximately 100 × 75 pixels.
4. With *FishGreen.bmp* selected, go to the Rollover palette.
5. Click on the New Rollover State button.
6. Go to the Adjust palette. Add a tint of 125. Be sure there is a noticeable difference in the Normal and Over layers on your Rollover palette.
7. Go to the Color palette and click on a green if it is not already on green. This changes the tint to green.
8. Click on the New Rollover State button.
9. Click on the 3D palette. Select Ripple from the drop-down box.
10. Save as *RippledRollover.liv*.
11. Using the Preview Mode Tool, preview the button in all three states.

Using Two Images in Rollovers

1. Go to the menu bar and choose File > Place. Browse to your CD and double-click on *WebMap.jpg*. Scale the image to 150 × 100 pixels.
2. Go to the menu bar and choose File > Place. Browse to your CD and double-click on *SepiaMap.jpg*. Scale the image to 150 × 100 pixels.

3. Click on the *SepiaMap.jpg*. This is the image you will use for the rollover state.
4. Go to the menu bar and choose Edit > Copy.
5. Click on the *WebMap.jpg*. On the Rollovers palette, click on the New Rollover State button.
6. Go to the menu bar and choose Edit > Paste Special > Paste Image.
7. Select *SepiaMap.jpg*. Delete it from the composition.
8. Save as *Mapping.liv*.
9. Preview the rollover using the Preview Mode Tool.

Hiding an Image in Rollovers

1. Go to the menu bar and choose File > Place. Browse to your CD and double-click on *PastelMap.jpg*.
2. Scale the image to 150 × 100 pixels.
3. With the image selected, go to the Object Layers palette and click on the New Layer button.
4. Go to the Textures palette and drag Cloud blue to Layer 1 on the Object Layers palette.
5. Go to the Opacity palette and lower the Object Layer Opacity to 10.
6. On the Rollover palette, click on the New Rollover State button.
7. With the Over state selected, click on the Opacity palette and raise the Object Layer Opacity back to 100.
8. Save as *CloudyMap.liv*.
9. Preview by clicking on the Preview Mode tool or pressing Q.

Creating a Remote Rollover

1. Create a new composition with the default settings.
2. Create a text object with the word "Stop" in it. It should be approximately 100 × 75 pixels. Apply a red color from the Color palette.
3. On the Rollovers palette, click on the New Rollover State button. In the drop-down box on the Over layer, click on Custom State. In the Custom State dialog box, name it "remote 1." Remove "Stop" and type "Yield." Change the color to yellow.
4. On the Rollovers palette, click on the New Rollover State button. In the drop-down box on the Over layer, click on Custom State. In the Custom State dialog box, name it "remote 2." Remove "Yield" and type "Go." Change the color to green.
5. Click on the Normal state. On the Opacity palette, move the Object Layer Opacity slider to 100.
6. On the remote 1 and remote 2 states, move the Object Layer Opacity to 100.
7. Save as *RedLight.liv*.

Targeting a Remote Rollover

1. Open *RedLight.liv*. This is the file that you created in "Creating a Remote Rollover."
2. Draw a six-sided octagon approximately 150 × 100 pixels. Apply a red color to it.
3. Go to the Rollovers palette and click on the New Rollover State button. Apply a yellow color to it.
4. Go to the Rollovers palette and click on the New Rollover State button. Apply a green color to it.
5. Drag the Target icon from the Normal state on the Rollovers palette to the "Stop" rollover. See the figure at right. Be sure that Normal is selected in the nested target.

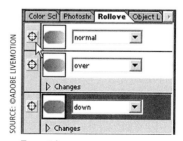

Target Icon

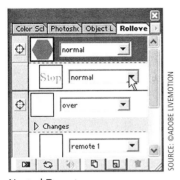

Nested Target

6. Drag the Target icon from the Over state to the Stop rollover. Be sure remote 1 is selected in the drop-down box.
7. Drag the Target icon from the Down state to the Stop rollover. Be sure remote 2 is selected in the drop-down box.
8. Save again.
9. Using the Preview Mode button, hover the mouse pointer over the six-sided octagon. This previews the Over state. Click on the six-sided octagon to preview the Down state.

Creating Moving Gradients

1. Create a new composition with the default settings.
2. Go to the Library palette and drag an instance of the up arrow to the composition. Add color to the up arrow.
3. Go to the Gradient palette and choose Linear and set the angle to 250. Move the end marker to 1/4-inch away from the start marker.
4. Go to the Rollovers palette and click on the Duplicate Rollover State button.
5. Choose Custom State from the drop-down box and type in "Gradient 1" on the Custom State dialog box for the name. Move the end marker all the way to the right and move the start marker 1/4-inch from the left edge of the color bar.
6. Go to the Rollovers palette and click on the Duplicate Rollover State button. Choose Custom State on the drop-down box and enter "gradient 2" on the pop-up menu. Move the start marker so it is about two-thirds of the way to the right on the Color bar.
7. Go to the Adjust palette and set the brightness to 15.
8. Draw a circle below the up arrow. Add an Over state and a Down state to the circle. Each state should be a different color.
9. On the Rollovers palette, drag the Target icon for the Normal state to the up arrow. Be sure Narrow is selected for the state.
10. Drag the Target icon for the Over state over the up arrow. Choose Gradient 1 from the Target state pop-up menu.
11. Drag the Target icon for the Down state over the Up Arrow. Choose Gradient 2 from the Target state pop-up menu.
12. Deselect all objects.
13. Save as *UpArrow.liv*.
14. Preview by clicking on the Preview Mode Tool.

Adding Sound to a Rollover

1. Create a new composition with the default settings.
2. Create a rollover with both an Over and a Down state.
3. You cannot add sounds to the Normal state. Click on the Over state.
4. Click on the Sounds palette. Click on one of the sounds and click Apply Sound on the Sounds palette.
5. Click on the Down state. Click on the Sounds palette and choose a sound. Apply the sound.
6. Save as *BadReception.liv*.
7. Preview the rollover with sound by clicking on the Preview Mode Tool.

Sounds Palette

Creating Two-Color Tile Backgrounds

1. Create a new 800 × 600 pixel composition. Clear the HTML check box. In the drop-down box next to Export, choose Trimmed Composition.
2. Using the Rectangle Tool, draw two rectangles from the top of the composition to the bottom. If you do not draw it all the way across, there is a chance it will not cover the entire Web page.

3. Apply appropriate colors to the two rectangles. You may want to let Color Scheme help you choose complimenting colors. Drag one of the rectangles to slightly overlap the other.
4. If the Export palette is not visible, go to the menu bar and choose Window > Export.
5. On the Export palette, in the first drop-down box, select GIF. Select the Preview check box. Click on the Transparency, Dither, and Interlace buttons next to the Web Adaptive drop-down box to select them. See right.
6. Go to the menu bar and choose File > Export.
7. Save as *TileFile.gif*.
8. To preview the background, create a new composition. Go to the menu bar and choose File > Place as Texture. Locate the saved GIF in your folder and double-click on the file.
9. Repeat steps 1 through 6, except create rectangles drawn horizontally. Save as *FileTile.gif*.

Export Palette

Using Dimmed Images for Backgrounds

1. Create a new 1024 × 1024 pixel composition.
2. Go to the menu bar and choose File > Place. Browse to your CD and double-click *SepiaCarnation.jpg*.
3. Leave blank space around the image. The fewer the colors, the smaller and faster to load the image will be.
4. Using the Adjust palette, dim the image by lowering the contrast and raising the brightness.
5. On the Export palette, in the first drop-down box, select GIF. Select the Preview. Click off Include Transparency Information, Dither, and Interlace.
6. Go to the menu bar and choose File > Export. Save as *CarnBack.gif*.
7. To preview, go to the menu bar and choose File > Place as Texture. Locate *CarnBack.gif* in your folders and double-click on the file.

ACTIVITY 5 • MINI-PROJECT

Create Images For School Use

1. Your school district uses presentation equipment each month at the board meetings and at parent meetings on all the campuses. They have asked your class to come up with some rollovers and backgrounds to "jazz up" the presentations.
2. Create a remote and target rollover announcing holidays for the next school year. The remote should have the name of the holiday and the target should have the date. Create rollovers for five different holidays. Consider color to represent the holiday.
3. Create images in rollovers for three of the campuses in your district.
4. Create two rollovers with moving gradients.
5. Create two rollovers with sound to use for information about the TAKS (Texas Assessment of Knowledge and Skills) test. It can have text or images on the rollover.
6. Create a background with two colors to use for your high school's presentation slide. Use school colors.
7. Create a dimmed background to use for general announcements.
8. The following criteria should be met:
   - ☐ Remote and target rollovers work properly and are accurate and creative.
   - ☐ Images appropriately used in rollovers for the campuses.
   - ☐ Images created with moving gradients.

☐ Images with sound appropriate and working.
☐ Background for the high school presentation slide has appropriate colors and is eye-catching.
☐ Dimmed background creative and eye-catching.

ACTIVITY 6 • ANIMATION

In this activity, you will become familiar with:

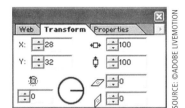
Transform Palette

■ Moving Objects Forward
■ Moving Objects Back
■ Receding Objects by Scaling
■ Changing Object Properties
■ Adding Backgrounds to Animation
■ Rotating an Object
■ Animating Text
■ Changing Colors on an Object
■ Changing an Object's Shape
■ Looping an Animation
■ Using Library Animations
■ Creating a Behavior Event
■ Exporting Animations

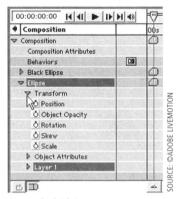
Expanded Objects

Moving Objects Forward

1. Create a new 550 × 500 pixel composition. Choose Entire Composition in the Export drop-down box. Select the Make HTML check box. This will be used as the default for the projects in Activity 6 unless otherwise noted.
2. Use the Ellipse Tool to draw the shape of a sun sized at 100 × 100 pixels. Use the Transform palette to watch the size of the sun as you draw. The sun should be positioned on the upper left side of the composition.
3. Color the sun yellow. You can use a Gradient so that it is two shades of yellow.
4. Go to the menu bar and choose Timeline > Show Timeline Window.
5. On the Timeline editor's objects hierarchy, click on Ellipse and press Enter.
6. Type "Sun" in the Name dialog box.
7. Expand the Sun's object list and click the triangle in front of Transform. See figure labeled Expanded Objects.
8. Click the stopwatch next to Position. See left.
9. Drag the current time marker to 02s (2 seconds). See below.

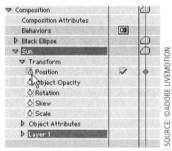
Position Stopwatch

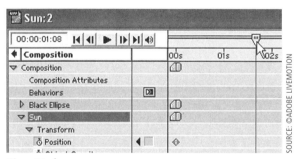
Time Marker

10. In the Composition window, drag the sun to the right side of the composition. Hold down the Shift key to constrain the movement when you have it where you want it.
11. Click in the gray area below the sun's hierarchy to deselect the object.

12. Click on the First Frame button at the top of the timeline editor.
13. Click on the Play button to preview.
14. Save as *Sun.liv*.

Moving Objects Back

1. On the timeline editor, drag the current marker to 03s (3 seconds).
2. In the Composition window, drag the sun back to its starting place. Hold down the Shift key to constrain it at the starting place.
3. Click on the timeline editor and click in the sun's hierarchy to deselect it.
4. Click on the First Frame button at the top of the timeline editor.
5. Click on the Play button to preview.
6. Save again.

First Frame

Receding Objects by Scaling

1. On the timeline editor, drag the current marker to the beginning mark, 00s.
2. Click on the stopwatch next to Scale to establish a starting size.
3. On the timeline editor, drag the current marker to 03s.
4. Set a keyframe by clicking on the blank box on the Scale line in the Create/Remove Keyframe column.

Play

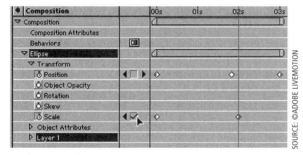

Scale Maintain

5. On the timeline editor, drag the current marker to 01s.
6. Using the Transform palette, resize the sun so that it is 50 × 50 pixels.
7. In the timeline editor, drag the current marker to 02s-05f (2 seconds, 5 frames).
8. Using the Transform palette, resize the sun back to 100 × 100 pixels.
9. Click on the First Frame button at the top of the Timeline editor.
10. Click on the Play button to preview.
11. Save again.

Changing Object Properties

1. Create a new 600 × 300 pixel composition. Choose Entire Composition in the Export drop-down box. Click on Make HTML.
2. Draw a 120 × 120 pixel circle. Add a gradient to it. Position it on the upper left side of the composition.
3. Using the Styles palette, add a drop shadow to the circle.
4. On the Object Layers palette, click the shadow layer. On the Layers palette, change the X Offset to 15, the Y Offset to 10, and the Softness to 10.
5. On the Opacity palette, make the Object Layer Opacity 60.
6. On the Object palette, click on Layer 1.
7. On the Gradient palette, move the end marker about 1/2-inch to the left. Set the Gradient Angle to 250 degrees.
8. On the 3D palette, choose Bevel. Change the settings so that they look like the figure to the right.

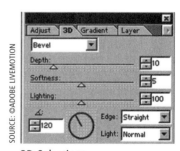

3D Selections

9. Show the timeline editor and rename the Ellipse to "Button."
10. On the timeline editor, drag the current marker to 01s-08f (1 second, 8 frames).
11. Drag the end point of the duration bar for the button to align with the current time marker's red line. See below.

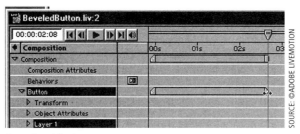

Duration Marker

12. Drag the current time marker to 00s.
13. Expand the button and shadow layer lists.
14. Click on the shadow layer. Click the stopwatch in the Offset row to set a new keyframe on that row.
15. Drag the current time marker to 01s.
16. In the Composition window, go to the Layer palette and change the X Offset to −10. You will see a new keyframe in the Offset row (a diamond).
17. Drag the current time marker back to 00s.
18. Expand the Layer list. Click on Layer. Click on the stopwatch for Color Gradient Angle.
19. Drag the current time marker to 01s.
20. In the Composition window, go to Gradient palette and change the angle to 280. On the 3D palette, change the effect angle to 30.
21. Deselect the Button frame.
22. Click on the First Frame button, then click on the Play button to preview.
23. Save again.

Adding Backgrounds to Animation

1. Create a new 600 × 300 pixel composition.
2. Add Bumpier texture to the composition for a background.
3. Draw a 50 × 50 pixel circle. Add a black and white radial gradient to it.
4. On the timeline editor expand the Ellipse object.
5. Click on the stopwatch in the Position row.
6. Drag the current time marker to 00s-05f. Drag the ball over to the right about 1/2-inch and down toward the bottom. Think about a bouncing rubber ball as you do this.
7. Drag the current time marker to 01s. Drag the ball over to the right about 1/2-inch and toward either the top of the screen or the bottom of the screen. It is your animation, so you can make it bounce where you want. Continue this pattern of moving the current time marker two times for each one second. Note that each time you do this, another keyframe is created (diamond).
8. Save as *BouncingBall.liv*.
9. Click on the First Frame button then click on the Play button to preview.

Rotating an Object

1. Create a new 600 × 300 pixel composition.
2. Draw three different-colored hearts that are also different sizes.
3. Click on the first heart.
4. On the timeline editor, expand the Transform Layer list.

5. Click on the stopwatch on the Rotate row.
6. Drag the current time marker to 01s.
7. On the Transform palette, drag the radius inside the circle a full circle to rotate the heart in a circle.
8. Click on the second heart.
9. On the timeline editor, expand the Transform Layer list.
10. Click on the stopwatch on the Rotate row.
11. Drag the current time marker to 02s.
12. On the Transform palette, drag the radius inside the circle a full circle to rotate the heart in a circle.
13. Repeat steps 8 through 12 for the third heart, dragging the current time marker to 03s.
14. Save as *Hearts.liv*.
15. Preview the animation.

Animating Text

1. Create a new 600 × 300 pixel composition.
2. Click on the Type Tool. Type your name in the text box. Add a gradient to it and change the size to 72. You can also change the font type.
3. On the timeline editor, move the current time marker to 01s.
4. Click on your name object. Press Enter and type your name in the pop-up box.
5. On the Layer palette, click on Softness and set it to 10.
6. Expand your name object and the Layer 1 list.
7. Click on the stopwatch next to Softness.
8. Drag the current time marker to 02s.
9. On the Layer palette, set the Softness to 0.
10. Expand the Transform Layer list.
11. Click on the stopwatch next to Scale.
12. Drag the current time marker to 01s.
13. Resize the text so that it is very small.
14. Drag the current time marker to 02s.
15. Save as *Name.liv*.
16. Preview.

Changing Colors on an Object

1. Create a new 600 × 300 pixel default composition.
2. Using the Library, drag an instance of a star onto the composition. Add a color of your choice to the star. Go to the Transform palette and resize the star to 150 × 150 pixels.
3. Select the star and display the timeline editor.
4. Click on the object name on the hierarchy list and press Enter. Type "Star" in the Name box.
5. Expand the Star list and the Layer 1 list.
6. Click the stopwatch next to the Color property. Drag the current time marker to 01s.
7. Choose a new color from the Color palette.
8. Drag the current time marker to 02s.
9. Select another color.
10. Drag the current time marker to 03s.
11. Select another color.
12. Save as *Star.liv*.
13. Preview.

Changing an Object's Shape

1. Create a new 500 × 250 pixel composition.
2. Use the Ellipse Tool to draw a 150 × 150 pixel circle.
3. Add a medium-dark color to the circle. Move the circle to the middle of the composition.
4. On the Layer palette, set the Softness to 2.
5. On the timeline editor, rename the object "Shape."
6. Drag the current time marker to 01s.
7. Expand the Shape list and the Transform list.
8. Click on the stopwatch for Position and Scale to set a keyframe at the current position.
9. Expand the Layer 1 list, then click on the stopwatch for Softness.
10. Move the current time marker to 00s.
11. Make sure the shape is selected.
12. Reshape the circle to 300 × 50 pixels.
13. Change the Softness to 5 on the Layer palette.
14. Save as *Shape.liv*.
15. Preview.

Looping an Animation

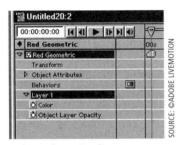

Independent Timeline

1. Create a new 550 × 500 pixel composition.
2. Drag four apple shapes from the Library. Apply a red color to each one of them.
3. Drag one of the apples away from the others.
4. Select the apple that is away from the other apples. This one will be animated. This also selects the object in the timeline window.
5. Go to the menu bar and choose Timeline > Time Independent. Note that an icon is displayed to the left of the object name on the timeline.
6. Double-click on the independent object name that will be animated.
7. Expand the Layer 1 list.
8. On the Opacity palette, set the Object Layer Opacity to 0.
9. Click on the stopwatch next to Object Layer Opacity.
10. Drag the current time marker to 01s.
11. On the Opacity palette, set the Object Layer Opacity to 100.
12. To loop the animation, click on the Loop button at the bottom of the timeline.
13. To preview the looping animation, click on the Preview Mode Tool in the Composition window. To stop the preview, click on the Edit Mode Tool in the Composition window.
14. Save as *Apples.liv*.

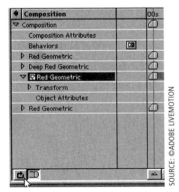

Loop Button

Using Library Animations

1. Create a new 550 × 500 pixel composition.
2. Go to the menu bar and choose File > Place. Browse to your CD and locate *Texas.jpg*.
3. Drag *Texas.jpg* to the Library. In the Name dialog box, type "Texas Logo."
4. Go to the Styles palette. Drag anim pulse 3x to the image on your composition.
5. Preview the style using the Play button on the timeline.
6. Expand the Transform, Object Attributes, and Layer 1 lists. Look at the lists to see where keyframes were added.
7. In a word processing document, write an explanation of where stopwatches were placed, keyframes were placed, and any other special symbols were used in the animation. Explain each one.
8. Save the word processing document as *LibraryAnimation*.
9. Save the animation as *AnimPulse.liv*.

Creating a Behavior Event

1. Create a new 550 × 500 pixel composition.
2. Create a sun using the Ellipse Tool and color it yellow. Move it to the right side of the composition.
3. Drag a cloud from the Library to the left side of the composition. Resize the cloud appropriately. Apply blue color to it. You may want to use a gradient for the cloud.
4. Select the cloud. Go to the menu bar and choose Timeline > Time Independent.
5. Show the timeline editor and rename each object appropriately.
6. Drag the composition duration bar endpoint to 01s.
7. Animate the cloud for position. Move it across the screen to the right to 01s.
8. Be sure the cloud is selected. Drag the current time marker back to 00s.
9. Click on the Behaviors button.

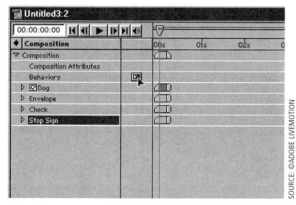

Behaviors Button

10. In the Edit Behaviors dialog box, choose Stop from the Add Behavior drop-down box. Choose Composition from the Target drop-down box. Click OK.
11. Drag the current time marker to 00s-01f.
12. Click on the Behaviors button. Type "start" in the Label box, then click OK.
13. Select the button. On the Rollovers palette, click on the New Rollover State button to create an Over state.
14. On the Rollovers palette, click on the Edit Behaviors button.
15. Choose Play from the Add Behavior drop-down box and choose Composition from the Target drop-down box.
16. Click on the New Rollover State button and create a Down state. Choose Out from the State drop-down box.
17. Click on the Edit Behaviors button on the Rollovers palette.
18. Choose Go To Label from the Add Behavior button drop-down box. Choose Composition from the Target drop-down box and choose start from the Label drop-down box. Click OK. See right.
19. Save as *Behaviors.liv*.
20. Preview by using the Preview Mode Tool. Hover the mouse pointer over the sun. The cloud should start moving toward the sun. Take the pointer off the sun and the cloud will move back to the starting point.

Edit Behaviors

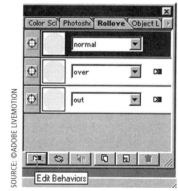

Rollover Behaviors

Exporting Animations

1. Open *Behaviors.liv*.
2. Go to the menu bar and choose File > Export As.
3. Name the file *Behaviors.swf*.
4. Go to your browser and open *Behaviors.swf* in the browser to preview.

ACTIVITY 6 • MINI-PROJECT

Create Animations for a Recreation Area

1. The HARC (Hill Area Recreational Center) has decided to place a kiosk in the registration office. This kiosk will give the guests answers to frequently asked questions.
2. The activities at the HARC include paddle boats, beach, water slides, picnic area, volleyball courts, mountain biking trail, refreshment center, and game room. Some special events planned for the summer are weekly volleyball tournaments, guided mountain biking trips each Saturday, beach party the last Friday of each month, and 4th of July fireworks display. Cost to enter the park is $15 per car.
3. Create four animations to use in the presentation at the kiosk. Vary the type of animation to include changing an object's shape, scaling an object, changing object properties, rotating an object, animating text, and changing color. Use objects from the library, objects created using the tools, and objects created by you with a scanner or digital camera.
4. The following criteria should be met:
   - ☐ Animations demonstrate creativity.
   - ☐ Animations useful to the types of activities at the recreation center.
   - ☐ Animations use a variety of animation techniques; at least six different animation techniques used.
   - ☐ Images and objects used are of good quality and appropriate for the use.
   - ☐ All animations work properly.

PART 3 • SIMULATION

Using LiveMotion

1. Visit http://www.sixflags.com/parks/fiestatexas/home.asp or another popular theme park's Web site if that one is not available. Study some of the information that the park thinks is important. They will use some of this same information around the park in kiosks and on presentations in a marketing plan.
2. Create six rollovers that use similar colors to the Web site to use on presentations and on kiosks around the park. Prepare a color scheme to use throughout this project. Text can be implemented from the Web site for other pages as you see in the navigation view. Vary the types of objects used to create these rollovers.
3. Create a matte using one of the rides as the image.
4. Using the colors from this Web site, create six backgrounds and rules to use in the presentations.
5. Use animation to create a banner ad for the newest ride or for use in advertising one of the sponsors. See the example on the Web page.
6. Create three targeted remote objects advertising the information on the Web site under Park Info.
7. Animate the park name using the color scheme. Create a behavior event for the animation.

8. The following criteria should be met:
   - ☐ Creativity and variety used in the rollovers in drawing objects used for creation as well as styles used.
   - ☐ Appropriate color scheme implemented throughout the project.
   - ☐ Banner ad is eye-catching and appropriate and uses intermediate-level skills in animation.
   - ☐ Backgrounds, rules, and matte appropriate in color and size and indicate appropriate level of skill.
   - ☐ Targeted remote objects work and are appropriate in their use.
   - ☐ Park name animation demonstrates creativity and uses the color scheme.

Part 4 | Jasc Animation Shop

> **Jasc Animation Shop**
> **Publisher: Jasc Software, Inc.**
> Animation Shop is a part of the Paint Shop Pro image management program. It contains a wizard to make instant text banners as well as animations from your images.

ACTIVITY 1 • TEXT BANNERS

In this activity, you will become familiar with:

- Getting Started
- Background
- Banner Size
- Timing
- Text Format
- Text Color
- Transition Style
- Flood Fill
- View Animation
- Frame Properties
- Saving

Getting Started

1. You can open Animation Shop from the Start menu or from within Paint Shop Pro.
2. To open only Animation Shop, go to Start > Programs > Jasc Software > Animation Shop 3. Your instructor may have it set up as a shortcut on your desktop. In that case, double-click the shortcut icon to begin using Paint Shop Pro.
3. If you are already in Paint Shop Pro and want to use Animation Shop, go to the menu bar and choose File > Jasc Software Products > Launch Animation Shop. Animation Shop may also be set up as a shortcut on your desktop. In that case, double-click the shortcut icon to begin Animation Shop.

Background

1. To activate the Banner Wizard, go to the menu bar and choose File > Banner Wizard.
2. In the Banner Wizard—Background dialog box, you have three choices for a background. Leave it on the default, which is opaque.
3. Click on Next.

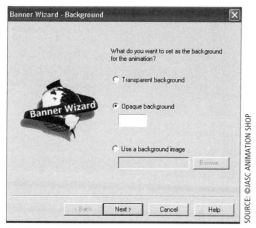

Background Dialog Box

Banner Size

1. In the Banner Wizard—Size dialog box, click in the drop-down box to look at the choices in creating a banner size. Leave it on the default, 468 × 60: Full banner. Note that you can also customize the size of the banner.

Size Dialog Box

2. Click on Next.

Timing

1. In the Banner Wizard—Timing dialog box, you can adjust the speed of the animation as it rotates through the frames. You can also view how many frames the animation will take, and whether you want it to loop indefinitely or stop after it has completed going through the frame sequence. You can even tell it how many times to play the frames.

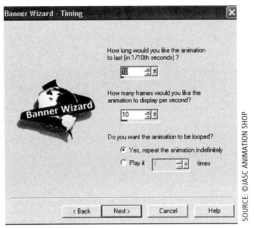

Timing Dialog Box

2. A good starting point is to leave it on the default and then make adjustments after you have previewed the animation.
3. Click on Next to accept the defaults.

Text Format

1. In the Banner Wizard—Text dialog box, type the text you want in the box. For this activity, type the name of your high school.

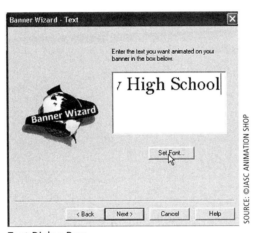

Text Dialog Box

2. In the Add Text dialog box, choose a font name, style, and size. You can also select some text effects as well as the alignment of text.

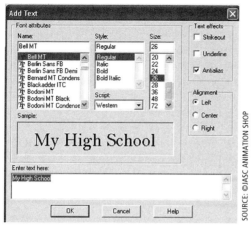

Add Text

3. Choose Berlin Sans FB Demi or a similar font. Leave the style as it is. This particular font type will have changed the style to bold.
4. Select 36 for the size.
5. Click on OK, then Next in the Banner Wizard—Text dialog box.

Text Color

1. In the Banner Wizard—Text Color dialog box, you can choose opaque or image text. Click on the opaque text color box.

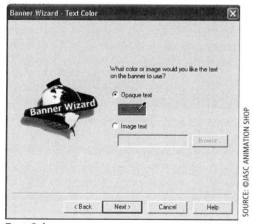

Text Color

2. In the Color dialog box, choose a color that matches one of your school colors as closely as possible.

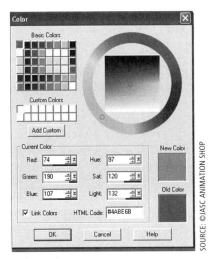

Color Dialog Box

3. Click OK in the dialog box, then click on Next in the Banner Wizard—Text Color dialog box.

Transition Style

1. In the Banner Wizard—Transition dialog box, choose Flag from the Transition Name drop-down box.

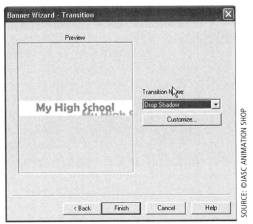

Transition Dialog Box

2. Click on Customize. Note that you can customize each of the transition names for even more variety. Click OK to leave it on the defaults.
3. Rendering frames will begin, which takes a minute or so. When the Finish button is no longer dimmed, click on it.

Flood Fill

1. On the Preview screen, you see each frame. The toolbar has some of the same tools that you used in Paint Shop Pro. Click on the Flood Fill tool.

Flood Fill

2. Choose the other school color from the Color palette and fill every other frame by clicking in the frame. Below each frame is the frame number. Move to the next frame by clicking and dragging in the scroll bar.

View Animation

1. Click on the View Animation icon.
2. Click on the View Animation icon again to stop the preview.

Frame Properties

1. After using the View Animation icon, you realize that this animation is going too fast. Select all the frames by pressing Ctrl + A. You can also click on the first frame, hold down the Shift key, and select the last frame.
2. With all the frames selected, right-click on the selection. On this shortcut menu, you can make any changes to what you selected during the Banner Wizard. Choose Frame Properties.
3. In the Frame Properties dialog box, on the Display Time tab, change to a higher number to slow down the animation. In this case it was very fast, so type "30" in the Display time (in 1/100th sec) box.
4. Click on View Animation to preview.

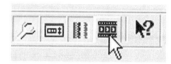

View Animation

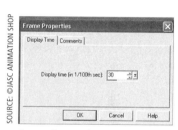

Frame Properties

Saving

1. Go to the menu bar and choose File > Save as. The default is to save it as a GIF, which is what you want to do.
2. In the Save As dialog box, type "*HighSchool*" in the File name box.
3. Click on Save.
4. In the Animation Quality Versus Output Size dialog box, you need to decide whether file size is important. You do not want to choose Smaller File Size over Quality unless there is a real space problem on your disk or computer.

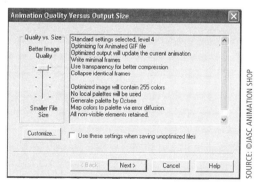

Animation Quality

5. Click on Customize. Note the other options available to you. Click on Cancel.
6. Click on Save.

ACTIVITY 1 • MINI-PROJECT

Create Banners for Businesses

1. Using the Banner Wizard, create the following banners:
   Trinity Care Center
   Bren-Tex Mills
   R & G Salvage Company
2. Save as *Trinity.gif*, *Bren.gif*, and *RG.gif*.
3. The following criteria should be met:
   ☐ Variety of font styles and colors used.
   ☐ Timing is appropriately set.
   ☐ Variety of transitions used.
   ☐ Creativity demonstrated in the three banners.
   ☐ Banners saved appropriately.

ACTIVITY 2 • IMAGE ANIMATION

In this activity, you will become familiar with:

■ Animation Wizard
■ Zoom Factor
■ Transitions
■ Image Effects
■ New Animation
■ Text Effects
■ Opening an Image

Animation Wizard

1. Go to the menu bar and choose File > Animation Wizard.
2. In the Animation Wizard dialog box, you can define the sizes of the images to fit in the frame or let the first frame be the guide for the rest of the images. Accept the default by clicking on Next.

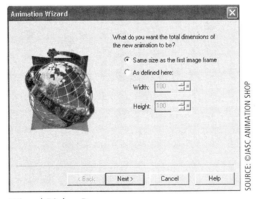

Wizard Dialog Box

3. You can then choose the canvas color for the animation. You can choose transparent or opaque. The default for opaque is black, but you can click on the Color box and select other colors. Click on Transparent, then Next.

4. If the image does not fill the frame, you have several choices. You can have it centered in the frame or in the upper left corner. Choose centered in the frame. The part of the frame that is left blank can be filled with the canvas color or the preceding image contents. Leave this on With the Canvas Color. Select the Scale "frames to fit" check box. Click on Next.

5. You can repeat the animation indefinitely or specify how many times you want it to play. Leave it on repeat the animation indefinitely. Change the length of time for each frame to play to 10. Click on Next.

6. You are now ready to add your images. Click on the Add Image button. Browse to your CD and double-click on *01College.jpg*. Repeat this for *02College.jpg* and *03College.jpg*. Note that you can remove images or reorder them with the Move Up and Move Down buttons. Click on Next.

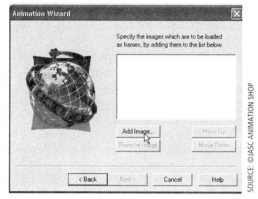

Add Image

7. Click on Finish in the next dialog box to begin building the animation. This may take a few minutes.

Zoom Factor

1. Click in the Zoom Factor drop-down box to change the Zoom to 1:3. This allows you to see all three slides.

2. You can also click on the Zoom tool or use the middle wheel on your mouse to zoom in or out.

Zoom Factor
SOURCE: ©JASC ANIMATION SHOP

Transitions

1. Right-click on the first frame and choose Insert Image Transition.

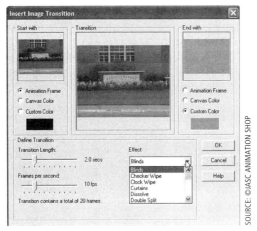

Insert Image Transition

2. In the Insert Image Transition dialog box, click in the Effect drop-down box and select Dissolve.
3. It will take a moment to render the preview; then click OK.
4. Repeat this procedure for each of the frames so that it can render the preview.
5. Save as *College.gif*. Accept the default for image optimization.
6. When the Optimization Progress is complete, click Next.
7. Click Next on the Optimization Preview dialog box.
8. Click Finish on the Optimization Results dialog box.

Image Effects

1. Use the Animation Wizard to create an animation consisting of *01Beta.jpg*, *02Beta.jpg*, and *03Beta.jpg*. These files are found on your CD.
2. The image size should be 100 × 100 pixels with a transparent canvas color.
3. The images should be centered in the frame with the "Scale frames to fit" check box selected.
4. Each frame should be displayed in 1/100th of a second at 20.
5. Once the image has been rendered, right-click on the first frame and choose Insert Image Effect.

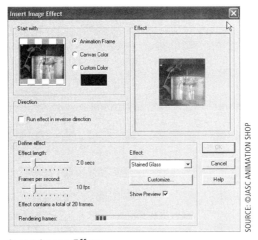

Insert Image Effect

6. In the Insert Image Effect dialog box, choose Stained Glass from the Effect drop-down box. Note your other choices on the Insert Image Effect dialog box for future reference.
7. Save as *Beta.gif*.

New Animation

1. Go to the menu bar and choose File > New.

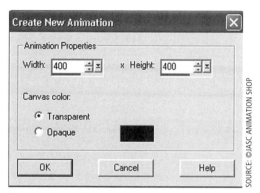

Create New Animation

2. In the Create New Animation dialog box, type 400 for Width and 400 for Height. Leave the canvas color on Transparent. Click OK.
3. Right-click on the frame and choose Insert Frames > From File.
4. In the Insert Frames from File dialog box, click on Add File. Browse to your CD and double-click on *Aquarium.jpg*. Click OK.

Text Effects

1. Right-click on the frame and choose Insert Text Effect.
2. In the Insert Text Effect dialog box, type "Where's the fish?" in the Define text box.
3. Change the Effect to Flag.
4. Choose a font type and color.
5. When the image has been rendered, click OK.
6. Click on the View Animation icon to try the animation.
7. Save as *Aquarium.gif*.

Opening an Image

1. Go to the menu bar and choose File > Open. Browse to your CD and double-click on *Button.psp*.
2. Right-click on the frame and choose Insert Image Effect.
3. Choose Rotate for the Image Effect.
4. Click on the View Animation icon to preview.
5. Save as *Rotating.gif*.

ACTIVITY 2 • MINI-PROJECT

Create a Business Image

1. Choose a business in which you are interested. Take a digital or other camera to the business and request permission to take at least three pictures. The pictures should be of the building with the business name, the inside offices, and some action taking place in the business.

2. Save the images as *01Business.jpg*, *02Business.jpg*, and *03Business.jpg*. If you are using a regular camera, get the photos developed and scan them, saving them with the same file names as if you were using a digital camera.
3. Create three different animations using transitions and image effects.
4. Save as *01Anim.gif*, *02Anim.gif*, and *03Anim.gif*.
5. Place all three animations on a disk and take them to the business for their use on a Web page or presentation.
6. The following criteria should be met:
   ☐ Photographs are of good quality.
   ☐ Animations are creative in use of the tools available in the software.
   ☐ Animations saved effectively.
   ☐ Timing on the animations is appropriate.
   ☐ Student participated in this business partnership project by taking the animations to the business for their use.

Part 4 • SIMULATION

Using Animation Shop

1. Create banners and animations that can be used by your city on presentations or Web pages.
2. Using the banner wizard, create three banners with the city name on them. Save as *01City.gif*, *02City.gif*, and *03City.gif*. Vary the colors and transitions to demonstrate skill.
3. Access a minimum of six pictures of various sites in your city. Take the pictures yourself with a digital or other camera or download them from the Internet. You can request pictures from your chamber of commerce. Save the images as *01Sites.jpg*, *02Sites.jpg*, *03Sites.jpg*, *04Sites.jpg*, *05Sites.jpg*, and *06Sites.jpg*.
4. Create at least three animations using a variety of the six images. You do not have to use all six images on every animation. You can add text effects as well as image effects. Be creative! Save as *01CityAnim.gif*, *02CityAnim.gif*, and *03CityAnim.gif*.
5. Use Paint Shop Pro drawing, text, and shape tools to create an image of your own that would represent your city. Save as *MyCity.psp*.
6. Animate the *MyCity.psp* image. Save as *AnimMyCity.gif*.
7. The following criteria should be met:
   ☐ Banners are creative and effectively use the tools available.
   ☐ Pictures of the city sites are of good quality.
   ☐ Animations using the pictures of the city sites are creative and effectively use transitions, image, and text effects.
   ☐ The drawing representing the city is appropriate and creative.
   ☐ The timing on the banners and animations is appropriate, as is the size of the animation.

Microsoft PowerPoint

> **Microsoft PowerPoint**
> **Publisher: Microsoft Publishing**
> PowerPoint is a presentation graphics software capable of creating dynamic slide shows.

ACTIVITY 1 • PLANNING THE PRESENTATION

In this activity, you will become familiar with:

- AUDIENCE Planning Sheet
- Presentation Planning Sheet

AUDIENCE Planning Sheet

1. Prepare the following planning sheet for each presentation you create in this course.
2. In a team of three or four students, brainstorm and discuss possible answers to the questions on the planning sheet. Discuss what kind of impact the answers to the questions would have on the preparation of the presentation. Before beginning the discussion, elect someone on your team to record the discussion. Elect someone on your team to present the discussion to the class. Elect someone on your team to serve as parliamentarian to make sure everyone gets equal discussion time and that everyone participates.

AUDIENCE Planning Sheet

Analyze	Who is the audience?	
	How can you connect with the members of the audience?	
	What is the purpose of the audience being there?	
	What is their mood?	
Understanding	What is the audience's level of knowledge on the topic of the presentation?	
Demographics	What ages, genders, and educational backgrounds are represented in the audience?	
Interests	Are the members of the audience there because they chose to attend or because they were required to attend?	

Environment	Is the platform or lectern placed so that the audience can see the projection screen?	
	Do you have limited space for movement?	
	How big is the room?	
	Can everyone see and hear you?	
	Do you have a working remote control?	
	Do you have a cordless microphone?	
	What is the light like in the room? Can it be altered?	
Needs	What does the audience need or want to get from the presentation?	
Customization	What can you do to make this presentation appropriate for this audience?	
Expectations	What is the audience expecting?	

Presentation Planning Sheet

1. Use the same team as you did for the AUDIENCE planning sheet to plan a presentation. The team should decide on the topic and the audience the presentation will be delivered to.
2. Elect someone to record the plan. Elect someone to present the plan to the class. Elect a parliamentarian to be sure that everyone participates and gets equal input into the presentation.

Presentation Planning Sheet

Theme	What will be the theme of the presentation?	
Title	What is the title of the presentation?	
Main Points	State the three main points of your presentation.	
Point 1	What other information do you want to include under this point?	
Point 2	What other information do you want to include under this point?	
Point 3	What other information do you want to include under this point?	
Resources	Where will the information for the presentation come from?	
Color	What colors will be used in the presentation?	
Graphics	What graphics will be used in the presentation?	
Sound	Will sound be used in the presentation? What type?	

Animation	Will animation be used in the presentation? Where and what type?	
Last Slide	What will be on the last slide?	

ACTIVITY 1 • MINI-PROJECT

Planning a Presentation

1. Your instructor has given you the task of planning a presentation to present to the school board. Some ideas for the presentation's topic:

    Present the community service projects that you completed as a member of a student organization this school year.

    Plan a presentation on a school-sponsored trip you took this year.

    Plan a presentation for the senior banquet.

2. Determine where the presentation will take place in your building and visit the facility.
3. Research the school board.
4. Prepare an AUDIENCE planning sheet and a presentation planning sheet. Both can be found on your CD.
5. The following criteria should be met:

    ☐ Topic is appropriate for the assignment.

    ☐ School board was researched and evident in the AUDIENCE planning sheet.

    ☐ AUDIENCE planning sheet is well thought out and thorough.

    ☐ Presentation planning sheet is appropriately completed, with evidence of thought and rationalization in planning.

ACTIVITY 2 • BASICS

In this activity, you will become familiar with:

- Task Pane
- Standard Toolbar
- Formatting Toolbar
- Drawing Toolbar
- Normal View
- Outline Pane
- Slide Pane
- Notes Pane
- Smart Tags
- Slide Sorter View
- Slide Show View
- Saving

SOURCE: ©MICROSOFT POWERPOINT

Task Pane

Task Pane

1. The Task pane lists the most commonly used operations. It is found on the right side of the screen. If your Task pane is not visible, go to the menu bar and choose View > Task Pane.
2. The commands that are used most often on the Task pane are creating a blank presentation file, opening an existing presentation file, and using a template.
3. The Task pane can be closed if you want more space on your screen.

Standard Toolbar

1. The Standard toolbar is found on the row underneath the menu bar. It contains shortcut icons to the most often used tools. It can also be customized to add or take away some of the icons.

Standard Toolbar.

2. Hover the mouse pointer over each icon on the Standard toolbar to see the ScreenTip. Try to say what the icon does before the ScreenTip appears.

Formatting Toolbar

1. In newer versions of Windows, the Formatting tools are found on the same line as the standard toolbar.

Formatting Toolbar.

2. If you want them on separate lines, go to the menu bar and choose Tools > Customize. In the Customize dialog box, select the "Show Standard and Formatting toolbars on two rows" check box.

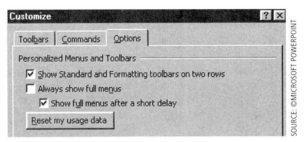

Customize

3. Go to the menu bar and choose Tools > Customize > Options. If you don't like your menus to pause before they show all the choices, select the "Always show full menus" check box. Click on Close.
4. Hover the mouse pointer over each icon on the Formatting toolbar to see the ScreenTip. Try to say what the icon does before the ScreenTip appears.

Drawing Toolbar

1. The Drawing toolbar is docked at the bottom of the screen.

Drawing Toolbar.

2. If you do not see the Drawing toolbar, go to the menu bar and choose View > Toolbars > Drawing to turn the toolbar on.

Normal View

1. Normal view is the main startup window in PowerPoint. It contains four panes: Outline pane, Slide pane, Notes pane, and Task pane.
2. All the panes can be increased or decreased in size by hovering the mouse pointer on the edge of the pane and clicking and dragging when the two-headed arrow appears.

Outline Pane

1. The Outline pane has two tabs: the Outline tab and the Slides tab.
2. Click on the Outline tab in the Outline pane. Type "Learning PowerPoint."

Outline Pane
SOURCE: ©MICROSOFT POWERPOINT

Slide Pane

1. The Slide pane shows one slide at a time as it will appear in the slide show.
2. Click in the second box of the Slide pane. Type your name and your school name underneath it.

Notes Pane

1. Click in the Notes pane and type a paragraph introducing yourself. In a presentation, the Notes pane takes the place of index cards in a speech.
2. You can format the text in the Notes pane to increase the size, color, and font.
3. You can also print the Notes pane for your use during your presentation.
4. Click in the Outline pane right after your name. Press Enter. This takes you to the next line. Press Shift + Tab to decrease the indent, which takes you to a new slide.

Smart Tags

1. These buttons appear (floating on your screen) as needed to assist in completing a task quickly.
2. Click on the button and a drop-down box of choices appears.
3. Look to see if you have any smart tags on your screen. If you do, try the drop-down box. If not, you will get an opportunity to try them later.

Slide Sorter View

1. Slide Sorter View is used to sort slides, delete slides, and preview transitions and animations. The slides are in thumbnail view so it is not effective for editing.
2. Go to the menu bar and choose View > Slide Sorter. You can also click on the Slide Sorter button in the Views toolbar located in the bottom left tray of your screen.
3. Click on Slide 1 in Slide Sorter View. Hold down the left mouse button and drag the slide to the right until you see the vertical line. Drop the slide in place once you see the vertical line.
4. Click on Slide 1, which is now the blank slide. Press Delete to remove it from the slide show. Note that the current selected slide is framed with a border.
5. To return to Normal View, double-click the slide.
6. In Normal view, click on the Outline pane and then the Outline tab. Click after your school's name in the first and only slide on your screen. Press Enter, then Shift + Tab to add a new slide. Type in the Title placeholder "Slide Views."

Slide Sorter View
SOURCE: ©MICROSOFT POWERPOINT

Slide Show View

1. Slide Show View is the full-screen preview of your presentation. You can access it in several different ways.

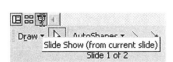

Slide Show

Shortcut Menu

2. Go to the menu bar and choose View > Slide Show. This begins the slide show on whatever slide the pointer was on. You want to be sure the pointer is on the first slide when using this method.
3. You can also use the View toolbar at the bottom left of your screen. This starts the slide show on whatever slide the pointer is on—the current slide.
4. A quick way to start your slide show is by pressing F5. This begins the slide from the first slide, no matter what slide is your current slide. If you are in front of a group and beginning the presentation, this is the best way to start the slide show.
5. Start the slide show by pressing F5. Try out the following ways to maneuver around the slide show:
   a. Click the left mouse button once to move to the next slide.
   b. Press the Backspace key to move back one slide.
   c. Type "2" and press Enter. This jumps the slide show to Slide 2.
   d. Hover the mouse pointer in the bottom left corner of the slide show to access the shortcut menu. Choose Pointer Options > Pen. You can change colors of the pen. Use the pen to circle your name. Type "e" to erase the circle. The pen writings will also erase on their own when you leave that slide.
   e. Right-click on the screen. This also accesses the shortcut menu.
   f. Type "b." This turns the screen black, so if you want to pause and talk about something with the audience and not have the slide show running, you can use this. Type "b" again to bring the screen back. You can also change to a white screen by typing "w."
   g. End the show by pressing Esc.

Saving

1. Go to the menu bar and choose File > Save As. Name the file *Learning.ppt*.
2. The file can also be saved as a graphic. This is a good way to save if you intend to include it in a word processing document. Go to the menu bar and choose File > Save As. In the Save As type drop-down box, select GIF (Graphic Interchange Format). Since there are two slides in this presentation, choose Every Slide in the message about saving Current Slide Only or Every Slide.
3. If you are unsure about the software available where you will be presenting, you may want to save the file as a PowerPoint show (PPS). To do this, go to the menu bar and choose File > Save As. In the Save As type drop-down box, select PowerPoint Show. You should be aware that you can then present without the PowerPoint software, although you may lose any special enhancements, including font types that you may have used. Those fonts would have to be stored on the computer that you are using for the presentation in order to show.

ACTIVITY 2 • MINI-PROJECT

Create an Introduction

1. Invite a guest speaker from a local Toastmasters club, or another professional who uses presentation software. Ask this person to give tips on using presentation software during a speech as well as effective speech delivery.
2. Before the speaker arrives, write a list of at least five questions or tips of your own.
3. After listening to the speaker, create a PowerPoint presentation introducing the speaker. Type the name of the presentation and the speaker's name. In the Notes pane, type a brief introduction of the speaker.

4. The following criteria should be met:
   - ☐ Questions or tips appropriate to the topic.
   - ☐ Appropriate behavior displayed during presentation.
   - ☐ Introduction slide information is accurate.
   - ☐ Introduction in Notes pane includes appropriate and accurate information.

ACTIVITY 3 • BLANK DOCUMENT

In this activity, you will become familiar with:

- ■ Slide Layout
- ■ Slide Placeholders
- ■ Line Style and Color
- ■ Slide Design
- ■ Color Schemes
- ■ Animation Schemes
- ■ New Slide
- ■ Line Spacing
- ■ Clip Art Gallery
- ■ Recoloring Pictures
- ■ Master Slides
- ■ Background
- ■ Bullets
- ■ Pictures from Files
- ■ SWF Files
- ■ Media Clip
- ■ AutoShapes
- ■ WordArt
- ■ Order
- ■ Group
- ■ Diagrams
- ■ Proofing Tools
- ■ Action Settings

Slide Layout

1. On the Standard toolbar, click on the New Blank Document icon.
2. The slide layout sets the format of the text and graphic content of each individual slide. When you create a blank presentation or add a new slide, the Slide Layout Task pane appears.
3. Hover the mouse pointer over each Task pane layout to display the name. Most of the time the Title Slide layout is the first slide of a presentation. Leave the slide layout on Title Slide. If you change your mind after typing on the slide, you can still change the layout format.

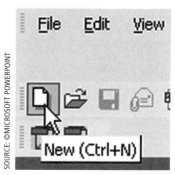

New Slide Show

Slide Placeholders

1. On the Title Slide, click inside the first placeholder. Type "PRESENTATION PLANNING" in all caps.
2. Type your name and your school's name in the second placeholder.
3. Placeholders have two selection modes. A slanted-line selection box means that the object's content can be edited. When you are typing in the placeholder, you should see a slanted-line selection around the box. A dotted-line selection box means that the object can be changed as a whole. A dotted line appears when you are resizing or moving the whole object.

Line Style

SOURCE: ©MICROSOFT POWERPOINT

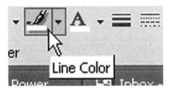

Line Color

SOURCE: ©MICROSOFT POWERPOINT

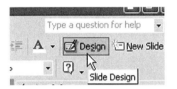

Slide Design

SOURCE: ©MICROSOFT POWERPOINT

Color Schemes

SOURCE: ©MICROSOFT POWERPOINT

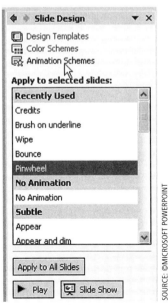

Animation Schemes

SOURCE: ©MICROSOFT POWERPOINT

4. Placeholders are text boxes that can be resized in the same way as other graphics. Hover the mouse pointer over any handle and it changes to a two-sided arrow. Hold down the left mouse button and drag to resize. If you want to resize for top/bottom or left/right at the same time, hold down the Ctrl key as you drag the placeholder.

5. Resize the text box to exactly fit around your name and your school's name. Most of the time you would not do this, because the default on the placeholders is no line.

Line Style and Color

1. With the pointer still in the placeholder, click on the Line Style icon on the Drawing toolbar. Choose 6 pt. with the three lines, not solid.

2. Click on the Line Color icon on the Drawing toolbar. Choose Yellow.

Slide Design

1. Click on the Slide Design icon on the Formatting toolbar. Notice that the Slide Design Task pane opens.

2. Hover the mouse pointer over some of the Slide Designs. Click on several of them to try them on your current presentation. Notice that the color of the box changes to match the default color scheme of the design you are trying.

3. Click on Shimmer.

4. You can create your own Slide Designs as you have learned in Flash or LiveMotion. You are not limited to only the designs you see on this screen.

Color Schemes

1. Below Design Templates in the Task pane, click on Color Schemes. Choose a blue color scheme for this design.

2. You can personalize your slide show by choosing your own colors, but it is sometimes tricky to get the right color for the lighting. PowerPoint has done this work for you and in most cases, the colors they have put together work.

Animation Schemes

1. Below Design Templates in the Task pane, click on Animation Schemes.

2. Animations are divided into four categories: No Animation, Subtle, Moderate, and Exciting. At the top of the categories, you also have the Recently Used animations listed.

3. Choose an animation, then click on the Play button at the bottom left of the Task pane. Try several of them, then leave it on Light Bulb.

4. Click on Slide Show at the bottom of the Task pane to get the full preview of the Light Bulb animation.

5. If you have more than one slide, you can add the animation scheme to as many slides as you want. In the Outline pane, you would click on the first slide, hold down the Shift key, and click on the last slide. With all the slides selected, click on the animation scheme of your choice.

6. Save as *Planning.ppt*.

New Slide

1. Click on the New Slide icon on the Formatting toolbar. Note that this is different from the New Slide Show icon on the far left of the Standard toolbar. The New Slide Show icon creates an entire new slide show, and the New Slide icon creates a new slide within the current slide show.

2. The default slide layout for the second slide is Title and Text. Leave the default slide layout for this slide.
3. Type "Planning Basics" in the Title placeholder.
4. Type the following in the bulleted list: "Audience," "Purpose," "Place," "Format," "Special Needs."

Line Spacing

1. Select the five items you typed in the bulleted list placeholder.
2. Go to the menu bar and choose Format > Line Spacing.
3. Change the After paragraph spacing to .2 lines. This adjusts the spacing between the bulleted items. Since the list did not fill up the entire slide, doing this makes the slide look not so empty with more spacing between the items. You could also increase the font size here, but it is best that the font size remain uniform throughout the presentation as much as possible unless you are trying to create some special effect to make a point.

Clip Art Gallery

1. Click the back button on the Task pane until you are back at Slide Layout.
2. Scroll down with the scroll bar on the right until you locate Other Layouts. Select the title, text, and clip art by double-clicking on it.

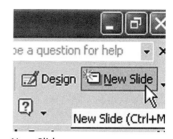

New Slide

SOURCE: ©MICROSOFT POWERPOINT

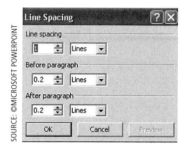

Line Spacing

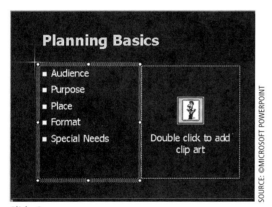

Slide 2

SOURCE: ©MICROSOFT POWERPOINT

3. Double-click on the clip art placeholder to open the Select Picture dialog box.

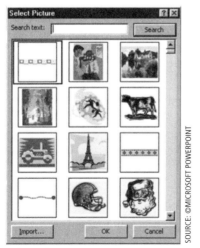

Select Picture

SOURCE: ©MICROSOFT POWERPOINT

4. Type a keyword in the Search text box. Think about the topics on the slide and locate a picture that is an image of one or more of those topics. You may want to try several synonyms. When you locate a picture that is appropriate for this slide, double-click on the clip art to insert it.

Recoloring Pictures

1. Click on the clip art to open the floating Picture toolbar. If it does not open, go to the menu bar and choose View > Toolbars > Picture.
2. Click on the Recolor Picture icon, as shown below.

Picture Toolbar

SOURCE: ©MICROSOFT POWERPOINT

3. In the Recolor Picture dialog box, you can choose to change colors or fills. Changing fills changes the background and not the lines. You need to change the colors. Change to any color to match the color scheme in your presentation. Click OK.
4. Resize the image and move the placeholders as needed. You can move placeholders by clicking anywhere on an outside border other than the handles, holding down the left mouse button, and dragging them to the new location.
5. Save again.

Master Slides

1. Click on the New Slide icon.
2. The Master Slide controls all the slides. If you want to make a format change in text such as size, it is best to make it in the Master Slide so it is consistent throughout your presentation.
3. Go to the menu bar and choose View > Master > Slide Master. You can also get to the Slide Master by holding down the Shift key and clicking on the Normal View icon on the View toolbar located on the bottom left corner of your screen.
4. There are two different Slide Masters. One of them is the Title Slide and the other one represents the rest of the slides. You can toggle between the two in the Outline pane.
5. Click in the Title placeholder. The default font size is 44. Change it to 48.
6. Click in the Object Area and click on the first bullet. This selects all levels. Click to edit Master text styles. Change the font size to 40.
7. Click on the Normal View icon to leave the Master Slides view.

Background

1. Type in the Title placeholder "Audience."
2. Type the following questions as bullets:
   What is the audience size?
   Are they required to attend?
   What are their color preferences?
   What style of images do they prefer?
3. In each question, select a word to emphasize and change the text color.
4. You can change backgrounds on one slide only or on all slides at the same time. Go to the menu bar and choose Format > Background.

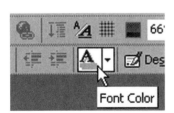

Font Color

SOURCE: ©MICROSOFT POWERPOINT

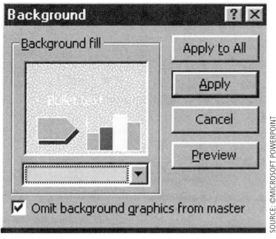

Background

5. In the Background dialog box, select the "Omit background graphics from master" check box. You don't always have to turn off the graphics, but sometimes it is a nice change in the presentation or necessary because of other graphics on the slide.
6. Choose a color from the drop-down box for the color scheme.
7. Click on Apply to apply only to this slide.
8. Save again.

Bullets

1. Click on the New Slide icon.
2. In the Title placeholder, type "Purpose."
3. In the bulleted list, type the following:
   Informative
   Educational
   Brainstorming Session
4. Select the bulleted list. Go to the menu bar and choose Format > Bullets and Numbering.
5. In the Bullets and Numbering dialog box, click on the Bulleted tab.

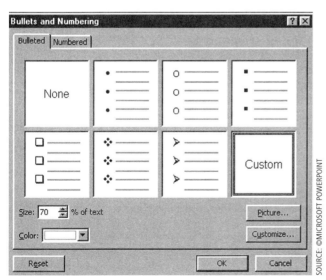

Bullets and Numbering

6. On this tab, you can change the size of the bullet and the color of the bullet. You can also use a customized symbol or a picture for a bullet. Click on Customize.
7. In the Symbol dialog box, you can choose from several fonts. Click in the Font drop-down box and choose Wingdings. Double-click on a suitable symbol for this slide.

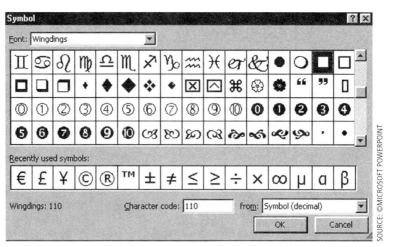

Symbol Dialog Box

8. Click OK in the Symbol dialog box and click OK in the Bullets and Numbering dialog box.
9. Select the list and change the Before and After paragraph spacing.
10. Save again.

Pictures from Files

1. Go to the menu bar and choose Insert > Picture > From File. Browse to your CD and double-click on *Backpack.jpg*.
2. Resize and move the image as needed.
3. Format the background for white without graphics.
4. Format the bullets and fonts to go with the color scheme and for the best view on the white background.

SWF Files

1. Click on the New Slide icon.
2. Choose Title and Text slide layout.
3. Click in the Title placeholder. Type "Place."
4. Click in the bulleted list placeholder. Type the following questions:
   Is the room large?
   Is the room small?
   Is there a projector?
   Is there good lighting? Can the lights be dimmed?
5. Go to the menu bar and choose View > Toolbars > Control Toolbox.
6. Save again.
7. Click on the More Controls icon and select Shockwave Flash Object.
8. When the pointer turns into a plus sign, click and drag the box where you want to place your SWF file.
9. Right-click on the box that you just drew and choose Properties.

Control Toolbox

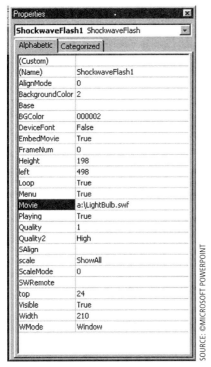

Properties

10. If ShockwaveFlash is not displayed in the drop-down box, click on the arrow in the drop-down box and select it.
11. Click on the Alphabetic tab.
12. In the blank next to Movie, type the exact path name of the file. Get path name instructions from your instructor.
13. Change Embed to True.
14. Close the Properties dialog box.
15. Save again.
16. Click on the Slide Show icon in the bottom left corner of the screen to preview the animation.
17. Save again.

Media Clip

1. Click on the New Slide icon.
2. For the slide layout, choose Title, Media Clip, and Text.
3. Type "Delivery Format" in the Title placeholder.
4. In the bulleted list placeholder, type "Speaker," "Kiosk," "Self-running," and "Web page."
5. Double-click on the media clip placeholder. Choose Mozart's Symphony No. 40. When it asks if you want it to automatically play in the slide show, click Yes.
6. Click on the Slide Show icon in the View toolbar to preview the media clip.
7. Save again.

AutoShapes

1. On the Drawing toolbar, choose AutoShapes > Basic Shapes > Cube. Draw a cube on top of the Media Clip icon.

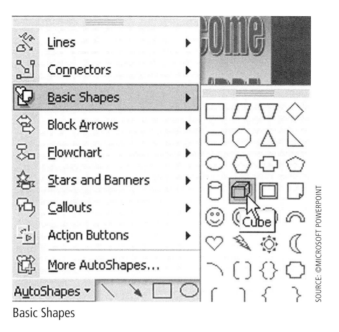

Basic Shapes

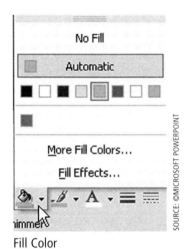

Fill Color

2. Click on the arrow next to the Fill icon on the Drawing toolbar.
3. Choose Fill Effects. In the Fill Effects dialog box, choose Two Colors, Horizontal. Note the other options, such as Preset, for later use.

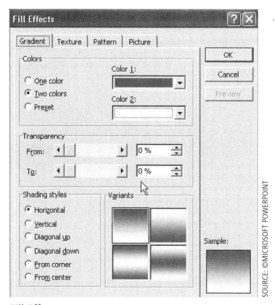

Fill Effects

Insert WordArt

WordArt

1. Click on the WordArt tool.
2. Choose a design and click OK.
3. In the Edit WordArt Text dialog box, type "Welcome (Press Enter) FBLA/BPA!"

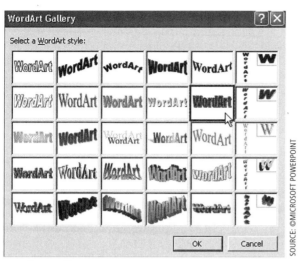

WordArt Gallery

4. Click on the WordArt object on your screen, hold down the left mouse button, and drag to position the WordArt on the front of the cube.
5. Resize the WordArt the same as you would a placeholder.
6. Click on the green circle at the top of the WordArt and drag to rotate it slightly to the left.
7. When you click on the WordArt, the WordArt floating toolbar should appear. If it does not, go to the menu bar and choose View > Toolbars > Word Art. Hover the mouse pointer over each of the icons to see what is available. Choose Format WordArt.

Rotate

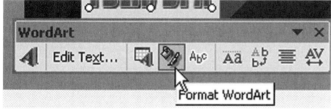

WordArt Toolbar

8. In the Format WordArt dialog box, adjust the fill color and the line color to create a WordArt that stands out on the cube and against the background.
9. Save again.

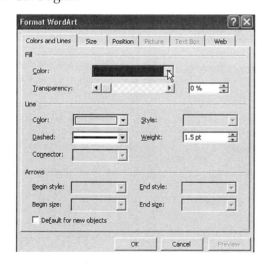

Format WordArt

Apply Content

Insert Diagram

Order

1. When you have several objects stacked on top of each other, it is sometimes necessary to place them in an order. If the WordArt is not showing then you need to click on it, right-click, and select Order, then Bring Forward.
2. If the Clip Media icon is showing, right-click and select Order then Send Backward.

Group

1. Once you have stacked objects and have them formatted the way you want, it is a good idea to group them. This way if you move them, they move as a group and you don't have to move each individual one and try to get the position the way you want it again.
2. Select them first by clicking on the WordArt, holding down the Shift key, and clicking on the cube. They should now both be selected.
3. On the Drawing toolbar, click on Draw > Group. You should notice that there are handles only around the group rather than around each individual object.
4. If you find it necessary to ungroup them, go to the Drawing toolbar and click on Draw > Ungroup.

Diagrams

1. Click on the New Slide icon. This slide will be the Summary slide. It is especially important, as it is the last impression you will leave on your audience.
2. Go to the Slide Layout Task pane and choose Content Layout > Apply to Selected Slides.
3. On the slide, click on Insert Diagram.
4. In the Diagram Gallery dialog box, choose Radial Diagram.
5. Format the background for this slide to a light yellow color and no graphics.
6. Click on AutoFormat on the Diagram toolbar.

Diagram Toolbar

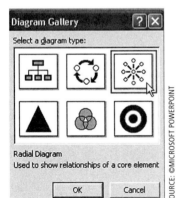

Diagram Gallery

7. Choose AutoFormat. On the Diagram Style Gallery, click on Fire.

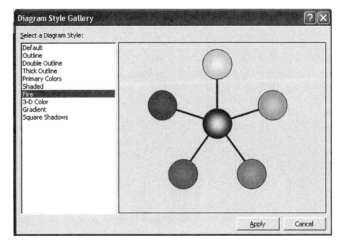

Style Gallery

8. Click on the middle circle and type "Summary." Resize the font to Size 40.
9. Click on each of the other circles and type "Review of Points" in one, "Contact Information" in the next, and "Sources" in the last one. For "Review of Points" and "Contact Information," press Enter as needed to fit them in the circle.
10. Select the text in the circles and remove the shadow. To do this, go to the menu bar and choose Format > Font. Clear the Shadow check box. Change font colors as needed for the best readability on this slide.
11. Save again.

Proofing Tools

1. Go to the menu bar and choose Tools > Spelling.

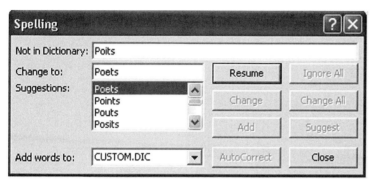

Spelling

SOURCE: ©MICROSOFT POWERPOINT

2. Verify the spelling of all words and change as needed.
3. If Style Checker is not on, choose Tools > Options. Click on the Spelling and Style tab. Select the Check style check box. Click on Style Options to review all the options. Leave them as the default.

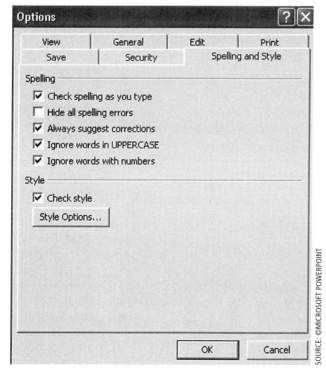

Style Checker

SOURCE: ©MICROSOFT POWERPOINT

4. Use the scroll bars on the right side of your slide show to scroll through the presentation. You can also scroll through each page quickly by using the middle wheel on your mouse. If there are any light bulbs, click on them to view the suggested change and make any changes necessary.
5. Save again.

Action Settings

1. Click on the Summary Radial to select it. Right-click and select Action Settings.

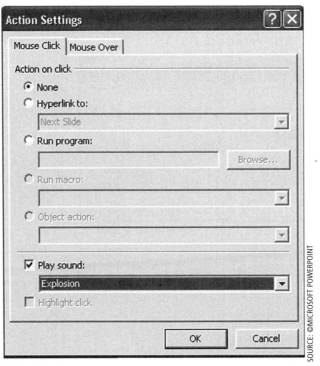

Action Settings

2. In the Action Settings dialog box, click on the Mouse Click tab and click the Play sound box to check it. Select the Explosion WAV from the drop-down box.
3. In the Action Settings dialog box, click on the Mouse Over tab and click the Play sound box to check it. Select the Drum Roll WAV from the drop-down box.
4. Save again.

ACTIVITY 3 • MINI-PROJECT

Create a Sales Presentation

1. Choose a brand of computer to research. Create a six-to-ten-slide presentation to sell the computer.
2. Information for the presentation should come from Web sites, brochures, or interviews with salespeople. The final slide should include all resources for this project in MLA style. Check http://www.mla.org/ for the proper style. Include notes on at least one slide.
3. The following criteria should be met:
   - ☐ Design appropriate for type of presentation.
   - ☐ Animation scheme added to at least one slide.

- [ ] One piece of clip art used with recoloring appropriate for color scheme.
- [ ] One slide has a background change appropriate for information on the slide.
- [ ] Minimum of one picture taken from another source (Internet, digital camera, or scanned).
- [ ] One SWF file created and used.
- [ ] Minimum of one diagram used.
- [ ] WordArt or AutoShape used appropriately at least once.
- [ ] Media clip inserted on at least one slide.
- [ ] Line spacing formatted to create the best-looking slides.
- [ ] Changes made to the Master Slide that created consistent font size throughout the presentation.
- [ ] Appropriate notes included on at least one slide.
- [ ] Information presented on slide appropriate for type of presentation.
- [ ] Slides are error-free.
- [ ] Title and summary slides contain appropriate information in correct format.

ACTIVITY 4 • AUTOCONTENT WIZARD

In this activity, you will become familiar with:

- Getting Started
- Header and Footer
- Promote and Demote
- Organizational Charts
- Format Painter
- Linking
- Deleting Slides
- Summary Slide
- Clip Art Background
- Text Box
- Format Font
- Customizing Animations
- Re-Ordering Animations

Getting Started

1. Go to the menu bar and choose File > New. In the Task pane, choose From AutoContent Wizard.
2. If the Office Assistant shows up to give you help, click on the No button.
3. Click Next on the wizard and it will take you to selecting a presentation type. Click on Corporate, then Employee Orientation, then Next.
4. The presentation style will be an on-screen presentation. Click on Next.
5. Type "Web Development Corporation" for the presentation title. Type your name in the Footer box. Leave the date and the slide number on the footer. Click on Next.
6. Click on Finish.
7. Save as *WDC.ppt*.

Header and Footer

1. In most cases when you give an on-screen presentation, you will not put headers and footers on the slide show. However, you may want them on the handouts. Go to the menu bar and choose View > Header and Footers.
2. In the Header and Footer dialog box, click on the Slide tab and clear all the check boxes.

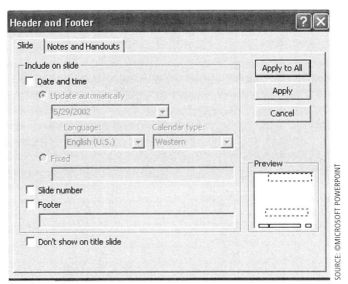

Header and Footer

SOURCE: ©MICROSOFT POWERPOINT

3. On the Notes and Handouts tab, you can add a header and a footer. Select the "Update date automatically" check box. Change the format of the date to Month, Day, Year and add your name as the footer. Click on Apply to All.
4. Save again.

Promote and Demote

1. In the Title, remove everything except the word "Topics."
2. Go to Slide 2. From Bullet 1, remove "& company vision."
3. Remove the Other Resources and Required Paperwork bullets.
4. Go to Slide 3. Leave the title as it is. Remove the bulleted items and replace with:
   Bullet 1: Founded in 1996
   Bullet 2: Mission Statement
   Increase Indent (Demote): To provide efficient Web development, desktop publishing, and presentation planning services via the Internet

To demote a line, press the Tab key or click on the Increase Indent icon on the Standard toolbar. To promote a line, press Shift + Tab. If you are at the beginning of the line and press Shift + Tab, nothing will happen. If you are in the Outline pane and press Shift + Tab, you will be promoted to a new slide.

Increase Indent

SOURCE: ©MICROSOFT POWERPOINT

Organizational Charts

1. Go to Slide 4. Click on the outer edge of the bottom placeholder until the edge is dotted. Press Delete to remove the placeholder.
2. Go to the menu bar and choose Format > Slide Layout.
3. In the Task pane, double-click on Title and Contents.
4. In the Diagram Gallery dialog box, click on Insert Organizational Chart.
5. On the top level of the organization chart, type "Cliff Samrio" and below his name type "President."
6. Click on two of the boxes in the second row to remove them. Type in the one remaining box "Karen Samrio" and below her name "Vice President."
7. With the pointer on Karen Samrio's box on the Organization Chart toolbar, click on Insert Shape twice.

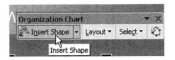

Insert Shape

SOURCE: ©MICROSOFT POWERPOINT

8. Type the following names and titles in the three boxes on the third level:
   Vic Jayson, Desktop Publishing Specialist
   Sandra Newmann, Web Development Specialist
   Fernando Vasquez, Presentation Specialist
9. Type the following names and titles in the boxes on the fourth level:
   Under Desktop Publishing Specialist: Jon Saunders, Employee; Joan Eckert,
   Employee
   Under Web Development Specialist: Cyrus Jackson, Employee; Randy
   Randolph, Employee
   Under Presentation Specialist: Laura Collier, Employee
10. On the Organization Chart toolbar, click on Layout and Scale Organization
    Chart. Use the pointer on the edge of the placeholder to click and drag to resize
    the chart appropriately.
11. Go to the menu bar and choose Format > Background. Click on the box to turn
    off the graphics and change to a white background.
12. On the Organization Chart toolbar, click on AutoFormat. Select a diagram style
    of your choice. Click on Apply.
13. Save again.

Format Painter

1. Go to Slide 5. Delete the information in the bulleted placeholder. Type the following four bulleted items: "Termination," "Dress Code," "Work Schedule,"
   "Absenteeism"
2. Type the following in the Notes pane:

   *Termination: You are free to resign your position at any time you wish, and for
   any reason you think is appropriate. While we would appreciate notice if you plan
   to resign, it is a matter of courtesy and is not required by law. We have the right
   to terminate any employee at any time, with or without notice, for any reason not
   prohibited by specific contracts or laws.*

   *Dress Code: Please be aware that what you wear to work is a reflection of your
   professional attitude and that of the organization. Certain requirements must be
   observed. When meeting with clients, clothing should not be low-cut, revealing, or
   extremely tight-fitting. Extremely casual dress is generally not considered appropriate for client meetings.*

   *Work Schedule: Since you are working from home, your schedule is your own as
   long as all deadlines are met. The specific deadlines for your assignments will be
   explained to you by your supervisor.*

   *Absenteeism: Absences should be approved by your supervisor as far in advance as
   possible. As much as possible, you should not accept assignments you will not be
   able to complete. If you are unable to finish an assignment, please call your supervisor as soon as possible. Repeated violation of incomplete assignments will be
   cause for written warnings, possible discipline, and termination.*

3. Bold "Termination." Double-click on the Format Painter icon on the Formatting
   toolbar. Paint the bold on "Dress Code," "Work Schedule," and "Absenteeism."
   Click on the Format Painter icon to turn it off.
4. You have placed your entire script in the Notes pane for reference if necessary.
   Double-click on the word "resign" under "Termination." Click on the Bold and
   Italics icons on the Formatting toolbar. Double-click on the Format Painter tool and
   go through and paint bold and italics on all keywords or phrases you are planning
   to emphasize in your presentation. Click on the Format Painter icon to turn it off.

Format Painter
SOURCE: ©MICROSOFT POWERPOINT

Linking

1. Go to Slide 6. Replace the bulleted information with the following:
   Employee paid health insurance; no dental
   Vacation: 2 weeks after 1 year
   Sick leave: 10 days per year
   Personal leave: 2 days per year
   Life insurance: $25,000
   No retirement benefits
   Training: $1,000 paid toward training each year
   Each of the above lines should be bulleted.
2. Go to Slide 7. Replace the bulleted information with the following:
   Bullet 1: Purpose
   Bullet 2: To assist the employee in improving performance
       To receive feedback from clients
   Bullet 3: Outline the review process
   Bullet 4: Supervisor evaluates employee once every six months
       Client evaluations upon completion of each assignment
3. Go to Slide 8. Delete "Contact name/phone for each area." Replace with "Web page." Press Tab to demote. Type "http://www.wdc.com."
4. Select http://www.wdc.com. Click on the Insert Hyperlink icon on the Standard toolbar.
5. In the Insert Hyperlink dialog box, click in the Address line and type "http://www.swep.com."
6. Create a second bullet under the Web page. Type "Email Personnel."
7. Select Email Personnel. Click on the Insert Hyperlink icon on the Standard toolbar. In the Insert Hyperlink dialog box, click on E-mail Address. Type the e-mail address "personnel@wdc.com." It will automatically add "mailto" in front of the e-mail address. Click OK.

Insert Hyperlink

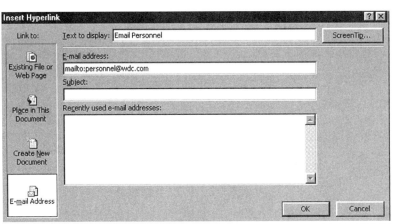

Email Hyperlink

8. Create a third bullet under Email Personnel and type "Company Handbook." Select the Company Handbook text. Click on the Insert Hyperlink icon. In the Insert Hyperlink dialog box, click on Existing File or Web page. In the Look in folder, browse to your CD and double-click on *CompanyHandbook.doc*. Click OK. You will now be able to click on this link during the presentation and go to the document located on your computer. Try this now by clicking on the Slide Show icon on the View toolbar. Click on Company Handbook on your slide. It should take you to the document.
9. Save again.

Deleting Slides

1. Delete the Required Paperwork slide (Slide 9) by clicking on it in the Outline pane.
2. Press Delete. You can also delete files from the Slide Sorter View.
3. Delete the last slide titled "Summary."

Summary Slide

1. Go to Slide Sorter View by clicking on the Slide Sorter icon on the View toolbar.
2. Select Slides 3–8 by clicking on Slide 3, holding down the Shift key, and clicking on Slide 8.
3. Click on the Summary Slide icon on the Slide Sorter toolbar.
4. The Summary Slide is created as Slide 3. Move it to the end of the slide show. You have a slide similar to this as Slide 2. This type of summary slide can be used in either or both places. Delete the word "Slide" from the title.

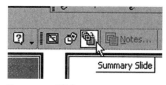

Summary Slide
SOURCE: ©MICROSOFT POWERPOINT

Clip Art Background

1. Create a new slide.
2. Format the background to white with no graphics.
3. Reapply the design layout as a blank slide.
4. Go to the menu bar and choose Insert > Picture > Clip Art. Search for "lakes."
5. Resize the lake image to the size of the slide.
6. On the Picture toolbar, click on the Color icon. Choose Washout.

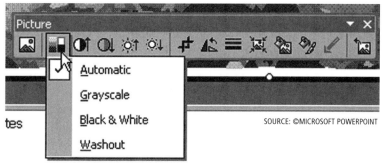

Picture Toolbar

7. Right-click on the middle of the image and choose Order > Send to Back.

Text Box

1. Click on the Text Box tool on the Drawing toolbar.
2. Click and drag to draw a text box in the middle of the slide. Change the line style and color.
3. Search for a motivational quote on the Internet that would inspire new employees in a company. Type the quote including the author's name in the text box.

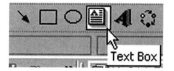

Text Box
SOURCE: ©MICROSOFT POWERPOINT

Format Font

1. Select the text and click on the Center icon on the Formatting toolbar.
2. Go to the menu bar and choose Format > Font.

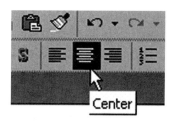

Center
SOURCE: ©MICROSOFT POWERPOINT

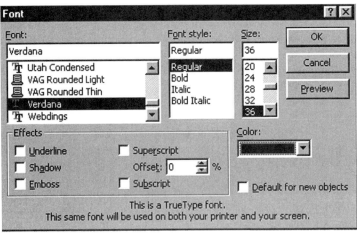

Font

3. In the Font dialog box, change the font type to Verdana or a similar font. Change the size and color.
4. Save again.

Customizing Animations

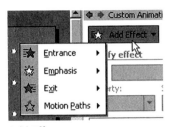

Add Effect

1. On Slide 1, click in the Subtitle placeholder.
2. Go to the menu bar and choose Tools > Custom Animation.
3. In the Custom Animation Task pane, click on Add Effect.
4. Choose Entrance > Diamonds.
5. Click in the Title placeholder and choose a custom animation for it.

Re-Ordering Animations

1. On the Custom Animation Task pane, click on the second animation. Click on the Re-order button at the bottom of the Custom Animation Task pane. Note that on the Normal view of the presentation, the placeholders have a small number indicating their animation order at the top left of the placeholder.
2. Go through the slide show assigning custom animations to at least two other slides.
3. Go to the menu bar and choose View > Master > Slide Master.
4. Click in the Title placeholder and increase the size of the font to 44.
5. Click in the Subtitle placeholder and increase the size of the font to 40.
6. In the Outline pane, click on Slide 2.
7. Click in the Title placeholder and change the font size to 44.
8. Click on the first bullet to select all the bulleted items and change the font size to 36.
9. Click on the Normal View icon on the View toolbar.
10. Save again.

ACTIVITY 4 • MINI-PROJECT

Create a Presentation on a Job Shadowing Experience

1. Participate in a job shadowing experience or interview a friend or family member in a career of your choice.
2. For more information on job shadowing, visit http://www.jobshadow.org.

3. Use the AutoContent Wizard Employee Orientation to create a six-to-ten-slide presentation on the business you job shadowed or from your interview. Get other appropriate information from brochures, interviews, and Web sites.
4. The following criteria should be met:
   - ☐ Information accurate and appropriate on presentation.
   - ☐ Headers and footers included and appropriate.
   - ☐ At least one clip art background included and appropriate for the information on the slide.
   - ☐ Summary slide created.
   - ☐ One organization chart included and appropriately formatted for the color scheme.
   - ☐ Text boxes and other objects ordered and grouped as needed.
   - ☐ At least one custom animation created and appropriate for the slide.
   - ☐ A minimum of two types of links used.
   - ☐ Participated in job shadowing experience successfully or provided an effective interview.

ACTIVITY 5 • FROM DESIGN TEMPLATE

In this activity, you will become familiar with:

- ■ Choosing a Template
- ■ Creating a Self-Running Show
- ■ Adding Narration
- ■ Picture Background
- ■ 3-D Settings
- ■ Replace Fonts
- ■ Pack and Go
- ■ Grayscale View
- ■ Printing

Choosing a Template

1. There are some advantages to choosing a template first in preparing your presentation. By choosing first, you have a color scheme that can save time. You get a definite idea as to how the finished presentation will look and at any time, and if you decide to change the design you can.
2. Go to the menu bar and choose File > New. With the New Presentation Task pane open, click on From Design Template.
3. Scroll through the choices of designs. Select the Proposal design.
4. Input the following slides:
   Slide 1 (Title Slide)
   Title placeholder: KIOSKS
   Subtitle placeholder: Student Name, School Name
   Slide 2 (Bulleted Slide)
   Title placeholder: Summary
   Bullets: Definition, Types, Uses, Key Features
   Slide 3 (Bulleted Slide)
   Title placeholder: Definition
   Bullet: Small Building
   or
   Bullet: Computer
   Bullet: Free-standing used by visitors
   Bullet: Considered robotic
   Bullet: Communicates with user

Design Template

Bullet: Interacts with user
Slide 4 (Bulleted Slide)
Title placeholder: Types
Bullets: Interactive, User makes selections, Find information, Print
  information, Passive, Run continuously, No user intervention
Slide 5 (Bulleted Slide)
Title placeholder: Uses
Bullets: Libraries, Gift Registries, Information Booths, Automated Bank
  Teller Machines, Hotels, Churches and Schools
Slide 6 (Bulleted Slide)
Title placeholder: Key Features to Consider
Bullets: Use of Sound and Video, Flashy, Innovative Ideas, Ease of Use,
  Hardware Stability

5. Add clip art of a computer to Slide 2. Format the background for a solid color.
6. Go to Slide Sorter View and select all slides. Add the same slide transition to all slides.
7. Add entrance animations to the two objects on Slide 1. Be sure they are in the correct order.
8. Save as *Kiosks.ppt*.

Creating a Self-Running Show

1. Go to the menu bar and choose Slide Show > Set Up Show.

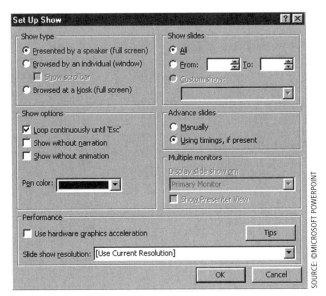

Set Up Show

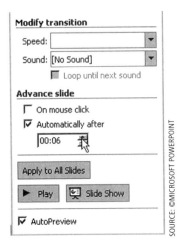

Advance Slide

2. In the Set Up Show dialog box, under Show options, select the "Loop continuously until 'Esc'" check box. Under Advance slides, select the "Using timings, if present" check box.
3. Click OK.
4. Go to Slide Sorter View. Select all the slides. Ctrl + A will also select all the slides.
5. In the Custom Animation Task pane, under Advance slide, select the "Automatically after" check box and change the seconds to 6 in the box. Clear the "On mouse click" check box.
6. Save again.

Adding Narration

1. In Normal view, click on Slide 2.
2. Go to the menu bar and choose Insert > Movies and Sounds, then click on Record Sound.
3. In the Record Sound dialog box, select Recorded Sound in the Name box and type over it "Slide 2."
4. In the Record Sound dialog box, click on the red circle to begin the recording. Speak into the microphone, telling the viewers what is on Slide 2. When you have finished, click on the blue square to stop. The recording should be only about ten seconds long.
5. In the Custom Animation Task pane, click on the down arrow next to Media 4. Select Timing from the drop-down menu.
6. In the Play Sound dialog box, click on the Timing tab. In the Start drop-down box, select With Previous.

Record Sound

SOURCE: ©MICROSOFT POWERPOINT

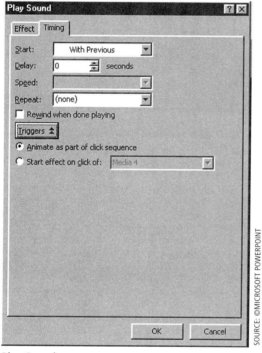

Play Sound

7. Preview in Slide Show View.
8. Save again.

Picture Background

1. Go to the end of the slide show. Add a new blank slide with a blank slide layout.
2. Right-click on the slide background and choose Background.
3. In the Background dialog box, click on Omit background graphics from master. Click on the Color drop-down box and choose Fill Effects.
4. In the Fill Effects dialog box, click on the Picture tab.

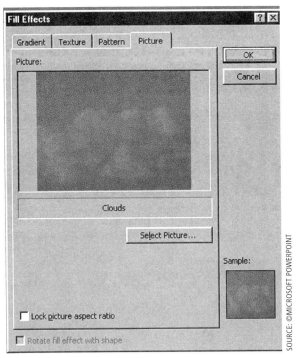

Fill Effects

5. Click on Select Picture. Browse to your CD and double-click on *Clouds.jpg*. Click OK.
6. In the Background dialog box, click on Apply.
7. Save again.

3-D Settings

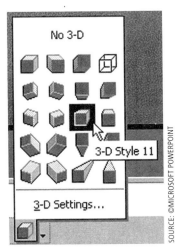

3-D Settings

1. On Slide 7 (the last slide), add a WordArt titled "Kiosks." Format the color to match the picture background.
2. Draw a text box on the slide and type in the text box "For more information, search the Internet."
3. With the text box selected, click on the 3-D icon on the Drawing toolbar.
4. Choose 3-D Style 11.
5. Save again.

Replace Fonts

Replace Font

1. Go to the menu bar and choose Format > Replace Fonts.
2. Leave Arial in the Replace drop-down box and choose Verdana from the With drop-down box.
3. Click on Replace, then Close.
4. Go to the Master Slide and adjust any font sizes that need adjusting.
5. Change line spacing as needed on all slides.

Pack and Go

1. Go to the menu bar and choose File > Pack and Go.

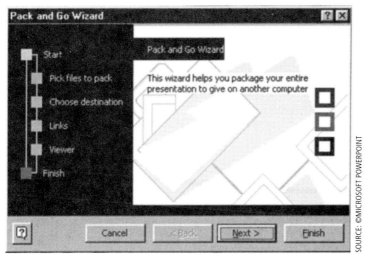

Pack and Go

SOURCE: ©MICROSOFT POWERPOINT

2. Click on Next on the Wizard.
3. Leave it on packaging the active presentation. Click on Next.
4. The file should be copied to a floppy, Zip disk, or CD. Click on Next.
5. Choose to include linked files and embed TrueType fonts. Click on Next.
6. Don't include the Viewer and click on Next.
7. Click on Finish to compress the file to your floppy disk.

Grayscale View

1. Click on the Color/Grayscale icon on the Standard toolbar.
2. On the floating Grayscale View toolbar, click on Setting. Try some of the settings, then choose White. Viewing in grayscale can save memory; if you print in grayscale, you can save ink.

Printing

1. Go to the menu bar and choose File > Print.

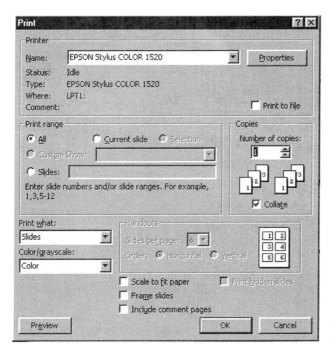

Print

SOURCE: ©MICROSOFT POWERPOINT

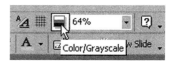

Grayscale

SOURCE: ©MICROSOFT POWERPOINT

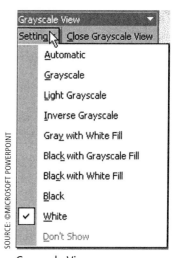

Grayscale View

SOURCE: ©MICROSOFT POWERPOINT

2. In the Print dialog box, in the Print what drop-down box, select Handouts. In the Slides per page drop-down box, choose 3. In the Color/grayscale drop-down box, choose Grayscale. Depending on the type of presentation, you may want to print handouts. If you choose to copy the handouts, they will copy better if they are not in color. Choosing 3 slides per page gives room on the right side for the participants to take notes. Note that you can print 1, 2, 3, 4, 6, and 9 slides per page.
3. You can also choose to print the notes page.
4. Cancel without printing unless otherwise instructed by your instructor.
5. Save again.

ACTIVITY 5 • MINI-PROJECT

Create a Self-Running Announcement Presentation

1. Many times students are not on campus when the announcements are read or presented by television. The principal has decided to set up a self-running presentation in the office. This will also allow visitors to be aware of what is taking place on the campus each week.
2. Keep notes all week on the announcements. Create a presentation from your notes. The presentation should have at least six to ten slides. Be sure to set the time adequately for the reading of the announcements on that slide.
3. The following criteria should be met:
   ☐ Announcements accurate from the past week.
   ☐ Design used is appropriate for the school and customized with a color scheme using the school colors; some creativity is evident.
   ☐ Presentation is set up as self-running and adequately timed.
   ☐ One picture background used, taken with a digital camera or scanned, of the school or activity within the school. Picture is of good quality.
   ☐ Introductory slide is narrated appropriately.
   ☐ Pack and Go used effectively to move the slide show to the kiosk.
   ☐ At least one slide uses a 3-D setting on an AutoShape or text box.
   ☐ Presentation is error-free.

ACTIVITY 6 • OPENING OUTLINES FROM WORD

In this activity, you will become familiar with:

■ Opening a Word Outline in PowerPoint
■ Cut and Paste
■ Office Clipboard
■ Find and Replace
■ Play CD Sound Track

Opening a Word Outline in PowerPoint

1. Go to the menu bar and choose File > Open.
2. In the drop-down box for file type, change to All Outlines.
3. Browse to your CD and double-click on *SIFEOutline.doc*. When an outline is created in Word and then opened in PowerPoint, the Heading 1/Level 1 lines are placed in Title placeholders. Heading 2/Level 2 lines are placed in Bullet placeholders, and the Heading 3/Level 3 are a demoted bullet. The file cannot be open in Word while you are opening it in PowerPoint.

4. Save as *SIFE.ppt*.
5. Change Slide 1 to a Title slide.
6. Change Slide 2 to Title and 2-Column Text layout. Remove the bullet from Slide 2.

Cut and Paste

1. Select "Compete" through the rest of the slide. Click on the Cut icon on the Standard toolbar.
2. Click in the second column and click on the Paste icon on the Standard toolbar.
3. Save again.

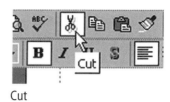

Cut

Office Clipboard

1. Go to the menu bar and choose Edit > Office Clipboard. This opens the Clipboard Task pane.
2. The Clipboard can hold up to 24 items. The Task pane shows each of them. You can paste one item at a time, paste all the items, or clear all the items.
3. On Slide 6, decrease the font size to 24.
4. Select all lines. Go to the menu bar and choose Format > Line Spacing. Change the Before paragraph spacing to 6.

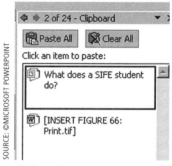

Clipboard

Find and Replace

1. Scroll back to Slide 1. Go to the menu bar and choose Edit > Replace.

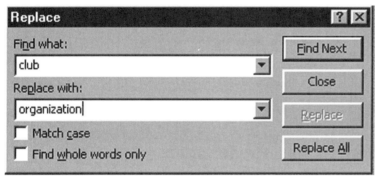

Replace

2. In the Replace dialog box, type "Club" in the Find what box. Type "Organization" in the Replace with box. Click on Find Next. Click on Replace. Continue until you have replaced all instances in the presentation.
3. Click on Close.
4. Save again.
5. Add a design to the presentation.

Play CD Sound Track

1. Place an audio CD in the CD drive.
2. Go to Slide 2.
3. Go to the menu bar and choose Insert > Movies and Sounds > Play CD Audio Track.
4. In the Movie and Sound Options dialog box, select one of the tracks to play. Click OK.

Sound Options

5. Click on Yes to have the tracks play automatically.
6. Go to http://www.sife.org. Place the SIFE logo on Slide 2. You may need to format the background to accommodate the design.
7. Add other appropriate clip art, transitions, and animations, formatting text boxes, font size, and color changes as needed.
8. Insert *Rookie.jpg* from your CD on an appropriate slide.
9. Save again.

ACTIVITY 6 • MINI-PROJECT

Create an Outline for a Presentation

1. In a team of three or four students, create an outline of one of the chapters from Unit 4. Each team should outline a different chapter. Remember not to make the outline too detailed, but keep it to the basic points.
2. Each student should input the outline in Word. The outline should have at least three levels with a minimum of eight Level 1 heads. Save as *ChapterOutline.doc*.
3. Open the outline in PowerPoint. Format appropriately. Cut and paste any information that does not fit in the slide onto another slide. Change slide layouts as needed. Add notes to three slides.
4. Insert a CD to play at least one track on an appropriate slide.
5. Save as *OutlineChapter.ppt*.
6. The following criteria should be met:
   ☐ Team worked well together and each student participated.
   ☐ Outline was input into Word appropriately.
   ☐ Outline includes three levels, with minimum of eight Level 1 heads.
   ☐ Everything in the presentation is visible; size and color appropriate; line spacing and design appropriate.
   ☐ Outline is not too detailed; details included in the Notes pane of the presentation on at least three slides.
   ☐ CD inserted and played appropriately.

ACTIVITY 7 • TABLES AND CHARTS

In this activity, you will become familiar with:

- Insert a Table
- Merging Cells
- Fill Color
- Resizing Rows and Columns
- Border Color
- Insert Chart
- Format Value Axis
- Format Category Axis
- Format Data Point
- Chart Type

Insert a Table

1. Create a new blank PowerPoint presentation.
2. On the Title slide, in the Title placeholder, type "Shilo Online Corporation."
3. In the Subtitle placeholder, type "Annual Review, Year 2003."
4. Insert a new slide.
5. Change the slide layout to Title and Content. Click on the Insert Table icon in the placeholder.
6. In the Insert Table dialog box, choose 4 Columns and 6 Rows.
7. On the Tables and Borders floating toolbar, click on Table, then Insert Table.

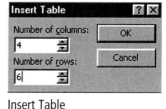

Insert Table

SOURCE: ©MICROSOFT POWERPOINT

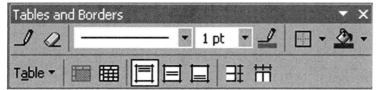

Tables and Borders

SOURCE: ©MICROSOFT POWERPOINT

8. In Row 3, type "No. of Employees as of 1/01, 42, 50, 56."
9. In Row 4, type "Retired, 2, 1, 6."
10. In Row 5, type "Resigned, 4, 5, 3."
11. In Row 6, type "No. of Employees as of 12/31, 36, 44, 53."

Merging Cells

1. Select row 1, columns 2, 3, and 4.
2. On the Tables and Borders floating toolbar, click on the Merge Cells button.

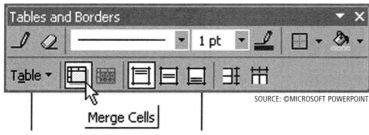

Merge Cells

3. In row 2, columns 2, 3, and 4, type "2001, 2002, 2003." Select the three cells and click on the Center icon on the Formatting toolbar.

Fill Color

1. Select rows 1 and 2, columns 2, 3, and 4.
2. Click on the Fill Color icon on the Tables and Borders toolbar. Don't worry too much about the color, as you will add a design to the presentation later.

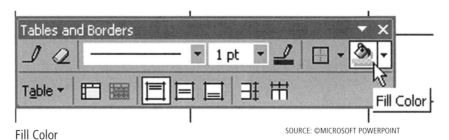

Fill Color

SOURCE: ©MICROSOFT POWERPOINT

3. In row 1, columns 2, 3, and 4 (merged cells), type "Last Three Years." Click on the Center icon on the Formatting toolbar.

Resizing Rows and Columns

1. Hover the mouse pointer between the rows. When it turns into a two-headed arrow, double-click or click and drag to resize the column.
2. Repeat step 1 to adjust the row height.
3. Click in the Title placeholder and type "Employee Retention."

Border Color

1. On the Tables and Borders floating toolbar, click on Border Color. Choose a color.

Border Color

SOURCE: ©MICROSOFT POWERPOINT

2. The pointer should turn into a pen. Draw a border around the table.
3. Save as *SOC.ppt*.

Insert Chart

Click icon to add content

Insert Chart

SOURCE: ©MICROSOFT POWERPOINT

1. Add a new slide.
2. Change the slide layout to Title and Contents.
3. Click on Insert Chart on the slide layout.
4. Type the information in the datasheet that you see on the following page. Close the datasheet by clicking the Close button in the upper right corner.

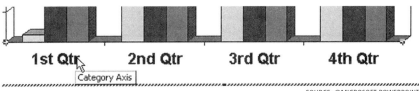
Datasheet

SOURCE: ©MICROSOFT POWERPOINT

Format Value Axis

1. Double-click on the Value Axis.
2. In the Format Axis dialog box, click on the Scale tab. Change the Minimum to 14, the Maximum to 22, and the Minor and Major to 1.

Format Category Axis

1. Double-click on the Category Axis.

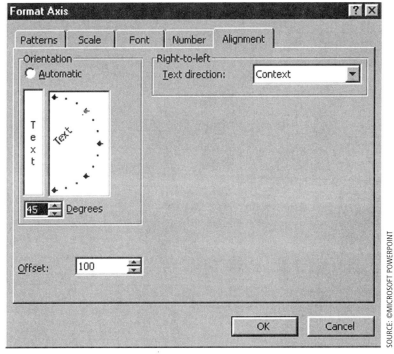

Category Axis

SOURCE: ©MICROSOFT POWERPOINT

2. In the Format Axis dialog box, click on the Alignment tab.

Format Axis

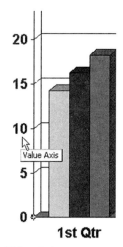

Value Axis

SOURCE: ©MICROSOFT POWERPOINT

3. Drag the angle to 45 degrees. Click OK.
4. Apply the design titled Balance to the presentation.

Format Data Point

1. Double-click on the Series 2002 column.

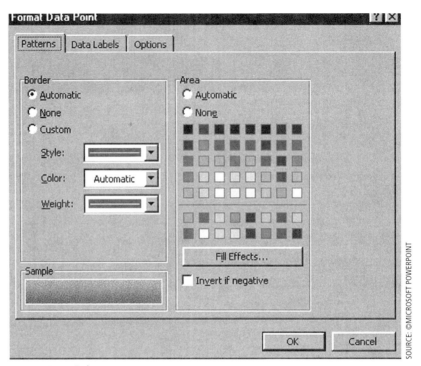

Format Data Point

2. In the Format Data Point dialog box, click on the Patterns tab.
3. Click on Fill Effects.
4. In the Fill Effects dialog box, click on Two colors.
5. Click OK, then OK again to return to your chart. You can experiment with other patterns if you like.
6. Save again.

Chart Type

1. Go to the menu bar and choose Chart > Chart Type. Double-click on one of the types of line charts to change this chart type to a line chart from a column chart.
2. Save as *SOCLine.ppt*.

ACTIVITY 7 • MINI-PROJECT

Create a Chart and Table for Sports

1. Go to http://www.sunbowl.org/history-legends.asp.
2. Create a presentation with Contents for the slide layout. Create a chart using information on the Sun Bowl inductees since 1994. The chart should have at least three columns. One column should be for the name, one column for the year, and one column for other brief information (such as whether they were a coach, player, and so on).

3. Merge the cells to create a title in the table. Type "Sun Bowl Legends" for the title.
4. Create a column heading row and fill with a color.
5. Add a border to the table.
6. Add an appropriate design to the table.
7. Save as *SunBowl.ppt*.
8. Use the following information for team rankings to create a line chart.
9. Format the Value Axis and Category Axis appropriately.
10. Format the Data Point to appropriately represent each team.

TEAM	TOTAL
Miami (FL)	2.62
Nebraska	7.23
Colorado	7.28
Oregon	8.67
Florida	13.09
Texas	17.79

11. Save as *Top6.ppt*.
12. The following criteria should be met:
    - ☐ Table contains appropriate information.
    - ☐ Design of table is appropriate for the subject.
    - ☐ Cells merged for title.
    - ☐ Column headings appropriate and filled with appropriate color.
    - ☐ Border added to table.
    - ☐ Table is error-free.
    - ☐ Data for chart was input correctly.
    - ☐ Correct chart type used.
    - ☐ Value Axis and Category Axis appropriately formatted.
    - ☐ Data Point formatted with colors or patterns to represent each team.
    - ☐ Chart is error-free.

PART 5 • SIMULATION

Using PowerPoint

1. Create three presentations. One of them will be presented in class. Prepare an AUDIENCE planning sheet for each presentation.
2. *Presentation 1:* (Selling) This will be a team idea with each team member creating his or her own presentation. Come up with an idea for a new product. Think about some things you have seen on the market recently. Discuss them with your team and think about something you could use, or have thought about that would make life easier. For instance, a recent new product has been a very small bookstand that can be used at the computer. It looks like a mouse, has a slot to hold the paper, comes in neon colors, and is inexpensive. Think of some advantages of your new product idea to help sell it in the presentation. You can draw a sketch or create a model. Use a digital camera or scanner to get an image of your new product on your presentation. Be sure to name the product and discuss with your team ideas of what could go on your presentation.

   Presentation 2: (Educating) All of us have something that we excel in. It could be band, a sport, dancing, a particular class, or writing. Create a presentation teaching the class about something that you already have knowledge about.

Presentation 3: (Informative) Research a plant or animal disease on the Internet. Inform the class about this disease.

3. Charts, tables, and diagrams need to be in only one of the presentations. They can be spread out as long as you have demonstrated each skill in one of the three presentations.

4. The following criteria should be met:

   ☐ Facts thorough and accurate in the presentation.
   ☐ Knowledge or research is evident.
   ☐ Formatting of text is appropriate; variety of font types, sizes, and colors used.
   ☐ Text boxes appropriately placed, sized, and formatted.
   ☐ WordArt effectively used at least once.
   ☐ Appropriate design and layout selected for all three presentations.
   ☐ Appropriate animation and color schemes selected for all three presentations.
   ☐ A minimum of one SWF file included in presentation.
   ☐ A media clip or sound clip from a CD was inserted.
   ☐ Line spacing adjusted as needed for all slides.
   ☐ At least two different bullets used.
   ☐ At least one instance of 3-D settings used.
   ☐ At least one table, chart, or graph included in one of the three presentations.
   ☐ Oral presentation has notes in the Note pane.
   ☐ Oral presentation demonstrates preparation and practice. (Student does not look down at notes most of the entire time.)
   ☐ Voice enthusiastic and loud enough during presentation.

Web Publishing Systems

Unit 5

The power behind Web design changes very fast. We are able to continuously create faster and flashier Web pages. Microsoft, Macromedia, and Adobe continue to be on top of the latest techniques in the field of Web design. Software updates allow more flexibility with image management, browser uniformity, and ease of use. In today's fast-paced business world, it is important to be able to update Web pages continually with ease.

You will be given the opportunity to explore Microsoft FrontPage in this unit. FrontPage has one of the best image management toolbars in Web design. Being able to resample to save Web page download time and create an image with a transparent background with a click of the mouse button are two simple features that save time for a Web designer.

You will be given the opportunity to explore Macromedia Dreamweaver. Dreamweaver is probably the most popular Web design software on the market today. It offers ease of use and yet it can be a very dynamic, powerful Web editor if you explore the advanced features. Layout tables and layout cells enable a Web designer to place images and text virtually anywhere on the document. Another great time-saving device in this software is the ability to create flash files and flash text within the software.

Finally, you will be given the opportunity to explore Adobe GoLive. GoLive is flexible in enabling you to place objects virtually anywhere on the page. The Objects palette is a great time-saving device that enables you to use drag-and-drop methods to create dynamic Web pages quickly. This software organizes its own folders and places the data information in one easy-to-find location. If you like to use frames in Web development, you will find this software a plus for you.

Part 1

Microsoft FrontPage

> **Microsoft FrontPage**
> **Publisher: Microsoft Corporation**
> FrontPage is a low-cost Web design program. Its popularity comes from the seamless design that easily integrates with other popular Microsoft products.

ACTIVITY 1 • GETTING STARTED

In this activity, you will become familiar with:

- Task Pane
- Views Bar
- New Page
- Page View
- Folders View
- Reports View
- Navigation View
- Hyperlinks View
- Tasks View
- Folder List
- Renaming
- Adding Pages
- Expanding and Collapsing the Structure

Task Pane

1. Go to the menu bar and choose File > New. The FrontPage Task pane displays to the right. This is quick access to frequently used menu items.
2. On the FrontPage Task pane, click on Empty Web.
3. In the Web Site Templates dialog box, click on One Page Web.

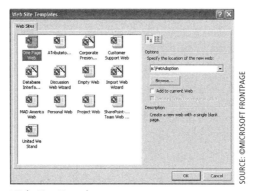

Web Site Templates

4. In the "Specify the location of the new Web," drop-down box, you can accept the default (which is to place it on your hard drive in Documents and Settings\My Documents\My Webs) or you can specify where you want to save the Web page. When you specify where you want it saved, you should name it *PetAdoption*.

5. Click OK to open the Create New Web dialog box, showing the progress of the Web page being created.

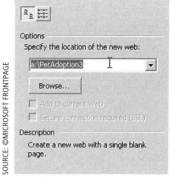
Specify Location

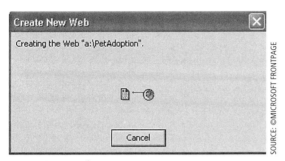
Create New Web

Views Bar

If the Views Bar is not on your screen, go to the menu bar and choose View > Views Bar. The Views Bar contains the most commonly used Views icons to easily toggle back and forth between Views.

Views Bar
SOURCE: ©MICROSOFT FRONTPAGE

New Page

Go to the menu bar and choose File > New. This will create the *index.htm* page for the new Web page. You can also use the shortcut Ctrl + N to create a new page.

Page View

Click on Page view. This is the page on which the Web pages are created. On this page, you can add text and graphics. It works similarly to a word processing document or desktop publishing document. Click on the Page view icon. Page view includes three tabs at the bottom of the screen: Normal, HTML, and Preview. The Normal tab is the view you use to type your information or insert your objects. HTML can be used if you need to make changes to the code. There are some HTML tags that FrontPage does not include. You can insert those directly into the HTML tab if you want to use them. The Preview tab is similar to previewing your Web page in the browser.

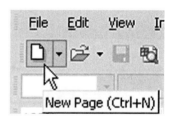
New Page
SOURCE: ©MICROSOFT FRONTPAGE

Page Views
SOURCE: ©MICROSOFT FRONTPAGE

Folders View

Click on Folders view. This is an organized page, graphic, and file structure of your Web page. It is in alphabetical order. Web pages can be opened by double-clicking on the file names. Web pages can be renamed and deleted in this view.

Reports View

Click on Reports view. Pages, graphics, and files can be analyzed by running reports. It checks for slow pages, unlinked pages, recent changes, broken hyperlinks, incomplete tasks, and the published status of your Web page.

Navigation View

Click on Navigation view. This view establishes the hierarchal structure of your Web site. This is the easiest place to add new pages to the Web site. You can add external hyperlinks to the Web site through the Navigation view.

Hyperlinks View

Click on Hyperlinks view. This view allows you to view all the internal and external pages, images, and documents that are hyperlinked within your Web page. You can see any broken hyperlinks that need to be fixed or deleted.

Toggle Pane

SOURCE: ©MICROSOFT FRONTPAGE

Tasks View

Click on Tasks view. In this view the Webmaster can assign specific tasks to designers. Priority levels can be assigned and dates and times that tasks were assigned can be viewed.

Folder List

Pages can easily be opened and edited in the Folder List. Edits, such as renaming a Web page, can take place in this view. Click on the Toggle pane on the Standard toolbar to turn on the Folder List.

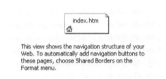

This view shows the navigation structure of your Web. To automatically add navigation buttons to these pages, choose Shared Borders on the Format menu.

Index

SOURCE: ©MICROSOFT FRONTPAGE

Renaming

1. Click on Navigation view on the Views Bar. Click on the Toggle Pane to turn on the Folders List.
2. This opens up the navigation structure on your work area and the Folders List to the left of it. The only page displayed on the work area should be *index.htm*. See the figure labeled Index.
3. Right-click on the *index.htm* icon on your work area and choose Rename. Type in the box "Pet Adoption." Note that in the Folder List, the file name is *index.htm*. That should not change.

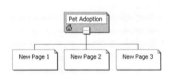

Tier 2

SOURCE: ©MICROSOFT FRONTPAGE

Adding Pages

1. Click on the Pet Adoption icon. This is considered Tier 1. With the mouse pointer on that tier, click on the New Page icon three times. This will add three pages to Tier 2.
2. Right-click on each of the icons and choose Rename. From left to right the names should be Guidelines, Pets for Adoption, and Statistics.
3. In the Folder List, rename each file. The names in step 2 are the names for the Web page, but the files still need to have a name. It is recommended that the names not be spaced or capitalized. Right-click on the New_Page_1 and choose Rename. Type "*guidelines.htm*" in the box. Repeat this instruction for the other two files. Name them *petsforadoption.htm* and *statistics.htm*.
4. Click on the Pet Adoption icon on Tier 2. Click on the New Page icon. This adds a Tier 3 to the navigation structure. Rename this page "Cat Information." Rename the file in the Folder List *catinfo.htm*.

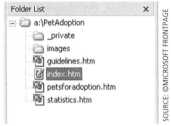

Folder List

SOURCE: ©MICROSOFT FRONTPAGE

Expanding and Collapsing the Structure

On the icon in the navigation structure there is a plus or minus sign on the icon in the middle of each tier. Click on the plus sign to expand the structure. If the icon is a minus sign, click on the minus sign to collapse the structure. This is especially helpful in extremely large Web pages.

Expand

SOURCE: ©MICROSOFT FRONTPAGE

ACTIVITY 1 • MINI-PROJECT

Create a Web Page Structure

1. Follow the steps to begin a Web page for each of the following:
   a. cityof(name of your city)
      Tier 2: City Council, Information, Budget
      Tier 3: Calendar placed from the Information page.
   b. sundevcorp
      Tier 2: Locations, History
      Tier 3: Florida and Texas placed from the Locations page.
   c. sabreelectric
      Tier 2: Current Jobs, Owners, Employment Opportunities
      Tier 3: Application placed from the Employment Opportunities page.
2. The following criteria should be met:
   - ☐ In the Navigation view, each Web page has the structure with the correct page names.
   - ☐ In the Folders List, each Web page has appropriate file names for the structure.
   - ☐ Capitalization and spelling is correct on file names.
   - ☐ Through teacher observation and questioning, student is familiar with each view and steps to begin a Web page using FrontPage.

ACTIVITY 2 • FORMATTING

In this activity, you will become familiar with:

- Background
- Save
- Get Background
- Page Tabs
- Insert File
- Formatting Fonts
- Shading Text
- Line Spacing
- Inserting Pictures
- Tables
- Picture Properties
- Alternative Text
- Load Time
- Resampling a Picture
- Horizontal Line
- Shared Borders
- E-Mail Link
- Navigation Bar
- Creating Hotspots
- WordArt
- Table AutoFormat
- Table Properties
- Copying and Pasting Images
- Drawing Tables
- Thumbnail Images
- Spell Checker

Background

1. Double-click on the Pet Adoption icon in the navigation structure to open the Web page in Page view.
2. Go to the menu bar and choose Format > Background. You can choose to change the color of the background or insert a background picture.

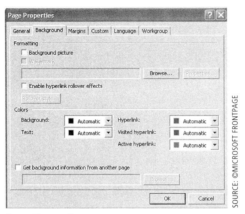

Page Properties

3. In the Page Properties dialog box, select the Background picture check box. Click on the Browse button, browse to your CD, and double-click on *paws.gif*. Click OK.

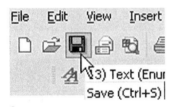

Save

SOURCE: ©MICROSOFT FRONTPAGE

Save

1. Click on the Save icon on the Standard toolbar or press Ctrl + S.
2. When you click on Save the first time, you have placed a new image on your Web page and you will get the Save Embedded Files dialog box. It must save this image in the same folder with your Web pages in order for the image to work. You can Rename the image, Change Folder, and some other options. Click OK to accept the defaults.

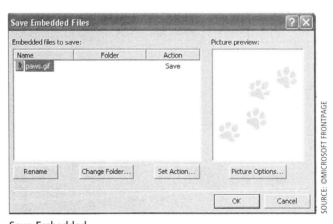

Save Embedded

Get Background

1. Click on Navigation view on the Views Bar. Double-click on the Guidelines icon on the navigation structure.
2. On the Page view in Guidelines, go to the menu bar and choose Format > Background. (You can also right-click anywhere on the screen in Page View and choose Background.)
3. In the Page Properties dialog box, click on Get background information from another page, then click on Browse.
4. In the Current Web dialog box, double-click on *index.htm* to use the background you have already formatted on that page.

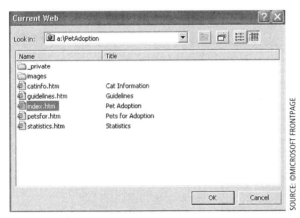

Current Web

5. Click on the Navigation view in the Views Bar. Double-click on the Pets for Adoption page. Go to the menu bar and choose Format > Background. Get background information from another page, then click on Browse. Double-click on *index.htm* to use the background on this page also.
6. Repeat step 5 for the Statistics page.
7. Go to the menu bar and choose File > Save All.

Page Tabs

1. At the top of Page view, you will see page tabs for each of the pages opened. You should have four pages open of this Web page.

Page Tabs

2. Click on *guidelines.htm* to make that the current page.

Insert File

1. Go to the menu bar and choose Insert > File.
2. In the Select File dialog box, double-click on *AdoptionGuidelines.doc*. This causes the file to convert from RTF format to HTML. You will see a quick dialog box on your screen telling you it is doing this.

Select File

Formatting Fonts

1. Select Pet Adoption Guidelines. Change the Font to Verdana, 18 pt., white.
2. Click on the Center icon to center the title horizontally.

Shading Text

1. With the title selected, go to the menu bar and choose Format > Borders and Shading.
2. In the Borders and Shading dialog box, click on the Shading tab.

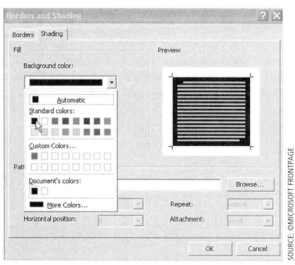

Borders and Shading

3. Click on the black color box, then click OK.

Line Spacing

1. Place your cursor in front of the title "Pet Adoption Guidelines."
2. Press Shift + Enter to insert a blank line above the title. You want the shaded area to be the same amount above and below the title. If you press the Enter key, FrontPage automatically returns two line spaces. In this case, you only need one line space. You can also change line spacing by going to the menu bar and choosing Format > Paragraph. You can change line spacing in the drop-down box.
3. Select all text after the title and change the font to Arial Black.
4. Click on the Save icon on the Standard toolbar.

Inserting Pictures

1. Click on the *index.htm* page tab.
2. Go to the menu bar and choose Insert > Picture > From File. Browse to your CD and double-click on *PetBanner.gif*. Center the image, then place the mouse pointer underneath the image.

Tables

1. Go to the menu bar and choose Insert > Table.

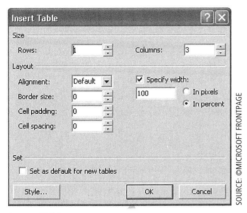

Insert Table.

2. Create a table with 1 row and 3 columns. Change the border size to 0. Leave all other defaults as they are.
3. In the middle cell of the table, type the following:
   292 Brazos Road
   Bryan, TX 77833
   979/555-0101
   http://www.petadoption.com
4. Format the preceding text for Arial, 18 pt., red, centered.
5. Click in the left cell. Go to the menu bar and choose Insert > Picture > Clip art. Search for a clip art picture of a dog.
6. Resize the dog picture.

Picture Properties

1. The dog picture should be approximately 125 × 112 pixels. You can check this by clicking once on the picture, right-clicking, and choosing Picture Properties. Your picture does not need to be the exact measurement, but it should be a similar size.

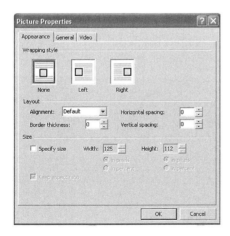

Picture Properties

2. Click on the picture and click on the Center icon on the Standard toolbar.
3. Repeat these instructions to add a cat picture to the right cell of your table.

Alternative Text

1. In the Picture Properties dialog box, click on the General tab.
2. Under Alternative representations Text, type "Kittens." When you do this, if someone's browser does not allow them to see the image, they will at least know what the image represents.
3. Add alternative text for all your images.

Load Time

Load Time
SOURCE: ©MICROSOFT FRONTPAGE

In the bottom right corner of your screen, a message box tells you approximately how much time it will take this page to load. It is measured at a connection of 28.8 Kbps, which is still the average connection speed. Even though you may have a faster connection, many of those who view your Web page will not. You should keep an eye on this time as you add images. Many Web viewers will cancel and leave a page if it takes too long to load.

Resampling a Picture

Resample
SOURCE: ©MICROSOFT FRONTPAGE

1. One thing that will help the load time is to resample a picture after you have resized it. Resizing the picture changes the view size on the screen, but it does not change the file size of the picture. If you do not resample, it still takes the same amount of time to load. Click on the picture.
2. The Picture toolbar should dock on the right side of your screen when you click on the picture. If it does not, go to the menu bar and choose View > Toolbars > Picture Toolbar.
3. Click on the Resample icon on the Picture toolbar.
4. Be sure you have resized and resampled the image of the cat and the dog.

Horizontal Line

Horizontal Line Properties
SOURCE: ©MICROSOFT FRONTPAGE

1. Click below the table so your cursor is no longer in the table. If you press the Tab key on a table, it will add another row in the table. You do not want more rows, but instead you need your cursor below the table. Go to the menu bar and choose Insert > Horizontal Line.
2. Right-click on the Line and choose Horizontal Line Properties.
3. Change the height to 5 and the Color to Red. Leave all other choices as the default.
4. Press the Enter key.

Shared Borders

1. Go to the menu bar and choose Format > Shared Borders.
2. In the Shared Borders dialog box, click on All pages and Bottom. Click OK.
3. Type in the Shared Border area:
   Copyright Pet Adoption, Inc. 2003
   For more information contact Julius Jennings.
4. Go to the menu bar and choose File > Save All.
5. Click on the Navigation view on the Views Bar and go to one of the other Web pages in Page View to check the Shared Border.

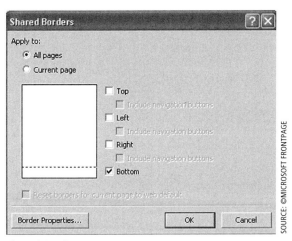

Shared Borders

E-Mail Link

1. Select Julius Jennings. Click on the Insert Hyperlink icon on the Standard toolbar.
2. In the Edit Hyperlink dialog box, click on E-mail address. Type "jjennings@petadoption.com" in the E-mail address line. It will automatically add "mailto:" in front of what you type. Click OK.

Insert Hyperlink
SOURCE: ©MICROSOFT FRONTPAGE

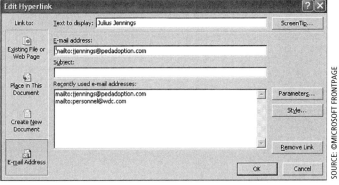

Edit Hyperlink

3. Add another red horizontal line below the Navigation Bar.

Navigation Bar

1. Click below the red horizontal line. Go to the menu bar and choose Insert > Navigation.

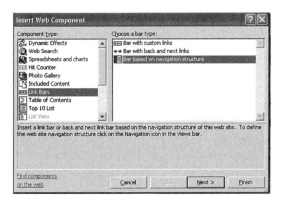

Insert Web Component
SOURCE: ©MICROSOFT FRONTPAGE

2. In the Insert Web Component dialog box, click on Bar based on navigation structure. Click on Next.
3. Click on Next again in the dialog box to choose an orientation. Click on Finish.
4. In the Link Bar Properties dialog box, leave it on Child level and click OK. Center the Navigation Bar if it is not already centered.

Bar Properties

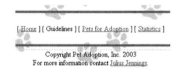

Tier 2 Links

5. Save again.
6. Go to each of the other Web pages and add a Navigation Bar. Each Tier 2 should have a Same level and Home. See the Tier 2 Links figure to the left.
7. Tier 3 will need a Parent level and Home page link. You can double-click on the Navigation Bar at any time to access the Link Bar Properties dialog box if you need to make a change.

Creating Hotspots

1. From your Navigation view, double-click on the Pet Adoption page to edit the page.
2. A hotspot can serve as a link on an image. Click on the dog picture in the table. The Picture toolbar should dock on the right side of your screen. Click on the Rectangular Hotspot tool.
3. The mouse pointer should now look like a pencil or pen when hovered over the Web page. Draw a rectangle around the dog's head.
4. The Insert Hyperlink dialog box opens. Click on Create New Document. Type "dog" in the Name of new document box.

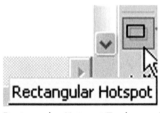

Rectangular Hotspot Tool

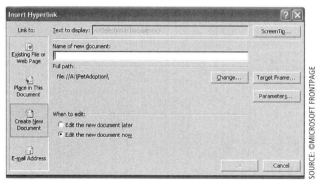

New Document

5. In the Insert Hyperlink dialog box, click on Target Frame.
6. In the Target Frame dialog box, click on New Window and OK.

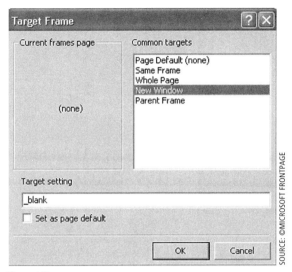

Target Frame

7. Click OK in the Insert Hyperlink dialog box. This opens the new page in Page view ready for you to edit. When you click on Target Frame and set it to open in a new window, users who click on this hotspot open a new window with the page in it. This is best used for external hyperlinks, to keep visitors from leaving your Web site accidentally.

WordArt

1. Click on the Insert WordArt tool on the Drawing toolbar docked at the bottom of your screen. If the Drawing toolbar is not visible, go to the menu bar and choose View > Toolbars > Drawing.
2. In the Edit WordArt Text dialog box, type "Popular Dog Names." Click OK.
3. Click on the WordArt and resize. When you click on the WordArt, the floating WordArt toolbar should pop up on your screen. If it does not, go to the menu bar and choose View > Toolbars > WordArt. Experiment with some of the tools available in WordArt.

Insert WordArt

SOURCE: ©MICROSOFT FRONTPAGE

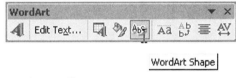

WordArt Toolbar   SOURCE: ©MICROSOFT FRONTPAGE

Table AutoFormat

1. Insert a two-column table below the WordArt. Input the names from the table to the right.
2. Click in one of the cells of the table. Go to the menu bar and choose Table > Select > Table.
3. Go to the menu bar and choose Table > Table AutoFormat.
4. In the Table AutoFormat dialog box, choose Grid 1 and select the AutoFit check box. Click OK.

Max	Buddy
Lady	Ginger
Jake	Casey
Molly	Sadie
Sam	Maggie
Shadow	Buster

Popular Dog Names

Table AutoFormat

Table Properties

1. Go to the menu bar and choose Table > Table Properties.

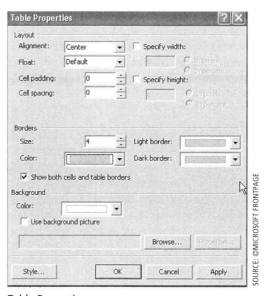

Table Properties

Popular Cat Names

2. In the Table Properties dialog box, change the layout alignment to Center. Change the border size to 4 and add a color that matches the WordArt for this page. Click on Apply, then OK.
3. Right-click on Page View anywhere on the Web page and choose Page Properties. Choose an appropriate background color.
4. Repeat these instructions for the picture of the cat in the right cell of the table. Add a table of Popular Cat Names, as seen in the figure to the left.

Copying and Pasting Images

1. Open the *statistics.htm* Web page. Type the title "Statistical Disposition of Animals." Format the font for 24 pt., Baskerville Old Face or a similar font, and black.

2. Use Microsoft Excel to open *Disposition.xls* from your CD.
3. Click on the chart. Go to the menu bar and choose Edit > Copy.
4. Click back on *statistics.htm* in FrontPage. Go to the menu bar and choose Edit > Paste.
5. Save again.

Drawing Tables

1. Open the *catinfo.htm* page from your folder list. Go to the menu bar and choose Insert > Picture > From File. Browse to your CD and double-click on *CatBanner.gif*. Press Enter, then click on the Align Left icon on the Formatting toolbar.
2. Go to the menu bar and choose Table > Draw Table. The floating Tables toolbar should pop up on your screen.
3. Click on the Draw Table icon.
4. Click on your screen below the banner and draw an approximate size for your table. See the table at right. Draw one vertical line to create two columns. Draw horizontal lines as needed.
5. Input the information from the Cat Table figure into your table.
6. On the Tables toolbar, click on Table AutoFormat and choose Simple 1.
7. Go to the menu bar and choose Table > Table Properties. Center the table.
8. Change the line properties so that they fit in with the color scheme on the page.
9. Save again.

Thumbnail Images

1. Click on "Pets for Adoption" so that it is in Page view for you to edit.
2. Add a title similar to the one shown in the Pets figure to the right.
3. Insert a table to place the images from your CD into the first column. The images are *Lucky.jpg*, *Angel.jpg*, and *Peaches.jpg*.
4. Place each pet's name in the second column opposite each picture.
5. Resample each image.
6. Click on the first image, then click on Auto Thumbnail on the Picture toolbar. Repeat this for the other two images.
7. Click on the Save icon on the Standard toolbar. When you do, notice that the Save Embedded Files dialog box pops up and has two images to save for each one. One of those is the thumbnail image.

Spell Checker

1. Go to any view other than Page view.
2. Go to the menu bar and choose Tools > Spelling. Click on Entire Web.
3. Follow the dialog box and correct any words that are not spelled correctly.
4. Save again.

ACTIVITY 2 • MINI-PROJECT

Create a Web Version of a Magazine

1. Bring an instructor-approved computer magazine from home or use one that your instructor has available. It should be an issue within the last three months.
2. Create a Web version of the magazine. You will not be able to include the entire magazine. Name the Web page with the name of the magazine.
3. On the *index.htm* page, scan a logo or image to use that represents the magazine. Create links to the next tier of Web pages. Decide on a background. You can use backgrounds already created or create your own with previously learned software.

Draw Table
SOURCE: ©MICROSOFT FRONTPAGE

Cat's Age	Human Years
1	15
2	25
4	40
7	50
10	60
15	75
20	105

SOURCE: ©MICROSOFT FRONTPAGE

Cat Table

SOURCE: ©MICROSOFT FRONTPAGE
Pets

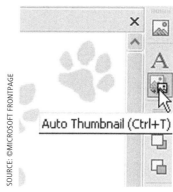
SOURCE: ©MICROSOFT FRONTPAGE
Auto Thumbnail

SOURCE: ©MICROSOFT FRONTPAGE
Save Embedded

4. Decide on three topics that you want to cover from the magazine. Create a minimum of three Web pages on the second tier. Use a combination of text and graphics. Reword any text you use.

5. Create at least one Tier 3 Web page.

6. Use the Pet Adoption Web page as a guideline as to what to include in this mini-project.

7. The following criteria should be met:

☐ Web page is set up correctly with proper name and details at the bottom for reference.

☐ Three Web pages on the Tier 2 with appropriate titles and content.

☐ Background is appropriate with recurring theme or colors throughout Web site.

☐ Fonts are appropriate size, type, and color.

☐ Line spacing adjusted where needed.

☐ Minimum of one table with Table AutoFormat used.

☐ Pictures are appropriate size and type with alternative text on each one. There are a minimum of three images on the Web site.

☐ Load time is appropriate for all pages (within 45 seconds).

☐ Minimum of one horizontal line with changed properties.

☐ Minimum of one example of shared borders on the Web site.

☐ Navigation bars provided that enable easy navigation from one page to another and back to the Web page.

☐ Minimum of one example of a hotspot created on an image.

☐ Minimum of one WordArt.

☐ Web site is error-free.

ACTIVITY 3 • USING THEMES

In this activity, you will become familiar with:

■ Themes
■ Modifying Themes
■ Page Banner
■ Hover Buttons
■ Formatting Images
■ Bullets
■ Marquee
■ Time and Date
■ Hit Counter
■ DHTML Effects

Themes

1. Go to the menu bar and choose File > New > Page or Web. Name it *AttackonAmerica*.

2. Choose Empty Web from the Task pane.

3. Click on the New Page icon on the Standard toolbar.

4. On your Views Bar, click on Navigation view. Double-click on *index.htm* to open it in Page view.

5. Go to the menu bar and choose Format > Theme.

6. In the Themes dialog box, scroll through to look at the themes available. Click on Freedom.

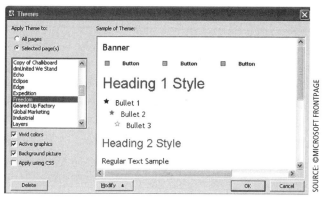

Themes

Modifying Themes

1. Click on Modify. You can modify three items on the theme: Colors, Graphics, or Text.
2. Choose Colors.
3. In the Modify Theme dialog box, choose a color that is as close to a red, white, and blue theme as you can get. Click OK and click OK again in the Modify Theme dialog box.

Modify

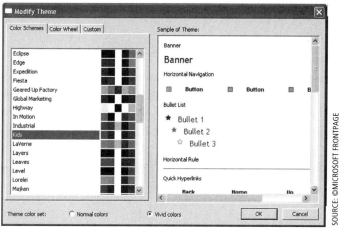

Modify Theme

4. Click Yes to saving changes to the Freedom theme.

Page Banner

1. Go to the menu bar and choose Insert > Page Banner.

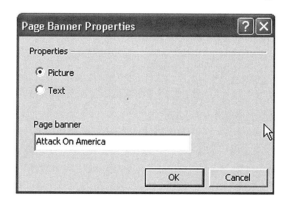

Page Banner

2. In the Page Banner Properties dialog box, type in the Page banner box "Attack on America."

Hover Buttons

1. Go to the menu bar and choose Format > Shared Borders. Click on Apply to All pages and Left. You could also add navigation buttons, but for this Web page, you are going to add Hover Buttons to navigate.
2. With the mouse pointer inside the shared border that you created, go to the menu bar and choose Insert > Web Component.
3. In the Insert Web Component dialog box, click on Hover Button for an effect. Click on Finish.

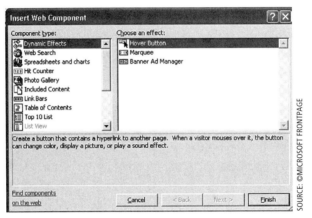

Hover Buttons

4. In the Hover Button Properties dialog box, type "Home" in the Button text box. Click on Browse and double-click on *index.htm*. Change the effect to Color fill and the effect color to red. Click OK.

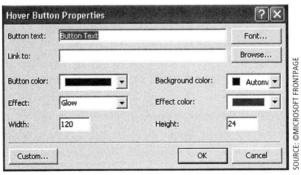

Hover Button Properties

5. Press Shift + Enter to go to the next line.
6. Repeat steps 3 through 5 for the following buttons:

Images	Link to: *images.htm*
News	Link to: *news.htm*
What next?	Link to: *whatnext.htm*
Comments	Link to: *comments.htm*

7. Save again.

8. Go to the Views Bar and choose Navigation view. Add the four pages you just created buttons for to the Web page. Rename the pages and the files.
9. Save all the pages.

Formatting Images

1. Add a horizontal line underneath the banner. Return and add a two-column, one-row table.
2. In the left cell of the table, go to the menu bar and choose Insert > Picture > From File. Browse to your CD and double-click on *Flower2.jpg*.
3. Resize the image. The image should be approximately 240 × 170 pixels. Resample the image.
4. On the Picture toolbar, click on Bevel.
5. On the Picture toolbar, click on Color and choose Grayscale from the menu.
6. Save again.

Bevel
SOURCE: ©MICROSOFT FRONTPAGE

Bullets

1. Type in the right cell of the table: "More than 3,000 people died in the September 11 attacks."
2. Click on the Bullet icon on the Formatting toolbar. The bullet used is the one that goes with the chosen theme.
3. Type three bulleted items: "New York," "Washington," and "Pennsylvania."
4. Format the text as yellow, Arial, 14 pt.
5. Go to the menu bar and choose Format > Paragraph. In the Paragraph dialog box, set the indentation before text to 5 and spacing before and after to 6.

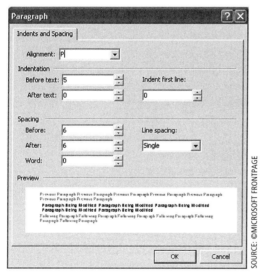

Paragraph

Marquee

1. Go to the menu bar and choose Format > Marquee.
2. In the Marquee Properties dialog box, type "September 11, 2001" in the Text box. Change the background color to blue.

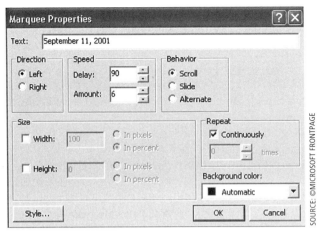

Marquee Properties

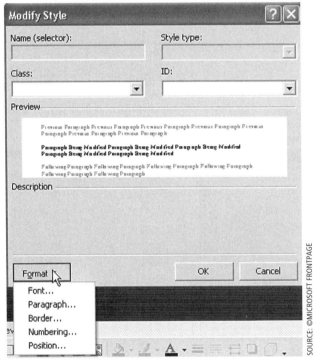

Modify Style

3. Click on Style. In the Modify Style dialog box, click on Format Font. Change the font to Comic Sans, 18 pt., red. Click OK until you have returned to the Front-Page screen.

Time and Date

1. Press the Enter key after the Marquee. Go to the menu bar and choose Insert > Date and Time.
2. Choose the Date format as shown to the left. Click OK.

Date and Time

Hit Counter

1. Go to the menu bar and choose Insert > Web Component.
2. Choose a counter style, then click on Finish.

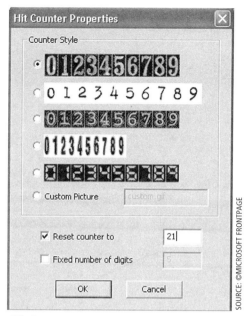

Hit Counter

SOURCE: ©MICROSOFT FRONTPAGE

3. In the Hit Counter Properties dialog box, click Reset counter to 21. It is best not to start the counter with 0. Click OK.
4. Select the Date and Hit Counter text and change the color to yellow. The counter will not work until the Web page is uploaded to the Internet.

DHTML Effects

1. Click on the banner image.
2. Go to the menu bar and choose Format > Dynamic HTML Effects.

DHTML Effects

SOURCE: ©MICROSOFT FRONTPAGE

3. In the On drop-down box, choose Mouse over.
4. In the Apply drop-down box, choose Formatting.
5. In the Effect drop-down box, choose Border. Format the border as shown below.

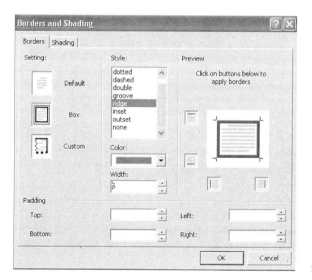

Border

SOURCE: ©MICROSOFT FRONTPAGE

6. Click on the X in the top right corner to close the toolbar.
7. Save again.

ACTIVITY 3 • MINI-PROJECT

Create a Music Web Site

1. Create a Web site and use your favorite music as the topic. The Web site should include a biography about your favorite singer or singers, lyrics, and other information such as concert dates.
2. Use an appropriate theme for the Web site.
3. The following criteria should be met:
   - [ ] Web site organized logically and contains required elements of biography and lyrics.
   - [ ] Theme is appropriate.
   - [ ] Page banner used on each Web page.
   - [ ] Hover buttons used appropriately.
   - [ ] First page is eye-catching.
   - [ ] Bullets used at least once.
   - [ ] Minimum of one marquee used appropriately.
   - [ ] Date and hit counter used at bottom of page for documentation.
   - [ ] DHTML effects used at least once.
   - [ ] Web site is error-free.
   - [ ] Images used appropriately and creatively. Some formatting of images occurred. A minimum of three images used.

ACTIVITY 4 • USING FRAMES

In this activity, you will become familiar with:

- Using the Wizard
- Saving
- New Page
- Resizing Frames
- Transparent Color
- Creating Links and Pages
- Inline Frames
- Inserting an SWF File
- Adding an Inline Frame
- Frame Properties
- Clip Art Wash Out
- Clip Art Send Backward
- Adding Meta Tags

Using the Wizard

1. Go to the menu bar and choose File > New > Page or Web.
2. On the Task pane, click on Web Site Templates.
3. In the Web Site Templates dialog box, click on Empty Web and type in the location *a:\wdc*. (You may need to get instructions from your instructor on the exact location for your Web.) Click OK.
4. Go to the menu bar and choose File > New > Page or Web.
5. On the Task pane, choose Page Templates.

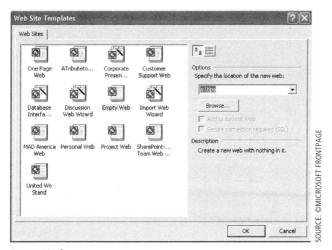

Empty Web

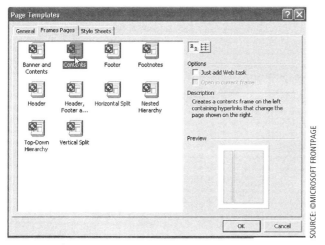

Page Templates

6. In the Page Templates dialog box, click on the Frames Pages tab. Click on Contents, then OK.

Saving

1. Click on the Save icon on the Standard toolbar.

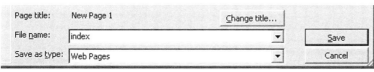

Save

SOURCE: ©MICROSOFT FRONTPAGE

2. Leave the file name as "index." Click on the Change title button. In the Set Page Title dialog box, type "Tips and Shortcuts." Click on Save. You can also change the title of the page by going to the menu bar and choosing File > Properties.

Page Title

SOURCE: ©MICROSOFT FRONTPAGE

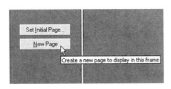

New Page

New Page

1. In the Contents frame, click on the New Page button.
2. Type the following in the Contents frame:
   Home
   Design Tips
   Formatting Shortcuts
   Document Shortcuts
   Editing Shortcuts
3. Format the text in the Contents frame as 14 pt. with a blank line between each entry.

Resizing Frames

1. Widen the frame by hovering the mouse pointer over the frame line. When the pointer changes to a two-headed arrow, click and drag to resize the frame. You can also go to the menu bar and choose Frames > Frame Properties to change the height and width.
2. Format the background as a light yellow.

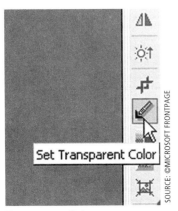

Transparent Color

Transparent Color

1. Below the four lines of text, insert clip art of a disk. Search for "computer." The image should have a background that is any color other than yellow. Resize and resample the image.
2. Click on the Set Transparent Color icon on the Picture toolbar.
3. The FrontPage dialog box explaining that the image will be converted to GIF format pops up on your screen. Click OK.

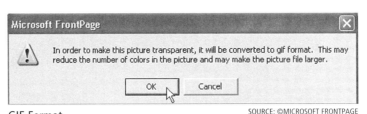

GIF Format

4. Click on the background in the image. Your pointer should be the Transparent tool. It will make the background transparent. (You do not have to use the same image as long as the one you use has a background that you can make transparent.)

Disk

Creating Links and Pages

1. Click on New Page in the Page View area.
2. Go to the menu bar and choose Insert > File. Browse to your CD and change Files of Type to All Files. Double-click on *FrontPage.doc*.
3. Add a horizontal line between the title and the first paragraph. Format the Horizontal line as light yellow, 5 pixels in height.
4. Insert the date after Last Updated.
5. Select Rolando Vasquez. Be sure there is a mail link to rvasquez@hotmail.com.
6. Click on the Save icon on the Standard toolbar. Name this page *frontpage.htm*. Click on Rename and type "*disk.gif*" to rename the image. This will help you associate it with what the image actually is. You will be asked to name the other page. Name it *frontpage1.htm*.
7. Select Home. Click on the Insert Hyperlink icon on the Standard toolbar. Click on Existing File or Web page. Browse to *frontpage1.htm*. Click OK.
8. Select Design Tips. Click on the Insert Hyperlink icon.

9. In the Insert Hyperlink dialog box, click on Create New Document. Type "*tips.htm*" in the Name box. Click Edit the new document later. Click OK. Repeat this step to create links and pages for *formatting.htm, document.htm,* and *edit.htm.*

10. Go to the menu bar and choose File > Save All.

11. Go to Navigation view. Double-click on *tips.htm* in the folder list.

12. Insert the file *TopTen.doc* from your CD in the *tips.htm* page. Reformat as needed to make the font size the same throughout the page. Select all text and click on Numbered List on the Formatting toolbar. Add a WordArt title, "Top Ten Tips." (You can also open the *TopTen.doc* file in Word and copy and paste it into the *tips.htm* page.)

13. Go to Navigation view. In the folder list, double-click on *formatting.htm.* Insert *Formatting Shortcuts.doc* into this page. Save. Repeat this instruction for *edit.htm* and *document.htm*, inserting *Editing Shortcuts.doc* and *DocumentShortcuts.doc* into those pages.

14. Go to the menu bar and choose File > Save All.

Inline Frames

1. Go to Navigation view. Double-click on *index.htm* to open the Frames page. On the Contents frame under Editing Shortcuts, type "*Inline Frames.*"

2. Select "Inline Frames" and click on the Insert Hyperlink icon on the Standard toolbar. Create a new page titled *inlineframes.htm.* Edit the new document now.

Inserting an SWF File

1. With the new Inline Frames page open, go to the menu bar and choose Insert > Web Component.

2. In the Insert Web Component dialog box, scroll down on the Component type to Advanced Controls. In Choose a control, click on Plug-in. Click on Finish.

3. In the Plug-In Properties dialog box, browse to your CD for the Data source and double-click on *InlineFrames.swf.*

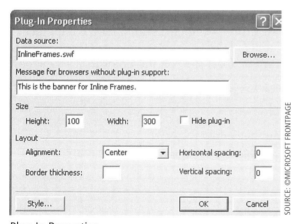

Plug-In Properties

4. Type the following in the "Message for browsers without plug-in support" text box: "This is the banner for Inline Frames."

5. Change the height to 100 and the width to 300. See above.

Adding an Inline Frame

1. Go to the menu bar and choose Insert > Inline Frame.

2. Click on the New Page icon in the Inline Frame.

Frame Properties

1. Double-click on the outline of the frame.

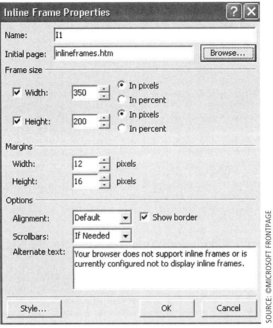

Frames Properties

2. In the Inline Frame Properties dialog box, change the width to 350 in pixels and the height to 200 in pixels. Change the layout alignment to Center. Click OK.
3. Go to the menu bar and choose Insert > File. Browse to your CD and double-click on *InlineFrames.doc*.

Clip Art Wash Out

Wash Out

1. With the mouse pointer at the beginning of the text in the inline frame, go to the menu bar and choose Insert > Picture > Clip art. Search for a computer.
2. Insert a picture in the inline frame.
3. Select the picture. On the Picture toolbar, click on the Color icon and choose Wash Out.

Clip Art Send Backward

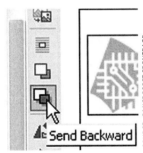

Send Backward

1. On the Picture toolbar, click on the Send Backward icon.
2. Resize the picture so that it fits below most of the text in the inline frame.

Adding Meta Tags

1. Go to Navigation view and double-click on *index.htm*. Click on the HTML tab at the bottom of the page. You will insert a description and keyword meta tag into the HTML code. This will not affect the Web site or show anywhere except in the code. It is used by search engines to pick up important information to assist in surfers locating your Web site.
2. See the top figure on following page to locate the line that reads "<meta name="Generator" content="Microsoft FrontPage 5.0">." Click at the end of that line and press Enter.
3. Type the following description meta tag: "<meta name="description" content="Welcome to Tips and Shortcuts.">."

```
<html>

<head>
<meta name="GENERATOR" content="Microsoft FrontPage 5.0">

<meta name="ProgId" content="FrontPage.Editor.Document">
<meta http-equiv="Content-Type" content="text/html; charset=windows
<title>FrontPage</title>
</head>

<body>
```

Insertion Point

4. Press the Enter key and type the following keywords meta tag: "<meta name="keywords" content="FrontPage 5.0, shortcuts, tips, Web site, HTML">."
5. Save All.

ACTIVITY 4 • MINI-PROJECT

Create an Information Site on Small Business

1. Go to http://www.small-business.co.il/ or search for other Web sites with tips on starting a business.
2. Create a Web site with frames. Name the Web site "Small Business Success."
3. The Web site should contain at least three Tier 2 Web pages and one Tier 3 Web page.
4. One of the Web pages should contain the plans for a business of your own. The plans should contain an animated logo using Flash or LiveMotion, company name, the purpose of the business, hours of operation, vision of the business, and desired location.
5. The following criteria should be met:
   - ☐ First page is eye-catching and contains useful information.
   - ☐ Design of frames in Web site makes it easy to navigate.
   - ☐ Information provided for small business success is accurate and appropriate in content.
   - ☐ Minimum of one inline frame created appropriately.
   - ☐ Minimum of one eye-catching SWF file created.
   - ☐ Business plan is clear and concise and demonstrates critical-thinking skills.
   - ☐ Web site is error-free.
   - ☐ Meta tags used for keywords and description in HTML code.
   - ☐ Recurring theme or color throughout the Web page.
   - ☐ Minimum of one image used as a watermark.

ACTIVITY 5 • USING FORMS

In this activity, you will become familiar with:

- ■ Creating a Form
- ■ Textbox
- ■ Textbox Properties
- ■ Modify Style
- ■ Drop-Down Box
- ■ Submit and Reset

Creating a Form

1. Go to the menu bar and choose File > New > Page or Web.
2. Click on Empty Web on the Task pane.
3. In the Web Templates dialog box, click on Empty Web and name the Web "Scholarship."
4. Click on New Page.
5. In Navigation view, double-click on *index.htm* to open the new page.
6. Go to the menu bar and choose Insert > File.
7. In the Select File dialog box, change the Files of type to All Files. Browse to your CD and double-click on *StudentScholarship.doc*.
8. Use the Delete key to remove extra blank lines and move lines to the margin that have been moved over.

Textbox

1. Place the mouse pointer next to "Name." Go to the menu bar and choose Insert > Form > Textbox.
2. Drag the Textbox up next to Name. Delete the Submit and Reset buttons.

Textbox Properties

1. Double-click on the Textbox.
2. In the Textbox Properties dialog box, type "Name" in the Name box. Change the width in characters to 75.

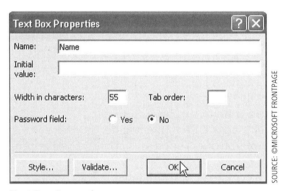

Text Box Properties

Modify Style

1. Click on Style. In the Modify Style dialog box, click on the Format button and select Border. Choose a double border for the Name box. You can also choose to modify colors, fonts, and sizes.
2. Click OK until you are back in Page view.
3. Create a Textbox for Home Phone that is 25 characters long. Name it appropriately. Create Textboxes for all other fields except for State and Member.

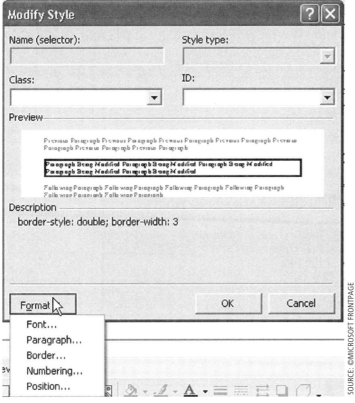

Modify Style

Drop-Down Box

1. Create a drop-down box for State. Go to the menu bar and choose Insert > Form > Drop-down box.
2. In the Drop-Down Box Properties dialog box, type "State" for the Name.

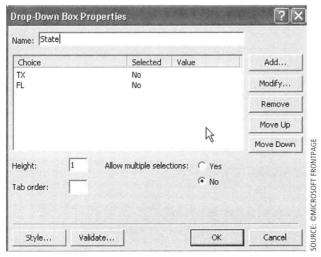

Drop-Down Box Properties

3. Click on the Add button. In the Add Choice dialog box, type "FL" in the Choice box. Click OK.
4. Click on the Add button again. In the Add Choice dialog box, type "TX" in the Choice box. Click OK.
5. Repeat these instructions for the Member box. The drop-down choices should be "BPA" and "FBLA."

Submit and Reset

1. Place the mouse pointer at the end of the document. Go to the menu bar and choose Insert > Form > Textbox. Delete the textbox, leaving the Submit and Reset buttons and the form boundary around the Submit and Reset buttons.
2. Click on the Center icon on the Formatting toolbar.
3. Click on Submit. Right-click and choose Form Properties.

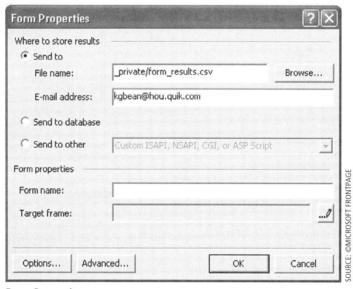

Form Properties

4. In the Form Properties dialog box, type an e-mail address in the E-mail address line. Click on the Options button.
5. In the Saving Results dialog box, click on the E-mail Results tab. Click in the Subject Line and type "Student Scholarship." Click OK twice.
6. Because this requires personal Web extensions to work properly, you will get a message asking if you want to remove the e-mail recipient. Click on No.
7. Save again.

ACTIVITY 5 • MINI-PROJECT

Create a Survey for a School Store

1. In a team of three or four students, design an online survey for the beginning of a school store.
2. In the survey, ask about specific types of school supplies students might purchase at school and the frequency, types of candy, and other items that might be useful to them in a school store. Other questions should pertain to hours of operation that they would find the store useful.

3. On this particular survey, it is important for verification that you have each student's name, address, and phone number as well as their classification.
4. Each member of the team should create his or her own online form for the survey.
5. The following criteria should be met:
   - ☐ Online survey meets all requirements.
   - ☐ Survey questions worded so they can be easily understood.
   - ☐ Questions appropriate in helping to decide what products to stock in the school store.
   - ☐ Design is easy to read and to maneuver through.
   - ☐ Online survey is error-free.
   - ☐ Correct field types used (drop-down boxes, textboxes, and so on).
   - ☐ Survey looks professional on the screen. Fields are of appropriate length. Correct font size, type, and color were used.
   - ☐ Submit and Reset forms are set correctly and work.

PART 1 • SIMULATION

Using FrontPage

1. Create a Web site on car comparison. Choose three vehicles that are similar in type but different makes. For instance, you could do a comparison of three trucks or three midsized cars, but the comparison might be midsized cars made by Toyota, Ford, and Chevrolet. Use the Internet for your research as well as brochures from the companies.
2. The first page of the Web site should create interest about the vehicles. Use animation software to create a banner for the Web site and hover buttons to use for navigation.
3. Create the following Web pages for Tier 2:
   a. History—Choose one of the companies (such as Ford, Chevrolet, or Toyota) and write a history of that company.
   b. Price—Compare the prices of the three vehicles. This should be a very detailed comparison. Be sure you are comparing cars with the same equipment on them.
   c. Reliability—Compare reports on reliability of the vehicle. You should be able to obtain this information from the Internet.
   d. Economy—Compare the costs of keeping each of the vehicles maintained, repair costs, insurance costs, and gas mileage. Search on the Internet or interview insurance company employees and automotive shops to get the information.
   e. Shopping Tips—Prepare a presentation of at least six slides on what to look for when shopping for a car and/or the steps to take in preparing to buy a car. Link this page to the presentation and include the presentation in the directory with your other files for this Web page. (When you link Power-Point, the Web viewer must have PowerPoint on his or her computer in order to view the slide show.)
   f. Summary—Write a summary as to which vehicle you would buy. Give detailed information that is supported on your Web page as to why you made this decision.
4. Create at least two Tier 3 Web pages.
5. Create at least one form. It can be a survey, an application, or a questionnaire. Use at least two different types of form fields.

6. The following criteria should be met:

- ☐ Information is thorough and accurate on all Web pages.
- ☐ Organization of Web pages is logical and lends to ease of navigation.
- ☐ Images are appropriate in size and type and come from a variety of sources, including digital and scanned.
- ☐ Continuity of theme or color throughout Web site.
- ☐ Web site is error-free.
- ☐ PowerPoint presentation is effective and linked properly.
- ☐ At least one chart or table is used in comparing vehicles. The chart or table is visually effective.
- ☐ Form is placed appropriately and works properly.
- ☐ Summary is well written, with excellent comparison examples leading to the decision.
- ☐ Proper meta tags for description and keywords were inserted into the HTML code.
- ☐ Student has demonstrated most of the skills learned in creating Web pages.

Macromedia Dreamweaver

ACTIVITY 1 • GETTING STARTED

In this activity, you will become familiar with:

- Status Bar
- New Site
- View Options
- Property Inspector
- Objects Panel
- History Panel
- Preferences
- Code and Design View
- Saving

Status Bar

1. Start Dreamweaver.
2. The Status Bar is in the lower right corner of your computer screen. In the Status Bar there is a current account of the file size and estimated download time for the current page, as shown below.

Status Bar

SOURCE: ©MACROMEDIA DREAMWEAVER

3. On the Status Bar, click on the Window Size menu. These are common monitor settings to choose from. Choose 600 × 300 pixels by selecting it then releasing the mouse button. There are other options on the Status Bar that you can explore later.

Window Size

SOURCE: ©MACROMEDIA DREAMWEAVER

New Site

1. On the Status Bar, click on the Show Site button.

Show Site

2. In the Site dialog box, click in the Site drop-down box and select Define Sites.

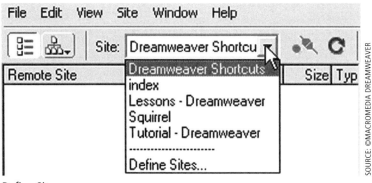

Define Sites

3. In the Define Sites dialog box, click on New.
4. Name the site "Squirrel." Get instructions from your instructor for the Local Root Folder and the HTTP Address.
5. Click OK.
6. A message box pops up on the screen that tells you the initial site cache will now be created. Click OK.

Site Cache

7. Be sure the mouse pointer is on the Squirrel Web site and click on Done in the Define Sites dialog box.
8. In the Site dialog box, go to the menu bar and choose File > New. In the file name box, type *index.htm*.
9. Double-click on *index.htm* to open it for editing.

View Options

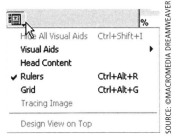

View Options

1. You can turn your rulers on and off from this menu. Click on the View Options button right below the menu bar at the far right. See the figure to the left.

2. Choose Rulers. This turns the rulers on or off depending on what their status was when you went to the menu.
3. You can also show the rulers by going to the menu bar and choosing View > Rulers. This allows you to show the rulers as well as change their measurement from pixels to inches or centimeters.

Property Inspector

1. Type "Squirrel" on the screen.
2. Below the text you have typed on your screen, insert an image. Go to the menu bar and choose Insert > Image. Browse to your CD and double-click on *Squirrel.jpg*. Resize the image so that it is 200 × 200 pixels.
3. Go to the menu bar and choose Window > Properties to open the Property inspector.

Property Inspector

SOURCE: ©MACROMEDIA DREAMWEAVER

4. Select the text on your screen. The Property inspector becomes a Text Property inspector.
5. Change the text to Verdana, +4, Blue. Center the text horizontally.
6. Click on the image of the squirrel. The Property inspector changes to an Image Property inspector. In the bottom right corner of the Image Property inspector is an upward arrow. This expands the menu. Click on it.
7. Center the squirrel image and type "3" in the Border box.
8. In the Image Property inspector, type "Squirrel" in the Alt box. If the image takes a while to load or a viewer's browser cannot display the image, the text will describe the image.

Objects Panel

1. Go to the menu bar and choose Window > Objects.
2. Click on the button below the title bar on the Objects panel. By default it is the Common button. Click on the down arrow and choose Characters from the pop-up menu. Experiment with the various symbols that can be inserted from this menu.
3. Continue to explore the Objects panel menu items and what each one does.
4. Click to the right of the title "Squirrels." Press the Enter key.
5. Click on the Objects panel and choose Common from the menu.
6. Locate the Insert Horizontal Rule icon and click on it.
7. The Horizontal Rule inspector opens up. Change the H (Height) to 5 and click in front of Shading to turn it off. If there is an extra blank line below the horizontal rule, delete it.

Objects Panel

SOURCE: ©MACROMEDIA DREAMWEAVER

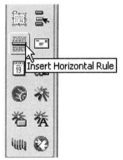

Horizontal Rule

SOURCE: ©MACROMEDIA DREAMWEAVER

History Panel

1. Go to the menu bar and choose Window > History.
2. The History panel has recorded all the commands on this document. You can drag the slider up to undo one or more of these commands.
3. To redo the command, click and drag the slider downward.
4. To undo the last command performed, go to the menu bar and choose Edit > Undo; to redo, choose Edit > Redo.

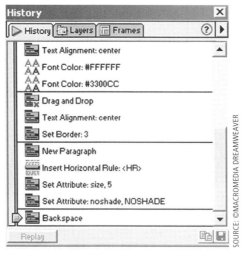

History Panel

Preferences

1. Go to the menu bar and choose Edit > Preferences.

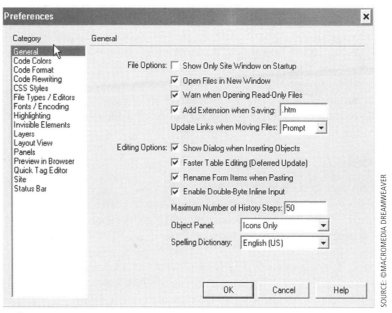

Preferences

2. Explore the different options available in Preferences. Leave it on the defaults. Click on Cancel.

Code and Design View

Code View

1. The Code View icon is located below the menu bar at the far left. It shows the HTML code for the Web page you have created. Click on Code View.
2. The button to the right of Code View splits the screen and shows the HTML code at the top and the Design View at the bottom.
3. Click on the Design View button. Usually this is the view you will work in.

Saving

1. Go to the menu bar and choose File > Save as.
2. Note that the file is already saved as *index.htm*. You saved it when you defined the site.
3. Click on Save to save again.

ACTIVITY 1 • MINI-PROJECT

Create a Web Site Structure

1. Define a Web site for recipes. Add three other Web pages: Dinner Entrees, Breads, and Desserts with file names *dinner.htm*, *breads.htm*, and *desserts.htm*.
2. Add an appropriate title on the *index.htm* page. Use the Property inspector to format the title.
3. Insert an appropriate image. Resize the image as needed.
4. The following criteria should be met:
   - ☐ All Web pages titled and defined appropriately.
   - ☐ Title formatted appropriately.
   - ☐ Image inserted properly and sized appropriately.
   - ☐ No errors on the Web page.

ACTIVITY 2 • FORMATTING THE WEB PAGE

In this activity, you will become familiar with:

- ■ Copying and Pasting Text
- ■ Paragraph Format
- ■ Line Breaks
- ■ Drop Cap
- ■ Outdent and Indent
- ■ Web Page Title
- ■ Preview in Browser
- ■ Show Site
- ■ Unordered List
- ■ Ordered List
- ■ Special Characters
- ■ Background
- ■ Text Page Links
- ■ Insert Date
- ■ Email Link

Copying and Pasting Text

1. Use Word to open *IntroSquirrels.doc* from your CD. Select the text in this document. Go to the menu bar and choose Edit > Copy. Close Word.
2. On your *index.htm* file, click below the image of the squirrel. Press Enter.
3. Go to the menu bar and choose Insert > Horizontal Line. Format the properties of the line so that it is the same as the other horizontal line on this page. Press Enter.
4. Go to the menu bar and choose Edit > Paste. This should paste the paragraph about squirrels into the Web page.
5. Save again.

Paragraph Format

1. Select the text that you pasted into the Web page.
2. In the Property inspector, click in the Format drop-down box and select Heading 3.
3. In the Text Color box, change the color to blue.
4. Click on Align Left.

Line Breaks

1. Place your cursor in front of the word "These." This is at the beginning of the fourth sentence.
2. Press Shift + Enter to insert a line break.
3. Press Shift + Enter to insert another line break.

Drop Cap

1. Highlight the first letter of the paragraph.
2. In the Property inspector, select Size +4.

Outdent and Indent

Text Indent
SOURCE: ©MACROMEDIA DREAMWEAVER

1. In the Property inspector, click on Text Indent twice. This indents the paragraph from both the left and the right sides.
2. In the Property inspector, click on Text Outdent if you decide that was too much indenting. This reverses the indent.

Web Page Title

1. Click in the Title box underneath the menu bar. Select Untitled and type "Squirrel."

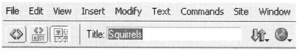

Document Title
SOURCE: ©MACROMEDIA DREAMWEAVER

2. Save again.

Preview in Browser

1. Go to the menu bar and choose File > Preview in Browser > Explorer (or the name of the browser you are using).
2. After previewing the Web page, click the Close button on the browser.

Show Site

1. On the Status Bar, click on the Show Site button.
2. In the Site—Squirrels dialog box, go to the menu bar and choose File > New File. Type in the name box *BabyFacts.htm*. Double-click on *BabyFacts.htm* to open the file for editing.
3. Click on the Close button in the Site dialog box.

Unordered List

Unordered List
SOURCE: ©MACROMEDIA DREAMWEAVER

1. On the new page, type in the Title box "Baby Facts." Format as Heading 1, Red, Align Center.
2. In the Property inspector, click on the Unordered List icon.

3. Type the following list:

 Gestation from 33 to 60 days
 Born in early spring
 Litter usually consists of four babies
 Weighs approximately one ounce
 Length is approximately one inch
 Blind for the first six weeks

4. Format the font as Georgia, +1.
5. Text Indent 3 times.
6. Select the first fact. Go to the menu bar and choose Text > List > Properties.

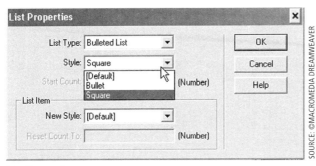

List Properties

7. In the List Properties dialog box, click on the Style drop-down box and select Square. All the bullets change to squares in the unordered list.

Ordered List

1. On the Status Bar, click on the Show Site icon.
2. In the Site—Squirrels dialog box, go to the menu bar and choose File > New File. Type in the file name box *Schedule.htm*.
3. Type "The Squirrel" for the heading in Brown, Times New Roman, +2, centered horizontally.
4. In the Property inspector, click on Ordered List.
5. Type the following:

 Most active two to three hours after sunrise.
 Resume activity two hours after sunset.
 Goes to bed long before dark.
 Rarely leaves its nest at night.
 Completes most of its activity during midday in winter.

6. Select the Ordered List. In the Property inspector, format the ordered list as Paragraph Format, Geneva Font, +1, Orange and Text Indent 3 times.
7. Save again.

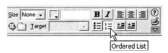

Ordered List

SOURCE: ©MACROMEDIA DREAMWEAVER

Special Characters

1. Place your cursor after the title "The Schedule."
2. In the Objects panel, click below the title bar to choose the object type. Choose Character.
3. Click on the Insert Other Character icon.
4. From the characters, choose the em dash. Click OK. See the figure labeled Em Dash on the following page.
5. Click after the em dash and type "of a Squirrel."
6. Save again.

Insert Other Character

SOURCE: ©MACROMEDIA DREAMWEAVER

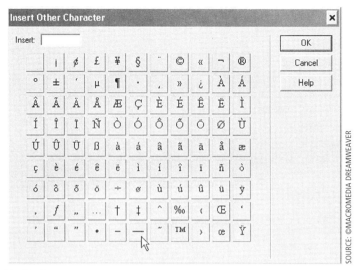

Em Dash

Background

1. Go to the menu bar and choose Modify > Page Properties.

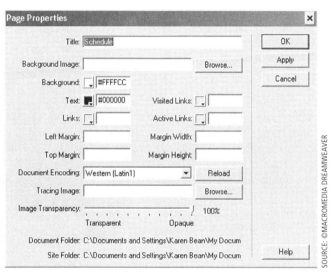

Page Properties

2. Click on the Background Color box and choose a light yellow.
3. Click on Apply, then OK.
4. Click on the Show Site icon on the Status Bar.
5. Double-click on *Baby Facts.htm*.
6. Go to the menu bar and choose Modify > Page Properties.
7. On the Background Image line, click on Browse. Browse to your CD and double-click on *acorns.gif*.
8. Click on Apply, then OK.
9. Save again.
10. Open *Index.htm*, which you created earlier.
11. Add a light orange background color to it.
12. Save again.

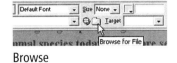

Browse

SOURCE: ©MACROMEDIA DREAMWEAVER

Text Page Links

1. With *index.htm* open, click below the last line of text on the page. Type "| (Shift + backward slash) Baby Facts |."
2. Select Baby Facts.
3. In the Property inspector, click on Browse for File.
4. In the Select File dialog box, browse to your CD and double-click on *Baby Facts.htm*.
5. Save again.
6. Repeat steps 1 through 5 for *Schedule.htm*.
7. In the Property inspector, click the Align Center icon.
8. Click on the Show Site icon on the Status Bar.
9. In the Site dialog box, click on the Site Map. This shows a diagram of the three Web pages and their hierarchy.
10. Save again.

Insert Date

1. Open *index.htm*.
2. Go to the bottom of the page by pressing Ctrl + End.
3. Click on the Insert Date icon on the Objects panel.
4. In the Insert Date dialog box, select the Update Automatically on Save check box. Leave all other defaults.

Insert Date

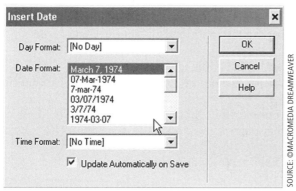

Date Dialog Box

5. Click OK.
6. After inserting the date, if changes need to be made, select the date and click on the Edit Date Format button in the Property inspector.

Date Properties

Email Link

1. Press Shift + Enter to insert a line break after the date.
2. On the Objects panel, click on Insert Email Link.
3. In the Insert Email Link dialog box, in the Text box, type "John J. Squirrel." In the E-Mail box, type "John@squirrels.com."

Email Link

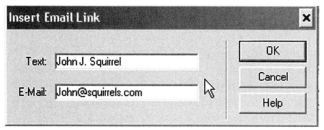

Email Dialog Box   SOURCE: ©MACROMEDIA DREAMWEAVER

4. Click OK.
5. If you need to make changes to the email link, click on the email link and go to the Property inspector to edit.

Email Properties   SOURCE: ©MACROMEDIA DREAMWEAVER

6. Save again.
7. Click on the Show Site icon in the Status Bar.
8. Double-click on *BabyFacts.htm* to open the Web page for editing.
9. At the bottom of the Web page, click on the Text Outdent icon on the Property inspector until the cursor is at the left margin. Click on the Center icon on the Property inspector.
10. Type the following: "| Home | | Schedule|."
11. Select Home. Click on Browse for File on the Property inspector. Double-click on *index.htm* to link to that page.
12. Select Schedule. Click on Browse for File on the Property inspector. Double-click on *Schedule.htm* to link to that page.
13. Save again.
14. Open *Schedule.htm*. Create links on this page to Home and Baby Facts, following steps 9 through 12.
15. Save again and close the Web page.

ACTIVITY 2 • MINI-PROJECT

Create a Personal Web Page

1. Decide on two or three colors to use for a theme for a personal Web site.
2. Create a GIF to use with your name or a title introducing your Web site. You can use any image management or animation software you have learned.
3. Acquire a picture of yourself either by digital camera or scanning.
4. Scan at least three pictures of your family. This can also include family pets.
5. Define the site as "Personal." Add three other pages: Family, Activities, and Career Goals.
6. On the *index.htm* page, insert the title image, the personal picture, and text links to the three other pages.
7. Add a title to each of the other three pages using the Property inspector to format the text for color, size, and alignment.
8. Add at least three pictures of your family to the Family page.
9. On the Activities page, add at least one piece of clip art and an unordered list of your activities. Use Indent and Outdent as needed.

10. On the Career Goals page, write an ordered list of your career goals. Choose one career goal and write at least five steps you plan to take to achieve that goal.
11. Add text links to all pages.
12. The Web pages should have at least two color changes on backgrounds and a background image on at least one Web page.
13. End each page with an inserted date and email address.
14. Save all pages.
15. The following criteria should be met:
    - ☐ Appropriate backgrounds as required.
    - ☐ Appropriate title image for the *index.htm* page.
    - ☐ Personal picture is good quality and appropriately sized.
    - ☐ Family Web page has a title appropriately formatted with quality pictures and text links to Home, Activities, and Career Goals pages.
    - ☐ Activities Web page has a title appropriately formatted with quality clip art and text links to Home, Family, and Career Goals pages.
    - ☐ Career Goals Web page has a title appropriately formatted with practical steps to achieve the career goal.
    - ☐ Web site is error-free.
    - ☐ All links work.

ACTIVITY 3 • USING TABLES AND LAYERS

In this activity, you will become familiar with:

- ■ Rollover Images
- ■ Hotspots
- ■ Navigation Bar
- ■ Library
- ■ Creating a Table
- ■ Table Alignment
- ■ Column Width
- ■ Border and Background Color
- ■ Cell Padding
- ■ Cell Spacing
- ■ Insert Columns and Rows
- ■ Merge and Split Cells
- ■ Layout Tables
- ■ Layout Cells
- ■ Column AutoStretch
- ■ Fixed Width Column
- ■ Adding Text to Layout Cells
- ■ Importing Word HTML
- ■ Draw Layers
- ■ Add Content to Layers
- ■ Resize Layers
- ■ Add Background Color to Layers
- ■ Layers Panel

Rollover Images

1. Click on the Show Site icon.
2. In the Site drop-down box, select Define Sites.
3. In the Define Sites dialog box, click on New.
4. In the Site Name box, type "Dreamweaver Shortcuts." Get the local root folder and HTTP address information from your instructor. Click OK.

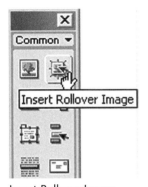

Insert Rollover Image

SOURCE: ©MACROMEDIA DREAMWEAVER

5. In the Define Sites dialog box, with your cursor on the new site name, click Done.
6. Go to the menu bar and choose File > New File.
7. Type *index.htm* in the file name box. Double-click on *index.htm* to open it for editing.
8. On the Objects panel, click on the Insert Rollover Image icon.
9. In the Insert Rollover Image dialog box, type in the image name "Dreamweaver." Browse to find the original image, which is *Dreamweaver Shortcuts.gif*. Browse to find the rollover image which is *WeaverDream.gif*. Click OK.

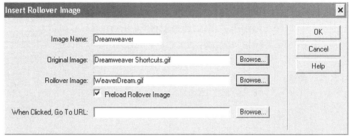

Rollover Image

SOURCE: ©MACROMEDIA DREAMWEAVER

10. Go to the menu bar and choose Modify > Page Properties. Choose a light yellow Background.
11. Save again.

Hotspots

1. On the Status Bar, click on Show Site. Go to the menu bar and choose File > New File. Name the New File *document.htm*. Repeat this instruction to add *menu.htm* and *object.htm*.
2. Double-click on *index.htm* to edit the file.
3. Below the rollover banner, insert the image *web.gif*.
4. Select the *web.gif* image by clicking on it.
5. In the Property inspector, click on the Oval Hotspot Tool icon. Draw the oval in the middle of the circle part of the *web.gif* image.

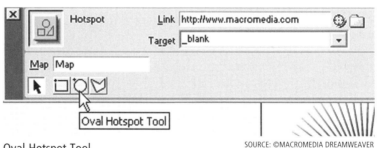

Oval Hotspot Tool

SOURCE: ©MACROMEDIA DREAMWEAVER

6. In the Property inspector, in the Link box, type "http://www.macromedia.com." In the Target drop-down box, select _blank so that the Web site will open in a new window. In the Alt box for Alternative Text, type "Macromedia Web site."

Navigation Bar

1. Click below the *web.gif* image. In the Property inspector, click on the Center icon.
2. Go to the menu bar and choose Insert > Interactive Images > Navigation Bar.

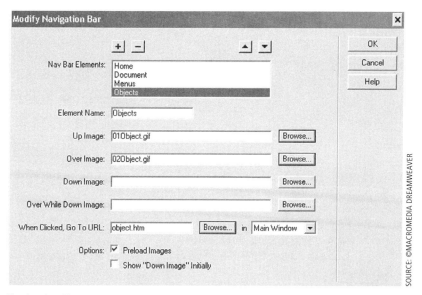

Navigation Bar

3. On the Insert Navigation Bar, type "Home" in the Element Name. Click on Browse in the Up Image box. Browse to your CD and double-click on *01Home.gif*. Click on Browse in the Over Image box. Browse to your CD and double-click on *02Home.gif*. Click on Browse in the Down Image box. Browse to your CD and double-click on *01Home.gif*. Click on Browse in the When Clicked, Go To URL box. Browse to your CD and double-click on *index.htm*.

4. Click on the plus sign above Nav Bar Elements.

5. Type "Document" in the Nav Bar Elements file name box. Type "Document" in the Element Name box. Browse for the Up Image and double-click on *01Document.gif*. Browse for the Over Image and double-click on *02Document.gif*. Click on Browse in the Down Image box. Browse to your CD and double-click on *01Document.gif*. Browse for *document.htm* to place in the When Clicked, Go To URL box.

6. Click on the plus sign above Nav Bar Elements.

7. Type "Menus" in the Nav Bar Elements file name box. Type "Menus" in the Element Name box. Browse for the Up Image and double-click on *01Menu.gif*. Browse for the Over Image and double-click on *02Menu.gif*. Click on Browse in the Down Image box. Browse to your CD and double-click on *01Menu.gif*. Browse for *menu.htm* to place in the When Clicked, Go To URL box.

8. Click on the plus sign above Nav Bar Elements.

9. Type "Objects" in the Nav Bar Elements file name box. Type "Objects" in the Element Name box. Browse for the Up Image and double-click on *01Object.gif*. Browse for the Over Image and double-click on *02Object.gif*. Click on Browse in the Down Image box. Browse to your CD and double-click on *01Object.gif*. Browse for *object.htm* to place in the When Clicked, Go To URL box.

10. Click OK.

11. If you need to modify the Navigation Bar, go to the menu bar and choose Modify Navigation Bar.

12. Select the Navigation Bar by clicking on each button. Hold down the Shift key while pressing each button after the first one.

Library

1. Drag the Navigation Bar to the Library. If the Library panel is not visible, go to the menu bar and choose Window > Library. Type "Navigation Bar" in the file name box.

2. Click on the Navigation Bar. In the Navigation Bar Property inspector, click on Detach from Original.

Remove Source

3. Click on the Home button. Press Delete. You do not need a link to the Home page on this page since you are already on the Home page.
4. Save again by going to the menu bar and choosing File > Save.
5. Click below the Navigation Bar.
6. In the Property inspector, click on the Center icon.
7. Insert the current date in default format. Select the Update Automatically on Save check box.
8. Press Shift + Enter to insert a line break after the date.
9. On the Objects panel, click on Insert Email Link. Type for the text "Karen Collier." Type for the email "karen@dreamweaver.com."
10. Select the date and email address.
11. Go to the menu bar and choose Window > Library.
12. On the Assets for Site panel, click on the arrow. Select New Library Item. Type "Date and Email" in the file name box.
13. Double-click on the Library item to edit it.
14. Change "Karen" to "Karin." Double-click on the email address and change "karen" to "karin" in the email address.
15. Close the Library Editor and save the changes to the date and email.
16. Delete the date and email from your Web page. Drag a new instance below the Navigation Bar with the correction to your Web page.
17. Save again.

Creating a Table

1. Click on the Show Site icon in the Status Bar.
2. Double-click on *document.htm* to open it for editing.
3. Click in the Title box of the document and type "Document Shortcuts."
4. Copy and paste that title to the page. Format it as Heading 1, blue, centered. Press Enter.
5. Click on Align Left to move your cursor back to the margin.
6. On the Objects panel, click on the Insert Table icon.
7. In the Insert Table dialog box, type 10 in the Rows box and 2 in the Column box, and change the border to 5. Leave all other defaults. See below.

Insert Table

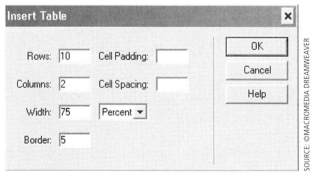

Table Dialog Box

8. Input the following information in the table. Press the Tab key after each entry. The Tab key will add extra rows as you need them.

Result	Keyboard Shortcut
New document	Ctrl Shift N
New window	Ctrl N
Open an HTML file	Ctrl O
Open in Frame	Ctrl Shift O
Close	Ctrl W
Save	Ctrl S
Save a Copy	Ctrl Alt S
Save All	Ctrl Shift S
Exit	Ctrl Q
Undo	Ctrl Z
Redo	Ctrl Y or Ctrl Shift Z
Cut	Ctrl X
Copy	Ctrl C
Paste	Ctrl V
Paste Into	Ctrl Shift V
Clear	Delete
Select All	Ctrl A
Page Properties	Ctrl J
Preferences	Ctrl U or Ctrl K

Table Alignment

1. Hover the mouse pointer over the top left corner of the table until the pointer changes to a four-headed arrow. Click on the corner to open the Tables Property inspector, as shown below.

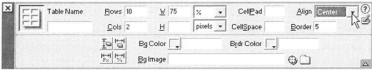

Tables Inspector Property

SOURCE: ©MACROMEDIA DREAMWEAVER

2. In the Tables Property inspector, click on the arrow in the Align drop-down box and select Center.

Column Width

1. Hover the mouse pointer over the right vertical line in the table. When it changes to a two-headed arrow, click and drag to decrease the column width. See below.

Document Shortcuts

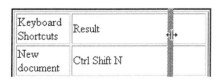

Decrease Width

SOURCE: ©MACROMEDIA DREAMWEAVER

2. Repeat this instruction for the middle vertical line. No lines should wrap. If they do, increase the column width until they are not wrapped.
3. Select the first row with the column headings. Center and bold the column headings.

Border and Background Color

1. In the Tables Property inspector, click on Bg Color and change to a light yellow.
2. Click on Brdr Color and change to a dark blue.

Border Background

Cell Padding

1. In the Tables Property inspector, click on CellPad and type "5". Press Enter.
2. Observe the difference in your table. Try typing in "20" for CellPad. Change CellPad back to 5 after observing the difference. Cell padding adjusts the space between the borders and the cell content.

Cell Spacing

1. In the Tables Property inspector, click on CellSpace and type "5". Press Enter.
2. Observe the difference in your table. Try typing "20" in CellSpace. Change CellSpace back to 5 after observing the difference. Cell Space adjusts the width of the table's cell borders.

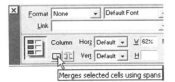

Cell Merge

Insert Columns and Rows

1. Click inside the first cell of the table.
2. Go to the menu bar and choose Modify > Table > Insert Column.

Merge and Split Cells

1. Select the column by hovering the mouse pointer over the top of the column until the pointer changes to a black down arrow. Click on the column.
2. In the Tables Property inspector, click on the "Merges selected cells using spans" icon. See top, left figure.
3. Press Caps Lock. Type "D." Press Enter. Type "O." Press Enter. Continue until you have the word "DOCUMENT" typed in the first column.
4. Select the word DOCUMENT. Format for Heading 1, +6, centered, blue.
5. Save again.

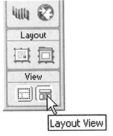

Layout View

Layout Tables

1. Click on the Show Site icon in the Status Bar.
2. Double-click on *menus.htm* to open the page for editing.
3. Type "Menus" in the Title box.
4. On the Objects panel, click on the Layout View icon. You must be in Layout View to create a layout table.
5. On the Objects panel, click on the Draw Layout Table icon. A layout table contains all the contents of the Web page. Draw a 600 × 600 pixel table on your page.

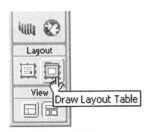

Draw Layout Table

Layout Cells

1. On the Objects panel, click on the Draw Layout Cell icon.
2. Draw a layout cell approximately 250 × 60 pixels. Type "Menu Shortcuts" in the layout cell. Format the text as Heading 1, Arial, yellow, centered.
3. Hover the mouse pointer on the edge of the layout cell. When the border turns red, click on the edge of the layout cell. This turns on the Layout Cell Property inspector.
4. In the Layout Cell Property inspector, change the background color to blue.

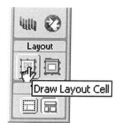

Draw Layout Cell

SOURCE: ©MACROMEDIA DREAMWEAVER

Cell Background

SOURCE: ©MACROMEDIA DREAMWEAVER

5. Click on the layout cell and drag it over to the approximate center of the layout table.

Column AutoStretch

1. Click on a column heading.
2. On the drop-down menu, click on Make Column Autostretch. This stretches the column so that it takes up any available horizontal space in the browser window.

Fixed Width Column

1. Click on a column heading.
2. On the drop-down menu, click on Add Spacer Image. A dialog box appears asking if you want to create a spacer image. Click OK.
3. Draw another layout cell below the title. Drag down to draw it to 350 pixels.

Adding Text to Layout Cells

1. Open *MenuShortcuts.doc* in Word. Copy Column 1 to your clipboard. Minimize Word.
2. Open *menus.htm*. Paste into the layout cell you drew in "Fixed Width Column," step 3.
3. Draw another layout cell even with the right edge of the title and down to 350 pixels.

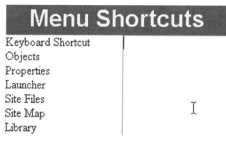

Menus Layout

SOURCE: ©MACROMEDIA DREAMWEAVER

4. Maximize *MenuShortcuts.doc* in Word. Copy Column 2 to your clipboard. Minimize Word.
5. Open *menus.htm*. Paste into the layout cell you drew in step 3.
6. Format the column headings in the layout cell for bold.
7. Format the second column to align right.

8. Add a line break after the column headings. Resize the layout cells as needed.
9. Save again.
10. Draw a layout cell below the table. Leave a little space between the table and the new layout cell. Drag an instance of the email and date from the Library to the new layout cell. Resize the layout cell as needed.
11. Draw a layout cell on the left side of the table. Drag an instance of the Navigation Bar from the Library. In the Library Property inspector, click on Detach from Original. Delete the Menu button.
12. Save again.

Importing Word HTML

1. Go to the menu bar and choose Modify > Page Properties. Click on Browse in the Background Image box. Browse to your CD and double-click on *objects.jpg*.
2. Go to the menu bar and choose File > Import > Import Word HTML. Browse to your CD and double-click on *ObjectsShortcuts.htm*. If you are using Word XP and get a message that it cannot determine the version, choose Word 2000. Click OK.
3. In the Clean Up Word HTML dialog box, click on Cancel.

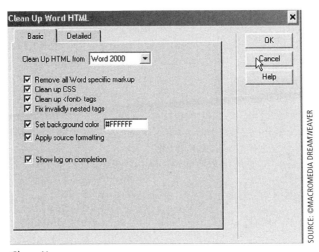

Clean Up

4. The table is imported into a new Untitled HTM file. There may also be some extraneous code imported. Select only the table by clicking and dragging. Go to the menu bar and choose Edit > Cut. Close the document without saving.
5. Open *objects.htm*. Go to the menu bar and choose Edit > Paste.
6. In the Tables Property inspector, in the Align drop-down box, select Center.
7. Place your cursor outside the table at the beginning of the document.
8. Press Enter to add a line at the beginning of the document.

Draw Layers

1. On the Objects panel, click on the Draw Layer icon.
2. Click and drag to draw a layer beginning right below 0 pixels from 200 pixels to 550 pixels. Drag down to 50 pixels.

Add Content to Layers

1. Click inside the layer.
2. Go to the menu bar and choose Insert > Image. Browse to your CD and double-click on *Obj.gif*. (This WordArt was created in Word, cut and pasted as a new image to image editing software, and saved as a GIF.)

Draw Layer

SOURCE: ©MACROMEDIA DREAMWEAVER

Resize Layers

1. Hover the mouse pointer over the border of the layer.
2. When the pointer changes to a two-headed arrow, click and drag to resize the layer so that it is the same size as the image.
3. Drag the layer to position it centered over the table.

Add Background Color to Layers

1. Select the layer. In the Layer Property inspector, click on Bg Color and select a light yellow from the palette. It helps in aligning objects if the layer is a different background color. You should now be able to see that the image is sized inside the layer. Resize if necessary.
2. Preview the page in your browser, then make any adjustments in the position of the layer that are needed.
3. Press Enter below the table to add a new line. Create text links to the other pages:
   |Home| |Document| |Menus|
4. Below the text links, drag an instance of the email and date information from the Library.
5. Save again.

Layers Panel

1. Go to the menu bar and choose Window > Layers.

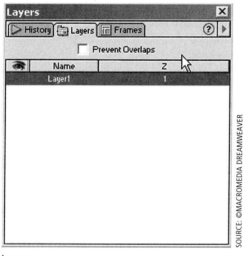

Layers

2. This opens the Layers panel to help you organize if you have more than one layer. Double-click on the file name *Layer1*. Type "Title" for the layer name.
3. In the Object Property inspector, click on the Draw Layer icon.
4. Draw a small layer over in the left margin. Type in the layer "Learn the Shortcuts!"
5. Change the color of the text to a color that matches the WordArt title. Format as Heading 3.
6. On the Layers panel, name the layer "Note."
7. Save again.

ACTIVITY 3 • MINI-PROJECT

Create a State Web Page

1. Create a Web page about your state. Search the Internet to gather information that can be used on the Web page, such as state flower, motto, tree, history of the state, and any other interesting facts.
2. One of the Web pages should include a table with at least ten of the largest cities in the state and their population.
3. The following criteria should be met:
   - ☐ Use of at least one rollover image.
   - ☐ Navigation bar created for the Web site and added to the Library.
   - ☐ Minimum of one index page and three other Web pages.
   - ☐ Minimum of at least one layer with a background color or image.
   - ☐ Minimum of one layout table and layout cell created.
   - ☐ Creation of buttons using image management software to use for navigation buttons. Must have a minimum of one different image for up and down state.
   - ☐ Content in Web page is appropriate and interesting.
   - ☐ Web site is error-free.

ACTIVITY 4 • USING FRAMES

In this activity, you will become familiar with:

- ■ Dividing a Page into Frames
- ■ Frame Borders
- ■ Adding Content to Frames
- ■ Link Properties
- ■ Frames Panel
- ■ Linking to Frames
- ■ Flash Text
- ■ Editing HTML
- ■ Flash Buttons
- ■ Tabular Data

Dividing a Page into Frames

1. Define a site titled "Kennels." Add a new page to the site and name it *index.htm*. Open the new page for editing.
2. Go to the menu bar and choose Modify > Frameset > Split Frame Left. Hover the mouse pointer over the vertical line dividing the frame. When the pointer changes to a two-headed arrow, drag the vertical line to 200.
3. Click on the left frame. Go to the menu bar and choose File > Save Frame As. In the Save as dialog box, type "TOC" in the File name box.
4. Click on the right frame. Go to the menu bar and choose File > Save Frame As. In the Save as dialog box, type "Welcome" in the File name box.
5. Select the Frameset by clicking on any frame border.

Frame Borders

1. In the Frameset Property inspector in the Borders text box, change Default to Yes in the drop-down box. Type "10" in the Border Width text box and change the color to red.

2. Go to the menu bar and choose File > Save Frameset As. In the Save as dialog box, type "KennelsFrameset" in the File name box.
3. Add three new files to the site: *owners.htm, hours.htm,* and *pricing.htm.*

Adding Content to Frames

1. Open *TOC.htm* which you created earlier. Type in the Title text box "TOC."
2. Type the following, pressing Enter after each one: "Owners," "Hours of Operation," "Pricing," and "Schedule." Format the font as Heading.

Link Properties

1. Go to the menu bar and choose Modify > Page Properties.

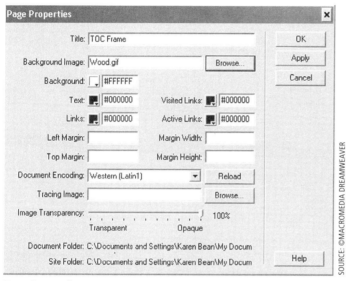

Page Properties

2. In the Page Properties dialog box, click in the Background Image box. Browse to your CD and double-click on *Wood.gif.*
3. Change Links, Visited Links, and Active Links to black. Click on Apply, then OK.
4. Go to the menu bar and choose File > Save.
5. Click in the right frame. Type in the Title text box "Welcome."
6. Go to the menu bar and choose Insert > Image. Browse to your CD and double-click on *Welcome.gif.* (Each time you insert an image, you will get a dialog box asking you to save this image into the same directory as your Web page. Choose Yes and continue saving the image to the folder the dialog box specifies.) In the Property inspector, click on the Align Center icon. Insert a line break by pressing Shift + Enter.
7. Go to the menu bar and choose Insert > Image. Browse to your CD and double-click on *Logo.gif.* Insert a line break by pressing Shift + Enter.
8. Add the following text under the logo:

   Our mission is to give our clients the best service. ABC Kennels understands that leaving your pet at home is never easy. We are committed to providing your pets with loving and reliable service from experienced professionals who will ensure their happiness and well-being along with your peace of mind.

9. Format the mission statement as Heading 5.
10. On the Objects panel, click on the Insert Date icon. Insert a line break after the date by pressing Shift + Enter.

11. On the Objects panel, click on Insert Email Link. In the Insert Email Link dialog box, type "Email Us!" in the text box. Type "art@abckennels.com" in the E-Mail box.

Frames Panel

1. Go to the menu bar and choose Window > Frames.
2. On the Frames panel, click on (No Name) on the right side of the panel. In the Frame inspector, click in the Frame Name box and type "Welcome."

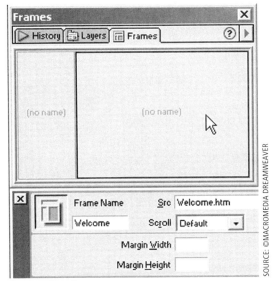

Frames Panel

3. Click on the left side of the frame on your screen. Click on (No Name) on the left side of the Frames panel. In the Frame inspector, type "TOC" in the Frame Name box.
4. Below the Pricing text on the left side of the frame, insert the image of *Cat.jpg*. Resize if needed.

Linking to Frames

1. Select Owners. In the Property inspector, click inside the Link box. Click on the yellow folder. Browse to your CD and double-click on *owners.htm*. Click on the Target drop-down box and choose Welcome. This is the name of the frame window you want it to open in.
2. Select Hours of Operation. In the Property inspector, click inside the Link box. Click on the yellow folder. Browse to your CD and double-click on *hours.htm*. Click on the Target drop-down box and choose Welcome. Repeat this instruction for Pricing and Schedule.
3. Save each of the frames and the frameset.
4. On the Status Bar, click on the Show Site icon. Double-click on *owners.htm* for editing.
5. Type the following on this page:
   Owned and Operated since 1981 by:
   Arturo and Bea Champick
   100 Kennel Range Road
   Junction, TX 78419
   915/555-0001
6. Format the first line as Heading 2 and all the other lines as Heading 3.
7. Save the frame.

Flash Text

1. On the Objects panel, click on the Insert Flash Text icon.
2. In the Insert Flash Text dialog box, click in the Font text drop-down box and select Comic Sans MS. Change the size to 30. Click on the Align Center icon. Change the color to brown and the rollover color to red. Type the following in the text box:

   We are always OPEN, but (Press Enter)
   we accept new animals from (Press Enter)
   6 AM to 6 PM, 7 days a week! (Press Enter)
3. Type in the Save as text box *"HoursText.swf."*
4. Click on Apply, then OK.
5. Save again.

Flash Text Icon

SOURCE: ©MACROMEDIA DREAMWEAVER

Editing HTML

1. Click on the Show Code View icon under the File menu.
2. Select Untitled Document within the Title tags. Type "Pricing."
3. Click on Show Code View. After the line with Meta Content, press the Enter key and type the following:

   <meta name="description" content="ABC Kennels is a pet kennel for all your needs.">
   <meta name="keywords" content="dogs, cats, boarding, kennel, pet sitting">

```
<html>
<head>
<title>Pricing</title>
<meta http-equiv="Content-Type" content="text/html; charset=iso-8859-
</head>
<body bgcolor="#FFFFFF" text="#000000">
</body>
</html>
```

Editing HTML

SOURCE: ©MACROMEDIA DREAMWEAVER

Flash Buttons

1. On the Objects panel, click on the Insert Flash Button icon.
2. In the Insert Flash Button dialog box, choose StarSpinner for the Style. In the Button Text box, type "Our Rates." Change the size to 20. Save as *Pricing.swf*.

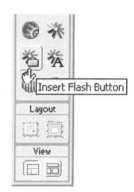

Flash Button

SOURCE: ©MACROMEDIA DREAMWEAVER

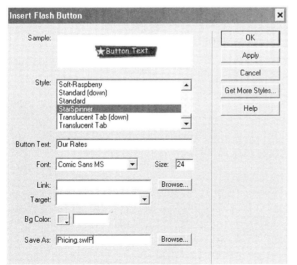

Button Dialog Box

SOURCE: ©MACROMEDIA DREAMWEAVER

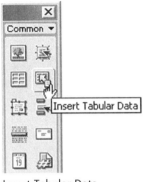

Insert Tabular Data

3. Click on Apply, then OK.
4. Draw a layer and place the flash button in the layer. Drag to the center of the page.

Tabular Data

1. On the Objects panel, click on Insert Tabular Data.
2. In the Insert Tabular Data dialog box, click on Browse for the Data File. Browse to your CD and double-click on *Tabular.txt.*

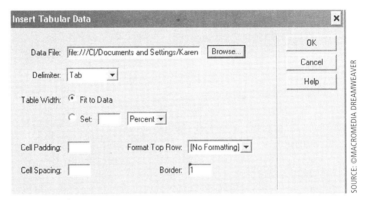

Tabular Dialog Box

3. Click OK.
4. Click on the top left of the table to get to the Tables Property inspector. Choose Center from the Align drop-down box.
5. Click in the last cell of the table and click on the Align Right icon on the Property inspector.
6. Go to the menu bar and choose Modify > Page Properties. Change the background to yellow to match the flash button.
7. Click on the top left edge of the table. On the Tables Property inspector, type "5" in the Border text box and change the Brdr Color to match a brown in the flash button.
8. Save again.

ACTIVITY 4 • MINI-PROJECT

Create an Online Computer Store

1. Create an online computer store carrying peripherals. The store will carry printers, scanners, and monitors.
2. Research the Internet and locate five items of each peripheral so that you are carrying at least fifteen items on your Web site.
3. Use frames for the Web site.
4. Use at least one flash text and flash button.
5. Create a table in Word using a tab between columns. Save the table as a TXT file. Import into Dreamweaver.
6. Edit the HTML code to include meta tags for description and keywords.
7. The following criteria should be met:
   ☐ Appropriate name for the business.
   ☐ Frames Web site set up appropriately with all links working.
   ☐ Fifteen appropriate items with descriptions and prices included on the Web site.
   ☐ Appropriate flash text and flash button included.
   ☐ HTML code edited with appropriate description and keywords.

☐ Table created and saved in Word appropriately and imported into Dreamweaver without error.

☐ Web site is error-free.

☐ Web site is appealing to the eye and organized.

ACTIVITY 5 • USING FORMS

In this activity, you will become familiar with:

- Creating Forms
- Checkboxes
- Radio Buttons
- Insert List
- Submit Button
- Email Results

Creating Forms

1. Define a new site titled Election. Create a new file in the site and name it *index.htm*. Double-click to open *index.htm* for editing.
2. Type at the top of the page "Student Council Election." Format as Heading 1, blue, centered.
3. On the Objects panel, select Forms from the drop-down menu. Click on the Insert Form icon.
4. The Insert Form icon creates a red dashed-line box that surrounds the form. In the red dashed-line box, type "President." Format the text as Heading 3, red.

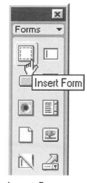

Insert Form
SOURCE: ©MACROMEDIA DREAMWEAVER

Checkboxes

1. On the Objects panel, click on Insert Checkbox. Click to the right of the checkbox and type "Wade Johnson." Press Shift + Enter to insert a line break.
2. Click on Insert Checkbox. Move the mouse pointer one space to the right of the checkbox and type "Matilda Jonesboro." Press Shift + Enter to insert a line break.
3. Click on Insert Checkbox. Move the mouse pointer one space to the right of the checkbox and type "Luther Smithson." Press Shift + Enter to insert a line break.
4. Click on the drop-down box on the Objects panel. Choose Common. Click on the Insert Horizontal Rule icon. Press Shift + Enter to insert a line break.

Insert Checkbox
SOURCE: ©MACROMEDIA DREAMWEAVER

Radio Buttons

1. Below the horizontal rule, type "Vice President." Format as Heading 3, red.
2. Normally, radio buttons would be the best type for this form, but for learning purposes, you will insert a variety of boxes, buttons, and fields. On the Objects panel, click on the drop-down box and choose Forms. Click on the Insert Radio Button icon.
3. Move the mouse pointer one space to the right and type "Marilyn Smiley." Format as Heading 3, blue. Press Shift + Enter to insert a line break.
4. Click on the Insert Radio Button icon.
5. Move the mouse pointer one space to the right and type "Sara Lee." Format as Heading 3, blue. Press Shift + Enter to insert a line break.
6. On the Objects panel, click on the drop-down box and choose Common. Click on the Insert Horizontal Rule icon. Press Shift + Enter to insert a line break.

Insert Radio Button
SOURCE: ©MACROMEDIA DREAMWEAVER

Insert List

1. Below the horizontal rule, type "Secretary." Format as Heading 3, red.

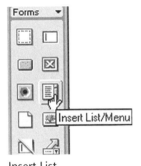

Insert List

SOURCE: ©MACROMEDIA DREAMWEAVER

2. On the Objects panel, click on the drop-down box and choose Forms. Click on the Insert List/Menu icon.
3. On the Property inspector, click on the List Values button.

Initial List Values

SOURCE: ©MACROMEDIA DREAMWEAVER

4. Add the three names as shown below. Each time another name is added, click the plus sign. Press Shift + Enter to insert a line break.

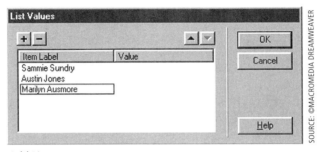

Add List

5. On the Objects panel, click on the drop-down box and select Common. Click on the horizontal rule. Press Shift + Enter to insert a line break.
6. Type "Treasurer." Format as Heading 3, red.
7. On the Objects panel, click on the drop-down box and select Forms. Click on Insert Radio Button.
8. Move the mouse pointer one space to the right and type "Jamie Sykora." Format as Heading 3, blue. Insert radio buttons for Jon Rodriguez and Daniel Saunders. Add a horizontal rule. Press Shift + Enter to insert a line break.
9. Type "Webmaster." Format as Heading 3, red. Create a list with these names: Jaylon Jazcik, Frankie Fuentes, Larry Williams. Add a horizontal rule. Press Shift + Enter to insert a line break.

Submit Button

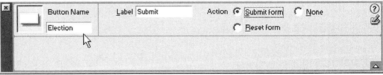

Insert Button

SOURCE: ©MACROMEDIA DREAMWEAVER

1. On the Objects panel, click on Insert Button.
2. On the Property inspector, type "Election" for the button name.

Button Name

SOURCE: ©MACROMEDIA DREAMWEAVER

3. Save again.

Email Results

1. Go to the menu bar and select Edit > Preferences. On the Preferences dialog box, click on Code Rewriting.
2. Under Special Characters, deselect Encode <, >, &, and " in Attribute Values Using &. Click OK.
3. Click on the red dashed-line border to select the form tag.

4. In the Property inspector Action field, type:
   "mailto:user@domain.com?subject5Election."
5. Save again.

ACTIVITY 5 • MINI-PROJECT

Create an Online Magazine Survey

1. In a team of three or four students, create a list with at least ten questions to use in an online survey. The survey should determine readers' interest in certain magazines.
2. Decide on five magazine titles to use in the list.
3. Brainstorm with your team to decide on questions and what type of form field should be used.
4. Use Text Fields, Radio Buttons, Lists, Checkboxes, and Submit Buttons.
5. Each team member should create his or her own form.
6. The following criteria should be met:
   ☐ Questions are appropriate and organized.
   ☐ Field types are appropriate for the question and set up correctly.
   ☐ Form is error-free.
   ☐ Formatting of Web page creates an easy-to-read reply form.
   ☐ Submit button set up correctly for feedback.

PART 2 • SIMULATION

Using Dreamweaver

1. Create a Web page with tips on interviewing, writing résumés, and dressing for success.
2. Title the Web page "Job Search" with a file name of *index.htm*. The Web page should have at least three other pages on Tier 2. Title the Web pages "Interview Tips, Résumé Tips, and Dress for Success" with file names *interview.htm*, *resume.htm*, and *dress.htm*. Create at least one Tier 3 Web page, which would be a link from one of the three pages on Tier 2.
3. Get the information to use for your Web pages by searching the Internet.
4. The following criteria should be met:
   ☐ Required number of Web pages created and properly linked.
   ☐ At least three images on the Web site from two different sources (digital, scanned, or clip art).
   ☐ Rollover buttons created using image editing or animation software.
   ☐ Created flash text, flash button, or SWF file.
   ☐ All text used is formatted effectively for color, size, and style.
   ☐ Effective use of layers. Minimum use of two layers.
   ☐ Effective use of tables. Minimum use of two tables.
   ☐ Use of form creation at least once.
   ☐ At least one layout table used.
   ☐ At least one layout cell used.
   ☐ Navigation Bar created for Web site and placed in Library.
   ☐ Email link and date added at least at the bottom of the first Web page.
   ☐ Minimum use of one unordered or ordered list.
   ☐ Background color changes are appropriate and Web content is readable.
   ☐ At least one background image used.
   ☐ Appropriate content for subject.
   ☐ One hotspot created linking to an external Web site.

Part 3

Adobe GoLive

> **Adobe GoLive**
> **Publisher: Adobe**
> GoLive is Web design software. It allows flexibility in the placement of images and text by the use of floating boxes. The software can also insert a number of tags that are Web-browser specific.

ACTIVITY 1 • GETTING STARTED

In this activity, you will become familiar with:

- New Site Setup
- Inspector
- Document View
- Adding Pages
- Site Folder
- Page Properties
- Layout Rulers
- Head Section
- Keyword Tag

New Site Setup

New Site

SOURCE: ©ADOBE GOLIVE

1. Go to the menu bar and choose File > New Site > Blank.
2. In the Create New Site dialog box, click in the Site Name box and type "International Business" in the box.
3. Tab to In Folder and type "International" in the box.
4. Browse to the directory and folder instructed by your instructor. See left.
5. Click OK.

Inspector

1. On the site window, double-click on *index.html* to open the Web page for editing.

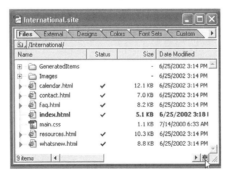

International Site

SOURCE: ©ADOBE GOLIVE

2. Go to the menu bar and choose Window > Inspector.
3. In the Window inspector, click on the Page tab. Type "International Web Site" in the Title box.
4. Go to the menu bar and choose File > Save to save all the changes.

Document View

1. When you open the document, the default is Layout Editor view. This is the view used to add objects and text to your page and set attributes such as size and color using the palettes.
2. Click on the Frame Editor tab. If you want to create a Web site with frames that divide the page, you would use this view.
3. Click on the HTML Source Editor tab. If you need to make a change to the HTML code, then you would use this view.
4. Click on the HTML Outline Editor tab. This allows you to view the document in Outline view.
5. Click on the Preview tab. This allows you to preview the document before uploading it to your Web site.

Adding Pages

1. On the site window, click on the Files tab.
2. Right-click and choose New Page.
3. Type for the file name of the Web page "*Canada.htm.*"
4. Create new pages for *Germany.htm*, *Japan.htm*, and *Mexico.htm*.

Site Folder

1. A site creates two folders that hold its contents. These are called the root folder and the data folder. You can recognize the data folder by the word *data* after the site name.
2. The data folder is not uploaded, but the root folder contains the pages and media that need to be uploaded to publish the Web site.

Page Properties

1. Click on the Page icon. See the figure labeled Page Properties.
2. This opens the Page tab on the Inspector. Type in the title box "International Business Protocol."
3. Click in the Background Color box and select a background color other than white. It should be a light color.
4. Save again.

Layout Rulers

1. Click on the Ruler icon above the vertical scroll bar to turn the ruler on.
2. The rulers help you place and resize objects.

Head Section

1. Click on the triangle next to the Page icon in the upper left corner of the document window to open the head section pane.
2. Go to the menu bar and choose Window > Objects.
3. In the Objects palette, click on the Head tab.
4. Hover the mouse pointer over the Meta tag under the Head tab on the Objects palette.

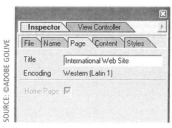

Inspector

New Page

Page Properties

Ruler Icon

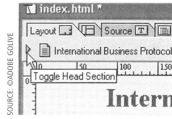

Head Section

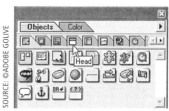

Head Tab

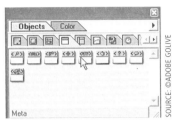

Meta Tag

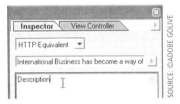

Meta Inspector

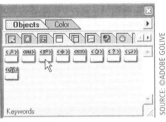

Keyword Tag

Add Keywords

5. Drag the Meta tag object to the head section pane of your document window.
6. In the Meta inspector, type "Description" in the bottom box. In the Content scrolling text box, type "International Business has become a way of life in our global economy."

Keyword Tag

1. Hover the mouse pointer over the Keywords icon under the Head tab on the Objects palette.
2. Click on the Keywords icon and drag it next to the Meta tag on the Head section of your document.
3. On the Inspector palette, type the keywords shown in the bottom left figure in the scrolling text box and click Add after each word. Keywords help search engines locate your site.

ACTIVITY 1 • MINI-PROJECT

Create a Web Site Structure

1. Define a Web site for an insurance agency. You may use a specific insurance agency that you have researched. Add three other Web pages: *RateQuote.html*, *AboutInsurance.html*, and *InsuranceTypes.html*. Save them in a folder titled *Insurance*. Give an appropriate title to each Web page.
2. Add an appropriate title on the *index.html* page to name the Web site.
3. Add a Meta tag and Keyword tag to the Head section.
4. The following criteria should be met:
   - ☐ All Web pages titled and defined appropriately.
   - ☐ *Index.html* has an appropriate title.
   - ☐ All necessary folders created appropriately.
   - ☐ Backgrounds have a color change.
   - ☐ No errors on the Web page.
   - ☐ Meta tag is a good description of the Web site contents and is well-written.
   - ☐ Keyword tag has a minimum of five keywords that appropriately describe the Web site.

ACTIVITY 2 • FORMATTING THE WEB PAGE

In this activity, you will become familiar with:

- ■ Adding and Formatting Text
- ■ Adding an Image
- ■ Text Links
- ■ Previewing the Web Page
- ■ Background Graphic
- ■ Page Margins
- ■ Numbered List
- ■ Font Size
- ■ Bold Text
- ■ Line
- ■ Modified Date
- ■ Email Link

Adding and Formatting Text

1. Open the *International Business* folder. Double-click on *index.html*. In the open *index.html* file, type "International Business Protocol."
2. Select the text. Click on the Color palette. Choose the Color Wheel as shown in the figure labeled Color to the right.
3. Choose any color red and drag and drop it onto the selected text. See the figure labeled Drag Color.
4. Practice dragging and dropping several different colors. Leave the color on blue.
5. On the Paragraph Format menu, choose Header 1 and the Align Center icon.

Text Formatting

Adding an Image

1. If the Objects palette is not open, go to the menu bar and choose Window > Objects.
2. Drag an Image placeholder below the title. See the figure labeled Image.
3. If the Image inspector is not visible, go to the menu bar and choose Window > Inspector.
4. On the Source line, click on the file folder. Browse to your CD and double-click on *BusinessLogo.gif*.
5. In the Image inspector, click on the Basic tab. In the Width and Height boxes, type 250 × 250 pixels to adjust the size. In the Alignment drop-down box, select Middle. Type "Business Around the World image" in the Alt Text box. See the figure labeled Image Formatting.
6. Save again.

Text Links

1. Type the names of the four new pages below the image. See below.

   |Canada| |Germany| |Japan| |Mexico|

   Text Links

2. Select Canada. On the Paragraph Format toolbar, click on the New Link icon.
3. In the inspector, click on the Link tab. Click on the yellow folder icon on the link reference. Browse to your *International* folder and double-click on the *Canada.html* file. Note that you can also click in the New Link icon in the inspector.
4. Type "Canadian Protocol" in the Title box.
5. Click on the drop-down arrow next to Target. Select blank. This will cause the link to open in a new window.
6. Link the other three Web pages.
7. Save again.

Previewing the Web Page

1. Click on the Layout Preview tab.

Layout Preview Tab

Color

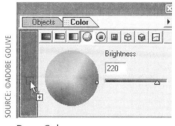

Drag Color

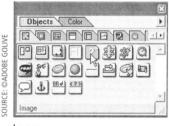

Image

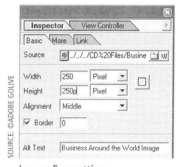

Image Formatting

New Link

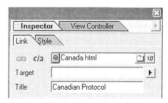

Link Inspector

Page Title

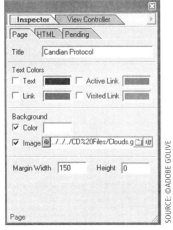

Margins

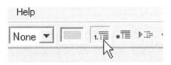

Numbered List

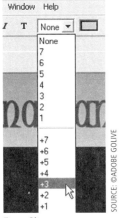

Font Size

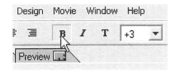

Bold

2. Try one of the text links. Each preview opens a new window. Close the window.
3. Click on the Layout tab.

Background Graphic

1. Click on the Page Properties icon.
2. In the Page inspector, click on Image and then the file folder to browse to your CD. Double-click on *Clouds.gif*.

Page Margins

1. Select the default page title "Welcome to Adobe GoLive 5.0." Overtype with "Canadian Protocol."
2. Click on the Page Properties icon next to the page title. See the top left figure.
3. Click in the Margin Width box and type "150." Click in the Height box and type "0." Because of the leftbound design for the background, the margin change is necessary.
4. In the Objects inspector, click on the Basic tab. Drag an Image icon to the top of the document.
5. In the Image inspector, click on the yellow file folder icon. Browse to your CD and double-click on *Canadian.gif*.
6. Click below the image you added to the page. If you need to, press the Enter key one time.

Numbered List

1. Click on the Numbered List icon.
2. Press Enter four times to add numbers 1 through 5 on the document.

Font Size

1. Select the numbers 1 through 5. Click on the drop-down box for the font size. See the figure labeled Font Size.
2. Select +3.
3. Click on the Color palette. Type the following numbers in the RGB boxes: 173, 182, 190. This color matches the banner. (You can find the color numbers that match by opening the banner in image management software. Use the Dropper tool to click on the color. Write down the RGB numbers to match the color.)
4. With the numbered list selected, drag and drop the color on the color box, as shown in the figure labeled Drop Color.

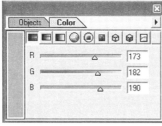

Color Matching

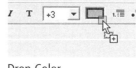

Drop Color

Bold Text

1. Click on the Bold icon to set bold text style.
2. Go to http://www.executiveplanet.com/community/. Click on Canada and read about the Canadian culture in business. Type five of the most interesting cultural differences on your document.

Line

1. On the Objects palette, drag and drop the Line icon below the numbered item 5.
2. In the Line inspector, click on the left line style (solid line).
3. In the Height box, type "5."
4. Click on the icon to Center paragraph or Layout Box.

Line

Modified Date

1. On the Objects palette, click on the Smart tab.
2. Drag the Modified Date icon below the line.
3. Press Shift + Enter to move to the next line. The cursor will not move to the next line until you start typing.

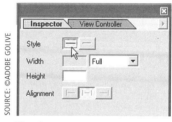

Line Inspector

Email Link

1. Type "business@canadian.com."
2. With the text selected, click on the Link icon in the Link inspector.
3. In the box next to the yellow file folder, type "mailto:business@canadian.com."
4. Go to the menu bar and choose File > Save.
5. Repeat the steps starting with "Background Graphic" for each of the countries on your Web site. Insert the appropriate banner for each country and change the email addresses for each country. You will use the following files from the CD: *French.gif*, *German.gif*, *Japanese.gif*, and *Mexican.gif*.
6. Save each page as you finish it.

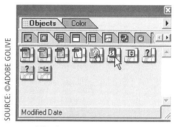

Modified Date

ACTIVITY 2 • MINI-PROJECT

Create and Format Content for an Insurance Agency Web Site

1. Use the Web site structure you created in Activity 1 to create the content for the insurance agency Web site. Research an insurance agency on the Internet to get the information for the content.
2. The following criteria should be met:

   ☐ *Index.html* page includes a properly formatted title as well as an appropriate image sized properly.

   ☐ *Index.html* page includes text links to the other three pages with a modified date and email on the page.

   ☐ At least one Web page of the four pages has a background graphic.

   ☐ At least one horizontal line inserted and formatted on one of the pages. The line is in an appropriate place.

   ☐ Numbered list used effectively on one of the content pages.

   ☐ Web page has a professional look with all links working, Alt Text on images, and an effective color combination.

   ☐ Logo, mission statement, or slogan included on the *index.html* page.

   ☐ No errors on the Web pages.

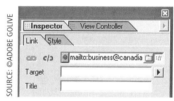

Line Inspector

Page Title

SOURCE: ©ADOBE GOLIVE

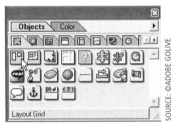

Grid Icon

Layout Grid

SWF Icon

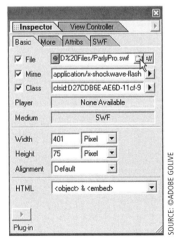

SWF Inspector

ACTIVITY 3 • USING ANIMATION

In this activity, you will become familiar with:

- Overtype
- Layout Grid
- SWF Files
- Background Color
- Layout Text Box
- Scrolling Marquee
- Font Format
- Rollovers
- Pasting Text
- Underline
- Line Break
- Font Sets
- Inserting Tables
- Formatting Tables
- Importing Text
- Floating Boxes
- Formatting Floating Boxes

Overtype

1. Go to the menu bar and choose File > New Site > Blank.
2. In the Create New Site dialog box, type "Parliamentary Procedure" for the Site Name and In Folder. Click OK.

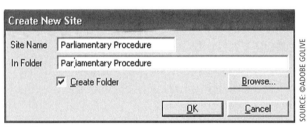

New Site

3. On the *index.html* Web page, select "Adobe GoLive 5.0" and overtype it with "Parliamentary Procedure." See the figure labeled Page Title.

Layout Grid

1. On the Objects palette, click on the Basic tab. Click on the Layout Grid icon and drag it to the current Web page.
2. In the Layout Grid inspector, change the width to 600 and the height to 400.

SWF Files

1. On the Objects palette, click on the Basic tab. Click on the SWF icon and drag it to the current Web page.
2. Click on the SWF object you placed on your document.
3. Click on the Basic tab in the Object inspector. Click on the yellow folder on the File line. See left.
4. Browse to your CD and double-click on *ParlyPro.swf*.

5. In the Object inspector, click the SWF tab. Click on the drop-down box on Scale and choose Exact Fit.
6. Using the grid lines, adjust the object so that it is centered horizontally and begins at the top of the page.
7. Click on the Preview tab.

Background Color

1. Click on the background on your document.
2. In the inspector, click in the box next to Background to select it. Click on the color box to change the background color.
3. On the Color palette, click on the cube. Scroll to select LightYellow for your background.

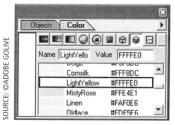
Background Color

Layout Text Box

1. On the Objects palette, click on the Basic tab and drag a layout text box below the banner on your document.
2. Horizontally center the layout text box on the grid by clicking and dragging.

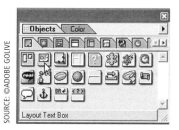
Layout Text

Scrolling Marquee

1. On the Objects palette, click on the Basic tab and drag a marquee into the layout text box on your document. (The marquee does not need to be in the layout text box unless you want to format the text on the marquee.)
2. Resize the layout text box and the marquee. Note that a gray arrow hovered over the resizing boxes on the edge of the object will resize and the gray box will move the object.
3. In the inspector, choose the Scroll option from the Behavior drop-down box. Click on Forever for Loops. Click on Right for the scrolling direction.
4. Click on the Color palette and drag and drop the AliceBlue color to the marquee.
5. Click on the More tab on the inspector. You can resize the marquee by typing in a number. Type "300" in the Width box and "25" in the Height box. Use the drop-down box to change Align to Middle.

Marquee Icon

Font Format

1. On the toolbar at the top of the screen, click on the drop-down box for size and change the font size to +1.
2. Click on the Color palette. Select a dark blue color and drag and drop it to the color box on the toolbar. See the bottom right figure.
3. Click on the Preview tab.
4. Save again.

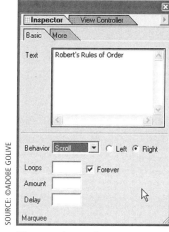
Marquee Inspector

Rollovers

1. Go to the menu bar and choose File > New.
2. Click on "Welcome to Adobe GoLive 5.0" next to the Page Properties icon and overtype it with "History." Click on the Page Properties icon and change the background to a light yellow.
3. Go to the menu bar and choose File > Save as *History.html*. Save it in the *Parliamentary Procedure* folder along with the *index.html* file.
4. Repeat steps 1 through 3 to create two other Web pages named *Links.html* and *Rules.html*.
5. On the Objects palette, click on the Smart tab. Drag the Rollover icon to the left side of the document.

Font Format

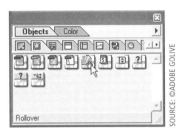

Rollover Icon

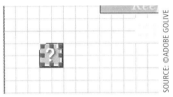

Rollover Placement

Rollover Inspector

6. See the figure labeled Rollover Placement for an approximate placement on the grid of the Rollover object.

7. In the Rollover inspector, click in the Name box and type "History." Click on Main and click on the yellow file folder to the right of the box underneath Main. Browse to your CD and double-click on *Obj1History.gif*.

8. Click in the box to the right of URL. Click on the yellow file folder and browse to your *Parliamentary Procedure* folder. Double-click on the file *History.html*.

9. Click on Over. Click on the box in front of Empty Reference to check it. Click on the yellow file folder and browse to your CD. Double-click on *Obj2History.gif*.

10. Click on Click. Click on the box underneath to check it. Click on the yellow file folder and browse to your CD. Double-click on *Obj3History.gif*.

11. Repeat steps 7 through 10 to add two more rollovers underneath the History rollover. Name them Rules and Links.

12. Click on the Preview tab. Check the links and the rollovers. You will use the following files from the CD: *Obj1Links.gif, Obj2Links.gif, Obj3Links.gif, Obj1Rules.gif, Obj2Rules.gif,* and *Obj3Rules.gif*.

13. Save again.

Pasting Text

1. On the Objects palette, click on the Basic tab. Drag a layout text box below the marquee.

2. Resize the layout text box so that it is as wide as the banner and as long as the rollovers.

3. In the layout text box, type "Definition." Format the text as Heading 3, Align Center.

4. Search the Internet for a definition of parliamentary procedure. Copy and paste the definition into the layout text box.

Underline

1. Quote your source using MLA style.

2. Underline the title of the Web page or textbook you used for your source.

3. Go to the menu bar and choose Type > Style > Underline.

4. Format the definition as Heading 4 and the source information as Heading 5.

5. Drag an Image icon from the Objects palette. For the reference in the inspector, browse to your CD and double-click on *IndexLine.gif*.

6. Press Enter after the Image. Type "Last Updated." Drag the Modified Date icon from the Objects palette.

Line Break

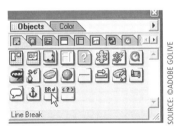

Line Break

1. On the Objects palette, click on the Basic tab.

2. Drag a line break next to Modified Date.

3. Type "Student Name." Select the text.

4. On the inspector, click on the Link icon. Type in the reference line "mailto:student@highschool.com."

5. Save again.

Font Sets

1. Go to the menu bar and choose File > Open.

2. Browse to your CD and double-click on *History.html*.

3. Type "History" at the top of the document. Format it as Header 1, +7, dark blue. Press Enter.

4. On the Objects palette, click on the Basic tab. Drag an Image icon to the screen below the History title.

5. In the Image inspector, click on the yellow folder and browse to your CD. Double-click on *RobertsRules.gif*.

6. In the Objects inspector, drag a layout text box below the image. Search for Robert's Rules of Order on the Internet and compose a short paragraph explaining the history.

7. Applying a font set enables you to control what font viewers will see, in case the font you chose first is missing on their computer. Select the text in the paragraph you composed. Go to the menu bar and choose Type > Font > Edit Font Sets.

8. In the Font Sets dialog box, click on New.

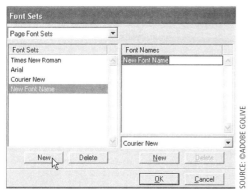

Font Sets

9. On the right pane of the Font Sets dialog box, click on the drop-down box and choose Comic Sans MS. The font set name becomes the name of the first font selected.

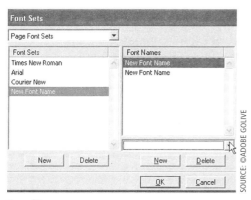

Font Names

10. Click on New on the right pane of the Font Sets dialog box. Choose Elephant from the drop-down box.

11. Click on New on the right pane of the Font Sets dialog box. Choose Garamond from the drop-down box. There should be a minimum of three fonts in the font set.

12. On the Objects palette, click on the Basic tab. Drag a Line icon below the composed paragraph. In the Line inspector, format the line as solid. Press Enter.

13. In the Objects inspector, click on the Basic tab. Drag three Image icons to the document below the line.

14. Click on the first Image icon. Click on Align Center on the toolbar.

15. In the Image inspector, click on the yellow folder and browse to your CD. Double-click on *Home.gif*.

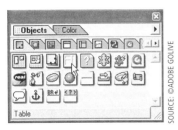

Table Icon

Table Inspector

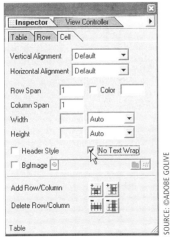

No Text Wrap

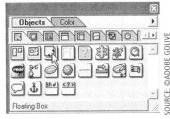

Floating Box Icon

16. In the Image inspector, click on the Link tab. Click on the yellow file folder and double-click on the *index.html* file in the *Parliamentary Procedure* folder.
17. Click on the second Image icon. Repeat steps 15 and 16 to insert the *Rules.gif* and *Links.gif* files from your CD and link them to the Rules and Links Web page in the *Parliamentary Procedure* folder.
18. Preview the Web page.
19. Save again.

Inserting Tables

1. Go to the menu bar and choose File > Open. Browse to the *Parliamentary Procedure* folder and double-click on *Rules.html*.
2. On the Objects palette, click on the Basic tab. Drag the Image icon to the middle of the top of the document.
3. In the Image inspector, click on the yellow file folder. Browse to your CD and double-click on *RulesBanner.gif*.
4. Click on the Page Properties icon and change the background color to WhiteSmoke.
5. On the Objects palette, click on the Basic tab. Drag the Table icon and drop it below the Rules banner.

Formatting Tables

1. In the Tables inspector, click on the Table tab. Click in the Columns box and type "2."
2. Click in the Border box and type "3."
3. Select the Color check box. Click on the Color box and on the Color palette, change the color to LemonChiffon.

Importing Text

1. On Import Tab-Text, click on Browse. See the figure labeled Table Inspector.
2. Browse to your CD and double-click on *ParliamentaryLaw.txt*.
3. Click on the edge of the first cell. In the Table inspector, click on the Cell tab. Select the No Text Wrap check box. Do this for all the cells.
4. Provide a way for the Web viewer to get to the index and the History and Links pages from this page. You can use text links, rollovers, or image links.
5. Preview the Web page.
6. Save again.

Floating Boxes

1. Go to the menu bar and choose File > Open. Browse to the *Parliamentary Procedure* folder and double-click on *Links.html*.
2. On the Objects palette, click on the Basic tab. Drag the floating box to the top of the document.
3. Click inside the floating box and type "Links, Links, and More Links."
4. Select the text. Format it as Heading 1, yellow, and bold.

Formatting Floating Boxes

1. Resize the floating box for an exact fit of the text and drag so that it is centered across the top of the document.
2. Click on the border of the floating box to select it.
3. In the Floating Box inspector, select the BGImage check box. Browse to your CD and double-click on *Marble.jpg*.

4. Click in the Name box in the Floating Box inspector and type "Links."
5. Drag a second floating box to the document. Search the Internet for Robert's Rules of Order. Copy a URL to the floating box. With the URL text selected, format it as Heading 3. Click on the Link inspector link and paste the URL into the Empty Reference.
6. Click on the Target drop-down box and select Blank. This allows the link to open a new browser window so the Web viewer does not leave your site to view the link.
7. In the Link inspector, type "URL" in the Name box.
8. Repeat steps 5 through 7 for two more floating boxes with links in them.
9. Add two more floating boxes with image icons in them. Use your available clip art to add images to the floating boxes. Arrange them on the document.
10. Preview the page.
11. Add text links, rollovers, or image links to the index (Home) and the History and Rules Web pages.
12. Save again.

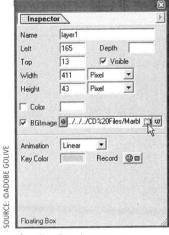

Floating Box Inspector

ACTIVITY 3 • MINI-PROJECT

Create a Web Site on Repetitive Stress Injury (RSI)

1. Using a search engine, search the Internet for information on repetitive stress injury.
2. Create a new Web site in a folder titled *RSI*. The Web site should contain *index.html* and at least three other pages.
3. The following criteria should be met:
   - ☐ Layout grid used for at least one of the Web pages.
   - ☐ Creation of at least one effective SWF file or other animated graphic using the program available to you.
   - ☐ Use of at least one scrolling marquee, effectively formatted and placed.
   - ☐ Creation of one set of fonts with at least two alternative fonts in the set.
   - ☐ Use of at least one table effectively used to support content. Table has at least two columns and contains at least two table formatting features.
   - ☐ Floating box used a minimum of two times.
   - ☐ Set of rollovers used to navigate the Web site.
   - ☐ Layout text box used at least once.
   - ☐ Web page is free of errors.
   - ☐ Content is appropriate for the subject and sources are noted on the Web site.

Target

ACTIVITY 4 • USING FRAMES

In this activity, you will become familiar with:

- ■ Creating a Frame Set
- ■ Formatting Frame Borders
- ■ Linking the Frameset
- ■ Editing the Frame
- ■ Resizing Frames
- ■ Date Inspector
- ■ Link Object
- ■ Unnumbered List

Frame Editor

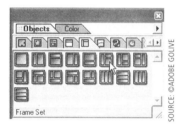

Frame Set

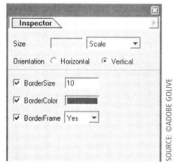

Frame Inspector

Creating a Frame Set

1. Create a new folder and name it "Texas."
2. Go to the menu bar and choose File > New.
3. Click on the Frame Editor tab at the top of the window. See the top left figure.
4. On the Objects palette, click on the Frames tab. Drag a frame set icon to your document.
5. Go to the menu bar and choose File > Save as. Browse to the *Texas* folder and save as *Frameset.html*.

Formatting Frame Borders

1. Select the frame set by clicking on any of its horizontal or vertical dividers.
2. In the Frame inspector, select the BorderSize check box and change it to 10. Select the BorderColor check box and change it to Red. Select the BorderFrame check box and select Yes. Follow these formats for both vertical and horizontal frames.
3. Click in each frame. In the inspector, type a name for the frame. In the top frame, type "Identity." In the left frame, type "Navigation." In the right frame, type "Information."
4. Save again.

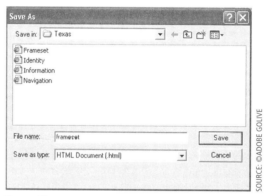

Frame Structure

5. Create HTML files for each of the frames. Name them *Identity.html*, *Navigation.html*, and *Information.html*. Be sure to change the titles of the Web pages to Identity, Navigation, and Information.
6. Create three new HTML files. Name them *Capitol.html*, *Facts.html*, and *MustSee.html*. Be sure to change the titles of the Web pages to Capitol, Facts, and MustSee.

Linking the Frameset

1. In the Frameset file, click in the Identity frame at the top.
2. In the Frame inspector, click on the yellow file folder. Browse to the *Texas* folder and double-click on *Identity.html*.

Editing the Frame

1. In the Frameset file, double-click on the Identity frame to open it for editing.
2. From the Objects palette, drag a floating box icon to the Identity document.
3. From the Objects palette, drag an image icon to the Identity document, dropping it into the floating box.

4. In the Image inspector, click on the Basic tab. Click on the yellow file folder. Browse to your CD and double-click on *Texas.gif*. (This file is animated. Animation will not work unless the image is within a floating box.)
5. Save again.
6. Preview the frameset by opening *Frameset.html* and clicking on the Preview tab.

Frame Resize

Resizing Frames

1. Click on the Frame Editor tab. Click in the Identity frame.
2. In the Frame inspector, type "120" for the size.
3. You can resize by clicking on the horizontal bar and dragging to adjust the size, or, in the Frame inspector, type in a number for the size.
4. Click in the Navigation pane. In the Frame inspector, change the size to 120. Click on the yellow file folder for URL. Browse to the *Texas* folder and double-click on *Navigation.html*.
5. Double-click on the Navigation pane to open the file for editing.
6. Turn on the rulers.
7. From the Objects palette, drag a floating box and then an image inside the floating box. See the figure labeled Navigation Placement for the placement of the floating boxes and images.
8. Click on the Page Properties icon. In the Page Properties inspector, click on the yellow file folder. Browse to your CD and double-click on *TexasBack.gif*.
9. Click in the first floating box. In the Image inspector, click on the Basic tab. Click on the yellow file folder. Browse to your CD and double-click on *Capitol.gif*.
10. In the Image inspector, click on the Link tab. Click on the Link icon then the yellow file folder. Browse to the *Texas* folder and double-click on *Capitol.html*.
11. Repeat steps 7 and 8 to insert the image and link the image to the correct page for Home (*Information.html*), Facts, and Information. You will use the *Home1.gif*, *Facts.gif*, and *MustSee.gif* files from the CD.
12. Save again.
13. Open *Frameset.html*. Click on the Preview tab.
14. If needed, toggle to *Navigation.html* and resize the frame.
15. Save again.
16. Open *Information.html*.
17. From the Objects palette, drag a floating box icon and an image icon to the document.
18. In the Image inspector, click on the yellow file folder. Browse to your CD and double-click on *Capitol.jpg*.
19. Click on the Page Properties icon and change the background color to blue.
20. Save again.
21. Open Frameset by going to the menu bar and choosing Window > Frameset.
22. Click on the Preview tab.
23. Make any adjustments in the image placement that is needed.

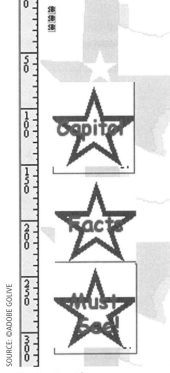

Navigation Placement

Date Inspector

1. On the *Information.html* page, add a floating box at the bottom center.
2. Drag the modified date icon to the floating box.
3. In the Date inspector, change the date format to the one demonstrated in the figure labeled Date Inspector.

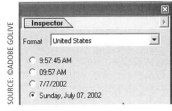

Date Inspector

Link Object

1. On the Objects palette, click on the Head tab. Drag the link icon to the floating box below the modified date.
2. In the Link inspector, select Empty Reference and type "mailto:Texas@texas.gov."

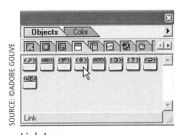

Link Icon

3. Select the reference tag on the document and type "Contact Us."
4. Click on the Preview tab to make any adjustments needed.
5. Save again.

Unnumbered List

1. Open *Facts.html*. Format the background to a color of your choice.
2. Type "Facts" at the top of the document. Format the text as Heading 1, color of your choice, and Align Center.
3. Add a horizontal line underneath the title.
4. Click on the Unnumbered List icon on the toolbar.
5. Go to http://www.state.tx.us/. Click on About Texas. Add at least 20 facts using the Unnumbered List format.
6. Format the background to a color of your choice and the text in the unnumbered list.
7. Save again.
8. Open *Capitol.html*.
9. Add a title and format the title and background for the page. You may add other elements such as a horizontal line if desired.
10. Using a layout text box, add a short paragraph about the history of the state capitol building. Use the Internet to research to gather the information. Format the text appropriately.
11. Save again.
12. Open *MustSee.html*.
13. Add a title and format the title and background for the page. You may add other elements if desired.
14. Using a two-column table, add at least ten sites to see in Texas, with where they are located in the second column. For example, in Column 1, you may type "The Alamo" and in Column 2, "San Antonio." Format the text, table, and background appropriately.
15. Save again.

Unnumbered List

SOURCE: ©ADOBE GOLIVE

ACTIVITY 4 • MINI-PROJECT

Create a Web Site on Preparing for a Competitive Event

1. Go to the Web site of Future Business Leaders of America, Business Professionals of America, or a University Interscholastic League to research preparation for competitive events. You may also use a competitive sports event as your topic.
2. Create a new Web site using frames and save it in a folder titled *Competition*.
3. Create a frame set using the left side frame as a table of contents or navigation bar. There should be three Web pages to navigate to: List of Events, Tips for Preparation, and Resources.
4. The following criteria should be met:
   - ☐ Frame set is appropriately set up and formatted.
   - ☐ Links to the frame set all work.
   - ☐ Frames are appropriately resized.
   - ☐ Content is appropriate and thorough.
   - ☐ Web design is appealing and professional-looking.
   - ☐ Web page contains no errors.
   - ☐ Images, rollovers, or banners are appropriately sized and of good quality. There are at least six uses of them on the Web site.

ACTIVITY 5 • USING FORMS

In this activity, you will become familiar with:

- Form Setup
- Text Field
- List Box
- Check Box
- Text Area
- Radio Button
- Submit Button
- Reset Button
- Form Inspector
- Tabbing Chains

Form Setup

1. Create a new folder and title it "Forms."
2. Go to the menu bar and choose File > New. Title the new document "Job Application." Save as *index.html*.
3. On the Objects palette, click on the Forms tab. Drag the form icon to the document.
4. Using Word, open *Job Application.doc*. Select all text in the document and copy it.
5. Click on GoLive on the taskbar. Go to the menu bar and choose Edit > Paste.
6. Select the top three lines in the document. Format the lines as Times New Roman, Align Center, Header 1, and blue.

Form Icon

Text Field

1. Delete the extra line breaks in the remaining text. Select all remaining text and format as Header 3.
2. On the Objects palette, click on the Forms tab. Drag the text field icon next to Name.
3. In the Text Field inspector, type "Name" in the Name box. Leave Value blank. In this box, you would type a default word or phrase that the applicant would overtype. This is not necessary in most cases.
4. Click in the Visible box and type "90." This determines the width of the box. Leave Max blank, which is the default. This would be the number of characters that would be allowed before it is truncated. If it is blank, the browser determines when to truncate.
5. Copy and paste the text field to Address and Phone Number. Click on the text field next to Address. In the Text Field inspector, change the Name to Address. Click on the text field next to Phone Number. Change the Name to PhoneNumber and the Visible to 82. You can also resize the text field on the screen so that it is the same width as the other two text fields.

Text Field

Text Inspector

List Box

1. On the Objects palette, click on the Forms tab. Drag the list box next to Dates Available in your document.
2. In the List Box inspector, in the Name field, type "Date Available." Clear the Multiple Selection check box.
3. Click on the first Label in the white box. Click on the box in front of the edit line below the white box to select it. This will make June 1 the default date. Type "June 1" for the Label and the Value. Click on the next item in the list and type

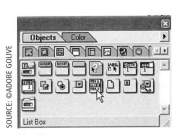

List Box

List Inspector

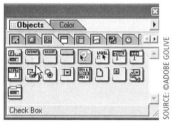

Check Box Icon

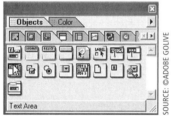

Text Area

Text Area Inspector

"June 15" for Label and Value. See the top left figure to complete the list box. You will need to click on the New button to add one more in the list.

4. Press the Backspace key to move Times Available up on the line with Date Available.

5. See below for the completed Times Available choices.

Times List

6. Save again.

Check Box

1. With your cursor to the right of Grade Average, press Shift + Enter. Type "ABCD."

2. On the Objects palette, click on the Forms tab. Drag the check box icon and drop it when the black vertical line is behind the A. Continue to drag and drop until you have a check box next to each grade.

3. Click on the first check box to select it. In the Check Box inspector, type "A" for Name. In the Value box, type "Grade A." Continue to name and give a value to each of the other three check boxes.

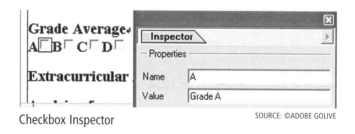

Checkbox Inspector

Text Area

1. On the Objects palette, click on the Forms tab. Drag the text area icon to the right of Extracurricular Activities.

2. In the Text Area inspector, type "Extracurricular Activities" in the Name box. Change the columns to 65.

3. Save again.

Radio Button

1. On the Objects palette, click on the Forms tab. Drag the radio button icon to the left of Mowing. Drag one to the left of each of the remaining positions: Painting, Tutoring, Clerical Work.

Radio Button

2. Click on the first radio button to the left of Mowing. In the Radio Button inspector, leave everything at the default.
3. Save again.

Submit Button

1. On the Objects palette, click on the Forms tab. Drag the submit button icon to the bottom of the document.
2. In the Submit Button inspector, type "Submit" for the Name and the Value. Leave all other defaults.

Reset Button

1. On the Objects palette, click on the Forms tab. Drag the reset button icon to the right of the submit button.
2. In the Reset Button inspector, click to check the Label box and type "Reset."
3. Save again.

Form Inspector

1. At the top left of your document, there is an F in a gray box. This is the icon to select the entire form. Click on the icon.
2. In the Form inspector, type "JobApplication" in the Name field.
3. Click on the Action box. Click on the yellow file folder and create a file titled *Results* in the *Forms* folder.
4. Save again.

Tabbing Chains

1. Go to the menu bar and choose Special > Start Tabulator Indexing. Small yellow index boxes appear on all the form fields that were created.
2. Click on each of the fields in the order in which you want them to tab. It will automatically number them. If you make a mistake, you can correct it by selecting the field, then making the change on the inspector.
3. When you are finished with all fields, go to the menu bar and choose Special > Stop Tabulator Indexing.
4. Save again.
5. You will need to preview in a browser.

ACTIVITY 5 • MINI-PROJECT

Create an Online Form to Receive Ideas for the Prom

1. Create an online form to gather ideas for this year's prom.
2. A minimum of information needed would be: Student's Name, Name of Instructor of their first class of the day (Homeroom Instructor).
3. Other questions suggested to gather input: preferred times of the prom, preferred locations, ideas for theme, colors, type of music, preferred decorations, preferred food, and ticket cost.
4. The following criteria should be met:
   - ☐ Form title is appropriately formatted and named.
   - ☐ Questions are appropriate and worded concisely.
   - ☐ At least four different types of form fields were used (Text Field, List Box, Radio Button, and so on).
   - ☐ Submit and reset buttons are included and appropriately set up.
   - ☐ Form fields are formatted for the right size and placed appropriately.

Radio Button Inspector

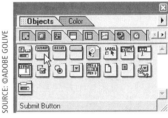

Submit Button

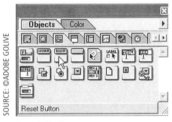

Reset Button

Form Inspector

Inspector Completed

☐ Form inspector is appropriately set up to gather information online.
☐ Form is free of errors.
☐ Order of tabbing is set up appropriately.

PART 3 • SIMULATION

Using GoLive

1. In a team of three or four students, brainstorm ideas for a Web site to promote the Summer Academy at your school.
2. Only 10 courses will be offered. Eight of those will be core courses, and two will be those that the administration thinks students will enjoy. Decide on which 10 courses will be offered.
3. On the Web site, give specifics on where and when the Summer Academy will take place. The exact beginning and ending dates will be needed, as well as times of the day. List the names of instructors who will teach the courses.
4. There will be a summer graduation celebration on the last day. Plan this event and create a flyer that can be converted to PDF to upload to the Web page.
5. Students must apply to attend the Summer Academy. Create an application form that will be one of the Web pages.
6. The Academy always has a theme or slogan for the summer. Decide on the slogan. Your team should all use the same slogan and Web site setup. Content may differ among each team member, as each team member is responsible for creating a Web page using the ideas.
7. At least one page of the Web site should focus on some tips for successful completion of the Summer Academy.
8. The following criteria should be met:
   ☐ The team worked together in creating ideas. Input was given and utilized by each team member.
   ☐ Web site contains at least four Web pages.
   ☐ Slogan or theme is well thought out and is presented creatively on the Web site.
   ☐ Information is placed in a logical, easy-to-read manner for the times and places of the classes, as well as the names of the classes and instructors. Formatting was used to create a dynamic page.
   ☐ Flyer is creative and contains all important information for the celebration. It was created using PDF appropriately.
   ☐ The online application contains all appropriate fields and field types. It is appropriately linked so that it can be completed by the students and sent to the Summer Academy personnel.
   ☐ Content on successful tips is appropriate and effectively formatted.
   ☐ Multimedia elements used in this unit are evident on the Web site in at least four items.
   ☐ Web site is error-free and professional.

Oral and Other Professional Communication Skills

Unit

6

Part 1 • Dragon NaturallySpeaking
Part 2 • ViaVoice
Part 3 • Adobe Premiere
Part 4 • MGI Cinematic

Voice recognition has arrived! Being able to communicate with your computer productively is now a reality, when not long ago it was only a vision. In many cases, it is the fastest and most productive way to produce documents.

Dragon NaturallySpeaking is an easy-to-use and accurate voice recognition program. It features many tools that you can customize for your particular use. You can import and train words that are specific to your type of business, as well as add contacts from an e-mail address book. You can also train commands for formatting the document. You can dictate in several modes, including numbers, which enables easy input of financial and statistical data by voice.

ViaVoice is a part of Windows XP. However, you can purchase upgraded versions of the program. With a minimum of training, you can begin to produce voiced documents. You can customize the dictionary and perform some basic formatting on the document through voice.

Our ability to communicate effectively continues to expand with each new technology. The ease of creating movies adds a whole new dimension to Web design and presentations.

Adobe Premiere can easily produce videos using still images or digital video. It is a flexible program that enables you to add titles and other clips to your movie. There are a number of tools available to draw shapes and a really cool way to create a shadow with your objects. If you want to really dazzle your audience and get their attention, you will love the ability to apply transitions and motions.

If you are looking for an inexpensive and easy program to use for creating videos, then MGI Cinematic is for you. This program enables you to create professional looking videos, as well as fun videos for home use. The CineMagic feature enables you to quickly create videos using styles, templates, and special effects.

Creating videos is no longer just for Hollywood. With programs such as Adobe Premiere and MGI Cinematic, you can now create videos to place on your Web pages and in your presentations. If you want to market a product, present a vacation spot, or even present a case in the courtroom, a video may be your best choice for getting your point across to an audience.

Dragon
NaturallySpeaking

Dragon NaturallySpeaking
Publisher: ScanSoft
Dragon NaturallySpeaking is voice recognition software that works best for continuous, natural speech recognition. This software enables you to create documents quickly and easily with your voice.

ACTIVITY 1 • GETTING READY

In this activity, you will become familiar with:

- Creating New Users on Installation
- Positioning the Microphone
- Audio and Volume Adjustments
- Training Dragon
- Adding and Managing Users

Creating New Users on Installation

1. When you install Dragon NaturallySpeaking, it automatically begins adding you as a new user. In the New User Wizard dialog box, type your name in the Your name box. Leave all other information as the default.
2. Click on Next.

New User

Positioning the Microphone

1. Before speaking into the microphone, always check the position of the microphone. Be sure it is turned toward your mouth.
2. Be sure that there is no background noise such as fans, music, and so on. You should be working in a quiet environment.
3. Click on Next.

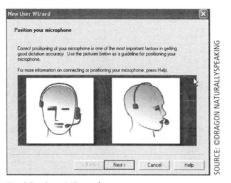

Positioning Microphone

Audio and Volume Adjustment

1. The next screen in the wizard checks the volume. You will need to read aloud for about 15 seconds. Click on Start Volume Check when you are ready to begin.

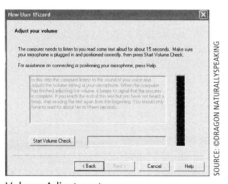

Volume Adjustment

2. Read the paragraph on the screen. When it is adjusted, you will receive a message on the screen.
3. Click on Next.
4. The sound quality check is next. Click on Start Quality Check.

Audio Input

5. Read the paragraph on the screen. When the program has checked the sound quality, it will stop you.
6. If your sound quality checks out okay, then click on Next. Otherwise, you will need to try it again.

Training Dragon

1. You are now ready to begin the training phase. Click on Go to begin.

Train Dragon

2. Read the phrase from the screen. When you have finished reading the phrase, the computer screen will move to another phrase. Continue to read until the computer screen stops and says you are completed with training.
3. Click on Next.
4. Part of the training is Paragraph Reading. Select the first choice from the list of passages, "Talking to Your Computer."

Paragraph Reading

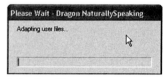

Adapting Files

SOURCE: ©DRAGON NATURALLYSPEAKING

5. Click on Next when you have finished reading the paragraph.
6. Your screen will contain a message about adapting the files after you have clicked Next. This may take a minute or so to complete.
7. Click on Finish to close the wizard. As shown below, leave the Begin dictating option selected.

Finish Wizard

Adding and Managing Users

1. You can easily have more than one user on the same computer. Go to the menu bar and choose NaturallySpeaking > Open/Manage Users.

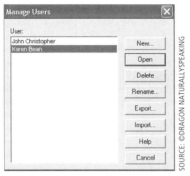

Manage Users

2. In the Manage Users dialog box, you can create a new user. If you make this choice, you will get the same New User wizard as on installation.
3. You can open an existing user, delete or rename a user, and export and import user files from this menu.
4. Click on Cancel to return to your toolbar.

ACTIVITY 1 • MINI-PROJECT

Adding a User

1. Add a pretend user using your favorite actor's name. Go through the voice training.
2. The following criteria should be met:
   - ☐ New user set up appropriately and thoroughly.
   - ☐ Appropriate name used for new user.

ACTIVITY 2 • VOICING A DOCUMENT

In this activity, you will become familiar with:

- Turning the Microphone On and Off
- Training Vocabulary
- Using Help
- Vocabulary Editor
- Importing Words
- DragonPad
- Recognition Modes
  - ○ Normal Mode
  - ○ Dictation Mode
  - ○ Command Mode
  - ○ Spell Mode
  - ○ Numbers Mode

Turning the Microphone On and Off

1. Click on the Microphone icon to turn it on or off. It is located on the toolbar at the top of your screen.

Toolbar

SOURCE: ©DRAGON NATURALLYSPEAKING

2. You can also turn the microphone on by clicking on NaturallySpeaking on the toolbar and selecting Turn Microphone On.

Training Vocabulary

1. With Microsoft Word open, browse to your CD and double-click on *VoiceRecognition.doc* to open it.
2. Print a copy of *VoiceRecognition.doc*.
3. All of the highlighted vocabulary are words that have a low rate of accuracy in voice recognition. Go to the toolbar and choose Words > Train.
4. In the Training dialog box, click in the box and type in the first word or phrase you want to train. In this case, type "technology."
5. Click on Train.
6. In the Train Words dialog box, click on Go. Say "technology," then click on Done.
7. Repeat steps 3 through 6 for all the highlighted words in *VoiceRecognition.doc*.
8. Practice voicing the document. Turn on the microphone. Open a blank Word document. Dictate the first sentence. Be sure to dictate the period at the end of the sentence.
9. Look back at the first sentence. If there are any errors, you can correct them by voice. Say "Select _____." (Fill in the blank with the word to replace the error.) Once the computer has selected the word for you, you can also choose the correct word with your mouse from the drop-down list. The drop-down list will pop up once the word is selected.
10. If you need to delete a word, say, "Delete."
11. Continue dictating and stop after each sentence to check for accuracy. Dictate the comma in the second sentence and all other punctuation throughout the document.

Using Help

1. Avoid making corrections in this practice document on your own. If you need help because the computer is not doing what you are voicing, use the Help menu to find the exact command to use. Go to the toolbar and choose Help > Help Topics.
2. Type "Capitalizing." Double-click on the subtopic "After dictating it."
3. Read the chart to get the correct dictation to use for capitalization.
4. When you have dictated the entire document, save as *MyDictation.doc*.

Vocabulary Editor

1. Go to the toolbar and choose Words > View/Edit.
2. In the Vocabulary Editor dialog box, choose Abbott Laboratories.

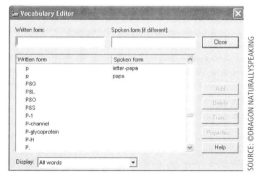

Vocabulary Editor

Microphone On

Train

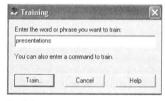

Training
SOURCE: ©DRAGON NATURALLYSPEAKING

Train Words
SOURCE: ©DRAGON NATURALLYSPEAKING

3. Click on Train.
4. In the Train Words dialog box, click on Go. Say "Abbott Laboratories." Then click on Done.
5. Click on Close to close the Vocabulary Editor when you have completed editing the following list of words:

> avant-garde
> averaging
> hearsay
> collusive
> Gettysburg

Importing Words

1. Go to the toolbar and choose Words > Import.
2. In the Import Words From List dialog box, click on Browse. Browse to your CD and double-click on *VocabularyList.txt*.

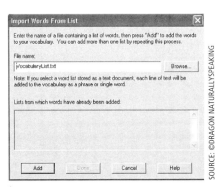

Import

3. Click on Add.
4. When the saving process is complete, click on Done.

DragonPad

1. Go to the menu bar and choose Tools > DragonPad.

DragonPad   SOURCE: ©DRAGON NATURALLYSPEAKING

2. Click in the document so that the cursor is on the first line. Use this document to record your practice in the "Recognition Modes" section that follows.

Recognition Modes

Normal Mode

1. Normal mode is the most flexible. It distinguishes dictation from commands by analyzing what you say between pauses.
2. Say "Normal mode on."
3. Say "Communication is the key to success."
4. Pause.

5. Say "Select success."
6. Pause again.
7. Say "Bold that."

Dictation Mode
1. Dictation mode is used to dictate rapidly without looking at your computer.
2. Say "Dictation mode on." Note that Dictation mode turns on the status bar. See the figure to the right.
3. Say several phrases that would normally be interpreted as a command. Some examples would be "Bold that," "Delete that," "Underline that," "Italicize that."

Dictation Mode
SOURCE: ©DRAGON NATURALLYSPEAKING

Command Mode
1. Command mode interprets everything as a command and nothing as dictated text.
2. Say "Command mode on."
3. Say "This is a test." Normally, Dragon NaturallySpeaking would not do anything for this statement.

Spell Mode
1. Spell mode enables you to speak without pauses and say any combination of letters, digits, or symbols. It is useful for dictating Internet addresses.
2. Say "Spell mode on."
3. Say "This Friday is our first football game."
4. Say "Select Friday."
5. Say "Bold that." It should not work. Change to Normal mode and repeat steps 3 through 5.
6. Change back to Spell mode and dictate each letter of www.spell.com.

Numbers Mode
1. Say "Numbers mode on."
2. Dictate "500, Tab, 300, Tab, 400, Enter."
3. Dictate "faculty, movie, dollar sign, test." The only thing out of that set that Numbers mode should have picked up was "dollar sign."
4. Save as *ModePractice.rtf*.

ACTIVITY 2 • MINI-PROJECT

Report on Voiceprint Technology

1. Research voiceprint technology on the Internet. Then, type a short report on this new technology.
2. Go through and highlight any words that may need training in your report. Use your judgment to make a decision on words that you think may be less accurate than others. Save as *WrittenReport.doc*.
3. Use voice technology to dictate and correct errors in the report. Save as *VoicedReport.doc*.
4. Use Spell mode to dictate Web addresses that were used as resources. Place these at the bottom of the document.
5. Type a list of words that are associated with voiceprint technology. Save as *VoicePrint.txt*. Import the list of words.
6. The following criteria should be met:
   - ☐ Written report is thorough with appropriate information about voiceprint technology.
   - ☐ Appropriate words are highlighted for training.

□ Proper technique was used in efficiently voicing and correcting the document.

□ List of words associated with voiceprint technology is appropriate and imported properly.

ACTIVITY 3 • MORE TOOLS

In this activity, you will become familiar with:

- ■ Accuracy Center
  - ○ Troubleshooting
  - ○ Adding Single Words
  - ○ Add Words from a Document
  - ○ Add Contacts
- ■ Command Browser
  - ○ Built-In
  - ○ Custom
- ■ Transcribe Recording

Accuracy Center

Troubleshooting

1. Go to the toolbar and choose Tools > Accuracy Center.

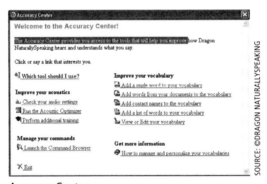

Accuracy Center

2. Click on Which tool should I use?
3. The Accuracy Assistant dialog box opens. This enables you to perform some basic troubleshooting. If you are having any of the problems listed, click on the link.

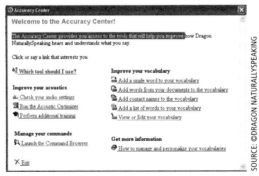

Accuracy Assistant

4. Click on Exit.

Adding Single Words

1. In the Accuracy Center dialog box, click on Add a single word to your vocabulary.
2. Think of your day yesterday and add a word that comes to your mind about the day. For instance, if you ate hamburgers for lunch, you may choose the word "hamburger." Train the word.

Add Words from a Document

1. Click on Add words from your documents to the vocabulary.
2. In the Add Words from Documents dialog box, click on Add Document.

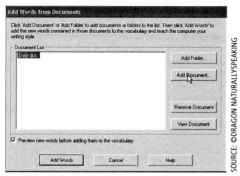

Add Words

3. Browse to your CD and double-click on *Daily.doc*.
4. Click on Add Words.
5. Click on Yes even if there were no new words to be added because the software already contained the words on the list.

Add Contacts

1. Click on Add contact names to the vocabulary.
2. In the Add Contacts dialog box, note the choices. You can add contacts from your email list and also scan sent email.
3. Get instructions from your instructor as to whether to add contacts. Otherwise, click on Cancel.

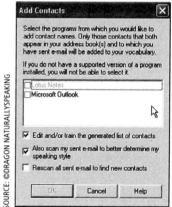

Add Contacts

Command Browser

Built-In

1. Go to the toolbar and choose Tools > Command Browser.

Command Browser

2. Click in the Application drop-down box and choose MS Word 2002.

3. Select the "undo action," "print this," and "align to the left" check boxes.
4. Click on Train.
5. Click on Next. Select the two most common commands that you would use and train them.

Custom

1. In the Command Browser dialog box, click on the Custom tab.

Commands Editor

2. In the MyCommands Editor dialog box, type "Closing" in the MyCommand Name box. Click on Train. Click on Go, then say the word. When it is finished, click on Done.
3. In the Description, type "closing lines for a letter."
4. Click on the Application specific radio button.
5. Click on the drop-down box and select Microsoft Word.
6. In the Content box, type the closing lines. See the Commands Editor figure above for the exact placement.
7. Click on Save.
8. Open a Word document.
9. Turn the microphone on.
10. Say "Closing."
11. Save as *Closing.doc*.

Transcribe Recording

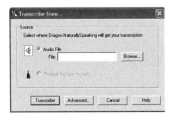

Transcribe Recording

SOURCE: ©DRAGON NATURALLYSPEAKING

1. Use the Sound Recorder to record a short introduction of yourself. Save it as *Intro.wav*. To be able to use this feature, your Sound Recorder must be able to record at 11.025–99.000kHz and 16 bit mono.
2. On the Dragon toolbar, click on Sound > Transcribe Recording.
3. In the Transcribe from dialog box, browse to your files and double-click on *Intro.wav*.
4. Click on Transcribe.
5. Use voice commands to edit the document. It transcribes in DragonPad.
6. Save as *Transcription.rtf*.

ACTIVITY 3 • MINI-PROJECT

Voice the Declaration of Independence

1. Go to http://www.law.indiana.edu/uslawdocs/declaration.html or another Web site with the text of the Declaration of Independence.

2. Using the Command Browser, create a custom heading. The heading should be at least two lines long.
3. You will only have time to record approximately the first two paragraphs. Go through the first two paragraphs and type a list of words that need to be trained. There should be at least ten words on the list. Save as *DeclarationVocab.doc*.
4. Add the words from *DeclarationVocab.doc* and train them.
5. Using the Sound Recorder, record the first two paragraphs of the Declaration of Independence. Save as *DecInd.wav*.
6. Transcribe the recording. Add the header to the DragonPad document. Save as *Declaration.rtf*. Use your voice to correct any errors.
7. The following criteria should be met:
   - [ ] Custom heading was appropriately created.
   - [ ] Appropriate list of words from the Declaration of Independence was chosen to add to the document.
   - [ ] Excellent-quality sound file. Good pronunciation, tone, loudness, and speed of dictation.
   - [ ] Transcription is appropriate and accurate.
   - [ ] Header is added appropriately to the transcribed document.

PART 1 • SIMULATION

Using Dragon NaturallySpeaking

1. Go to http://www.siue.edu/~dcollin/mathfame.html or search for famous mathematicians on the Internet.
2. Choose a mathematician. Print the information about the mathematician.
3. Train at least 20 difficult words from the reading.
4. Voice the report. Save as *Famous.doc*.
5. Open a new Word document. Insert a 12 × 12 table.
6. Across the top row, dictate the numbers 1 through 12. Dictate "Tab" in between each number. Down the first column, dictate the numbers 1 through 12. Use the correct command to move down. Fill in the blanks using your multiplication knowledge and dictate each number. Save as *Multiplication.doc*.
7. Dictate a letter in proper format to your math instructor. The letter should tell your math instructor at least two things you have learned in math this year that you did not know before and also discuss at least two ways you think you would use math in the future. Create at least one custom command. Some ideas for a custom command would be the inside address, date, or closing lines. Save as *MathLetter.doc*.
8. Go to http://www.stfx.ca/special/mathproblems/grade12.html or a similar site with math word problems. You may also use a word problem from your math homework or one that you have received from your instructor. Use Sound Recorder to dictate the word problem. Save as *WordProblem.wav*. Transcribe the recording and save as *ProblemWord.doc*.
9. The following criteria should be met:
   - [ ] Famous mathematician's report was voiced and is accurate.
   - [ ] Multiplication table was voiced using proper commands and is accurate.
   - [ ] Dictated letter is in appropriate format, contains required information, and is accurate.
   - [ ] Transcription from WAV file was completed properly and accurately.

Part 2

ViaVoice

> **ViaVoice**
> **Publisher: IBM**
> ViaVoice is a speech recognition program. It is part of the accessories available with Windows XP. The Language bar is used as the toolbar for this program.

ACTIVITY 1 • GETTING READY

In this activity, you will become familiar with:

- Accessing Speech
- Speech Properties
- Profile Wizard
- Microphone Wizard
- Test Positioning
- Voice Training
- Recognition Profile Settings
- The Language Bar
- Restore and Minimize

Speech

Accessing Speech

On your Windows taskbar, click on Start > Control Panel. Double-click on Speech.

Speech Properties

1. In the Speech Properties dialog box, click on the Speech Recognition tab.

Speech Properties

2. Click on New.

Profile Wizard

1. Read the information in the Profile Wizard dialog box. Type your name in the Profile box. (If your name is already there, type the name of a member of your family.)

Profile Wizard

2. Click on Next.

Microphone Wizard

1. Read the information in the Microphone Wizard—Welcome dialog box.

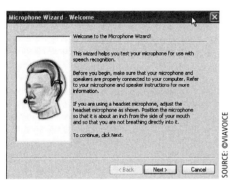

Microphone Wizard

2. Click on Next.

Test Positioning

1. Read the information in the Microphone Wizard—Test Positioning dialog box.

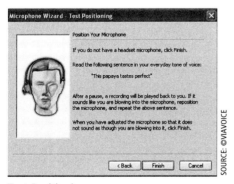

Test Positioning

2. Read the sentence as it instructs.
3. Click on Next.

Voice Training

1. Read the information in the Voice Training dialog box, then click on Next.

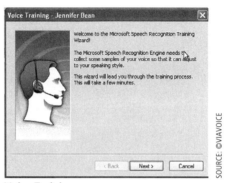

Voice Training

2. Make sure you are in a quiet environment and begin the voice training session.
3. When the voice training is complete, click on Next.
4. The profile update will begin. Click on Next when it is complete.

Profile Update

5. You can click on the More Training button in this dialog box. For now, click on Finish. You can always do more training later if your accuracy is not suitable.

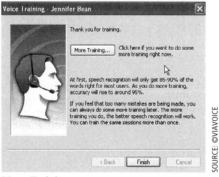

More Training

Recognition Profile Settings

1. On your Windows taskbar, click on Start > Control Panel. Double-click on Speech.
2. In the Speech Properties dialog box, click on Settings.

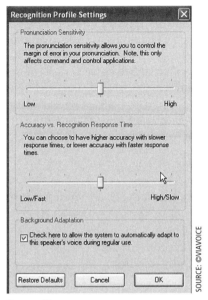

Recognition

3. You can fine-tune your margin of error by using the slider to change the Pronunciation Sensitivity and Accuracy vs. Recognition Response Time. For now, leave the settings on the default.

The Language Bar

1. The Language bar must be open in order to use ViaVoice. If your Language bar is not in the bottom right tray of your window (it has an EN on it for English) then you will need to restore the Language bar. Go to Start > Control Panel.
2. Click on Switch to Classic View.
3. Double-click on Text Services.

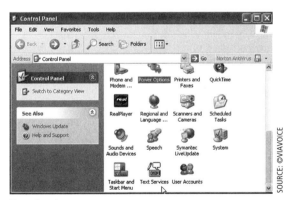

Text Services

4. Click on Language bar.
5. In the Language Bar Settings dialog box, select the "Show the Language bar on the desktop" check box.

Language Bar Settings

6. Right-click on the Language bar. The shortcut menu gives you several options for the toolbar. You can turn the text labels off to give you a smaller toolbar on your screen. You may also choose to have the Language bar in a vertical position on your screen.

Restore and Minimize

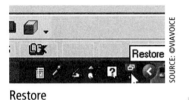

Restore

1. When the Language bar is in the tray at the bottom right of your screen, you can restore the Language bar to a floating toolbar by clicking on Restore on the toolbar. See the figure to the left.
2. Toggle the Language bar back to a docked toolbar at the bottom right of the screen by clicking on Minimize on the toolbar.

ACTIVITY 1 • MINI-PROJECT

Training for ViaVoice

1. Create another profile on your computer. Use the name of a friend or another person in your family.
2. The following criteria should be met:
   ☐ Training was completed thoroughly using proper tone.
   ☐ All distracting noises were removed from the environment.
   ☐ Voice is even and unhurried.
   ☐ Profile has no errors and was finished in a timely manner.

ACTIVITY 2 • VOICING AND EDITING A DOCUMENT

In this activity, you will become familiar with:

- Toolbar
- Microphone
- Moving the Toolbar
- Editing
- Voice Command
- Add to or Delete from the Dictionary
- Spelling Mode

Toolbar

If the toolbar is not available on your screen, double-click on the EN icon in your tray at the bottom right. If the EN icon is not in the tray, go back to the Language Bar section in Activity 1 to review how to restore the Language bar.

Microphone

1. Open Word.
2. On the toolbar, click on Microphone and Dictation to begin dictation. You will be able to tell they are on because the icon looks pressed in.

Wizard

ng

Microphone

3. Be sure to turn the microphone off when you are not dictating.
4. Browse to your CD and double-click on *VoiceRecognition.doc*. Print the document.
5. Voice the document without correcting errors. Dictate all punctuation. At the end of a line, say "Return." If you want to return more than once, say "Return" as many times as necessary.
6. As you dictate, a blue box scrolls across the screen and then creates the words when you stop dictating. See below.

Dictation

SOURCE: ©VIAVOICE

7. Save as *MyVoice.doc*.

Moving the Toolbar

1. If the toolbar is in your way, hover the mouse pointer over the left end of it until you get a four-headed arrow.

Moving

SOURCE: ©VIAVOICE

2. Click and drag to move the toolbar out of the way.

Editing

1. Click on Dictation to turn it off.
2. Proofread your passage for errors. If the software picked up the wrong word, select the word and dictate it again. Try it several times. If you cannot get it to understand the word, then type the word.

Voice Command

1. Use your mouse to select Voice Recognition at the beginning of the second paragraph.
2. Click on Voice Command.
3. Say "Bold."
4. Say "Font." Pause while the menu pulls down.
5. Say "Arial."
6. Say "Font Size." Pause while the menu pulls down.
7. Say "12."
8. Say "Undo." Watch it as it undoes the last voice command you issued.
9. Select the last sentence. Say "Delete."
10. Say "Format, Font, Font Color." Click on Red, then OK. Be sure to pause after each command as the computer accesses the menu.
11. In Voice Command mode, you can select text by saying "Select line," "Select next word," "Select last line," or "Select last paragraph." Try each of these voice commands.

Add to or Delete from the Dictionary

1. Open *CompuTech.doc* from your CD.

Speech Tools

2. On the Language bar, click on Speech Tools. Choose Learn from document.
3. Click on Add Words so that all the unrecognizable words will be added to the dictionary. Note that you can also delete the words individually.

Spelling Mode

1. Print *CompuTech.doc* that you have open on your screen.
2. Dictate the letter, including the company name at the top. Do not format until you have finished dictating.
3. You can correct a spelling error by voice recognition. Select the error by using your mouse.
4. In Dictation mode, say "Spelling mode." Spell the correction. You can delete the last thing you said by saying "Scratch that." If you continue to say, "Scratch that," it works as an Undo button, undoing more than one command. Do not pause between letters when dictating. It hears that as a space when you pause.
5. Select CompuTech at the top of the letter. Say "Font, Tahoma." Say "Font Size, 26." Say "Format, Font, Font Color." Click on Indigo.
6. Say "File, Page Setup, Layout." Click on Center for Vertical Alignment.
7. Save as *CompuTechLetter.doc*.

ACTIVITY 2 • MINI-PROJECT

Voicing Correspondence

1. Use your desktop publishing software to create a letterhead for your company. The company is Smythe and Smythe Attorneys, Inc., 937 Legal Lane, Amelia, OH 45101.
2. Handwrite a memorandum to the staff encouraging them to use voice technology in preparing their documents. The memorandum should have a short introduction paragraph, a list of at least four reasons to use voice technology, and a summary paragraph.
3. Voice the content of the memorandum. You can either use word processing software and import it into your memorandum or use your desktop publishing software if it is compatible with ViaVoice. Save as *StaffMemo*. (If you choose to use an extension as part of your document name, that extension will depend on the software you are using. For example, if you are using Microsoft Word, your title would be *StaffMemo.doc*.)
4. Use as many voice commands as possible to edit your memorandum.
5. The following criteria should be met:
   ☐ Letterhead contains all necessary information and projects a positive business image.
   ☐ Content of memorandum is well written and all criteria requested are included.
   ☐ Voice technology is used appropriately in inputting the content.
   ☐ The memorandum is error-free.

PART 2 • SIMULATION

Using ViaVoice

1. You have been invited to present at a seminar in Cincinnati, Ohio, on May 25. The topic will be voice technology. Create a name for your session and a short

description of what the attendees will learn about in the session. Voice this into a word processing document. Save as *VoiceSession*.

2. Your session is at 9 A.M. You will not be able to leave until noon. Use http://www.expedia.com or another site to search for the cheapest flight. (If you need to, you can change the date of the seminar so that it is three weeks from the current date.) Use word processing software to create a table with the flight information. You will fly from Houston, Texas, to Cincinnati, Ohio. Decide on the best time to leave and the best time to return. Save as *Flights*.

3. If you have MapPoint available, locate Cincinnati and Houston on the map. Determine the best place to stay overnight that is near the airport. You may decide to make this your family's vacation and sightsee along the way. Voice the best directions from Houston to Cincinnati. Save as *Directions*.

4. Voice an itinerary as if you were going to leave three days before the seminar and take three days to return. Where would you stay? What could you see in those locations? Save as *Itinerary*.

5. Voice a slide show into PowerPoint to use in your presentation. The presentation should include speaker's notes. It should also contain images, transitions, and animation and be at least ten slides long. You may use information from your textbook for your content, but you should also use at least two other Web sites. Put the references on the last slide in MLA format. If you are not sure of this format, visit http://www.mla.org. Save as *VoicePresentation.ppt*.

6. The following criteria should be met:
   ☐ Session name creates interest in the session and description is appropriate. There are no errors in the document.
   ☐ Flight possibilities are accurate and formatted for easy reading in a table. Color and other formatting techniques were used. There are no errors in the document.
   ☐ Directions are clear and error-free.
   ☐ Itinerary demonstrates effective use of map.
   ☐ Presentation is organized and contains valuable content.
   ☐ Presentation demonstrates transitions, animation, and images effectively. There is a consistent theme throughout the presentation that is in line with the title and description of the session.
   ☐ Proper reference citations.
   ☐ The presentation is error-free.
   ☐ Voice technology skills used effectively on all documents.

<table>
<tr><td>

Part 3

</td><td>

Adobe Premiere

</td></tr>
</table>

Adobe Premiere
Publisher: Adobe Publishing Systems, Inc.
Adobe Premiere is a digital video editing software that allows you to create movies. These movies can be exported to different media such as videotape or Web pages.

ACTIVITY 1 • GETTING STARTED

In this activity, you will become familiar with:

- Initial Workspace
- Project Settings
- Windows
- Palettes
- Settings Viewer
- Project Window
  - ○ Preview Area
  - ○ Project Window Menu
  - ○ View Icons

Initial Workspace

1. Open Adobe Premiere. When you initially open the program, you must select an initial workspace.

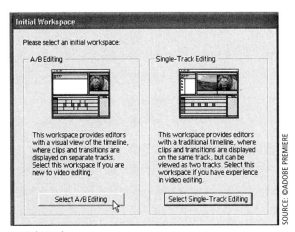

Initial Workspace

2. Click on the Select A/B Editing button. This is the best workspace to use if you are new to video editing.

Project Settings

1. In the Load Project Settings dialog box, leave it on the default of DV – NTSC Standard 32kHz.

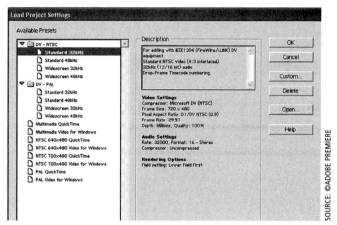

Available Presets

2. Click OK.

Windows

1. Click on the Close button in the Timeline window. If a window is closed to allow more work space and you want to open it again, go to the menu bar and choose Window > Timeline. This toggles the window back open.
2. Click on the Close button in the Transitions window. Go to the menu bar and choose Window > Transitions. This toggles the window back open.

Palettes

1. Go to the menu bar and choose Window > Show Transitions. (If the Transition palette is already open, click on the Transition tab on your screen.)
2. Click on the right arrow to open the folder you want to look at.
3. Double-click on one of the files to see what the transition will look like.

Settings Viewer

1. Go to the menu bar and choose Project > Project Settings > General. You can make changes to the settings as needed. Leave them at the default and click on Next.

Project Settings

2. Continue to click on Next until you have scrolled through the setting windows for Video, Audio, Keyframe, and Rendering and Capturing. Click OK in the last dialog box. You can also view the project settings by going to the menu bar and choosing Project > Settings Viewer. You cannot change the project settings in this dialog box.

3. In the Settings Viewer dialog box, click on Project Settings to go to the Project Settings dialog box to make changes.

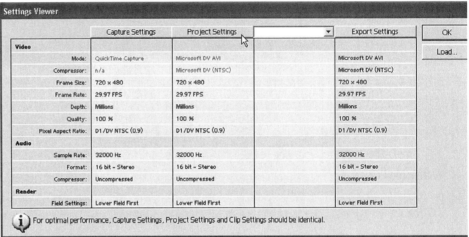

Settings Viewer						
		Capture Settings	Project Settings	▾	Export Settings	OK
						Load...
Video						
	Mode:	QuickTime Capture	Microsoft DV AVI		Microsoft DV AVI	
	Compressor:	n/a	Microsoft DV (NTSC)		Microsoft DV (NTSC)	
	Frame Size:	720 x 480	720 x 480		720 x 480	
	Frame Rate:	29.97 FPS	29.97 FPS		29.97 FPS	
	Depth:	Millions	Millions		Millions	
	Quality:	100 %	100 %		100 %	
	Pixel Aspect Ratio:	D1/DV NTSC (0.9)	D1/DV NTSC (0.9)		D1/DV NTSC (0.9)	
Audio						
	Sample Rate:	32000 Hz	32000 Hz		32000 Hz	
	Format:	16 bit - Stereo	16 bit - Stereo		16 bit - Stereo	
	Compressor:	Uncompressed	Uncompressed		Uncompressed	
Render						
	Field Settings:	Lower Field First	Lower Field First		Lower Field First	

ⓘ For optimal performance, Capture Settings, Project Settings and Clip Settings should be identical.

Settings Viewer

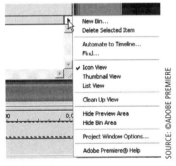

Preview

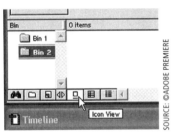

Project Menu

View

Project Window

Preview Area
The Preview Area displays information about the selected bin or clip. You must select the bin or clip in order for it to preview.

Project Window Menu
Click on the arrow to display a menu of commands used in the Project window.

View Icons
These buttons control how the clips are viewed in the Project window.

ACTIVITY 1 • MINI-PROJECT

Prepare the Premiere Desktop for a Project

1. Read the documentation with your digital camcorder or medium you intend to use for capture. Determine the project settings you will need to use for your movie projects.

2. Visit a store or Internet site that sells camcorders to locate three other camcorders. Determine from the documentation online what the project settings would be.

3. Use word processing software to create a table with this information. Save as *ProjectSettings*.

4. The following criteria should be met:
   ☐ Correct project settings are recorded for classroom camcorder.
   ☐ Appropriate other devices were researched with correct project settings.
   ☐ Table is organized and contains accurate information.

ACTIVITY 2 • CREATING A STILL PROJECT

In this activity, you will become familiar with:

- Creating Bins
- Importing Clips
- Storyboard
- Text Note
- Saving the Storyboard
- Automate to Timeline
- Creating Titles
- Formatting Text
- Creating Shapes
- Changing Object Color
- Adding Line Width
- Adding Shadows
- Moving and Resizing Objects
- Adding Gradient Color
- Saving the Title
- Adding the Title
- Previewing the Project

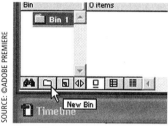

New Bin

Creating Bins

1. In the Project window, click on the New Bin icon.
2. Click inside the Bin folder to rename the bin. Rename the bins "Ranch" and "Heritage." Place them with Ranch first and Heritage below. You can move them by clicking and dragging.
3. Click on the Heritage folder and press Delete to remove it.

Importing Clips

1. Click on the Ranch folder.
2. Go to the menu bar and choose File > Import > File.

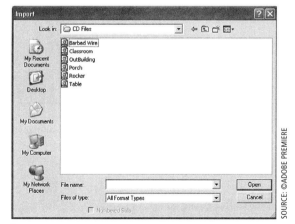

Import

3. In the Import dialog box, browse to your CD and double-click on *BarbedWire.jpg*.
4. Browse to your CD again and click on *Classroom.jpg*. Hold down the Ctrl key and click on the following files: *Stove.jpg, Porch.jpg, Rocker.jpg, Table.jpg,* and *BarbedWire.jpg*.

Storyboard

Note Area

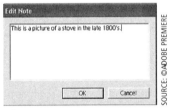

Edit Note

Automate Icon

5. With the five files selected, right-click and choose Select. This will import more than one file at a time.

Storyboard

1. Go to the menu bar and choose File > New > Storyboard.
2. Drag *stove.jpg* from the Project window to the top left corner of the storyboard.

Text Note

1. Double-click on the note area to add a note about the clip.
2. Type "This is a picture of a stove in the late 1800's."
3. Click OK.
4. Double-click on the picture in the storyboard to enlarge for better viewing. Close the window.

Saving the Storyboard

1. Add the other four clips to the storyboard. Add notes that you think describe the pictures.
2. You can click and drag the clips to rearrange them on the storyboard.
3. Click on the storyboard title bar. Go to the menu bar and choose File > Save As.

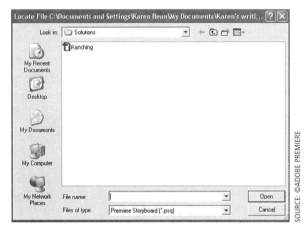

Save File

4. In the Save File dialog box, save the file as *Ranching.psq*. Click on Save. PSQ is the extension for a Premiere storyboard.

Automate to Timeline

1. Click on *Ranching.psq* in the Project window.
2. Click on the Automate to Timeline icon.
3. In the Automate to Timeline dialog box, leave the settings on default and click OK.

Automate Timeline

SOURCE: ©ADOBE PREMIERE

Creating Titles

1. Go to the menu bar and choose File > New > Title.
2. In the Title window, click on the Type Tool. See right.
3. Click in the window and type "Ranching Museum."

Formatting Text

1. Select the text you want to change.
2. Go to the menu bar and choose Title > Font. Change to a larger size and a different font.
3. Go to the menu bar and choose Title > Justify > Center.
4. Click on the text box. Hover the mouse pointer over the bottom right handle of the text box. When the pointer changes to a hand, click and drag to resize so the title is on two lines.
5. Select the text. Click on the Object Color box.
6. In the Color Picker, choose a blue.

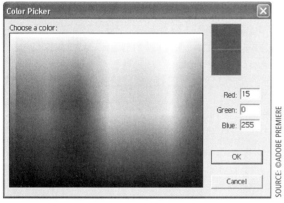

Color Picker

Creating Shapes

1. In the Title window, click on the Oval Tool. Note that if you click on the left side of the shape, you draw an outline. If you click on the right side of the shape, you draw a fill. In this case, select the left side (outline).
2. Click and drag an oval underneath the title in the Title window.
3. With the shape selected, click on the Selection Tool.

Changing Object Color

1. Click on the Object Color box. Change the color to any shade of blue.
2. Click on the Shadow Color box. Change the color to any shade of lighter blue.

Adding Line Width

1. Click on the Line Width slider.
2. Drag the Line Width to 16.

Adding Shadows

1. Use the Selection Tool to click on the oval.
2. Click and drag the shadow position to create a drop shadow.

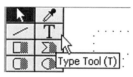

Type Tool

SOURCE: ©ADOBE PREMIERE

Ranching
Museum

Resize

SOURCE: ©ADOBE PREMIERE

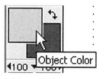

Object Color

SOURCE: ©ADOBE PREMIERE

Oval Tool

SOURCE: ©ADOBE PREMIERE

Selection Tool

SOURCE: ©ADOBE PREMIERE

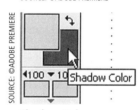

Shadow Color

Line Width

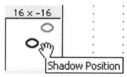

Shadow Position

SOURCE: ©ADOBE PREMIERE

Moving and Resizing Objects

1. Resize the oval object, then drag it so that it surrounds the text "Ranch Museum."
2. Resize again if needed so that none of the text is covered.

Adding Gradient Color

1. Use the Selection Tool to click on the text.
2. Click on the Gradient Start Color box. Change to a different color to complement your shape. See righthand figure for an example of the result.

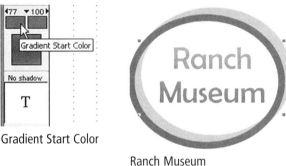

Gradient Start Color

Ranch Museum

SOURCE: LEFT AND RIGHT ©ADOBE PREMIERE

Saving the Title

1. Go to the menu bar and choose File > Save As.
2. Save as *RanchingTitle.ptl*. All titles are saved with PTL extensions.
3. Save the project.

Adding the Title

When you save the title, it is automatically added to the project. To add it to the Timeline, click and drag. Drop it at the beginning of the Timeline.

Previewing the Project

1. Go to the menu bar and choose Timeline > Preview. (You can also press Enter to begin the Building Preview.)
2. The Building Preview dialog box will appear and may take several minutes to complete. Any time you make a change to the Timeline, the Building Preview will have to build the changes.
3. Be sure when you start the preview that the Timeline Marker is at the beginning of the clip. You will see the preview in your Monitor window. Be sure that you have it placed so you can see it.

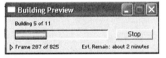

Building Preview

SOURCE: ©ADOBE PREMIERE

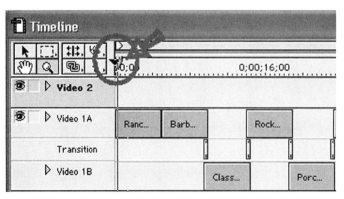

Timeline Marker

SOURCE: ©ADOBE PREMIERE

ACTIVITY 2 • MINI-PROJECT

Create a Still Video

1. Use a digital camera or a digital camcorder to take at least six still shots that tell a story or are about the same topic. Here are some ideas:
   Various areas in your school: the library, an office, a classroom, the cafeteria, a wall with the school mascot on it, and so on
   Football or other athletic practice
   An extracurricular activity or meeting

2. Import the six still clips into an Adobe Premiere project. Be sure the files have been saved properly. Save the project as *StillProject.psq*.

3. Create a title for the movie. Decide on a color scheme. Create a graphic shape with shadow and adjusted line width. Save the title as *StillTitle.ptl*.

4. Automate the project to Timeline.

5. Preview the project.

6. Save again.

7. The following criteria should be met:
   ☐ The six digital images are clear and of good quality.
   ☐ The six digital images fit into a particular topic and work well together.
   ☐ Title for video is appropriate. All requested elements are included: shape, color, gradient, shadow, and line width adjustment.
   ☐ Automated Timeline is appropriate, with the title added in the appropriate place.
   ☐ Preview demonstrates that all elements requested are included in the project. There are no gaps in the movie or errors in order.

ACTIVITY 3 • CREATING A VIDEO PROJECT

In this activity, you will become familiar with:

- Capturing Video
- Creating a Scratch Disk
- Importing Video
- Viewing a Video Clip
- Adding a Leader Clip
- Applying Transitions
- Superimposing Effects
- Applying Video Effects
- Adding Motion Effects
- Adding an Audio Clip
- Applying Audio Effects
- Exporting to a Movie File

Capturing Video

1. Go to the menu bar and choose File > Capture > Movie Capture.

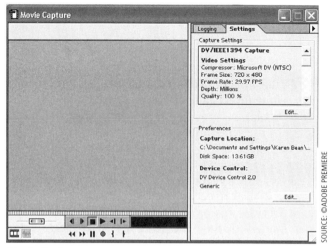

Movie Capture

Playback Video

2. In the Movie Capture dialog box, use the Playback buttons to control the video, or use the ones on the camcorder. Close the Movie Capture window.

Creating a Scratch Disk

1. Go to the menu bar and choose File > Capture > Movie Capture.
2. Go to the menu bar and choose Edit > Preferences > Scratch Disks and Device Control.

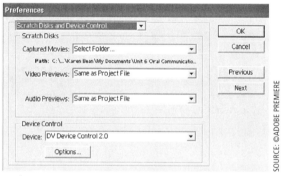

Preferences

3. In the Preferences dialog box, click on the drop-down box on Captured Movies. Choose Select Folder, and then browse to the folder you should use. (Get these instructions from your instructor.)
4. Click OK. The Scratch Disk is used for when you run out of RAM. Sometimes it becomes necessary to have more work area, as video captures can be extremely large in size.

Importing Video

1. Go to the menu bar and choose File > New Project. Browse to your CD and double-click on *Helicopter.mpg*.
2. Save the project as *HelicopterRide.ppj*.

Viewing a Video Clip

1. In the Project window, double-click on the icon for *Helicopter.mpg*.

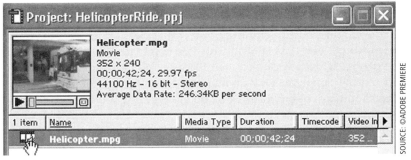

View Clip

2. Click on the Play button in the Clip window.

Play Video

3. Click on the Set Location marker to stop the video on a clip. Practice dragging the marker to different clips in the video. Close the Clip window.

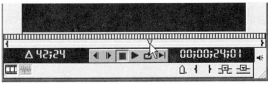

Set Location

SOURCE: ©ADOBE PREMIERE

Adding a Leader Clip

1. Go to the menu bar and choose File > New > Bin.
2. Click on the bin you just created.
3. Go to the menu bar and choose File > New > Bars and Tone.
4. The Bars and Tone window opens and adds it to the Project window in the bin you had selected.
5. Drag and drop the Bars and Tone icon from the Bars and Tone window to Video 1A on the Timeline window.
6. Drag and drop *Helicopter.mpg* next to it. Note that this MPG file already had audio with it, so it adds the audio to the Audio line.
7. Import *Copter.jpg* . This is a file created using PowerPoint and saved as a JPG. Drag and drop it before the Bars and Tone window.

Title Example

SOURCE: ©ADOBE PREMIERE

Applying Transitions

1. Create a title to add to the beginning of the video. See left.
2. Go to the menu bar and choose Window > Show Transitions.
3. Click and drop a 3D transition between the title and Bars and Tone. Drag and drop another one between Bars and Tone and the Helicopter clip. All transitions should be on the transition line on the Timeline. See below for the arrangement.

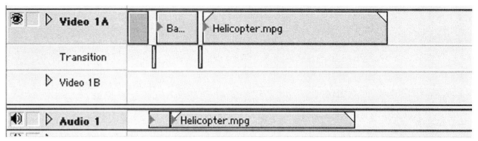

Transition Arrange

SOURCE: ©ADOBE PREMIERE

4. Save the project and preview.
5. Rearrange the transitions and clips. Drag the Bar and Tones to the end. See below. Click and drag to rearrange.

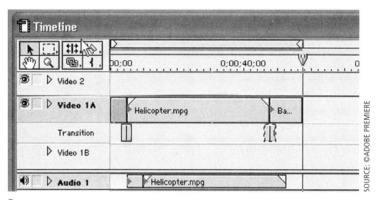

Rearrange

6. Save again and preview.
7. Make adjustments to the arrangement as you feel are necessary.

Superimposing Effects

1. Place a clip directly over another clip in the Timeline window.
2. Add a track by right-clicking Track 2. Drag the top clip to Track 2 and the other clip on Track 1 directly below it. Click on the top clip.
3. Go to the menu bar and choose Clip > Video Options > Transparency.

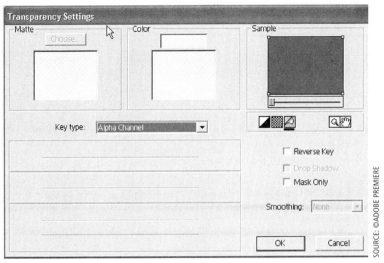

Transparency Settings

Effect Controls

4. In the Transparency Settings dialog box, click on the down arrow to display the key types.
5. Choose the Alpha Channel key type.
6. Save and preview the project.

Applying Video Effects

1. Go to the menu bar and choose Window > Show Video Effects.
2. Choose an effect. Drag and drop it to the Helicopter clip on the Timeline window.
3. Save and preview the project.

Adding Motion Effects

1. Click on the EndTitle clip to set a motion to it.
2. Go to the menu bar and choose Clip > Video Options > Motion.

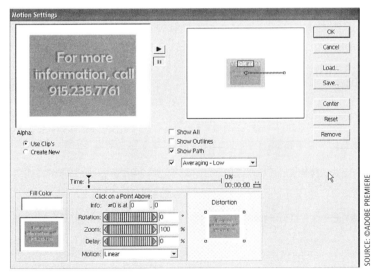

Motion Settings

3. See above for settings for this clip.

Adding an Audio Clip

1. Go to the menu bar and choose File > Import. Browse to your CD and double-click on *Ready2.wav*
2. Drag and drop *Ready2.wav* to the beginning of the audio track.

Applying Audio Effects

1. Click on the sound clip you want to add the audio effect to. In this case, click on *Ready2.wav*
2. Go to the menu bar and choose Window > Show Audio Effects.
3. Drag and drop it on the clip. The Effect Control palette opens. Make any adjustments necessary.
4. Save and preview the project.

Exporting to a Movie File

1. Go to the menu bar and choose File > Export Timeline > Movie.

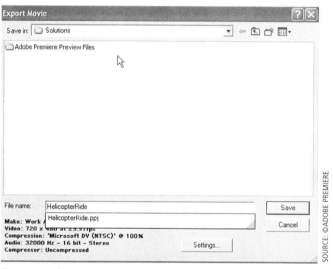

Export Movie

2. In the Export Movie dialog box, click on Settings.
3. Choose DV AVI file type.
4. Click OK.
5. In the file name box, type "HelicopterRide."
6. Click on Save.

ACTIVITY 3 • MINI-PROJECT

Create a Movie

1. With a partner, videotape each other doing a one minute how-to explanation. Save the project as *HowTo.ppj* Some suggestions:
   How to make peanut butter and jelly sandwiches (or making something else simple to eat)
   How to swing a golf club in the right way (or any other athletic skill)
   How to tie a particular kind of knot (or other scouting skill)
2. Use PowerPoint to add a title at the beginning of the movie.

3. Search on the Internet for audio clips to add to the project.
4. Add a final page, using the Title feature.
5. Include the following special effects: transitions, video effects, motion effects, and audio effects.
6. Export the movie to a file. Save it as *HowTo.avi*.
7. The following criteria should be met:

   ☐ Topic is appropriate and information is organized.
   ☐ Title page is visually appealing and appropriate in length.
   ☐ Audio clip is appropriate for the project.
   ☐ Final page is visually appealing and contains appropriate information.
   ☐ At least three special effects were used.
   ☐ All items are appropriately placed on the Timeline.

PART 3 • SIMULATION

Using Adobe Premiere

1. In a team of three students, create two 60-second commercials for a cleaning product. It can be a new cleaning product or one already on the market.
2. The first commercial should be made of still images. There should be at least eight images with a title slide. Save as *StillCommercial.ppj*.
3. The second commercial should be made using a digital camcorder. It should also contain a title slide. Save as *VideoCommercial.ppj*.
4. The following criteria should be met:

   ☐ Team worked well together.
   ☐ Commercials contain appropriate information that is useful in a marketing situation.
   ☐ The still commercial contains digital images of good quality.
   ☐ The video commercial contains video of good quality.
   ☐ Colors chosen for both commercials are appropriate and visually appealing.
   ☐ At least three effects were used on the commercials, with at least one transition on each commercial.
   ☐ All images, sound, transitions, and effects are placed appropriately on the Timeline.

Part 4

MGI Cinematic

> **MGI Cinematic**
> **Publisher: Roxio**
> MGI Cinematic is designed to easily create and enhance videos. It allows three choices in creating videos. You can use the Automatic Movie Generator or the StoryBuilder, or you can choose to work on your own.

ACTIVITY 1 • USING CINEMAGIC

In this activity, you will become familiar with:

- Video Capture
- Video Library
- Preview Selection
- Add Video
- Add Audio
- Style
- Make Movie
- Format Quality
- Name Your Movie

Video Capture

1. Open MGI Cinematic. Click on Capture Video.

Capture Video

2. You can choose to capture video from three different sources. See your instructor for which medium you have available in your classroom. For the purposes of learning this software, you will use video that has already been captured.

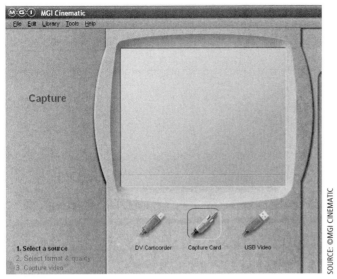

Capture Screen

Video Library

1. Go to the menu bar and choose Library > Add Files.

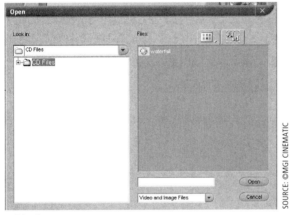

Add Files

2. In the Open dialog box, browse to your CD and double-click on *Waterfall.mpg*.

Preview Selection

1. Click on the *Waterfall.mpg* icon.
2. Click on the Preview Selection icon on the Library taskbar.

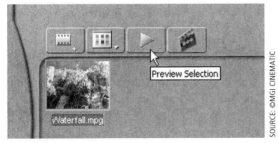

Preview Selection

3. In the Waterfall Preview dialog box, click on the Close button.
4. Click on the Done button on the Cinematic screen.

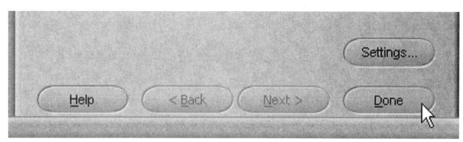

Done

Add Video

1. Click on the CineMagic icon.

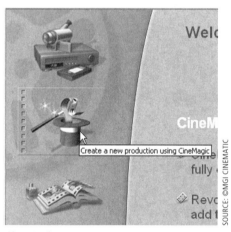

CineMagic

2. On the CineMagic screen, click and drag *Waterfall.mpg* from the Library to the Production window. You will see a box that explains it is preparing for use. It is compressing the video file.

Select Video

3. Click on Next in the Production window.

Next

Add Audio

1. Click on the Add file(s) to Library icon. Browse to your CD and double-click on *NightSound.wav*

Add Audio

2. Drag *NightSound.wav* from the Library to the Production window.

Drag Audio

3. Click on Next.

Style

1. Click on Nostalgia.

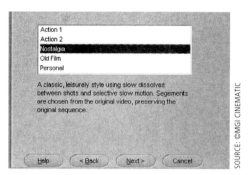

Select Style

2. Click on Next. CineMagic will begin creating your movie.

Make Movie

1. Click on Preview.
2. Click on Make movie. Click on Yes to save the movie. Save as *Waterfall.cmp*.

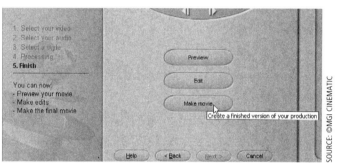

Make Movie

3. Click on Video File for the destination, then click on Next.

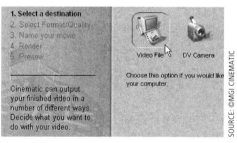

Destination

Format Quality

1. Click on the drop-down box for Format Quality.

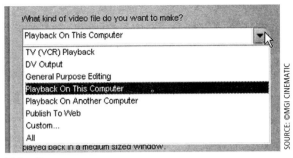

Video Types

2. Choose Playback On This Computer with Normal Quality. Click on Next.

Name Your Movie

1. Click on Browse to choose a place and name for your movie.

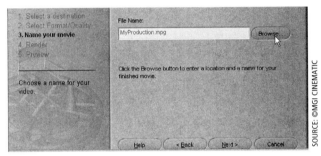

Movie Name

2. In the Save dialog box, choose a folder location and name the movie *Waterfall.mpg*.
3. Click on Next. The movie completes rendering and gives you a preview. Click on Finish.
4. Click on Home.

ACTIVITY 1 • MINI-PROJECT

Create a Video by CineMagic

1. Take a field trip to a business in your city. If a field trip is not possible, invite a speaker to the classroom. It could be a member of your advisory board. Learn about their business and discuss ways in which they would be able to use a video in their business.
2. Use a digital camcorder or camera during the field trip or visit the business after school to create at least a minute of images or video.
3. Use CineMagic to create a video of the business use.
4. Burn the movie to a CD to share with the business. Save as *FieldTrip.mpg*.
5. Use word processing software to write a summary of the business use. Explain how it would be used in the business. Save as *Rationale*.
6. The following criteria should be met:
   - ☐ Images are of good quality.
   - ☐ Business use is well thought out and practical.
   - ☐ Appropriate audio was added.
   - ☐ Explanation of video is clear, with no grammar or spelling errors.

ACTIVITY 2 • USING STORYBUILDER

In this activity, you will become familiar with:

- Template
- Introduction
- Select Audio
- Add Video
- Text
- Ending

Template

1. Click on the StoryBuilder icon.

StoryBuilder

2. Select the template A Day at the Beach. Click on Next.

Template

Introduction

1. Select Ocean from the drop-down box.

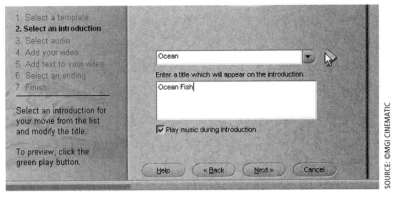

Introduction

2. Type "Ocean Fish" in the title box.
3. Click on Preview, then click on Next.

Select Audio

1. In the Music drop-down box, click on "floating away."
2. Click on the green arrow to preview the music.
3. Click on Next.

Add Video

1. Click on Add file(s) to Library. Browse to your CD and double-click on *Fish.mpg*.
2. Drag *Fish.mpg* from the Library window to the Production window.
3. Click on Next.

Text

1. In the text box, type "Fish, Fish, Fish." Press Enter after the second "Fish" and space center the third "Fish" somewhat under the first two "Fish."

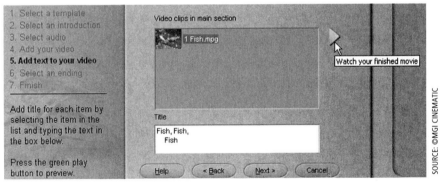

Text

2. Click on Preview, then on Next.

Ending

1. Choose Shells and Wave from the drop-down box.

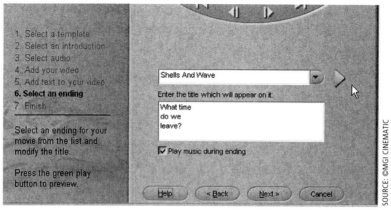

Ending

2. Type "What time do we leave?" in the text box. See above for the exact places to press the Enter key. Space it so that it is somewhat centered.
3. Click on Preview. Make any changes needed. Click on Next.
4. Click on Make movie.
5. Save the production as *Fish.mpg*.

ACTIVITY 2 • MINI-PROJECT

Use StoryBuilder to Create a Video

1. Work with a partner to create a video for an e-commerce bookstore.
2. Use your school or public library to get books or other scenarios to use in the video.
3. Use Sound Recorder to create a WAV file to narrate the video as part of the marketing of your business. Be sure that the video is three times as long as the WAV file.
4. The following criteria should be met:
   - ☐ Partners worked well together.
   - ☐ Video is approximately one minute long.
   - ☐ Partners used creativity in developing the video.
   - ☐ Video is of good quality. Images are clear.
   - ☐ Introduction, template, and ending demonstrate a clear theme that is evident throughout the video.
   - ☐ WAV file is of good quality.

ACTIVITY 3 • CREATING A PRODUCTION ON YOUR OWN

In this activity, you will become familiar with:

- ■ Selecting Images
- ■ Color Panel
- ■ Add Titles
- ■ Motion
- ■ Transitions
- ■ Special Effects
- ■ Overlays
- ■ Adjust Speed
- ■ Open an Existing File

Selecting Images

1. Click on the Work on Your Own icon.

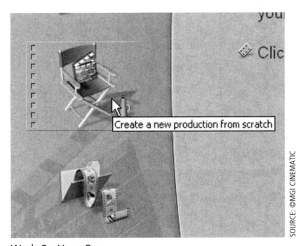

Work On Your Own

2. Click on the Add file(s) to the Library icon. Browse to your CD and double-click on the *Animal Haven* folder. Select all ten images in the folder by clicking on the first image, then holding down the Shift key, and clicking on the last image.
3. Click Open to add all ten images to the Library.

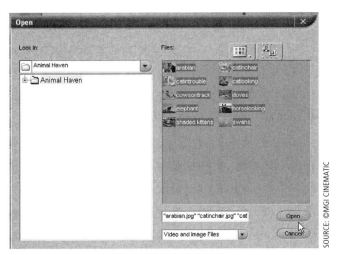

Select Images

Color Panel

1. Right-click on the first panel on the filmstrip. See the figure labeled Color Panel.
2. Select Insert Color Panel. Choose a brown color.

Add Titles

1. Click on the Text icon on the toolbar.

Color Panel

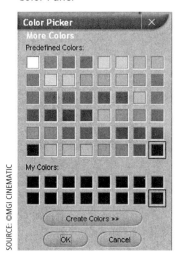

Color Picker

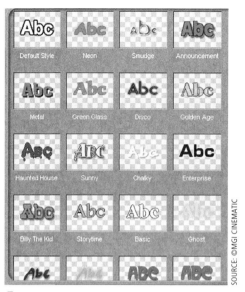

Text

2. Choose the Billy The Kid text style and type "Animal Haven."

Motion

1. Click on the Motion tab. See below.

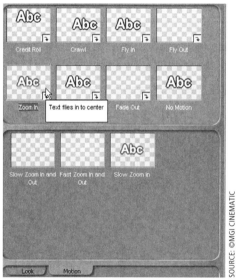

Motion

2. Choose Zoom In. Click on Slow Zoom In.
3. Drag each of the ten images to a panel on the filmstrip. You may order them however you choose.

Transitions

1. Click on Transitions on the toolbar.

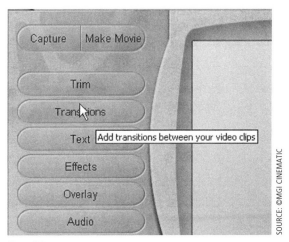

Transitions

2. Drag and drop a transition between each image. You may choose which transition. Use several different ones.
3. Click on Done.

Special Effects

1. Click on Effects on the toolbar.
2. Choose the Frame effect. Click on Portrait.

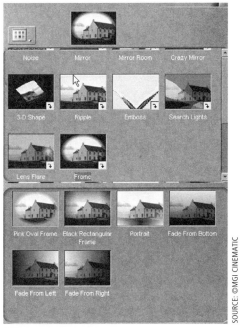

Effects

3. Click on Done.

Overlays

1. Click on Overlays on the toolbar.

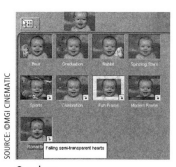

Overlays

2. Drag and drop Romantic to the last slide.
3. Click on Done.
4. Add an audio clip of your choice to the movie.
5. Click on Done.
6. Click on Make movie.
7. Save as *AnimalHaven.mpg*.
8. Go through the wizard to make the movie. Save it as *AnimalHaven.mpg*.
9. Click on Done.

Adjust Speed

1. Double-click on one of the images on the filmstrip. This brings it into the Production window.
2. Click on the Adjust Speed icon. See below.

Adjust Speed

3. Slow the speed.
4. Click on Home.
5. Click on Yes to save the existing file.

Open an Existing File

Open Existing File

1. Click on the Open an Existing File icon.
2. Browse to where you have saved *AnimalHaven.mpg* and select it.
3. Preview the movie.

ACTIVITY 3 • MINI-PROJECT

Create a Video on Your Own

1. Attend a school activity. Take at least ten digital images of the activity.
2. Use the On Your Own feature in MGI Cinematic to create a video using the images. Save as *SchoolActivity.mpg*.
3. Burn the video to a CD for use on your school announcements.
4. The following criteria should be met:
   - ☐ At least ten images of good quality were used.
   - ☐ A theme is evident throughout the video.
   - ☐ Color panel was appropriately created.
   - ☐ Title is appropriate for the video.
   - ☐ Motion is used appropriately.
   - ☐ Appropriate transitions are used between each image.

☐ Special effect was used that is consistent with the theme.
☐ No errors in wording in video.
☐ Audio is consistent with theme of video.

PART 4 • SIMULATION

Using MGI Cinematic

1. Use the Internet or other resources to research an exercise activity such as road biking, mountain biking, or golfing.
2. Use voice recognition software and word processing software to voice a two-page report on your research. Save as *ExerciseReport.*
3. Create a six- to ten-slide presentation on your report. Save as *ExercisePresentation.*
4. Add a video to one of the slides in your presentation. Use MGI Cinematic to create the video from at least ten images that you have taken, digital video footage, or other clip art available to you in your classroom. It can be a mixture of images and clip art. Be sure that you have a clear theme for your video. Save as *ExerciseVideo.mpg.*
5. The following criteria should be met:

   ☐ Content in research is appropriate and thorough.
   ☐ Report is error-free and in correct format.
   ☐ Presentation is an accurate summary of the report, with the ability to catch interest in the topic.
   ☐ Video is of good quality and interesting, and demonstrates knowledge of most of the tools available in MGI Cinematic.
   ☐ Video is appropriately placed in the presentation.

Index